THE
WEBSTER'S
DICTIONARY

1994 EDITION

Published by PSI & Associates, Inc.
13322 SW 128th Street, Miami, FL 33186
(305) 255-7959

INCLUDES
NEW
COMPUTER
SECTION

Copyright © MCMLXXIX Ottenhiemer Publishers, Inc.; Updated 1994 PSI & Associates, Inc.

Cover design by; 1994 Barbara Baron.

Published by; PSI & Associates, Inc.

ISBN# 1-55993-294-5

How to Use This Dictionary

example: **ăd-mīre′,** v., regard highly; **-r; ration**
     A   B   C   D

A. Each entry word is shown in bold-face type.
1. **(-)** shows the division between each syllable.
2. **(′)** indicates the accented syllable.
3. Pronunciation marks are shown only for vowels and are found above the vowel. Vowels without marks have no sound.
4. Irregular pronunciation is indicated in parentheses following the word.

    example: **cham-pāgne′ (shăm)**

5. If there is more than one pronunciation for a word, only the most common is generally given. In situations where different parts of speech of the same word are pronounced differently, each pronunciation is given.

    example: **ăl′têr-nāte,** v., do by turns; a. **(nàte),** every other; **tion**

B. The part of speech for each word is abbreviated (see Abbreviation Key) and is printed in italics.
1. Some words have one meaning for different parts of speech.

    example: **ăn′swêr,** n., v., reply

2. Some words have different meanings for each part of speech.

    example: **à-lêrt′,** n., alarm; v., warn; a., quick

3. Some words have similar meanings for different parts of speech.

    example: **gī′ànt,** n., a., (one) of great size

4. Some words are commonly used in the plural form and are indicated by pl.

    example: **băc-tē′rĭ-à,** n. pl.

C. The definition is in a short, concise form.
1. For most nouns, a, an, and the have been omitted before the definition.
2. For all verbs, to has been omitted before the definition.
3. Words often have many meanings; only the more common are given.

D. Endings of words derived from the entry word are printed in bold-face type following the definition.
1. Their parts of speech are not indicated unless they are different from those listed in the Suffix Key or not listed at all.

    example: **À-mĕr′ĭ-cà,** n., Western Hemisphere, United States; **-n,** n.

The new word becomes **American.**

2. If there is a hyphen (-) before the ending, it is added directly to the entry word to make a new form.

example: **ăd-mīre′,** *v.*, regard highly; **-r**

The new word becomes **admirer.**

3. If there is no hyphen (-) before the ending, then the ending replaces the last few letters or syllable so that the ending is comprised of a complete syllable or syllables.

example: **ăd-mīre′,** *v.*, regard highly; **ration**

The new word becomes **admiration.**

Pronunciation Key

Symbol	Key Word
ă	ăt
ā	āce
â	bâr
à	sofà
ä	äll
aͧu	aͧuto
ĕ	bĕd
bē	bē
ê	hêr
ė	mėchanic
eͧw	feͧw
ĭ	ĭn
ī	īce
î	sîr
ï (ē)	alïen
ŏ	ŏx
ō	gō
ô	ôr
ö	wörd
ȯ	gallȯp
oĭ	oĭl
oͧo	boͧok
oͦo	boͦot
oͧu	oͧut
oͧw	coͧw
ŭ	ŭp
ū	ūse
û	ûrn
ȳ (ī)	bȳ
ÿ (ē)	berrÿ
ẏ (ĭ)	mẏth

The following combinations are always pronounced as shown below unless otherwise noted.

Symbol		Key Word
ch		chain
ck	(k)	back
dg	(j)	edge
gh	(silent)	night
gn	(n)	gnat
ism	(ĭz-ėm)	egotism
kn	(n)	knot
ph	(f)	graph
pn	(n)	pneumonia
ps	(s)	psalm
qu	(k)	quit
rh	(r)	rhyme
wh	(w)	what
wr	(r)	write

Abbreviation Key

a.	adjective
adv.	adverb
art.	article
coll.	colloquial
conj.	conjunction
cont.	contraction
etc.	et cetera
ex.	example
int.	interjection
n.	noun
pl.	plural
prep.	preposition
pro.	pronoun
sing.	singular
v.	verb

Suffix Key

These suffixes or word endings are used throughout this dictionary. Each will always have the same pronunciation and be the same part of speech unless otherwise indicated in the entry word itself.

-åge	n.
-ål	a.
-āte	v.
-bĭl-ĭ-tÿ	n.
-ble (b'l)	a.
-blÿ	adv.
-cial, -tial (shil)	a.
-cious, -tious (shis)	a.
-dŏm	n.
-ėd	a.
-ēe	n.
-ēer	n.
-ėn	v.
-êr	n.

-ĕss	*n.*
-fŭl	*a.*
-hŏŏd	*n.*
-ĭc	*a.*
-ĭcs	*n.*
-ĭ-fÿ	*v.*
-ĭng	*a.*
-ĭon (yón)	*n.*
-ĭsh	*a.*
-ĭsm (ĭz-ėm)	*n.*
-ĭst	*n.*
-ĭ-tĭs	*n.*
-ĭ-ŭm	*n.*
-ĭze	*v.*
-lĕss	*a.*
-līke	*a.*
-lÿ	*adv.*
-mĕnt, -mėnt	*n.*
-nce	*n.*
-ncÿ	*n.*
-nĕss	*n.*
-nt	*a.*
-ôr, -ör	*n.*
-oŭs	*a.*
-shĭp	*n.*
-sion, -tion (shĭn)	*n.*
-sĭve	*a.*
-stêr	*n.*
-tĭve	*a.*
-tûre (chêr)	*n.*
-tūre (chŭr)	*n.*
-ÿ	*n.*

A

ă, *a.*, one, each   [eater
âard′vârk, *n.*, African ant-
à-băck′, *adv.*, backwards
ăb′àcŭs, *n.*, counting
    frame with beads
à-băft′, *adv.*, *prep.*, behind
ăb-à-lō′nē, *n.*, mollusk
    yielding mother-of-pearl
à-băn′dòn, *v.*, give up;
    -ment; -er; -ed; -edly
à-bāse′, *v.*, degrade, hu-
    miliate; **-ment**
à-băsh′, *v.*, embarrass,
    shame; **-ment**
à-bāte′, *v.*, lessen; **-r;**
    -ment; table   [house
ăb-àt-tōir′, *n.*, slaughter-
ăb′bèss, *n.*, head nun
ăb′bēy, *n.*, monastery
ăb′bòt, *n.*, head monk
ăb-brē′vĭ-āte, *v.*, shorten;
    tor; tion; tory
ăb′dĭ-cāte, *v.*, resign office
    or power; **tor; tion**
ăb′dò-mĕn, *n.*, body be-
    tween chest and pelvis;
    minal
ăb-dŭct′, *v.*, kidnap; **-or;**
    -ion
ăb′êr-rāte, *v.*, deviate;
    tion
à-bĕt′, *v.*, aid in doing
    wrong; **-ter; -tor; -ment**
ăb-hôr′, *v.*, hate, detest;
    -rer; -rence; -rent
à-bīde′, *v.*, await, endure;
    -r
à-bĭl′ĭ-tў, *n.*, skill, talent
ăb′jĕct, *a.*, wretched,
    base; **-ion; -ness; -ly**
àb-jūre′, *v.*, renounce; **ra-
    tion; -r; ratory**
ăb-lāte′, *v.*, remove by sur-
    gery; **tion**
à-blāze′, *a.*, on fire
ăb-lū′tion, *n.*, washing the
    body; **tary**
ăb′nè-gāte, *v.*, re-
    nounce; **tor; tion**
ăb-nôr′màl, *a.*, not usual;
    -ity; -ly   [conveyance
à-bōard′, *adv.*, on or in a
à-bōde′, *n.*, residence

à-bŏl′ĭsh, *v.*, do away with
à-bŏm′ĭ-nāte, *v.*, loathe,
    hate; **tor; tion; nable**
ăb-ō-rĭg′ĭ-nē, *n.*, earliest
    inhabitant; **nal**
à-bôrt′, *v.*, miscarry; **-ion;
    -ionist; -ive**
à-bŏund′, *v.*, be plentiful
à-brāde′, *v.*, rub off; **-r;
    dant**
à-brā′sion, *n.*, scrape;
    sive   [side
à-brĕast′, *adv.*, side by
à-brĭdge′, *v.*, shorten;
    -ment
à-broäd′, *adv.*, outside
ăb′rò-gāte, *v.*, abolish;
    tor; tion; tive
à-brŭpt′, *a.*, sudden; **-ion;
    -ness; -ly** [sue in body
ăb′scĕss, *n.*, pus-filled tis-
àb-scĭnd′, *v.*, cut off
ăb-scŏnd′, *v.*, secretly run
    away; **-er**
ăb′sènt, *a.*, away; **-ee;
    sence; -eeism**
ab′sènt–mĭnd′èd, *a.*, for-
    getful; **-ly; -ness**
ăb′sò-lūte, *a.*, uncondi-
    tional; **-ness; -ly**
àb-sŏlve′, *v.*, forgive
àb-sôrb′, *v.*, suck up, take
    in; **-er; -ability; -ency;
    -ent; -able**
àb-stāin′, *v.*, refrain; **-er**
àb-stē′mĭ-oŭs, *a.*, moder-
    ate; **-ness**
ăb-străct′, *n.*, summary; *v.*,
    remove; *a.*, theoretical;
    -er; -ion; -ness; -ive; -ly
ăb-strūse′, *a.*, obscure;
    -ness; -ly
àb-sûrd′, *a.*, ridiculous;
    -ity; -ness; -ly
à-bŭn′dànt, *a.*, plentiful;
    dance; -ly
à-būse′, *v.*, mistreat; **sive;
    siveness**
à-bўss′, *n.*, deep pit
ăc-à-dĕm′ĭc, *a.*, scholas-
    tic; **-al; -ally**
ā-càp-pĕl′là, *a.*, without
    accompaniment

ăc-cēde', v., consent; -r;
-nce

ăc-cĕl'êr-āte, v., go faster;
tor; tion   [stress

ăc'cĕnt, n., emphasis; v.;
-uation; -uate; -ual

ăc-cĕpt', v., receive; -er;
-or; -ance; -ant; -able;
-ably; -ableness; -abil-
ity

ăc-cĕs'sô-rў, n., extra; rial

ăc'cĭ-dĕnt, n., chance,
mishap; -al

ăc-clāim', v., applaud

ăc-clà-mā'tion, n., ap-
plause; tory

ăc-clĭv'ĭ-tў, n., upward
slope

ăc'cô-lāde, n., honor,
award

ăc-cŏm'mô-dāte, v., make
fit, lodge; tor; tion; tive

ăc-côm'pà-nў, v., go
with; niment; nist

ăc-cŏm'plĭce, n., partner
in crime

ăc-côrd', v., agree; -ance;
-ant; -antly; -ingly

ăc-côr'dĭ-ôn, n., musical
instrument; adj., folding

ăc-cŏst', v., approach,
greet

ăc-coū'têr, v., equip;
-ment

ăc-crĕd'ĭt, v., authorize;
-ation

ăc-crūe', v., increase

ăc-cū'mū-lāte, v., collect;
tor; tion; tive; tively

ăc'cû-rà-cў, n., exactness

ăc-cūse', v., blame; -r;
singly   [ate

ăc-cŭs'tôm, v., habitu-
à-cêrb', a., bitter, sour;
-ity; -ate   [acid

ăc'ē-tāte, n., salt of acetic

ăc'ē-tōne, n., liquid paint
remover   [blowtorch

à-cĕt'ў-lēne, n., gas for

ăch-rô-măt'ĭc (ăk), a., colorless; -ly

ăc'ĭd, a., sour; -ity; -ify;
-ic

ăc-knŏwl'ĕdge, v., admit;
gment; -able

ăc'mē, n., summit

ăc'nē, n., skin disease with

pimples   [helper

ăc'ò-lўte, n., altar boy,

à-coūs'tĭc, a., of hearing;
-al; -ally; -s

ăc-quāint', v., make
aware; -ance

ăc'quĭ-ĕsce, v., consent;
-nce; -nt

ăc-quīre', v., get; -ment

ăc-quĭt', v., absolve; -ter;
-tal; -tance

ā'cre, n., land measure;
-age

ăc'rĭ-mō-nў, n., harsh
manner; nious

ăc'rô-băt, n., skilled gym-
nast; -ic

ăc'rô-nўm, n., word
formed from initials; -ic

ăct, n., deed; v., do, perform; -or; -ress; -ion

ăc'tĭve, a., busy, moving;
vity

ăc'tū-àl, a., real; -ity; -ize;
-ly   [statistician

ăc'tū-ār-ў, n., insurance

à-cū'ĭ-tў, n., keenness

à-cū'mĕn, n., sharpness

ăc'-ū-pŭnc-tûre,   n.,
Chinese pain-relieving
practice of inserting
needles into body

à-cūte', a., sharp; -ness;
-ly

ăd'àge, n., old saying

ăd'à-mànt, a., inflexible

ădd, v., sum up, total; -er;
-ition; -itional; -ition-
ally; -able; -ible; -ibil-
ity; -itive   [added

ăd-dĕn'dŭm, n., thing

ăd'dêr, n., snake

ăd-dīct', v., give to habit;
-ion; -ive

ăd'dle, v., confuse

ăd-drĕss', n., speech,
place of residence; v.,
speak or write to; -ee;
-er

ăd-dūce', v., cite, quote;
-r; -nt

ăd'e-nŏids, n., lymph tissue behind nose

ăd-ĕpt', a., very skilled;
-ness; -ly   [ciency

ăd'ē-quà-cў, n., suffi-
ăd-hēre', v., stick; -r; -nce;

A
B

-nt
ăd'ĭt, *n.*, mine entrance
ăd-jā'cĕnt, *a.*, near; **ncy**
ăd'jĕc-tĭve, *n.*, word quali-
   fying a noun; **val**
ăd-jōin', *v.*, next to
ăd-joûrn', *v.*, suspend,
   postpone; **-ment**
ăd'jŭnct, *n.*, addition; **-ly;**
   -ive; -ively
ăd-jūre', *v.*, charge under
   oath; **-r; ration; ratory**
ăd-jŭst', *v.*, conform; **-er;**
   -or; -ment; -able
ăd-lĭb', *v.*, improvise
ăd-mĭn'ĭs-têr, *v.*, govern
ăd-mire', *v.*, regard highly;
   -r; ration; rable; rably;
   rability; ringly
ăd-mĭt', *v.*, let in, acknowledge; **-tance; -tedly**
ăd-mŏn'ĭsh, *v.*, advise;
   nitor; -ment; nition; ni-
   tory
à-do' (dū), *n.*, fuss [brick
à-dō'bē, *n.*, sun-dried
ăd-ò-lĕs'cĕnce, *n.*, teen-
   age years; **scent**
à-dŏpt', *v.*, take as one's
   own; **-er; -ion; -ive;**
   -ively; -able
à-dôrn', *v.*, add beauty;
   -ment
Ăd-rĕn'ăl-ĭn, *n.*, hormone
   that stimulates heart
ăd'ŭ-lāte, *v.*, highly flatter;
   tor; tion; tory
à-dŭlt', *a.*, *n.*, mature (person); **-hood; -ness**
à-dŭl'têr-ȳ, *n.*, extramarital
   sexual relations; **rer**
ăd-vănce', *v.*, go forward;
   -r; -ment
ăd-văn'tàge, *n.*, benefit;
   geous; geously
ăd-vĕn'tûre, *n.*, exciting
   happening; *v.*, risk; **-r;**
   -ss; -some; turism; tur-
   ist; turous; turously;
   turousness
ăd'vêrb, *n.*, word modify-
   ing verb, adjective, or
   adverb; **-ial; -ially**
ăd'vêr-sār-ȳ, *n.*, oppo-
   nent; **sative**
ăd-vêrt', *v.*, refer, call attention to; **-ence; -ency;**

-ent; -ently
ăd-vêr-tīse', *v.*, make
   known; **-r; -ment**
àd-vice', *n.*, opinion
àd-vīse', *v.*, counsel; **-r;**
   sor; -ment; sory; -d;
   -dly; sable; sably; sa-
   bility; sableness
ăd'vo-cāte, *v.*, support;
   tor; cacy; tion; tory
āer'āte, *v.*, expose to air;
   tor; tion
āer'ĭ-ăl, *n.*, antenna; *a.*,
   like air, high up; **-ist**
āer'iē, *n.*, eagle's nest
āer-ō-dȳ-năm'ĭcs, *n.*,
   study of air movement
āer-ŏm'ė-têr, *n.*, air meas-
   urer [aircraft
āer-ò-nāu'tĭcs, *n.*, study of
aĕs-thĕt'ĭc, *a.*, of artistic
   beauty; **-ism; -al; -ally**
ăf'fà-ble, *a.*, friendly; **bil-**
   ity; bly
àf-fāir', *n.*, business, event
àf-fĕct', *v.*, influence; **-ive;**
   -ively; -ed; -edness
àf-fĕc'tion, *n.*, fondness;
   -ate; -al; tive; ter
ăf-fĭ-dā'vĭt, *n.*, sworn written statement
àf-fĭn'ĭ-tȳ, *n.*, connection,
   attraction; **tive**
àf-firm', *v.*, assert as true;
   -er; -ation; -ance; -ant;
   -ative; -atively; -able
àf-flā'tŭs, *n.*, inspiration
àf-flĭct', *v.*, cause pain;
   -ion; -ive; -ively
ăf'flū-ĕnce, *n.*, wealth; **nt;**
   ntly
àf fôrd', *v.*, bear the cost
àf-frāy', *n.*, public fight
àf-frònt', *v.*, offend
à-fĭĕld', *adv.*, astray
à-fôre-mĕn'tioned, *adj.*,
   mentioned before
à-frāid', *a.*, fearful
à-frĕsh', *adv.*, again
ăft, *adv.*, toward stern
ăf'têr-ėf-fĕct, *n.*, later
   result [quence
ăf'têr-măth, *n.*, conse-
ăf'têr-tāste, *n.*, lingering
   taste [reflection
ăf'têr-thôught, *n.*, later
ăf'têr-wàrd, *adv.*, later

à-gain' (gĕn), *adv.*, once more [contrary to

à-gainst' (gĕnst), *prep.*,

à-gápe', *a.*, *adv.*, surprised [precious stone

ăg'ate (ĭt), *n.*, hard, semi-

āge, *n.*, period of time; *v.*, grow old; **-less**

ā'gĕn-cў, *n.*, means, bureau acting for another

à-gĕn'dă, *n.*, list of things to do

ā-gent, *n.*, one acting for another, active force; **-ial**

ăg-glŏm'êr-āte, *v.*, collect into a heap; **tion; tive**

ăg-grăn'dĭze, *v.*, increase power; **-r; -ment**

ăg'grà-vāte, *v.*, make worse, annoy; **tion**

ăg-grĕs'sion, *n.*, attack; **sor; sive**

ăg-griĕve', *v.*, injure

à-ghăst', *a.*, horrified

ăg'ĭle, *a.*, quick, light movement; **lity**

ăg'ĭ-tāte, *v.*, disturb, excite; **tor; tion**

ăg-nŏs'tĭc, *n.*, one who doubts God's existence; **-ism; -ally**

ăg'ō-nў, *n.*, great pain, distress; **nize**

à-grăr'ĭ-àn, *a.*, of land, rural; **-ism**

ăg'rĭ-cŭl-tûre, *n.*, science of farming; **rist; ral; rally**

à-grŏn'ò-mў, *n.*, science of farm production; **mist; mic; mical** [shore

à-grŏund', *a.*, *adv.*, on

ā'gūe, *n.*, fever with chills; **guish**

à-hĕad', *a.*, *adv.*, forward

à-hoy'(ŏi), *inter.*, sailor's

āid, *n.*, *v.*, help [call

āil, *v.*, be in ill health; **-ment**

āim, *n.*, intention; *v.*, point; **-less; -lessness; -lessly**

āir, *n.*, gases surrounding earth; *v.*, ventilate; **-iness; -y; -ily**

āir'crăft, *n.*, flying machine [for aircraft

āir'fīeld, *n.*, landing field

āir fôrce, *n.*, military branch using airplanes

āir'līne, *n.*, aircraft transport company; **-r**

āir'māil, *n.*, mail sent by aircraft [flying machine

āir'plāne, *n.*, power-driven

āir'pôrt, *n.*, landing place for aircraft

āir rāid, *n.*, airplane attack

aīsle (ĭl), *n.*, passageway along rows of seats

à-kĭn', *a.*, related, similar

ăl'à-băs-têr, *n.*, white stone

à-lârm',*n.*, warning signal, fear; *v.*, frighten; **-ist**

à-lăs', *int.*, cry of sorrow

ălb, *n.*, priest's white robe

ăl'bà-trŏss, *n.*, large seabird of the South Seas

ăl-bē'ĭt, *conj.*, although

ăl-bī'nō, *n.*, animal lacking coloration of hair, eyes, skin; **nism**

ăl'bŭm,*n.*, book with blank pages for collecting

ăl-bū'mĕn, *n.*, egg white, complex protein; **minoid; minous**

ăl'chė-mў, *n.*, medieval chemistry; **mist; mize; mic; mical; mically**

ăl'cò-hôl, *n.*, intoxicating liquid

ăl'cŏve, *n.*, recess of a room [cilman

ăl'dêr-măn,*n.*, local coun-

āle, *n.*, kind of beer

à-lêrt', *n.*, alarm; *v.*, warn; *a.*, quick [for fodder

ăl-făl'fà, *n.*, legume used

ăl'gė-brà,*n.*, mathematics of equations; **-ist; -ic; -ical; -ically**

ā'lĭ-às, *n.*, assumed name

ăl'ĭ-bī, *n.*, excuse

à-līght', *v.*, dismount; *a.*, burning

à-līgn', *v.*, line up; **-ment**

ăl'ĭ-mĕnt, *n.*, food; *v.* (mĕnt), nourish; **-ation; -ary; -al; -ally**

ăl'ĭ-mō-nў, *n.*, support money in divorce

à-līve', *a.*, living, alert

ăl'kà-lĭ, *n.*, acid neutralizer; **loid; -ze; -c; -ne, -nity**

äll, *a.*, *n.*, *adv.*, entire, every

àl-lāy', *v.*, calm

àl-lĕge', *v.*, declare without proof; **gation**

àl-lē'giànce, *n.*, loyalty

ăl'lé-gô-rÿ, *n.*, symbolic story; **rist; rize; rical; rically** [cally fast

àl-lĕ'grŏ, *a.*, *adv.*, musi-

ăl'lêr-gÿ, *n.*, sensitivity of body to things; **gist; gic**

àl-lē'vĭ-āte, *v.*, relieve; **tor; tion; tive; tory**

ăl'lēy, *n.*, narrow lane

àl-lī'ánce, *n.*, union, league

àl-līt'ĕr-ā-tion, *v.*, repetition of initial word sounds; **rate; tive; tively**

ăl'lŏ-cāte, *v.*, allot, distribute; **tion; cable**

àl-lŏt', *v.*, assign shares; **-ment**

àl-loᴡ', *v.*, let; **-ance; -able; -ably** [ture

ăl'loy' (**lŏi**), *n.*, metal mix-

àl-lūde', *v.*, refer

àl-lūre', *v.*, entice; **-ment**

àl-lū'sion, *n.*, casual mention; **sive; sively**

ăl'lÿ, *n.*, helper, associate; *v.* (**àl-lÿ'**), unite

ăl'mà màt'êr, *n.*, school attended

ăl'mà-năc, *n.*, calendar with extra data

ăl-mīght'ÿ, *a.*, all-powerful

ăl'mŏnd, *n.*, edible nut

ălms, *n.*, money, food, etc., for poor

à-lōne', *a.*, *adv.*, by oneself

à-lŏng', *prep.*, beside; *adv.*, forward, together

à-lŏof', *a.*, *adv.*, distant

ălp, *n.*, high mountain

ăl-păc'à, *n.*, llama domesticated for its wool

ăl'phà-bĕt, *n.*, ordered letters of a language; **-ize; -ical; -ically**

ăl-rĕad'ÿ, *adv.*, previously

ăl-rīght', *a.*, adequate; *int.*, yes

ăl'tàr, *n.*, holy platform or table

ăl'têr, *v.*, change; **-ation; -able; -ative**

ăl'têr-cāte, *v.*, quarrel; **tion**

ăl'têr-nāte, *v.*, do by turns; *a.* (**náte**), every other; **tion**

àl-têr'nà-tĭve, *n.*, choice; **-ly**

ăl-thŏugh', *conj.*, even if

ăl-tĭm'è-têr, *n.*, instrument measuring height

ăl'tĭ-tūde, *n.*, height; **dinal**

ăl'tŏ, *n.*, lowest female voice

ăl-tò-gĕth'êr, *adv.*, wholly

ăl'trū-ĭsm, *n.*, selflessness; **ruist; ruistic; ruistically**

à-lū'mĭ-nŭm, *n.*, light metal; **nize; nous**

à-lŭm'nŭs, *n.* (*pl.* **nī**), graduate

àl-vē'ŏ-lŭs, *n.* (*pl.* **-lī**), small cavity

ăl'wāys, *adv.*, forever

à-măl'gà-māte, *v.*, unite; **tor, tion; tive**

à-măss', *v.*, collect; **-er; -ment**

ăm'à-têur, *n.*, nonprofessional; **-ism; -ish; -ishly; -ishness**

à-māze', *v.*, surprise; **-ment; zingly** [woman

ăm'à-zŏn, *n.*, strong

ăm-băs'sà-dôr, *n.*, topranking diplomat; **-ship; dress** [brown

ăm'bêr, *a.*, yellowish-

ăm-bĭ-dĕx'troŭs, *a.*, using both hands equally

ăm-bĭg'ū-oŭs, *a.*, vague; **guity**

ăm-bĭ'tion, *n.*, drive to succeed; **tious**

ăm-bĭv'à-lénce, *n.*, conflicting feelings; **nt; ntly**

ăm'ble, *v.*, walk leisurely

ăm'bū-lánce, *n.*, vehicle to carry sick [tack

ăm'bŭsh, *n.*, surprise at-

à-mēl'ĭŏ-rāte, *v.*, improve; **tor; tion, tive; able**

ă-mĕn', *int.*, so be it

ă-mē'nà-ble, *a.*, easily led

à-mĕnd', v., change; -er;
-ment; -able [sation
à-mĕnds', n. pl., compen-
à-mĕn'ĭ-tў, n., pleasant-
ness
A-mĕr'ĭ-cà, n., western
hemisphere, United
States; -n
à-mêrse', v., punish by
fine; -ment
ăm'è-thýst, n., purple gem
ā'mĭ-à-ble, a., good na-
tured; bility
à-mĭd', prep., among
à-mĭss', a., adv., wrong
ăm'ĭ-tў, n., friendly
relations [gas
ăm-mō'nĭ-à, n., pungent
ăm-nē'sĭà, n., memory
loss; sic
ăm'nĕs-tў, n., pardon
à-moē'bà, n., one-celled
animal; bic
ā-môr'àl, a., without moral
sense; -ity; -ly
ăm'ô-roŭs, a., full of love;
-ness; -ly
à-môr'phoŭs, a., shape-
less; hism; -ly; -ness
ăm'ôr-tīze, v., pay gradually; zation; zable
à-moŭnt', n., sum; v.,
equal
ăm'pēre, n., unit of electrical current; rage
ăm-phĭb'ĭ-àn, n., one
adapted to land and
water; bious
ăm'ple, a., plentiful; -ness
ăm'plĭ-fў, v., increase;
fier; fication [dance
ăm'plĭ-tūde, n., abun-
ăm'pū-tāte, v., surgically
cut off; tor; tee; tion
à-mūse', v., entertain; -r;
-ment, sable
ăn, art., one
ăn-à-cŏn'dà, n., large
snake that crushes its
prey
ăn'à-grăm, n., new words
from letters of another
word; -matize; -matic;
-matical; -matically
à-năl'ò-gў, n., likeness;
gist; gize; gous; gical;
gically

à-năl'ў-sĭs, n., examina-
tion of parts of whole;
lyst; lyze; lytic; lytical;
lytically [ness
ăn'âr-chў (kў), n., lawless-
hist; hism; histic; hic
à-năth'è-mà, n., reli-
gious curse; mize
à-năt'ò-mў, n., study of
body structure; mist;
mize; mical; mically
ăn'cĕs-trў, n., family lineage; tor; ral; rally
ăn'chŏr (kŏr), n., iron object to secure ship; -age
ăn'chò-rīte (kò), n., hermit
ăn'chō-vў, n., small her-
ān'ciènt, a., old [ring
ăn-dän'tē, a., adv., slow
ănd'ĭrŏn, n., fireplace support for wood
ăn'ĕc-dōte, n., brief story;
tal; tic; tical
à-nē'mĭ-à, n., low count of
red blood cells; mic
ăn-ĕs-thĕt'ĭc, n., drug
causing feeling loss;
tist; tize
à-new' (nū), adv., again
ān'gèl, n., God's messen-
ger; -ic
ăn'gêr, n., fury, rage; gry
ăn'gle, n., shape of two
lines meeting at a point,
corner
ăn'glêr, n., fisherman
ăn-gôr'à, n., kind of wool
ăn'guĭsh, n., v., distress
ăn'gū-làr, a., having an-
gles; -ity; -ly; -ness
ăn-hў'droŭs, a., without
water
ăn'īle, a., old-womanish
ăn'ĭ-màl, n., living be-
ing; -ist; -ism; -istic;
-istically; -ity; -ize
ăn-ĭ-mŏs'ĭ-tў, n., hostility
ăn'ĭ-mŭs, n., ill will
ăn'kle, n., joint connecting
leg and foot
ăn'klĕt, n., ankle orna-
ment, sock [ords
ăn'nàls, n., pl., yearly rec-
àn-nī'hĭ-lāte, v., destroy;
tor; tion; tive
ăn-nĭ-vêr'sà-rў, n., event
recurring yearly

ăn'nō-tāte, v., make notes about; tor; tion; tive

àn-noúnce', v., declare; -r; -ment

àn-noy' (noĭ), v., bother; -er; -ance

àn'nū-àl, a., yearly; -ly

àn-nŭl', v., do away with

ăn'ōde, n., positive electrode; dic

à-nóint', v., consecrate with oil; -er; -ment

à-nŏm'à-lÿ, n., deviation from norm; lism; listic; lous; lously; lousness

à-nŏn', adv., soon

à-nŏn'ÿ-moŭs, a., nameless; mity; -ly [more

àn-óth'êr, adj., prep., one

ăn'swêr, n., v., reply; -able

ănt, n., tiny wingless insect

ănt-ăc'ĭd, n., acid neutralizer

ăn'tē, n., poker stake

ăn-tē-bĕl'lŭm, a., before Civil War

ăn'tė-lōpe, n., deer

ăn-tĕn'nà, n., aerial

àn-tē'rĭ-ór, adj., at front

ăn'tė-rōom, n., waiting room

ăn'thĕm, n., national hymn

ăn-thŏl'ō-gÿ, n., literary collection; gist; gize; gical

ăn'thrà-cīte, n., hard coal

ăn'thrăx, n., cattle disease

ăn-thró-pŏl'ō-gÿ, n., study of man; gist; gical; gically

ăn'tĭ-bŏd-ÿ, n., body substance that fights toxins

ăn-tĭc'ĭ-pāte, v., expect; tor; tion; pant; tive; tory

ăn-tĭ-clī'măx, n., descent from important to trivial; mactic

ăn'tĭ-dōte, n., remedy to counteract poison; tal

ăn'tĭ-gĕn, n., substance causing body to make antibodies

ăn-tĭ-hĭs'tà-mĭne, n., drug to treat allergies

ăn'tĭ-mō-nÿ, n., metal; nic; nous; nial

ăn-tĭ-păs'tō, n., appetizer

ăn-tĭp'à-thÿ, n., dislike; thetic; thetical, thetically [posite

ăn'tĭ-pōde, n., exact op-

ăn-tïque', n., old relic

ăn-tĭ-Sĕ-mĭt'ĭc, a., against Jews; tism; mite

ăn-tĭ-sĕp'tĭc, n., a., (substance) inhibiting infection; sepsis -ize; -ally

ăn-tĭ-sō'ciàl, a., unfriendly

ăn-tĭth'ė-sĭs, n., contrast; thetical

ăn-tĭ-tŏx'ĭn, n., serum to prevent disease; xic

ăn'tó-nÿm, n., opposite meaning to word

ā'nŭs, n., bowel opening; nal [metal on

ăn'vĭl, n., block to hammer

ănx-ĭ'ė-tÿ, n., uneasiness; xious; xiously, xiousness

an'ÿ (ĕn), a., one or some of several

an'ÿ-how (ĕn), adv., in any case

an-ÿ-môre' (ĕn), adv., now

à-ôr'tă, n., main artery from heart

à-pāce', adv., swiftly

à-pârt'heid (hād), n., policy of racial segregation

ă-pârt'mĕnt, n., room(s) to live in

ăp'à-thÿ, n., lack of interest; hetic, hetically

ăp'êr-tûre, n., opening

ā'pĕx, n., highest point

à-phā'sĭ-à, n., loss of use or understanding of speech [plant juice

ā'phĭd, n., bug that sucks

ăph'ò-rĭsm, n., saying

ăp'ĭ-âr-ÿ, n., bee-keeping place; rist

à-pīece', adv., each [dant

à-plĕn'tÿ, a., adv., abun-

à-pŏl'ò-gÿ, n., expression of regret; gize; gizer

à-pŏs'tle, n., missionary

à-pŏs'tró-phē, n., punctuation mark [gist

à-pŏth'ė-cār-ÿ, n., drug-

ăp-pāll', v., shock; -ing

ăp-pà-ră'tŭs, n., equipment

ăp-păr′ĕl, *n.,* clothing

ăp-pà-rī′tion, *n.,* ghost; **-al**

ăp-pēal′, *v.,* make a request

ăp-pēar′, *v.,* seem; **-ance**

ăp-pĕl-lā′tion, *n.,* name; **tive**

ăp-pĕn′dĭx, *n.,* additional part [sire

ăp′pè-tīte, *n.,* strong de-

ăp-plăud′, *v.,* approve,

ăp′ple, *n.,* fruit [clap

ăp-plī′ance, *n.,* useful device

ăp′plĭ-cà-ble, *a.,* relevant; **bility**

ăp-point′, *v.,* assign; **-or; -ee; -ment**

ăp-pôr′tion, *n.,* allot; **′-ment**

ăp′pò-sĭte, *a.,* suitable; **tion; tional; tionally; -ly; -ness**

ăp-prē′cĭ-āte, *v.,* value; **tor; tion, tory, tive; tively; tiveness; ciable; ciably**

ăp-prĕn′tĭce, *n.,* helper learning a trade; **-ship**

ăp-prīse′, *v.,* notify

ăp-prōach′, *v.,* come near; **-able; -ability** [proval

ăp-prò-bā′tion, *n.,* ap-

ăp-prŏx′ĭ-māte, *v.,* come near; *a.* **(āte)** nearly; **tion; -ly**

ā′prĭ-cŏt, *n.,* fruit [ment

ā′prŏn, *n.,* protective gar-

ăp-rò-pōs′ (pō), *a., adv.,* relevant

ăpt, *a.,* suitable; **-ly; -ness**

ăp′tĭ-tūde, *n.,* fitness

ăq′uà, *n.,* water; **queous**

à-quăr′ĭ-ŭm, *n.,* a water tank for fish

à′què-dŭct, *n.,* channel for supplying water

ăr′à-ble, *a.,* fit for farming

à-răch′nĭd, *n.,* eight-legged insects

âr′bĭ-têr, *n.,* umpire

âr′bĭ-trāte, *v.,* settle a dispute; **tor; tion; tive; tional**

âr′bôr, *n.,* shaded place

ârc, *n.,* circle segment

ârch, *n.,* curved structure;

a., main

âr-chaē-ŏl′ò-gỹ (kē), *n.,* study of ancient times; **gist; gical; gically**

âr-chā′ĭc (kā), *a.,* old; **-ly**

ârch′êr, *n.,* shooter of arrows with bow; **-y**

âr-chĭ-pĕl′à-gō (kĭ), *n.,* group of islands

âr′chīves, *n. pl.,* public records; **vist; val**

âr′dör, *n.,* passion; **dent; dently**

âr′dū-oŭs, *a.,* hard; **-ly; -ness**

âr′ē-à, *n.,* surface; **-l**

à-rē′nà, *n.,* fighting area

är′gūe, *v.,* quarrel, dispute; **gument; gumentation; gumentative; gumentatively; guable; guably**

â′rĭ-à, *n.,* melody of opera

âr′ĭd, *a.,* dry

à-rīse′, *v.,* get up

à-rĭth′mè-tĭc, *n.,* science of numbers; **-ian, -al; -ally**

ârk, *n.,* boat, chest

ârm, *n.,* body's upper limb; *v.,* furnish weapons; **-ful**

âr-mà-dĭl′lō, *n.,* animal with armorlike covering

âr′mĭ-stĭce, *n.,* truce

âr′mör, *n.,* protective covering

âr′mör-ȳ, *n.,* arsenal

âr′mȳ, *n.,* unit of soldiers

à-rō′mà, *n.,* smell; **-tic; -tically**

à-roŭse′, *v.,* awaken, stir

âr-rāign′, *n.,* accuse; **-ment**

âr-rānge′, *v.,* put in order; **-ment**

âr-rēar′, *n.,* overdue debt

âr-rĕst′, *v.,* stop, seize

âr-rīve′, *v.,* come to a place; **-val**

âr′rŏw, *n.,* pointed rod to shoot with bow

âr′sè-năl, *n.,* storehouse of weapons [element

âr′sè-nĭc, *n.,* poisonous

ârt, *n.,* skill, creative work; **-ist; -istry; -y; -istic; -istically; -ful**

är'têr-ÿ, *n.*, blood vessel

är-thrī'tĭs, *n.*, joint inflammation; **tic**

är'tĭ-cle, *n.*, item

är-tĭc'ū-lāte, *v.*, say clearly; *a.* (**lăte**), able to speak; **tor; tion; -ly; -ness**

är'tĭ-făct, *n.*, simple man-made object

är'tĭ-fĭce, *n.*, clever trick

är-tĭ-fĭ'ciàl, *a.*, not real; **-ity; -ly**

är-tĭl'lêr-ÿ, *n.*, mounted guns; **rist**

är'tĭ-sàn, *n.*, craftsman

ăs, *adv.*, *prep.*, like; *conj.*, while [material

ăs-bĕs'tòs, *n.*, fireproof

às-cĕnt', *n.*, a way up

às-cĕt'ĭc, *a.*, *n.*, self-denying (person); **-ism; -ally**

ăs'cŏt, *n.*, neck scarf

às-crībe', *v.*, credit; **bable**

ā-sĕx'ū-àl, *a.*, sexless

ăsh, *n.*, fire residue, tree

ăsh'ĕn, *a.*, pale

à-shôre', *a.*, *adv.*, on land

ăs'ī-nīne, *a.*, silly

à-skănce', *adv.*, sideways

ăsp, *n.*, poisonous snake

à-spăr'à-gŭs, *n.*, stalky green vegetable

ăs'pĕct, *n.*, phase

ăs-pêr'ĭ-tÿ, *n.*, harshness

às-pêr'sion, *n.*, slander

ăs'phàlt, *n.*, tarlike mixture

ăs-phÿx'ĭ-āte, *v.*, suffocate; **tor; tion; xiant**

ăs'pĭc, *n.*, gelatin mold

ăs'pĭ-rā-tôr, *n.*, suction apparatus

ăs-pire', *v.*, be ambitious; **-r; ration**

ăs'pĭ-rĭn, *n.*, pain-reducing pill or powder

ăss, *n.*, donkey, fool

às-sāil', *v.*, attack; **-er; -ment; -ant; -able**

às-săs'sĭn, *n.*, killer; **-ation; -ate**

às-säult', *n.*, *v.*, attack

às-sĕnt', *n.*, *v.*, consent; **-er; -ation**

às-sêrt', *v.*, declare; **-er; -or; -ion; -ive; -ively;** -iveness

às-sĕss', *v.*, set tax value on; **-or; -ment**

ăs'sĕt, *n.*, valuable thing

às-sīgn', *v.*, allot; **-er; -or; -ee; -ation; -ment; -able**

às-sĭm'ĭ-lāte, *v.*, resemble, absorb; **tion; tion-ism; tionist; tive**

às-sō'cĭ-āte, *v.*, join; *n.* (**āte**), friend, partner; **tion; tive**

às-sôrt', *v.*, classify; **-ment**

às-suāge', *v.*, lessen; **-ment**

às-sūme', *v.*, take on; **-r; mable**

às-sūre', *v.*, make certain; **-r; rance**

às-sûr'gĕnt, *a.*, upward

ăs'têr, *n.*, flower

ăs'têr-ĭsk, *n.*, starlike sign

ăs'têr-ōĭd, *n.*, small planet; *a.*, starlike

ăsth'mà, *n.*, breathing disorder; **-tic**

à-stĭg'mà-tĭsm, *n.*, eye defect causing blurriness

à-stĭr', *a.*, *adv.*, in motion

às-tŏn'ĭsh, *v.*, surprise; **-ment**

à-strāy', *adv.*, in error

à-strīde', *adv.*, legs apart

às-trĭn'gĕnt, *a.*, contracting; **ncy; -ly**

às-trŏl'ō-gÿ, *n.*, science of human prediction by stars; **ger; gist; gical; gically**

ăs-trōn'ò-mÿ, *n.*, science of stars; **mer; mical; mically**

às-tūte', *a.*, clever

à-sŭn'dêr, *adv.*, apart

à-sÿ'lŭm, *n.*, refuge

ā'thē-ĭsm, *n.*, belief that God does not exist; **st; stic; stical; stically**

ăth'lēte, *n.*, skilled sport participant; **tics; tic; tically** [crosswise

à-thwart' (ôrt), *adv.*, *prep.*,

ăt'làs, *n.*, book of maps

ăt'mòs-phēre, *n.*, air surrounding earth; **ric**

ăt'ŏll, *n.,* coral island

ăt'ŏm, *n.,* basic component of matter; **-ize; -ic; -icity; -ics** [device

ăt'ŏm-īz-êr, *n.,* spraying

à-tōne', *v.,* make amends; **-ment**

ăt'ŏ-nÿ, *n.,* lacking body tone; **tonic; tonicity**

ā'trĭ-ŭm, *n.,* central court

à-trŏc'ĭ-tÿ, *n.,* cruelty; **cious; ciousness; ciously**

ăt'rŏ-phÿ, *n.,* waste away; **hic**

àt-tăch', *v.,* fasten; **-ment; -able**

ăt-tà-che' (shā), *n.,* diplomatic staff member

àt-tăck', *n., v.,* assault; **-er**

àt-tāin', *v.,* reach; **-ment; -able; -ability**

àt-tāin'dêr, *n.,* forfeiture of civil rights

àt-tāint', *v.,* dishonor

àt-tĕnd', *v.,* be present; **-ance; -ant**

àt-tĕn'tion, *n.,* notice, care; **tive; tiveness; tively**

àt-tĕst', *v.,* certify; **-er; -or; -ation** [roof

ăt'tĭc, *n.,* space just under

àt-tīre', *n., v.,* dress

ăt'tĭ-tŭde, *n.,* manner; **dinal; dinize**

àt-tör'nēy, *n.,* lawyer

àt-trăct', *v.,* draw toward; **-er; tion; tive; -able**

ăt'trĭ-būte, *n.,* quality

àt-trī'tion, *n.,* gradual wearing away

à-tÿp'ĭ-cǎl, *a.,* abnormal; **-ly**

äu'bûrn, *a.,* reddish-brown

äuc'tion, *n.,* public sale; **-eer**

äu-dăc'ĭ-tÿ, *n.,* bold courage; **cious; ciousness; ciously**

äu'dĭ-ble, *a.,* can be heard; **bility; bly**

äu'dĭ-ênce, *n.,* assembly of listeners

äu-dĭ-ō-vĭs'ŭ-ǎl, *a.,* about both hearing and seeing

äu'dĭt, *n.,* formal financial examination; **-or**

äu-dĭ'tion, *n.,* tryout

äu'gêr, *n.,* drill

äug-mĕnt', *v.,* increase; **-er; -ation; -ative; -able**

äu'gŭr, *v.,* foretell

äu-gŭst', *a.,* grand

äuk, *n.,* diving bird

au'rà (ô), *n.,* sensation about

äu'rĭ-cle, *n.,* heart chamber

äus-pĭ'ciŏus, *a.,* favorable; **-ness; -ly**

äu-thĕn'tic, *a.,* genuine; **-ity; -ate; -ator; -ation; -ally**

äu'thŏr, *n.,* creator, writer; **-ship; -less**

äu'thŏr-ize, *v.,* empower; **-r; zation**

äu-tō-bĭ-ŏg'rà-phÿ, *n.,* story by and about oneself; **her; hic; hically**

äu-tŏc'rà-cÿ, *n.,* dictatorship; **tocrat; tocratic**

äu'tŏ-grăph, *n.,* one's signature; **-y; -ic; -ically**

äu-tŏ-măt'ĭc, *a.,* spontaneous; **-ally**

äu-tŏn'ŏ-mÿ, *n.,* independence; **mist; mous**

äu'tŏp-sÿ, *n.,* examination of dead body

äu'tŭmn, *n.,* fall season

äux-ĭl'ia-rÿ, *a.,* additional, assisting

à-vāil', *v.,* be helpful; **-able; -ably; -ability**

ăv'à-rĭce, *n.,* greed for wealth; **cious; ciousness; ciously**

à-vĕnge', *v.,* take revenge; **-r**

à-vêr', *v.,* declare true

ăv'êr-àge, *n.,* sum divided by its parts; *a.,* normal

à-vêrt', *v.,* turn away

ā'vĭ-är-ÿ, *n.,* birds' cage

ā-vĭ-ā'tion, *n.,* science of airplanes; **tor; viate**

ăv-ŏ-cā'tion, *n.,* hobby; **-al**

à-vōĭd', *v.,* escape; **-able; -ably**

à-voW', *v.,* declare; **-er; -al**

à-wāre', *a.,* conscious

A
B

āwe, *n.,* reverence; *v.,* inspire; **-some**
āw'fŭl, *a.,* terrible; **-ly**
āwk'wård, *a.,* ungraceful; **-ness; -ly** [dow shade
äwn'ĭng, *n.,* outside winä-wrȳ', *a.,* twisted, wrong
äx, äxe, *n.,* chopping tool
äx'ĭ-öm, *n.,* obvious truth; **-atic; -atically**
äx'le, *n.,* rod on which wheel turns
äx'ön, *n.,* nerve cell
aȳe, *adv.,* yes [shrub
à-zāl'eä, *n.,* flowering
äz'ûre, *a.,* sky-blue

B

bäa, *n.,* sheep cry; *v.,* bleat
bäb'ble, *n.,* meaningless talk; *v.,* make sounds
bābe, *n.,* baby
bä-bōōn', *n.,* large monkey
bā'bȳ, *n.,* very young child
bā'bȳ-sĭt, *v.,* watch over children; **-ter**
bäc-cà-läu'rē-àte, *n.,* college bachelor's degree
bäc-cà-rat' (râ), *n.,* gambling card game
bäc-cĭv'ör-oŭs, *a.,* berryfeeding
bäch'-ė-lör, *n.,* unmarried man; **-hood**
bäck, *n.,* rear part of; *v.,* support; *a., adv.,* at the rear; **-er**
bäck'bīte, *v.,* slander
bäck'bōne, *n.,* spine, main support, courage
bäck'fīre, *n.,* unexpected result; *v.,* go awry
bäck'gäm-mön, *n.,* board game
bäck'groŭnd, *n.,* past events, less important place [rect, insincere
bäck'händ-ĕd, *a.,* indi-
bäck'ĭng, *n.,* endorsement
bäck'läsh, *n.,* sudden reaction [reserve
bäck'lŏg, *n.,* something in
bäck'sīde, *n.,* rump, buttocks
bäck'släp-pêr, *n.,* overly friendly person [virtue

bäck'slīde, *v.,* slip from
bäck'stäge, *a., adv.,* behind the stage, wings, etc. [withdraw
bäck'träck, *v.,* revisit path,
bäck'ŭp, *a.,* alternate, supportive
bäck'wård, *a., adv.,* behind, reversed
bäck'wä-têr, *n.,* stagnant water [pork meat
bā'cön, *n.,* salted, smoked
bäc-tē'rĭ-à, *n. pl.,* onecelled microorganisms; **-l; -lly**
bäd, *a.,* not good, evil; **-ly**
bädge, *n.,* membership pin [bother
bädg'êr, *n.,* animal; *v.,*
bäd-ĭ-náge', *n.,* playful talk
bäd'mĭn-tön, *n.,* game played hitting feather ball
bäf'fle, *v.,* confuse; **-r; -ment**
bäg, *n.,* soft container; *v.,* enclose in bag, hang loosely; **-ful**
bäg-à-tĕlle', *n.,* trifle
bā'gĕl, *n.,* hard roll
bäg'gäge, *n.,* traveler's equipment
bäg'pīpe, *n.,* Scottish reed instrument [diamond
bä-guĕtte', *n.,* narrow-cut
bāil, *n.,* deposit to ensure prisoner's appearance; *v.,* dip out water
bāi'lĭff, *n.,* deputy sheriff
bāi'lĭ-wick, *n.,* one's area of interest
bâirn, *n.,* child
bāit, *n.,* food to catch fish or animals; *v.,* entice
bäl'ánce, *n.,* weighing device, equality; *v.,* weigh, equalize
bäl'cö-nȳ, *n.,* projecting platform with rail
bäld, *a.,* hairless on head
bäl'dêr-däsh, *n.,* nonsense
bāle, *n.,* large bundle
bâlk, *n.,* hinder, stop; **-y**
bâll, *n.,* round object for games, social dance

băl'lȧd, *n.*, story-telling song; **-eer; -ry**

băl'lȧst, *n.*, heavy matter to balance ship

băl-lė-rī'nȧ, *n.*, woman ballet dancer

băl'let (lā), *n.*, artistic group dance

bȧl lĭs'tĭcs,*n.*, study of bullets

bȧl-lōōn',*n.*, air-filled bag; *v.*, expand   [vote

băl'lȯt,*n.*, paper for voting,

băl'lў-hōō, *n.*, loud talk

bȧlm, *n.*, healing ointment

bȧ-lō'nĕy, *n.*, nonsense

bȧl'sȧ, *n.*, light wood

bȧl'sȧm, *n.*, aromatic resins, oils   [for railing

băl'ŭs têr,*n.*, support post

băm-bĭ'nō, *n.*, baby

băm-bōō', *n.*, tall, hollow, woody grass stems

băm-bōō'zle,*v.*, trick, confuse; **-r; -ment**

băn, *n.*, public edict; *v.*, forbid

bȧ-năn'ȧ, *n.*, ·oblong yellow-skinned fruit

bănd, *n.*, strip that binds, group of musicians; *v.*, join together   [injury

bănd'ȧge,*n.*, strip to bind

băn-dăn'nȧ,*n.*, large print handkerchief

băn-deau'(ō), *n.*, headband   [fighter

băn-dė-rĭl-lĕ'rō, *n.*, bull-

băn'dė-rōle,*n.*, pennant

băn'dĭt, *n.*, robber   [tor

bănd'măs-têr,*n.*, conduc-

bănd'wăg-ȯn, *n.* (coll.), winning side   [forth

băn'dў, *v.*, hit back and

bāne, *n.*, ruin; **-ful**

băn'gle,*n.*, bracelet

băng'ŭp, *a.* (coll.), excellent

băn'ĭsh, *v.*, send away; **-ment**

băn'is-têr, *n.*, railing

băn'jō, *n.*, guitar-like instrument; **-ist**

bănk, *n.*, financial institution, shore, row of objects

bănk'rŭpt, *n.*, inability to

pay debts; **-cy**

băn'nêr, *n.*, flag·with slogan or motto

băn'quĕt,*n.*, elegant feast

băn'tȧm, *n.*, small fowl

băn'tȧm-weight (wāt), *n.*, 113–118-pound boxer

băn'têr.*v.*, joke; **-er;-ingly**

băp'tĭsm,*n.*, rite with water to join church; **st; tīze**

băr,*n.*, oblong solid piece, musical measure, legal profession, counter serving liquor; *v.*, close, exclude

bârb,*n.*, sharp point, biting remark; **-ed**

bâr'bė-cūe, *n.*, meat roasted over open fire; *v.*, roast, broil

bâr'bêr, *n.*, hair-cutter

bâr'bêr-rў,*n.*, spiny shrub with red berries

bâr-bĭ'tu-rȧte, *n.*, drug used as sedative

bârd, *n.*, poet   [uncover

bāre, *a.*, naked, mere; *v.*,

bāre'băck, *a.*, *adv.*, on horse with no saddle

bāre'fāced, *a.*, shameless; **-ness**

bāre'lў, *adv.*, scarcely

bâr'gaĭn, *n.*, agreement; *v.*, barter; **-er**

bârge, *n.*, flat-bottomed freight boat; *v.*, enter rudely

băr'ĭ-tōne, *n.*, male voice between tenor and bass

băr'ĭ-ŭm,*n.*, chemical element

bârk, *n.*, tree-covering, dog's cry; *v.*, snap; **-er**

bâr'lĕy,*n.*, cereal grain

bâr'māid,*n.*, woman serving drinks

bârm'ў, *a.*, foamy

bâr'nȧ-clė, *n.*, ship-clinging shellfish

bârn'stôrm, *v.*, perform in rural areas; **-er**

băr'ȯn, *n.*, nobleman; **-ess; -age**

bȧ-rō'nĭ-ȧl, *a.*, grand

bȧ-rōque', *a.*, overdecorated   [mitory

băr'răck, *n.*, soldiers' dor-

bӑr-rȧ-cū'dȧ, *n.*, fierce fish

bȧr-räge', *n.*, heavy attack

bȧr'rȧ-trÿ, *n.*, encouragement of causing lawsuits; **tor; trous**

bȧr'rêl, *n.*, large wooden cylindrical container

bȧr'rӗn, *a.*, sterile

bȧr-rӗtte', *n.*, hair clasp

bȧr'rĭ-êr, *n.*, obstacle

bȧr'rĭs-têr, *n.*, lawyer

bȧr'rōw, *n.*, pushcart, hill

bȧr'tӗnd-êr, *n.*, one serving liquor

bȧr'têr, *v.*, trade [turret

bȧr'tĭ-zȧn, *n.*, overhanging

bȧ-sält', *n.*, volcanic rock; **-ic**

bāse, *n.*, foundation, principle, goal; *a.*, low, dishonest; **-sic; -sal**

bāse'bäll, *n.*, team game with bat and ball, ball used

bāse'bôard, *n.*, wall molding next to floor

bāse'mӗnt, *n.*, lowest floor of building, cellar

bӑsh, *v.*, smash; *n.*, party

bӑsh'fŭl, *a.*, shy; **-ly; -ness**

bӑs'ĭl, *n.*, herb

bȧ-sĭl'ĭ-cȧ, *n.*, ancient Roman building, church

bā'sĭn, *n.*, washbowl, bay

bӑsk, *v.*, warm oneself

bӑs'kӗt, *n.*, woven wood container; **-ry**

bӑs'kӗt-bӑll, *n.* team game with basket, ball

bӑss, *n.*, fish, low, deep tone or voice

bӑs'sӗt, *n.*, dog

bӑs-sĭ-nӗt', *n.*, basketlike baby bed

bȧs-sōōn', *n.*, bass wind instrument; **-ist**

bӑss'wood, *n.*, tree

bāste, *v.*, moisten roasting meat; sew loose stitches

bӑs'tion, *n.*, fortified place

bӑt, *n.*, stout club, flying mammal; *v.*, strike, flutter; **-ter; -tery**

bӑtch, *n.*, quantity done

bȧ-teau'(tō), *n.*, flat-bottomed boat [washing

bӑth, *n.*, washing, water for

bȧ-thŏm'ė-têr, *n.;* apparatus measuring water depth

bā'thŏs, *n.*, sentimentality

bӑth'rōbe, *n.*, lounging garment

bȧ-thÿm'ė-trÿ, *n.*, science of water depth; **ric; rical; rically** [method

bȧ-tĭk', *n.*, cloth-dyeing

bȧ-tĭste', *n.*, fine thin cloth

bȧ-tŏn', *n.*, slender stick for leading music

bӑt-tӑl'iŏn, *n.*, large group of soldiers

bӑt'tӗn, *n.*, wood strip

bӑt'têr-ÿ, *n.*, set, power source, beating

bӑt'tle, *n.*, *v.*, fight

bӑt'tle-mӗnt, *n.*, low wall on tower

bäu'ble, *n.*, trinket

bäux'īte, *n.*, mineral having aluminum

bäwd'ÿ, *a.*, obscene; **ily; iness**

bäwl, *v.*, cry; **-er**

bāy, *n.* water inlet, alcove; *v.*, bark; *a.*, reddish-brown

bāy'bӗr-rÿ, *n.*, shrub

bāy'ȯ-nӗt, *n.*, blade on end of rifle [let

baÿ'oū, *n.*, marshy river in-

bȧ-zâar', *n.*, street of shops; charity sale

bȧ-zōō'kȧ, *n.*, weapon

bӗach, *n.*, sandy shore

bӗa'cȯn, *n.*, warning light

bӗad, *n.*, small round object for stringing, drop; **-y**

bӗa'dle, *n.*, parish officer

bӗa'gle, *n.*, hunting dog

bӗak'êr, *n.*, glass container

bӗam, *n.*, long thick piece of wood, ray, smile

bӗan, *n.*, vegetable, edible seed, its pod; *v.* (coll.), hit on head

bӗar, *n.*, animal; *v.*, carry, give birth, endure, produce; **-er**

bӗard, *n.*, hair on face, whiskers; **-ed; -less**

bӗar'ĭng, *n.*, one's manner,

posture; relationship

bĕast, *n.,* animal, gross person; **-ly; -liness**

bĕat, *n.,* throb, route, musical unit; *v.,* hit repeatedly, mix, flap, win; *a.,* tired; **-er**

beau (bō), *n.,* sweetheart

beaū'tĭ-fŭl, *a.,* eye-pleasing; **-ly**

beaū'tў, *n.,* pleasing quality; **teous** [animal

bēa'vêr, *n.,* dam-building

bĕck'ŏn, *v.,* summon

bĕ-clŏud', *v.,* darken, confuse

bĕ-cŏme', *v.,* change into, suit; **coming** [base

bĕd, *n.,* thing to sleep on,

bĕ-dâub', *v.,* smear

bĕ-dăz'zle, *v.,* confuse

bĕd'bŭg, *n.,* wingless bug

bĕ-dĕck', *v.,* adorn

bĕ-dĕv'ĭl, *v.,* torment; **-ment**

bĕd'fĕl-lōw, *n.,* friend

bĕ-dĭz'ĕn, *v.,* cheaply decorate

bĕd'lăm, *n.,* insane asylum; confusion

bēe, *n.,* insect that makes honey, group meeting

bēech, *n.,* tree

bĕef, *n.,* cow or bull meat; **-y**

bēe'līne, *n.,* direct route

bēep, *n.,* high-pitched sound; **-er**

bēer, *n.,* alcoholic drink brewed from malt; **-y**

bēet, *n.,* root vegetable

bēe'tle, *n.,* insect, mallet; *v.,* jut

bĕ-fäll', *v.,* happen

bĕ-fĭt', *v.,* be suitable; **-ting; -tingly**

bĕ-fŏg', *v.,* confuse

bĕ-fôre', *adv., prep., conj.,* earlier

bĕ-fŏul', *v.,* make dirty

bĕ-friĕnd', *v.,* help

bĕ-fŭd'dle, *v.,* confuse

bĕg, *v.,* ask for; **-gar; -garly** [cause

bĕ-gĕt', *v.,* give birth to,

bĕ-gĭn'nĭng, *n.,* origin

bĕ-gŏne', *v., inter.,* go

away

bĕ-gō'nĭ-å, *n.,* plant

bĕ-grŭdge', *v.,* envy

bĕ-guīle', *v.,* deceive, amuse

bĕ-hāve', *v.,* act, conduct oneself

bĕ-hĕst', *n.,* order [back

bĕ-hīnd', *a., adv., prep.,* in

bĕ-hŏld', *v., int.,* look

bĕ-hŏld'ĕn, *a.,* grateful

bĕ-hŏove', *v.,* be morally necessary [tan

beige (bāzh), *a.,* grayish-

bĕ-jew'ĕl, *v.,* decorate with jewels [cize

bĕ-lā'bôr, *v.,* beat, criti-

bĕ-lāy', *v.,* secure

bĕlch, *v.,* expel gas from mouth

bĕ-lēa'guêr, *v.,* besiege

bĕl'frў, *n.,* bell tower

bĕ-līe', *v.,* falsify; **-r**

bĕ-lief', *n.,* faith, trust, opinion

bĕ-liēve', *v.,* take as true, think; **-r; lievable; lievability; lievably**

bĕ-lĭt'tle, *v.,* make seem unimportant; **-r; -ment**

bĕll, *n.,* cuplike object that can ring

bĕlle, *n.,* pretty girl

bĕll'hŏp, *n.,* hotel porter

bĕl'lĭ-cōse, *a.,* quarrelsome

bĕl'lōw, *v.,* roar

bĕl'lōws, *n., sing. & pl.,* device that makes air

bĕll'wĕth-êr, *n.,* male sheep that leads flock

bĕl'lў, *n.,* abdomen, stomach

bĕ-lōw', *a., adv., prep.,* lower, beneath

bĕlt, *n.,* strap around waist, area; *v.,* hit; **-ed**

bĕ-mīre', *v.,* make dirty

bĕ-mōan', *v.,* mourn

bĕnch, *n.,* long hard seat; **-er**

bĕnd, *n., v.,* curve; **-er; -able** [lower, under

bĕ-nēath', *a., adv., prep.,*

bĕn'ĕ-dĭct, *n.,* newly married ex-bachelor

bĕn-ĕ-dĭc'tion, *n.,* blessing; **tory**

běn′ė-fĭt, *n.*, charitable act, help; **ficial; ficially**

bė-nĭgn′, *a.*, kind, not harmful; **-ity; -ant; -ly**

běn′ĭ-sŏn, *n.*, blessing

běn′zēne, *n.*, clear liquid from coal tar

běn′zīne, *n.*, liquid used in gasoline and for dry cleaning

běn′zō-cāine, *n.*, anesthetic ointment

bė-quēath′, *v.*, give by will; **-al** [will

bė-quĕst′, *n.*, that left by

bė-rāte′, *v.*, scold

bė-rēave′, *v.*, deprive, leave lonely; **-ment; -d**

bė-ret′ (rā), *n.*, flat round cap

běr-i-běr′ĭ, *n.*, disease of vitamin B deficiency

běr′rў, *n.*, small juicy fleshy fruit

bêr-sêrk′, *a., adv.*, violent rage; **-er** [anchor, job

bêrth, *n.*, bed, place to

bêr′thȧ, *n.*, woman's wide

běr′ўl, *n.*, mineral [collar

bė-rўl′lĭ-ŭm, *n.*, metallic element

bė-sēech′, *v.*, beg for; **-ingly**

bė-sět′, *v.*, attack; **-ting**

bė-siēge′, *v.*, attack, overwhelm; **-r**

bė-smēar′, *v.*, soil

bē′sŏm, *n.*, broom

bė-sŏt′, *v.*, make drunk; **-ted** [with spangles

bė-spăn′gle, *v.*, decorate

bė-spăt′tėr, *v.*, spread dirt, slander

bė-spēak′, *v.*, order, engage beforehand

běs′tiȧl, *a.*, beastlike, savage; **-ity; -ize; tiary**

bė-stĭr′, *v.*, exert

bė-stōw′, *v.*, give; **-al**

bė-strew′, *v.*, cover over

bė-strīde′, *v.*, straddle

bět, *n.*, wager; *v.*, pledge a thing as result of con-

bė-tāke′, *v.*, go [text

bē′tėl, *n.*, climbing plant

bė-tīde′, *v.*, happen

bė-tō′kėn, *v.*, indicate, show

bė-trāy′, *v.*, deceive; **-er; -al**

bė-twēen′, *adv., prep.*, in the middle of, connecting [measure angles

běv′ėl, *n.*, tool to draw or

běv′êr-ȧge, *n.*, any drink

běv′ў, *n.*, group

bė-wāre′, *v.*, be careful

bė-wĭtch′, *v.*, cast a spell, enchant; **-ment; -ery**

bė-yŏnd′, *adv., prep.*, farther on

běz′ėl, *n.*, metal holding ring's jewel; tool's cutting edge

bī-ăn′nū-ȧl, *a.*, twice a year; **-ly** [prejudice

bī′ȧs, *n.*, diagonal line,

bĭb, *n.*, under-chin apron

Bī′ble, *n.*, sacred book, Old and New Testament; **licist**

bĭb-lĭ-ŏg′rȧ-phў, *n.*, list of writings; **pher; phic; phical; phically**

bĭb-lĭ-ŏp′ė-gў, *n.*, art of bookbinding

bĭb′lĭ-ȯ-phīle, *n.*, book collector; **list; lism; listic**

bĭb′ū-loŭs, *a.*, spongy; fond of liquor; **-ly; -ness**

bī-căm′êr-ȧl, *a.*, having two legislative bodies

bī-cĕn-tĕn′nī-ȧl, *n., a.*, (period of) two hundred years; **tenary** [cle

bī′cĕps, *n.*, large arm muscle

bĭck′êr, *v., n.*, squabble; **-er** [tooth

bī-cŭs′pĭd, *n.*, two-pointed

bĭd, *n., v.*, command, offer; **-der; -ding; -able**

bĭd′dў, *n.*, chicken, gossipy woman

bīde, *v.*, stay, reside

bī-ĕn′nī-ȧl, *a.*, every two years; **-ly** [coffin

biêr, *n.*, framework to hold

bĭff, *n., v.* (coll.), strike, hit

bī′flĕx, *a.*, two-curved

bī-fō′cȧl, *n.*, two-part lens for near, far vision

bĭg′ȧ-mў, *n.*, having two spouses at once; **mist;**

mous
bĭg'heärt-ĕd, a., generous
bĭg'hôrn, n., wild sheep
bĭght, n., bend, curve
bĭ-kĭ'nï, n., woman's very
  brief two-piece bathing
  suit
bĭle, n., fluid of liver;
  lious [barrel, ship)
bĭlge, n., broadest part (of
bĭlk, v., swindle; **-er**
bĭll, n., list of charges
  owed, proposed law, pa-
  per money, bird's beak;
  v., present charges; **-er;**
  -able
bĭl'lĕt, n., soldiers' hous-
  ing, job
bĭll'fōld, n., wallet
bĭl'liărds, n., table. game
  with balls and cúe
bĭll'ĭng, n., actor's listing
  on playbill
bĭl'liön, n., thousand mil-
  lions; **-aire; -th**
bĭl'lōw, n., large wave; **-y**
bĭl'lÿ, n., policeman's stick
bĭ-mŏnth'lÿ, a., adv., every
  two months
bĭn, n., storage container
bĭ'nä-rÿ, a., double, two-
bĭ'nāte, a., in pairs [fold
bĭnd, v., tie, bandage, ob-
  ligate; **-er; -ing**
bĭnd'ĕr-ÿ, n., place for
  binding books
bĭnd'ĭng, n., book cover
bĭnge, n., spree
bĭn'gō, n., game
bĭn-ŏc'ŭ-lărs, n. pl., field
  glasses [terms
bĭ-nŏ'mĭ-ăl, a., having two
bĭ-ō-chĕm'ĭs-trÿ, n., study
  of chemistry of living
  matter
bĭ-ō-dė-grād'à-ble, a.,
  naturally decomposable
bĭ-ŏl'ȯ-gÿ, n., study of life;
  gist; gic; gical; gically
bĭ-ŏm'ė-trÿ, n., measurement of life; **rics; ric;
  rically**
bĭ-ō-phÿs'ĭcs, n., physics
  of living things; **cist;
  cal** [of living tissue
bĭ'ŏp-sÿ, n., examination
bĭ-pâr'tĭ-sàn, a., repre-

senting two groups;
  -ship; tition [mal
bĭ'pĕd, n., two-footed ani
bĭ-rä'ciàl, a., involving two
bĭrch, n., tree [races
bĭrd, n., feathered animal
  with wings [person
bĭrd'brāin, n., silly, stupid
bĭrd's'-eÿe, a., seen from
  above, overall
bĭ-rĕt'tà, n., priest's cap
bĭrl, v., spin, revolve
bĭrth, n., being born, beginning, origin
bĭrth'rāte, n., number of
  births per year [bread
bĭs'cuĭt, n., small, soft
bĭ-sĕx'ū-àl, a., of both
  sexes; **-ity; -ism; -ly**
bĭsh'ŏp, n., high-ranking
  Christian clergyman
bĭs'mŭth, n., metallic element; **-ic, -ous**
bĭ'sŏn, n., buffalo [soup
bĭsque, n., thick creamy
bĭt, n., bridle's mouth-
  piece, small piece
bĭtch, n., female dog; v.,
  complain
bĭte, n., mouthful, sting,
  wound; v., cut with teeth
bĭt'ĭng, a., cutting, sharp;
  -ly
bĭt'têr, a., sharp, sorrowful;
  -ness; -ly
bĭt'têrn, n., marsh bird
bĭt'têr-swēet, n., plant; a.,
  pleasant and sad
bĭ-tū'mĕn, n., mineral substance; **minize; mini-
  zation; minous**
bĭv'oŭ-ăc, n., temporary
  camp [two weeks
bĭ-wēek'lÿ, a., adv., every
bĭ-zârre', a., odd, fantastic
blăb, v., chatter; **-ber**
blăck, a., color of coal,
  dark, evil [against
blăck'băll, n., v., vote
blăck'bĕr-rÿ, n., fruit
blăck'bôard, n., chalk-
  board [fame
blăck'ĕn, v., darken, de-
blăck'guàrd, n., scoundrel; v., abuse with
  words; **-ly** [skin pore
blăck'hĕad, n., clogged

blăck'jăck, *n.,* steel-filled club, card game

blăck'līst, *n.,* list of undesirables [threat

blăck'māil, *n.,* coercion by

blăck'smĭth, *n.,* iron-worker, one who shoes horses [face

blăck'tŏp, *n.,* asphalt sur-

blăd'dêr, *n.,* body sac for urine

blāde, *n.,* broad, flat sur-face, cutting edge

blāme, *v.,* accuse, criti-cize; **mable; -ful; -less; -lessness**

blănch, *v.,* make white; **-er**

blănd, *a.,* soft, mild

blănk, *n.,* empty space

blăn'kėt, *n.,* bed cover; *v.,* cover

blāre, *n., v.,* loud sound

blâr'nēy, *n.,* smooth talk of flattery

blă-sé (sā), *a.,* bored

blăs'phė-mÿ, *n.,* irreverent talk; **eme; mous**

blăst, *n.,* sudden air gust, explosion

blā'tănt, *a.,* loud, obvious; **-ly; ncy**

blăth'êr, *n.,* foolish talk; **-er** [light; *v.,* mark

blāze, *n.,* bright flame,

blā'zêr, *n.,* sports jacket

blā'zŏn, *n.,* coat of arms; *v.,* adorn; **-ry**

blēach, *n., v.,* (chemical) to whiten

blēach'êrs, *n. pl.,* cheap stadium seats

blēak, *a.,* bare, harsh; **-ness; -ly**

blēar, *v.,* dim by tears; **-y -iness; -ily**

blēat, *n.,* sheep's cry

blēed, *v.,* lose blood; **-er**

blēep, *n.,* short, sharp sound [mar

blĕm'ĭsh, *n.,* defect, *v.,*

blĕnch, *v.,* become pale

blĕnd, *v.,* mix; **-er**

blĕss, *v.,* make holy, happy; **-ing; -ed**

blīght, *n.,* destruction, plant disease; **-er**

blīnd, *n.,* window shade; *a.,* unable to see; **-ness; -ly**

blĭnk, *v.,* open and close eyes, flash on and off; **-er**

blĭss, *n.,* happiness

blĭs'têr, *n.,* skin swelling

blĭtz, *n.,* destructive attack

blĭz'zård, *n.,* bad snow [storm

blōat, *v.,* swell

blŏb, *n.,* drop, lump of

blŏc, *n.,* alliance [mass

blŏck, *n.,* large solid piece, city square; *v.,* obstruct, hinder; **-er, -age**

blŏck'āde, *v.,* shut off a place

blōke, *n.* (coll.), chap

blŏod, *n.,* red liquid in body; **-y; -iness; -ily; -less; -lessness; -lessly**

blŏod'cûr-dlĭng, *a.,* hor-rible

blŏod'hŏund, *n.,* tracking dog

blŏod'shĕd, *n.,* killing

blŏod'shŏt, *a.,* red, inflamed [kill

blŏod'thîrst-ÿ, *a.,* eager to

blōom, *n., v.,* flower; **-er; -y**

blŏop'êr, *n.,* mistake

blŏs'sŏm, *n.,* flower; *v.,* bloom, develop

blŏt, *n., v.,* stain, disgrace, destroy; **-ter**

blōuse, *n.,* woman's shirt

blous'ŏn, *n.,* long full blouse

blōw, *n.,* wind, hit, shock; *v.,* move air by mouth, wind; **-er; -y** [gun

blōw'gŭn, *n.,* dart or pellet

blōw'hârd, *n.,* boastful person

blōw'tôrch, *n.,* torch shooting hot flame

blŭb'bêr, *n.,* fat; *v.,* cry

blŭdg'eŏn, *n.,* short heavy club

blūe, *a.,* color of sky, sad

blūe'bĕll, *n.,* flower

blūe'bĕrrÿ, *n.,* fruit

blūe'bîrd, *n.,* blue

A
B

songbird [tocrat
blūe′blŏod, n. (coll.), aris-
blūe chĭp, a., of stable stock
blūe-cŏl′làr, a., industrial
blūe′grăss, n., Kentucky grass, southern folk music
blūe′jāy, n., bird [plan
blūe′prĭnt, n., detailed
blŭff, n., steep bank, cliff; v., mislead; **-ness; -ly**
blū′ĭng, n., blue substance to whiten fabric
blŭn′dêr, n., error; v., stumble, err; **-er; -ingly**
blŭnt, a., dull, abrupt; **-ness; -ly**
blûr, n., v., smear, smudge; **-ry; -riness**
blûrt, v., say suddenly
blŭsh, v., redden, be embarrassed; **-er**
blŭs′têr, v., blow stormily, speak noisily; **-er; -y; -ous; -ingly**
bō′à, n., snake
bōar, n., wild hog
bōard, n., flat piece of wood, council, meals for pay; v., close with boards, get on, house; **-er**
bôard′ĭng-house, n., place where meals, food are paid for [walkway
bôard′wălk, n., wood
bōast, v., brag; **-ful; -fulness; -fully**
bōat, n., small watercraft; **-ing**
bŏb, n., girl's short haircut; v., move up and down; **-ber**
bŏb′bêr-ÿ, n., commotion
bŏb′bĭn, n., reel for thread
bŏb′bÿ, n., English police-
bŏb′căt, n., lynx [man
bŏb′ò-lĭnk, n., songbird
bŏb′slĕd, n., racing sled
bŏb-whīte′, n., small quail
bŏck, n., dark beer
bōde, v., be omen of
bŏd′īce, n., upper part of
bŏd′ĭng, n., omen [dress
bŏd′ÿ, n., whole physical structure, main part,

group; **lly** [guard
bŏd′ÿ-guàrd, n., person's
bŏg, n., small marsh; v., sink; **-gy** [tate
bŏg′gle, v., startle, hesi-
bō′gŭs, a., false
bō′gÿ, n., evil spirit
bōil, n., skin swelling; v., bubble, heat, seethe
bōil′êr, n., tank for heating water
bōis′têr-oŭs, a., rowdy; **-ly**
bōld, a., fearless, shameless, striking; **-ness; -ly**
bò-lĕr′ō, n., short vest
bōll, n., cotton seed pod
bōll′wēe-vĭl, n., insect
bō′lō, n., single-edged knife [sage
bò-lō′gnà, n., smoked sau-
bōl′stêr, n., long narrow pillow; v., strengthen
bōlt, n., flash, bar for locking, roll of cloth; v., fasten, rush out
bŏmb, n., explosive device; v., attack
bŏm′băst, n., pompous talk; **-ic; -ically**
bŏm′bĭ-nāte, v., buzz; **tation** [wealth
bò-nǎn′zà, n., source of
bŏn′bŏn, n., candy
bŏnd, n., anything binding, surety against theft
bŏnd′àge, n., slavery
bōne, n., hard tissue of skeleton; v., remove bones, study hard
bōn′êr, n., error
bŏn′fîre, n., large outdoor fire [sound
bŏng, n., deep ringing
bŏn′gō, n., antelope, pair of small drums
bŏn′nĕt, n., hat
bŏn′nÿ, a., handsome, pretty; **niness; nily**
bŏn-saī′, n., dwarfed tree
bō′nŭs, n., something extra
bōŏ′bŏŏ, n., (coll.) mistake
bōŏ′bÿ, n., stupid person
bōŏ-gĭe-wōŏ′gĭe, n., jazz music
bōŏ-hōŏ, v., weep loudly
bōŏk, n., bound printed

work; *v.*, list, engage ahead

bŏŏk′ĕnd, *n.*, device to keep book upright

bŏŏk′ĭng, *n.*, engagement

bŏŏk′kēep-ĭng, *n.*, record of business transactions; **keeper**

bŏŏk′măk-êr, *n.*, bet taker; **making**

bŏŏk′mō-bĭle, *n.*, travelling lending library

bŏŏk′plăte, *n.*, label to tell owner

bŏŏk′stôre, *n.*, place to buy books   [reader

bŏŏk′wŏrm, *n.*, avid

bōōm, *n.*, prosperous time, beam, deep hollow sound; *v.*, increase

bōōn, *n.*, benefit

bōōn′dŏcks, *n.*, *pl.*, wilderness

bôor, *n.*, rude person; **-ish** *a.*; **-ishly; -ishness**

bōōst, *n.*, *v.*, push up; **-er; -erism**   [*v.*, kick

bōōt, *n.*, shoe above ankle,

bōōth, *n.*, small enclosure, stall   [**-ger; -ged**

bōōt′lĕg, *v.*, sell illegally;

bōōt′ÿ, *n.*, spoils of war

bô′rȧ-cīte, *n.*, mineral

bôr′ăx, *n.*, white salt

bôr-dĕl′lō, *n.*, brothel

bŏr′dêr, *n.*, edge, boundary

bôre, *n.*, hole, dull person; *v.*, drill a hole

bôre′dŏm, *n.*, uninterested state

bôrn, *a.*, brought into life

bŏr′ŏugh, *n.*, self-governing district

bŏr′rōw, *v.*, temporarily take

bôrsch, *n.*, beet soup

bŏs′cȧge, *n.*, wooded place

bŏsh, *n.*, *int.*, nonsense

bŏs′ŏm, *n.*, woman's breast; **-y** *a.*

bŏss, *n.*, supervisor; *v.*, order; **-ism; -y**

bŏ′tăn-ÿ, *n.*, study of plant life; **nist; nize; nizer; tanical; ically**

bŏtch, *v.*, do poor work; **-er; -y** *a.*

bōth, *a.*, *pro.*, the two; *adv.*, *conj.*, equally

bŏth′êr, *v.*, annoy; **-some**

bŏt′tle, *n.*, container; **-er; -ful** *n.*

bŏt′tle-nĕck, *n.*, retardation of progress

bŏt′tŏm, *n.*, lowest part; **-less; -most** *a.*

bŏt′ŭ-lĭsm, *n.*, food poisoning

boū-cle′ (klā), *n.*, small curly yarn

boū′doir (âr), *n.*, lady's private room

boū-gȧin-vĭl′lē-ȧ, *n.*, flowering vine

bŏŭgh, *n.*, tree branch

boŭil-lȧ-bāisse′, *v.*, fish stew

boŭil′lŏn, *n.*, clear broth

boŭl′ė-vârd, *n.*, broad street   [**-r**

boŭnce, *v.*, spring back;

boŭnd, *n.*, *v.*, leap, limit; *a.*, tied, headed

boŭnd′ȧ-rÿ, *n.*, limit, border

boŭnd′êr, *n.*, cad

boŭn′tÿ, *n.*, bonus, generosity; **teous; tiful; tifulness; tifully**

boū-quet′ (kā), *n.*, bunch of flowers, scent

boûr′bŏn, *n.*, whiskey

boûr-geois′ (zhwȧ), *n.*, *a.*, middle class; **sie**

boŭt, *n.*, contest, spell

boū-tĭque′, *n.*, fashionable shop   [**vine**

bō′vĭd, *a.*, of ox family;

bow, *n.*, ship's front; *v.*, bend body, submit

bōw, *n.*, curve, arrow shooter, looped knot

bōwd′lêr-īze, *v.*, remove offensive parts; **ism; ization**   [part

bow′ĕl, *n.*, intestine, inner

bōwl, *n.*, deep rounded container; *v.*, roll ball

bōw′lĕg, *n.*, curved leg; **-ged**

bōwl′êr, *n.*, derby hat

bōwl′ĭng, *n.*, game with

ball and pins; **bowler**
bōw'màn, *n.,* archer
bŏx, *n.,* container, group of seats, evergreen shrubs; *v.,* fight
bŏx'câr, *n.,* enclosed railroad car
bŏx'ĭng, *n.,* sport of fighting; **boxer**
boy (bŏĭ), *n.,* male child; **-hood; -ish; -ishness; -ishly** [deal with
boy'cŏtt (bŏĭ), *v.,* refuse to
bō'zō, *n.,* uncouth fellow
brăb'ble, *v.,* squabble
brāce, *n.,* pair, clamp; *v.,* tighten, support
brāce'lĕt, *n.,* wrist or arm ornament
brāc'ĭng, *a.,* refreshing
brăck'ĕn, *n.,* fern
brăck'ĕt, *n.,* wall support
brăck'ĭsh, *a.,* salty; **-ness**
brăct, *n.,* modified leaf
brăd, *n.,* fastener, nail
brāid, *v.,* interweave strands; **-er**
brāin, *n.,* nerve tissue in skull; intelligence; *v.,* (coll.) hit head
brāin'chĭld, *n.,* idea
brāin'stôrm, *n.,* (coll.) sudden idea; **-ing** *n.*
brāin'wàsh, *v.,* indoctrinate
brāise, *v.,* cook, brown and simmer
brāke, *n., v.,* (device to) stop motion; **-age; -less**
brāke'măn, *n.,* conductor's assistant
brăm'ble, *n.,* prickly shrub
brăn, *n.,* wheat grain's skin or husk [tree limb
brănch, *n.,* part or division,
brănd, *n.,* mark burned on, label; **-er**
brăn'dĭsh, *v.,* wave
brăn'dȳ, *n.,* liquor from wine; **-died**
brăsh, *a.,* hasty
brăss, *n.,* metal of copper and zinc, (coll.) high official; **-y** *a.*
brás-sârd', *n.,* armor
brás-sìere', *n.,* undergarment for breasts

brăt'tle, *n.,* clatter
brà-và'dō, *n.,* pretended courage
brāve, *a.,* bold, courageous; **-ry; -ly**
brà'vō, *int.,* well done!
brăwl, *n., v.,* quarrel, fight; **-er**
brăwn, *n.,* muscular strength; **-y; -iness**
brāy, *n.,* donkey's cry
brāze, *v.,* make of brass; **-er** [**-ly**
brăz'ĕn, *a.,* bold; **-ness;**
brà'zĭl, *n.,* tree, nut
brēach, *n.,* violation
brēad, *n.,* leavened flour mixture baked, (coll.) money
brĕadth, *n.,* width
brĕad'wĭn-nêr, *n.,* money earner
brēak, *v.,* split apart, ruin, interrupt; **-er; -age; -able** [work
brēak'down, *n.,* failure to
brēak'êr, *n.,* wave
brĕak'fàst, *n.,* morning meal
brēak'throŭgh, *n.,* important advance
brēak'ŭp, *n.,* ending
brēak'wâ-têr, *n.,* barrier against waves
brĕast, *n.,* milk secreting gland, bosom, bust
brĕast'plāte, *n.,* chest armor
brĕath, *n.,* inhaling and exhaling air; **-less; -lessness; -lessly**
brēathe, *v.,* inhale and exhale air, live; **-r**
brĕath'tāk-ĭng, *a.,* thrilling
brēech, *n.,* lower part
brēed, *n.,* similar type; *v.,* produce, raise; **-er; -ing**
brēeze, *n.,* gentle wind
brēeze'wāy, *n.,* covered passageway
brĕth'rèn, *n., pl.,* spiritual brothers
brē'vĭ-ār-ȳ, *n.,* prayer book
brĕv'ĭ-tȳ, *n.,* briefness
brew, *v.,* prepare beer, boil, plot; **-er; -age**
brībe, *n.,* inducement to do

something wrong; **-r; -ry**

bric'à-brăc, *n.,* small objects of art

brick, *n.,* baked clay building block

brick'lė, *n., a.,* brittle

bride, *n.,* woman getting married

bride'groom, *n.,* man getting married

brides'māid, *n.,* bride's wedding attendant

bridge, *n.,* connection, structure spanning water or road, card game

bridge'wŏrk, *n.,* mounting of false teeth

bri'dle, *n.,* head harness for horse; *v.,* restrain

brief'cāse, *n.,* carrying case for papers

bri'êr, *n.,* thorny bush

brig, *n.,* boat, navy jail

bri-gāde', *n.,* unit of soldiers

brig'ånd, *n.,* bandit; **-age**

bright, *n.,* shining; cheerful; **-en,** *v.,* **-ness; -ly**

bril'liånt, *a.,* bright, intelligent; **liance; liancy; -ly**

brim, *n.,* edge; **-ful**

brine, *n.,* salt water; **-y,** *a.*

brink, *n.,* edge, verge

brisk, *a.,* quick, cool, active; **-ness; -ly**

bris'kėt, *n.,* animal's breast

bris'tle, *n.,* stiff prickly hair; **tly; tliness**

brit'tle, *a.,* stiff, fragile; **-ness; -ly** [**-er**

brŏach, *v.,* bring up, utter;

brŏad, *a.,* wide; **-ness; -ly**

brŏad'clŏth, *n.,* fine woolen cloth

brŏad-mīnd'ėd, *a.,* tolerant; **-ness; -ly**

brō-cāde', *n.,* rich cloth with metallic thread

brŏc'cò-li, *n.,* edible plant

brō-chĕtte', *n.,* skewer

brō'gàn, *n.,* heavy work shoe [shoe

brŏgue, *n.,* accent, coarse

broil, *v.,* cook by direct heat, become angry; **-er**

brŏk'ėn, *a.,* out of order, cracked

brŏk-ėn-heärt'ėd, *a.,* crushed by grief; **-ly**

brō'kêr, *n.,* hired agent; **-age**

brō'mīde, *n.,* sedative, platitude; **midic**

brŏn'chĭ-ål, *a.,* of windpipe; **chitis; chitic**

brŏn'cō, *n.,* wild horse

brŏnze, *n.,* metal alloy of copper and tin

brŏoch, *n.,* ornamental pin

brŏod, *n.,* family offspring; *v.,* worry; **-er, -y,** *a.*

brŏok, *n.,* stream; *v.,* endure

brŏom, *n.,* long-handled brush for sweeping, shrub

brŏth, *n.,* clear thin soup

brŏth'ėl, *n.,* house of prostitution

brŏth'êr-lў, *a.,* friendly

brow, *n.,* forehead

brow'bēat, *v.,* bully

brown, *n.,* color of chocolate; **-ish**

brown'ie, *n.,* elf, rich chocolate cookie

browse, *v.,* glance through, feed on leaves; **-er**

bruise, *v.,* hurt

brume, *n.,* fog

brunch, *n.,* one meal for both breakfast and lunch

brunt, *n.,* main impact

brush, *n.,* utensil with bristles for hair, paint; thicket; *v.,* use brush, touch [missal

brush'-ŏff, *n.* (coll.) disbrusque, *a.,* curt, blunt

brūte, *n., a.,* animal, cruel person; **brutish**

bŭb'ble, *n.,* film holding air and gas; *v.,* boil foam, belch; **bly**

bŭc'cà-nêer, *n.,* pirate

bŭck, *n.,* male deer, (coll.) dollar; *v.,* rear upward

bŭck'bôard, *n.,* wagon with seating

bŭck'ėt, *n.,* pail; **-ful**

bŭck'le, *n.,* clasp for belt

and shoes; v., join, bend
bŭck'shŏt, n., large lead
bullet [front tooth
bŭck'tōoth, n., protruding
bŭck'whēat, n., grain
bū-cŏl'ĭc, a., rural; **-ally**
bŭd, n., developing flower;
v., start to grow; **-der**
bŭdge, v., move
bŭdg'êr-ĭ-gâr, n., bird
bŭdg'ĕt, n., v., plan for expenses; **-er**; **-ary**
bŭff, v., polish; **-er**
bŭf'fà-lō, n., wild oxen
bŭf'fet (fā), n., counter for
serving food
bŭf-fōon', n., clown
bŭg'gÿ, n., horse-drawn
carriage; a., insane
bū'gle, n., small trumpet
buĭld, v., put together, construct; **-er**
bŭlb, n., underground bud;
bulbous
bŭlge, n., v., swell; **-y**, a.
bŭlk, n., mass; **-y**; **-iness**;
-ily
bŭll, n., male bovine, elephant, seal, etc., Papal
edict, nonsense; **-ish**
bŭll'dōze, v., bully, dig
out; **-er** [gun
bŭl'lĕt, n., metal shot from
bŭl'lè-tĭn, n., brief statement
bŭll'fĭnch, n., songbird
bŭll'frŏg, n., large frog
bŭll'hĕad-ĕd, a., stubborn
bŭll'hôrn, n., voice ampli-
fier [ingot
bŭl'lĭon, n., gold or silver
bŭl'lÿ, n., v., (one who)
frighten(s)
bŭl'rŭsh, n., marsh plant
bŭl'wârk, n., fortification
bŭm'ble-bēe, n., large bee
bŭmp, n., v., knock
against; **-y** [guard
bŭmp'êr, n., metal car
bŭmp'tioŭs, a., arrogant;
-ness; **-ly** [knot
bŭn, n., small roll, hair in
bŭnch, n., cluster, group
of things; **-y**; **-iness**
bŭnd, n., league; **-ist**
bŭn'dle, n., things held together

bŭng, n., barrel stopper
bŭn'gà-lōw, n., one story
house, cottage [-r
bŭn'gle, v., botch, spoil;
bŭn'ĭòn, n., foot swelling
bŭnk, n., shelflike bed
bŭnk'êr, n., storage bin,
sand pit in golf
bŭn'nÿ, n., rabbit
bŭnt, n., v., butt, push
bŭn'tĭng, n., decorative
cloth [marker
bŭoÿ, n., floating warning
bŭr, n., prickly seed case
bŭr'dĕn, n., load; **-some**;
-somely
bū'reau (rō), n., chest of
drawers, agency
bûrg, n., town; **-er**
bûr'gĕon, v., sprout, grow
bûr'ĭ-àl, n., burying a body
bûrke, v., get rid of
bûrl, n., knot in wood
bûr'lăp, n., coarse hemp
cloth
bûr-lĕsque', n., comic satire, sexy entertainment
bûr'lÿ, a., big and strong;
iness
bûrn'īsh, n., v., polish
bûrr, n., rough edge
bûr'rō, n., donkey
bûr'rōw, n., animal dug
hole or ground tunnel
bûr'sàr, n., college treas-
urer; **-y**; **-ial**
bûr-sī'tĭs, n., inflammation
of sac in joints
bûrst, v., explode; **-er**
bur'ÿ (bĕr), v., put in grave,
hide
bŭs'boy (bŏi), n., waiter's
assistant
bŭsh, n., shrub, low thickly
grown plant; **-y**, a.
bŭshed, a., bewildered,
(coll.) tired
busi'nĕss (bĭz), n., one's
work, commerce, con-
cern; **-man**; **-woman**
bŭst, n., sculpture from
chest up, breast; v.,
break, become bankrupt
bŭs'tle, n., commotion,
skirt padding in back; v.,
busily hurry
bus'ÿ (bĭz), a., active, in-

dustrious; **-ness**

bū'tāne, *n.*, flammable gas

būtch'êr, *n.*, meat slaugh-terer and cutter; **-er; -y; -ly**

bŭt'lêr, *n.*, male house servant   [ram

bŭtt, *n.*, thick end, stub; *v.*,

bŭtte, *n.*, lone steep hill

bŭt'têr, *n.*, yellowish fat churned from cream; *v.*, spread butter; **-y** *a.*

bŭt'têr-fĭn-gêrs, *n.*, one who drops things

bŭt'têr-flȳ, *n.*, insect with 4 large colored wings

bŭt'têr-scŏtch, *n.*, hard, sticky candy

bŭt'tŏck, *n.*, half of rump

bŭt'tŏn, *n.*, small disk or knob for fastening gar-ments

bŭt'trĕss, *n.*, wall support.

bŭx'ŏm, *a.*, plump, jolly

buȳ, *v.*, get by paying money, purchase; **-er**

bŭz'zárd, *n.*, bird of prey

bȳ'-ănd-bȳ', *adv.*, before long

bȳe'-bȳe', *n.*, int. goodbye

bȳ'gŏne, *a.*, past

bȳ'-prŏd-ŭct, *n.*, second-ary result

bȳ'-stănd-êr, *n.*, onlooker

bȳ'wāy, *n.*, side road

bȳ'wŏrd, *n.*, saying, prov-erb

C

căb, *n.*, taxi, train, truck operator's compartment

cȧ-băl', *n.*, plot (ter)

căb'ȧ-lȧ, *n.*, secret belief; **list; lism; listic; listically**   [house

cȧ-bä'nȧ, *n.*, private bath-

căb-ȧ-ret' (**rā**), *n.*, café with entertainment

căb'bȧge, *n.*, leafy vegetable [story house

căb'ĭn, *n.*, simple one-

căb'ĭ-nĕt, *n.*, furniture with shelves and/or drawers; advisory council; **-ry**

cā'ble, *n.*, thick wire or rope; *v.*, send message

overseas

cȧ-bōose', *n.*, trainmen's car at rear

căb'rĭ-ōle, *n.*, graceful curved furniture leg

căb-rĭ-ȯ-let' (**lā**), *n.*, two-wheeled carriage

căche (**căsh**), *n.*, hidden storage

cȧ-chet' (**shā**), *n.*, official seal   [hen

căck'le, *n.*, *v.*, shrill like

căc'tŭs, *n.*, desert plant

căd, *n.*, ill-bred man

cȧ-dăv'êr, *n.*, dead body; **-ic; -ous; -ousness; -ously**   [ant

căd'dĭe, *n.*, golfer's attend-

cā'dénce, *n.*, rhythmic flow of sound; **dency; dent**

cȧ-dĕt', *n.*, student of mil-itary school

cădge, *v.*, beg; **-r**

căd'mĭ-ŭm, *n.*, metallic element   [symbol

cȧ-dū'cē-ŭs, *n.*, medical

căf-ė-tē'rĭ-ȧ, *n.*, self-serv-ice restaurant

căf'fēine, *n.*, stimulant in coffee and tea

căf'tȧn, *n.*, long full robe

cāge, *n.*, barred enclosure for animals

cā'gĕy, *a.*, (coll.) sly

cāis'sŏn, *n.*, ammunition wagon   [**-ment**

cȧ-jŏle', *v.*, coax; **-r; -ry;**

cāke, *n.*, sweet baked dough; *v.*, solidify

cāke'wălk, *n.*, dance

căl'ȧ-mīne, *n.*, mineral for lotions and ointments

cȧ-lăm'ĭ-tȳ, *n.*, disaster; **tous; tousness; tously**

căl'cĭ-ŭm, *n.*, chemical element in bone, lime-stone

căl'cū-lāte, *v.*, compute; **lation; -d; -dly; lable; lably; lability**

căl'cū-lāt-ĭng, *a.*, shrewd

căl'cū-lŭs, *n.*, kind of higher mathematics

căl'drŏn, *n.*, large kettle

căl'ėn-dȧr, *n.*, list of months and days

căl'ĭbêr, n., degree of worth, gun measurement; brator; bration; brate

căl'ĭ-cō, n., cotton cloth

căl'ĭ-pêr, n., measuring tool

că'lĭph, n., Moslem ruler

căl-ĭs-thĕn'ĭcs, n., exercises [watertight

călk, v., fill cracks to make

căll, n., v., summon, shout, order; telephone

căll'êr, n., visitor

căl-lĭg'rà-phӰ, n., penmanship; pher; phist; graphic

căl'loŭs, a., insensitive; losity; -ness; -ly

căl'lōw, a., inexperienced; -ness [skin

căl'lŭs, n., hard place on

călm, n., stillness; a., quiet, tranquil; -ness; -ative; -ly

căl'ô-riē, n., unit of food energy; loric

căl'ŭ-mĕt, n., Indian peace pipe

căl'ŭm-nӰ, n., slander; niator; niation; niate; nious; niously

cà-lӰp'sō, n., West Indian music

că'lӰx, n., flower's protective leaves

căm, n., rotating machine part [curve

căm'bêr, n., slight convex

căm'brĭc, n., fine linen or cotton cloth [hump

căm'ĕl, n., animal with

căm'ĕ-ō, n., gem with carved figure

căm'êr-à, n., picture-taking device

căm'ĭ-sōle, n., woman's undergarment

căm'ou-flăge, n., disguise; -r

cămp, n., temporary lodging, for vacations, the military; -er

căm-pāign', n., planned actions, military battle

căm-pà-nĭ'lē, n., bell tower

căm'phör, n., substance for protecting clothes; -ate; -ic

căn, n., metal container; v., to be able to, may

cà-năl', n., artificial waterway; -ize; -ization

cà-nàrd', n., false story

cà-năs'tà, n., card game

căn'-căn, n., high kicking dance

căn'cĕl, v., make void, do away with; -er; -ler; -lation

căn'cêr, n., malignant growth; -ous

căn-dė-là'brŭm, n., branched candlestick; -bra pl. [cence

căn-dĕs'cĕnt, a., glowing;

căn'dĭd, a., frank, informal

căn'dĭ-dāte, n., office seeker; dacy

căn'dle, n., wax stick for burning

căn'dör, n., frankness

căn'dӰ, n., sweet food made with sugar; died

cāne, n., walking stick

cā'nīne, a., n., (of) dog

căn'ĭs-têr, n., small can or box [-ous

căn'kêr, n., ulcerous sore;

căn'nĭ-bàl, n., eater of human flesh; -ism; -istic; -istically

căn'nĭng, n., preservation of food

căn'nòn, n., large, mounted gun

căn'nӰ, a., shrewd, cautious

cà-noe' (nū), n., small boat moved by paddle(s)

căn'òn, n., church law, clergyman; -ical

căn'òn-īze, v., declare a saint; zation

càn'ô-pӰ, n., awning, rooflike covering

cănt, n., insincere talk, dialect, tilt, slant

căn'tà-lōupe, n., orange melon

căn-tà'tà, n., choral composition

căn-tēen', n., water container, military store

căn'têr, *n.,* horse's easy gallop [chant

căn'tĭ-cle, *n.,* religious

căn'tĭ-lē-vêr, *n.,* beam supported at one end

căn'tòn, *n.,* small district

căn'tōr, *n.,* synagogue's lead singer [cloth

căn'văs, *n.,* heavy hemp

căn'văss, *v.,* examine, solicit; **-er**

căn'yòn, *n.,* deep, narrow valley

căp, *n.,* brimless hat, bottle top; *v.,* cover, do better

cā'pà-ble, *a.,* able, skilled; **-ness; bly; bility**

cá-pā'cioŭs, *a.,* roomy; **-ness; -ly**

cāpe, *n.,* sleeveless loose outer garment; land jutting into water

cā'pêr, *n.,* prank; *v.,* leap about

căp'ĭl-lär-ў, *n.,* tiny blood vessel; *a.,* hairlike; **larity**

căp'ĭ-tàl, *n.,* large letter, place of government, wealth; *a.,* punishable by death, chief

căp'ĭ-tàl-ĭsm, *n.,* economic system of private investment; **ist; istic; istically**

căp'ĭ-tòl, *n.,* chief government building

că-pĭt'ū-lāte, *v.,* surrender; **lation** [rooster

cā'pŏn, *n.,* castrated

cá-prīce', *n.,* whim; **pricious**

căp'sīze, *v.,* overturn

căp'sŭle, *n.,* small case, ex. for dose of medicine; **lar; late** *a.*

căp'taĭn, *n.,* leader; **-cy; -ship**

căp'tiòn, *n.,* headline, title

căp'tioŭs, *a.,* critical; **-ness; -ly**

căp'tĭve, *n.,* prisoner *a.,* forced; **tivity**

căp'tûre, *v.,* seize, catch; **tor** [key

căp'ū-chĭn (shĭn), *n.,* mon-

câr, *n.,* wheeled vehicle,

automobile [falo

cā-rà-bāo', *n.,* water buffalo

căr'à-mèl, *n.,* chewy candy; **-ize**

căr'àt, *n.,* unit of weight for precious stones

căr'à-văn, *n.,* group of travellers

căr'à-wāy, *n.,* seed for flavoring

câr'bīne, *n.,* short rifle; **-er**

câr-bò-hŷ'drāte, *n.,* organic compound, energy food, ex. starch, sugar

câr'bòn, *n.,* chemical element, **-ation; -ate; -ize; -aceous; ic**

câr'bŭn-cle, *n.,* garnet, pus-bearing skin sore

câr'bŭ-re-tôr (rā), *n.,* device to mix air and gasoline [dead body

câr'càss, *n.,* animal's

câr-cĭ-nō'mà, *n.,* cancer

cârd, *n.,* stiff piece of paper, usually printed

câr'dĭ-ăc, *a.,* of heart

câr'dĭ-nàl, *n.,* Catholic high official, red songbird; *a.,* chief, red; **-ship; -ly**

cāre, *n.,* concern, worry; *v.,* be interested in, wish

cá-rēen', *v.,* lean

cá-rēer', *n.,* occupation in life; **-ist**

cá-rĕss', *n., v.* touch with love; **-er; -ive; -ively**

cāre'tàk-êr, *n.,* custodian, one who cares for building

câr'fāre, *n.,* price to ride bus

câr'gō, *n.,* ship's freight

căr'ĭ-boū, *n.,* reindeer

căr'ĭ-cà-tûre, *n.,* exaggerated portrait or description [ious

căr'iĕs, *n.,* tooth decay;

căr'ĭl-lòn, *n.,* set of bells

căr'ĭ-ōle, *n.,* horse carriage

cā'rĭ-òn, *n.,* dead flesh

câr'līne, *n.,* witch

câr'nàge, *n.,* killing of

many people

cȃr'năl, a., of flesh, sexual; **-ity; -ly**

cȃr-nā'tion, n., flower

cȃr'nĭ-vȁl, n., merrymaking, travelling show

cȃr'ŏl, n., joyful song

cȃr'ȯ-tēne, n., red or orange vegetable pigment

cȧ-rouse', v., drink at a party

cȃr'pĕl, n., flower part

cȃr'pĕn-tĕr, n., skilled worker in wood; **try**

cȃr'pĕt, n., heavy cloth floor covering

cȃr'pŭs, n., wrist and its bone; **pal**

cȃr'rĭage, n., wheeled vehicle for people, posture

cȃr'rȳ, v., take to another place, support, hold; **rier**

cȃrt, n., two-wheeled vehicle; v., carry; **-er; -age**

cȃr-tĕl', n., industrial monopoly

cȃr'tĭ-lȧge, n., elastic-like body tissue, gristle; **laginous**

cȃr-tŏg'rȧ-phȳ, n., map making; **pher; graphic**

cȃr'tȯn, n., large cardboard box

cȃr-tōon', n., humorous drawing

cȃr'trĭdge, n., metal case for bullet or gunpowder

cȃr-ȳ-ȁt'ĭd, n., female statue used as column

cȃs-cāde', n., waterfall

cāse, n., instance, lawsuit, holder

cā'sė-ĭn, n., milk protein

cāse'mĕnt, n., window frame

cā'sē-oŭs, a., of cheese

cȧsh'ew, n., nut

cȧsh-iĕr', n., one who deals with money

cȧsh'mēre, n., soft wool fabric

cȧ-sĭ'nō, n., gambling hall

cȧsk, n., barrel

cȧs'kĕt, n., coffin, chest

cȧs-sĕtte', n., film or tape holder   [game

cȧs-sĭ'nō, n., simple card

cȧs'sȯck, n., clerical garment   [bird

cȧs'sȯ-wȃr-ȳ, n., flightless

cȧst, n., v., throw, mold; n., actors in a play

cȧst'ȧ-wāy, n., shipwrecked person

cȧste, n., social class

cȧst'ĕr, n., wheel used as furniture leg

cȧs'tĭ-gāte, v., punish; **tor; tion; tory**   [dence

cȧs'tle, n., fortified residence

cȧs'trāte, v., remove testicles; **tion**

cȧs'ū-ȧl, a., by chance, informal; **-ty; -ness; -ly**

cȧs'ū-ĭst-rȳ, n., oversubtle reasoning; **istic; istical; istically**

cȧt'ȧ-clȳsm, n., disaster; **mic; mal**

cȧt'ȧ-cōmb, n., underground burial place

cȧt'ȧ-lĕp-sȳ, n., loss of consciousness; **leptic**

cȧt'ȧ-lŏg, n., v., list; **-er; -ist**

cȧt'ȧ-lȳst, n., agent causing chemical reaction; **lyze; lytic; lytically**

cȧt-ȧ-mȧ-răn', n., sailboat

cȧt'ȧ-pŭlt, v., hurl, launch

cȧt'ȧ-răct, n., waterfall, eye disease

cȧ-tȃrrh', n., nose and throat disease; **-al; -ous**

cȧ-tȧs'trȯ-phē, n., sudden disaster; **strophic; strophically**

cȧt'cȁll, n., shrill noise of disapproval

cȧtch, v., capture, get; **-er**

cȧtch'ȳ, a., arousing interest; **catchiness**

cȧt'ė-chĭsm, n., religious doctrine; **chist; chize; mal; chistic; chistical**

cȧt'ė-gȯr-ȳ, n., grouping; class; **rization; rize**

cȧ'tĕr, v., provide food, serve; **-er**

cȧt'ĕr-pĭl-lȧr, n., moth or butterfly larva

cȧt'ĕr-wȁul, n., v., howl like a cat

cȧ-thâr'sĭs, *n.*, release of emotion; **thartic**

cȧ-thē'drȧl, *n.*, imposing church [bladder

căth'ė-têr,*n.*, tube to drain

căth'ōde, *n.*, negative electrode

căth'ȯ-lic, *a.*, universal; **-ity; -ize**

căt'sŭp,*n.*, tomato sauce

căt'tȳ, *a.*, spiteful

căt'wălk,*n.*, narrow bridge

cau'cŭs,*n.*, political meeting

cau'dȧl, *a.*,taillike

cause, *n.*, reason, motive; *v.*, bring about; **sation; -ity; causal**

cause'wāy,*n.*, raised road

caus'tic, *a.*, burning, sarcastic; **-ity; -ally**

cau'têr-ize, *n.*, burn with hot iron; **zation** [ing

cau'tion, *n.*, danger warn-

căv'ȧ-liêr, *n.*, gentleman; *a.*, gay, arrogant

căv'ȧl-rȳ, *n.*, military troops on horseback

cāve, *n.*, hollow place in earth

cāve'-ĭn, *n.*, collapse

cāve'măn, *n.*, prehistoric man

căv'ĭ-âr, *n.*, fish eggs as appetizer

căv'ĭl, *v.*, find fault; **-er**

căv'ĭ-tȳ, *n.*, hole

cȧ-vôrt', *v.*, prance, frolic

căw, *n.*, crow's cry [per

caȳ-ĕnne',*n.*, hot red pep-

cēase, *n.*, *v.*, stop; **-less**

cē'dȧr,*n.*, tree

cēde, *v.*, give up, surrender [room

cēil'ĭng, *n.*, covering of a

cĕl'ė-brāte,*v.*, honor with festivity, perform ritual; **tor; tion; tory**

cĕl'ė-rȳ, *n.*, stalked vegetable [-ly

cė-lĕs'tiȧl, *a.*, heavenly;

cĕll,*n.*, small room, unit of living matter; **-ular** *a.*

cĕl'lȧr, *n.*, room(s) under a building

cĕl'lō,*n.*, stringed musical instrument

cĕl'lȯ-phāne,*n.*, transparent plastic sheeting

cĕl'lū-lōse, *n.*, substance in plant cell walls

cė-mĕnt', *n.* substance of mortar or concrete; *s.* stick

cĕm'ė-tĕr-ÿ,*n.*, graveyard

cĕnse, *v.*, burn incense

cĕn'sör, *n.*, official judge of media for acceptability **-ship**

cĕn'sŭs, *n.*, official population count

cĕnt, *n.*, 0.01 of a dollar

cĕn'tȧur, *n.*, mythical horseman

cĕn-tĕn'nĭ-ȧl, *a.*, of 100 years; **-ly**

cĕn'têr, *n.*, middle point

cĕn'tĭ-grāde, *a.*, of thermometer based on 100 degrees

cĕn'tĭ-pēde,*n.*, insect with many legs

cĕn-trĭf'ŭ-gȧl, *a.*, away from center; **-ly**

cĕn-trĭp'ė-tȧl, *a.*, toward a center; **-ly**

cĕn-tû'rĭ-ȧn, *n.*, ancient Roman military officer

cė-phăl'ĭc, *a.*, of the head; **lous; -ally**

cė-răm'ĭcs, *n. pl.*, are of pottery; **ist; ic**

cē'rē-ȧl, *n.*, *a.*, grain for food

cĕr-ė-bĕl'lŭm, *n.*, lower part of brain

cĕr'ė-brŭm, *n.*, main part of brain; **bral**

cĕr'ė-mō-nȳ, *n.*, formal act; **nial; nialist; nialism; nious; niousness; niously**

cêr-tĭf'ĭ-cȧte, *n.*, document of true facts; **tor, tory**

cêr'vĭx, *n.*, necklike part

cĕs-sā'tion, *n.*, stopping

cĕss'pŏŏl, *n.*, sewage pit

cė-tŏl'ȯ-gȳ, *n.*, study of whales; **gist; logical**

chāfe, *n.*, irritation from rubbing; *v.*, rub against

chăf'êr, *n.*, beetle

chȧ-grĭn' (shȧ), *n.*, embarrassment

chāin, *n.,* series as links, (*pl.*) bondage; *v.,* restrain

chāir'măn, *n.,* presiding officer; **woman; -ship**

chāise, *n.,* horse-drawn carriage, couch-like chair

chă-let' (**shă-lā**), *n.,* country house

chăl'ĭce, *n.,* cup, goblet

chăl'lĕnge, *n., v.,* dare, question, contest; **-r -able**

chăm'bêr, *n.,* room, hall

chăm'bêr-laĭn, *n.,* manager, supervisor

chă-mē'lĕ-ŏn (**kă**), *n.,* lizard who can change color

chăm-pāgne' (**shăm-pān**), *n.,* sparkling white wine

chăm-pāign' (**shăm-pān**), *n.,* plain

chăm'pĭ-ŏn, *n.,* winner, *v.,* defend; *a.,* best; **-ship**

chăn'cĕl, *n.,* space near church altar

chăn'cĕl-lŏr, *n.,* high official; **lery; -ship**

chăn-dĕ-liêr' (**shăn**), *n.,* hanging lighting fixture

chăn'dlêr, *n.,* supplier; **-y**

chănge'lĭng, *n.,* child substituted for another

chăn'nĕl, *n.,* passage, waterway, television frequency; *v.,* direct; **-ize; -ization**

chănt, *n.,* song, *v.,* speak in singsong; **-er**

chăn'tĭ-clēer (**shăn**), *n.,* rooster

chă'ŏs (**kā**), *n.,* confusion; **otic; otically**

chăp'ĕl, *n.,* room of worship

chăp'êr-ōn (**shăp**), *n.,* older person in charge of young one

chăp'laĭn, *n.,* clergyman

chăp'têr, *n.,* part, book division, branch

chăr, *v.,* burn

chăr'ăc-têr (**kăr**), *n.,* sym-

bol, role, personality, quality

chă-rāde' (**shă**), *n.,* pantomime game

châr'cōal, *n.,* partly burned wood

chârge, *n., v.,* load, command, blame, bill, attack; **-r; -able**

chăr'ĭ-ŏt, *n.,* ancient horse-drawn cart; **-eer**

chă-rĭs'mă (**kă**), *n.,* personal magnetism; **matic**

chăr'ĭ-tў, *n.,* good will, giving to the needy; **table; tableness, tably**

châr'lă-tăn, *n.,* quack; **-ism**

chârm, *n.,* trinket, spell; *v.* attract, fascinate; **-er; -ing**

chârt, *n., v.,* map, diagram; **-ist; -less**

chârt'êr, *n.,* license; *v.,* hire; **-er**

châr-treūse' (**shâr**), *n.,* yellowish-green

châr'wŏm-ăn, *n.,* cleaning lady

châr'ў, *n.,* careful

chāse, *n.,* hunt, pursuit; *v.,* run after; **-r**

chăsm, *n.,* deep crack in earth

chăs'sĭs (**ē**), *n.,* framework

chăste, *a.,* virtuous, pure; **-ness; -ly**

chăs'tĕn, *v.,* punish; **-er**

chă-teau' (**shă-tō**), *n.,* house [erty

chăt'tĕl, *n.,* movable prop-

chăt'têr-bŏx, *n.,* incessant talker

chau'vĭn-ĭsm (**shō**), *n.,* fanatical prejudice, **ist; istic, istically**

chēap, *a.,* low in price; **-ness; -en;** *v.,* **-ly**

chēat, *v.,* swindle, trick; **-er; -ingly**

chĕck, *n., v.,* halt, bill, test control, mark; *n.,* written order to one's bank

chĕck'êr, *n.,* square on chessboard, cashier, (*pl.*) game

chĕck'êred, *a.,* varied

chĕck′māte, *n.,* defeat

chĕek, *n.,* face below eye, impudence; **-y** *a.*

chĕer, *n.,* joy, glad shout; *v.,* comfort, encourage; **-ful; -fulness; -fully; -less; -y;** *a.,* **-ly**

chĕese, *n.,* food made from milk curd

chĕese′ clŏth, *n.,* thin cotton cloth   [cat

chĕe′táh, *n.,* leopard-like

chĕf, *n.,* cook

chĕm′ĭs-trў, *n.,* science of substances and elements

chĕm-ō-thĕr′á-pÿ (kĕm), *n.,* treatment of infection by chemical drugs; **pist; peutic; peutics; peuti-cally**

chĕr′ĭsh, *v.,* hold dear

chĕ-rōot′ (shá), *n.,* cigar

chĕr′rў, *n.,* small red fruit

chĕr′ŭb, *n.,* angel, sweet child; **-ic; -ically**

chĕss, *n.,* checkerboard game of skill

chĕst, *n.,* box with lid, cabinet, front part of body above abdomen

chĕv′rŏn (shĕv), *n.,* bar on sleeve for rank

chĕw, *v.,* grind with teeth, think; **-er, -y** *a.*

chĭc (shĭk), *a.,* stylish, smart   [ception

chĭ-cān′êr-ў (shĭ), *n.,* de-

chĭck′ĕn, *n.,* edible farm bird; *a.* (coll.) timid

chĭc′ŏ-rў, *n.,* plant for either salad or coffee

chĭde, *v.,* scold   [-ly

chĭef, *n.,* leader; *a.,* main;

chĭf-fŏn′ (shĭf), *n.,* sheer fabric

chĭg′gêr, *n.,* larva of a mite

chĭ′gnŏn (shĭ), *n.,* hair knot or roll

chĭld, *n.,* young person, offspring; **-hood; -less; -ish**

chĭl′ĭ, *n.,* hot seasoning

chĭl′ĭ-ăd, *n.,* thousand

chĭll, *n.,* cold feeling, shiver; *v.,* make cool; **-y** *a.;* **-iness; -ily**

chīme, *n.,* set of bells; *v.,* ring   [smoke

chĭm′nēy, *n.,* passage for

chĭn, *n.,* face below lips; *v.,* pull up by hands

chī′ná, *n.,* porcelain, dishes

chĭn-chĭl′lá, *n.,* rodent bred for its fur

chĭ′nō (shĭ), *n.,* strong cotton cloth

chĭntz, *n.,* shiny cotton cloth; **-y** *a.*

chĭp, *n.,* small piece, gambling disc; *v.,* break off bits; **-per**

chĭp′pêr, *a.,* lively

chī-rŏg′rá-phÿ (kī), *n.,* handwriting; **pher; graphic, graphically**

chī-rŏp′ŏ-dÿ (kī), *n.,* treatment of hands and feet; **dist**

chī-rŏ-prăc′tĭc (kī), *n.,* body treatment by massage; **tor**

chîrp, *n., v.,* shrill like a bird

chĭs′ĕl, *n.,* cutting tool

chĭt, *n.,* child, voucher

chĭt′ter-lings (chĭt lĭngz), *n.,* pig's intestine as food

chĭv′ál-rў (shĭv), *n.,* knight's qualities; **ric; rous; rousness; rously**

chīve, *n.,* onionlike plant

chlō′rĭne (klō), *n.,* gaseous element; **ric; rous**

chlō′rŏ-fôrm (klō), *n.,* liquid anesthetic

chlō′rŏ-phÿll (klō), *n.,* green pigment of plant cells; **-ous**

chŏc′ŏ-láte, *n.,* flavor from cacao beans, candy, drink

choĭce, *n.,* selection; *a.,* superior   [singers

choĭr (kwîr), *n.,* group of

chōke, *v.,* unable to breathe; **-r; -y** *a.*

chŏl′êr-á (kŏl), *n.,* intestinal disease

chŏ-lĕs′têr-ōl (kŏ), *n.,* substance in animal fat

chŏmp, *v.,* bite down

chōose, *v.,* pick, select

C
D

chŏp, v., cut; n., sharp blow, slice of meat; **-per**

chôrd, n., combination of musical notes

chôre, n., task, odd job

chôr'ē-ȯ-grăph (kôr), v., design a dance; **-er; -y; -ic; -ically**

chôr'tle, n., v., chuckle

chŏs'ĕn, a., selected

chŏw, n., dog, (coll.) food

chŏw'dĕr, n., thick soup

chrō-măt'ĭc (krō), a., of color, **-ism; -ity; -s; -ally**

chrō'mĭ-ŭm (krō), n., metallic element

chrō'mȯ-sōme (krō), n., carrier of genes in every human cell; **mal**

chrŏn'ĭc (krŏn), a., constant, recurring; **-ity; -ally**

chrȯ-nŏl'ȯ-gȳ (krȯ), n., arrangement of things in order; **gist; ger; logic; logical; logically**

chrȯ-nŏm'ė-têr (krō), n., very accurate clock

chŭb'bȳ, a., plump; **bi-ness**

chŭck, n., cut of meat; v., toss

chŭm, n., close friend; **-my; -miness; -mily**

chŭmp, n., (coll.) fool

chŭnk, n., short thick piece; **-y** a.

chŭrch, n., place for worship, religion; **-less; -ly**

chŭrl, n., boor; **-ish**

chŭrn,, v., make milk into butter, agitate

chūte (shŭt), n., sloping passage for sliding

cĭ-cā'dȧ, n., insect family

cĭc'ȧ-trĭx, n., scar; **trize**

cĭ-gâr', n., roll of tobacco leaves

cĭg-ȧ-rĕtte', n., cut tobacco rolled in paper

cĭl'ĭ-ȧ, n. pl., hairlike growths; **-ry** a.

cĭnch, n., saddle, (coll.) easy thing

cĭnc'tûre, n., belt

cĭn'dêr, n., burned wood, ash

cĭn-ė-mȧ-tŏg'rȧ-phȳ, n., art of photographing movies; **pher; graphic; graphical; graphically**

cĭn'nȧ-mȯn, n., spice

cī'phêr, n., zero, code

cîr'cȧ, adv., prep., about

cîr'cle, n., closed curved line where all points lie equally from center, group

cîr'cuĭt, n., boundary, path (of current)

cîr'cŭ-lāte, v., move around; **tor; tion; tive; tory**

cîr'cŭm-cīse, v., remove foreskin of penis; **sion**

cîr-cŭm'fêr-ĕnce, n., distance around a circle; **ential; entially**

cîr'cŭm-spĕct, a., careful; **-ion; -ly**

cîr'cŭm-stănce, n., happening; **stantial; stan-tially; stantiality**

cîr-cŭm-vĕnt', v., surround, outwit; **-ion; -ive**

cîr'cŭs, n., arena, show with animals, clowns, etc.   [ease

cîr-rhō'sĭs, n., liver dis-

cîr'rŭs, n., cloud formation

cĭs'têrn, n., tank for water

cĭt'ȧ-dĕl, n., fortress

cīte, v., summon by law, quote, mention; **citation**

cĭt'ĭ-zĕn, n., inhabitant; **-ry; -ship**

cĭt'rŭs, n., fruit as lemon, orange, etc; **ric; rous**

cĭt'têrn, n., guitarlike instrument

cĭv'ĭcs, n., study of citizenship

cĭv'ĭl, a., of citizens, polite, not military; **-ize; -iza-tion; -ly**   [person

cĭ-vĭl'ĭȧn, n., non-military

clăd, a., clothed

clāim, n., v., demand; **-er; -ant** n.; **-able**

clăm, n., edible mollusk

clăm'bêr, v., climb clumsily; **-er**

clăm'mȳ, a., moist and cold; **miness; mily**

clăm′ör, *n.*, loud noise; **-er**; **-ous**; **-ousness**; **-ously**

clăn,*n.*, group of relatives; **-nish**

clăn-dĕs′tĭne, *a.*, secret; **-ness**; **-ly**

clăp′bôard, *n.*, tapered board as house siding

clăp′trăp,*n.*, insincere talk

clăr′ĕt, *n.*, dry red wine

clăr′ĭ-fȳ, *v.*, make clear; **fier; fication**

clăr-ĭ-nĕt′, *n.*, woodwind instrument

clăr′ĭ-ȯn, *a.*, clear, sharp

clăsh,*n.*, *v.*, crash, conflict

clăsp, *n.*, *v.*, grip, embrace; **-er**

clăss,*n.*, like group, status

clás′sĭc, *a.*, standard, ancient Greek or Roman, excellent; **-ism**; **-ist**; **-ity**; **-ize**; **-al**; **-ally**

clăuse,*n.*, sentence part

clăus-trȯ-phō′bĭ-à,*n.*, fear of being enclosed; **bic**

clà′vêr,*n.*, *v.*, gossip

clăv′ĭ-chôrd, *n.*, pianolike instrument

clăv′ĭ-cle,*n.*, collarbone

clăw, *n.*, sharp nail on animal's foot; *v.*, scratch

clāy, *n.*, sticky earth used to make pottery

clēan, *a.*, free from dirt, pure, entire; *adv.*, completely; **-er**; **-ness**; **-able**; **-ly**; **-liness**

clēan′-cŭt, *a.*, trim, neat

clēar, *v.*, make bright, prove, remove; *a.*, sunny, easy to see, transparent; **-er**; **-ness**; **-ance**; **-able**; **-ly**

clēar′ĭng-house,*n.*, place for clearing bank checks

clēat, *n.*, extra piece to make thing secure, spike

clēav′àge,*n.*, division

clēav′êr, *n.*, thick bladed butcher knife

clĕf,*n.*, musical sign

clĕft,*n.*, split, crack

clĕm′ĕnt, *a.*, mild, merciful; **ency**; **-ly**

clĕnch,*v.*, close firmly

clêr′gȳ, *n.*, religious ministers; **-man** *n.*

clêrk, *n.*, office worker; `salesperson; **-ship**; **-ly**

clĕv′êr, *a.*, skillful, smart; **-ness**, **-ly**

clĭ-che′ (chā),*n.*, trite idea

clī′ĕnt, *n.*, customer; **-al**

clĭff,*n.*, steep rock

clĭff′hăng-êr, *n.*, suspenseful story

clī′màte, *n.*, weather conditions; **matic**

clī′măx, *n.*, highest point, summit; **mactic**; **matically**

clĭnch,*v.*, fix firmly, settle; `**-er**

clĭng, *v.*, stick; **-er**; **-y** *a.*

clĭn′ĭc, *n.*, place for medical practice and treatment; **-al**; **-ally**

clĭp, *n.*, fastening device; *v.*, cut short; **-per**

clĭp′pêr, *n.*, cutting tool, sailing ship

clĭque,*n.*, snobbish group

clōak, *n.*, loose outer garment; *v.*, disguise

clŏck, *n.*, *v.*, (device to) measure time

clŏck′wīse, *a.*, *adv.*, in direction of clock's hands

clŏd,*n.*, earth, dull person; **-dish**; **-dishness**; **-dishly**

clŏg, *n.*, shoe; *v.*, hinder, stop up; **-gy**, **-giness**

clois′têr,*n.*, monastery; *v.*, seclude; **tral**

clōse (ōz), *v.*, shut, stop, end

clōse, *a.*, near, shut in, stuffy; **-ness**; **-ly**

clŏt,*n.*, lump; *v.*, thicken

clŏth, *n.*, fabric

clōthes, *n.*, *pl.*, garments to wear [bate

clō′tûre, *n.*, stopping debate

cloud, *n.*, visible mass of vapor in air; **-y** *a.*; **-iness**; **-less**

clōve,*n.*, spice, bulb segment

clō′vĕn, *a.*, split

clō′vêr,*n.*, herb

cloy (ŏī), *v.*, make weary

C
D

clŭb, *n.,* heavy stick, social group, card suit; *v.,* hit with club

clŭb'foot, *n.,* deformed foot

clŭck, *n.,* sound of a hen

clūe, *n.,* fact to help solve mystery [**-y** *a.*

clŭmp, *n.,* mass, cluster;

clŭm'sÿ, *a.,* awkward

clŭtch, *n., v.,* hold tightly

clŭt'têr, *n.,* mess

cōach, *n.,* passenger car or carriage, trainer, *v.,* instruct, train

cō-ăd'jŭ-tănt, *n.,* assistant

cō-ăg'ŭ-lāte, *v.,* curdle, clot; **tor; tion; tive; lable; lability**

cōal, *n.,* carbon mineral, fuel; **-y** *a.*

cō-à-lĕsce', *v.,* mix; **cence; cent**

cō-à-lī'tion, *n.,* alliance; **-ist**

côarse, *a.,* rough, vulgar, **-en; -ness; -ly**

cōast, *n.,* shore, slide down; **-er; -al**

cōax, *v.,* persuade; **-er**

cŏb, *n.,* corn center, horse

cō'bält, *n.,* metallic element; **-ic; -ous**

cŏb'ble, *v.,* mend

cŏb'ble-stōne, *n.,* stone for paving streets

cŏb'blêr, *n.,* shoe repairman, drink, deep-dish fruit pie

cō'ble, *n.,* small fishing boat [snake

cō'brà, *n.,* poisonous

cō-cāine', *n.,* narcotic drug, anesthetic

cŏc'cŭs, *n.,* bacterium

cŏck, *n.,* rooster, male bird; *v.,* tilt, set

cŏck'chäf-êr, *n.,* beetle

cŏck'eÿed, *a.,* crooked, foolish

cŏck'le, *n.,* shellfish

cŏck'nĕy, *n.,* East Londoner's dialect; **-ish**

cŏck'pït, *n.,* pilot's room

cŏck'rōach, *n.,* insect

cŏck'tāil, *n.,* alcoholic drink

cŏck'ÿ, *a.,* self confident; **iness; ily** [der

cō'cōa, *n.,* chocolate powder

cō'cò-nŭt, *n.,* large hard edible fruit

cŏd, *n.,* fish

cŏd'dle, *v.,* treat tenderly

cōde, *n.,* set of rules, secret message; **-r**

cō'dēine, *n.,* drug for pain

cŏd'ĭ-cĭl, *n.,* addition to a will; **-lary** *a.*

cō-ĕf-fī'cĭent, *n.,* that which unites with another

cō-êrce', *v.,* force; **cible; cibly; cion; cive; cively**

cŏf'fēe, *n.,* dark drink made from beans

cŏf'fêr, *n.,* strongbox, funds

cŏf'fïn, *n.,* box to bury dead body in

cŏg, *n.,* tooth of wheel

cō'gĕnt, *a.,* valid; **gency**

cŏg'ĭ-tāte, *v.,* think; **tor; tion; tive**

cō'gnăc, *n.,* brandy

cŏg'nĭ-zănt, *a.,* aware; **zance, nition; zable**

cō'hôrt, *n.,* supporter

cŏif-fūre', *n.,* hair style

coil, *n.,* spiral; *v.,* wind around

coin, *n.,* metal piece of money; **-age**

cō-ïn-cīde', *v.,* happen together, agree; **dence; dent; dental; dently**

cō'ĭ-tŭs, *n.,* sexual intercourse; **tion**

cōke, *n.,* coal after heating

cō'là, *n.,* tree whose nuts have caffeine, soft drink

cò-lăn'dêr, *n.,* pan with holes for drainage

cōld, *n., a.,* low temperature, no heat, lack of feeling; **-ness; -ly**

cō'lē-ŭs, *n.,* plant

cŏl'ĭc, *n.,* abdominal pains, baby's fretfulness

cŏl-ĭ-se'ŭm, *n.,* stadium

cŏl-lăb'ò-rāte, *v.,* work together; **tor; tion; tive**

cŏl-lāge', *n.,* art form

cŏl-lăpse', *v.,* fall apart,

fail

cŏl'lȧr, *n.*, garment for neck

cŏl'lȧr-bōne,*n.*, long bone joining breast and shoulder bones

cŏl'lȧrd, *n.*, leafy vegetable   [tion

cŏl-lāte', *v.*, compare; tor;

cŏl'lēague, *n.*, associate

cŏl-lĕct', *v.*, gather; -or; -ion; -ive; -able

cŏl'lēge, *n.*, school of higher learning; gian *n.*; giate *a.*

cŏl-līde', *v.*, crash; lision

cŏl'līer, *n.*, coal miner; -y

cŏl-lō'quī-ȧl, *a.*, of informal speech; -ism; -ly

cŏl-lū'sion, *n.*, conspiracy; sive; sively

cō'lŏn, *n.*, punctuation mark (:), large intestine; litis   [officer

colo'nėl (kêr), *n.*, military

cȯ-lō'nĭ-ȧl-ĭsm, *n.*, policy of maintaining colonies; ist   [columns

cŏl-ȯn-nāde', *n.*, series of

cŏl'ȯ-nȳ, *n.*, land settled by outsiders; nist; nize; nizer; nization; nial

cŏl'ŏr,*n.*, pigment, shade, hue, red blue etc.; *v.*, paint, alter; -ful; -fulness; -fully; -ation; -less

cŏl'ŏr-blīnd, *a.*, unable to see color; -ness

cōlt,*n.*, young horse

cŏl'ŭm-bīne, *n.*, flowering plant   [row

cŏl'ŭmn,*n.*, pillar, vertical

cŏl'ŭm-nĭst, *n.*, newspaper writer   [state

cō'mȧ, *n.*, unconscious

cōmb, *n.*, *v.*, (device to) smooth hair

cŏm'bȧt, *n.*, battle; *v.*, (cȯm-bȧt') fight; -ant; -ive; -iveness; -ively

cŏm'bīne, *n.*, harvesting machine, association

cȯm-bīne', *v.*, join; -r; nation; native

cȯm-bŭs'tion,*n.*, burning; tive; tible; tibility; tibly

cŏm'ė-dȳ, *n.*, humorous entertainment   [tor

cȯ-mē'dĭ-ȧn,*n.*, comic ac-

cȯme'lȳ, *a.*, beautiful

cŏm'ėt, *n.*, heavenly body with glowing tail

cŏm'fŏrt, *n.*, ease, relief; *v.*, soothe; -able; -ableness; -ably

cŏm'fŏrt-êr,*n.*, quilt

cŏm'ĭ-tȳ, *n.*, politeness

cȯm-mȧnd', *n.*, *v.*, order; -er, -ment

cŏm'mȧn-dȧnt, *n.*, head officer   [property

cȯm-mȧn·deer', *v.*, seize

cȯm-mĕm'ȯ-rāte,   *v.*, celebrate; tor; tion; tive; tory

cȯm-mĕnce', *v.*, begin; -er; -ment

cȯm-mĕnd', *v.*, praise -able; -ably; -ation; -atory

cȯm-mĕn'sû-rāte,   *a.*, equal in measure; tion; rable; rability; rably

cŏm'mĕnt,*n.*, *v.*, remark

cȯm-mêr'cĭȧl, *n.*, T.V. or radio advertisement; *a.*, of trade; -ism; -ize; ization; -ly

cŏm'mêrce,*n.*, business

cȯm-mĭn'gle,*v.*, blend

cŏm'mĭ-nūte, *v.*, pulverize; tion

cŏm'mĭs-sār-ȳ, *n.*, retail store on military base; sarial

cȯm-mĭs'sion, *n.*, authority, monetary percentage of sales, military certificate; -er

cȯm-mĭt', *v.*, entrust, do, pledge; -ment; -tal

cȯm-mĭt'tēe, *n.*, group working for purpose

cȯm-mōde', *n.*, small dresser, toilet

cȯm-mō'dĭ-oŭs,*a.*, roomy; -ness; -ly

cŏm'mȯ-dȯre,*n.*, officer

cŏm'mȯn, *a.*, public, usual, vulgar; -ness; -able

cŏm'mon-wĕalth, *n.*, nation   [ance

com-mō′tion, *n.,* disturb-
com′mūne, *n.,* group living and sharing to-
gether; **nal; nally; nal-
ism; nalize; nalization**
com-mūn′ĭ-cāte, *v.,* transmit, make known; **tor;
tion; tive; tiveness;
tively; cable; cabil-
ity; cably**
com-mūn′ĭon, *n.,* sharing,
Christian ritual
com′mū-nĭsm, *n.,* economic system of com-
mon ownership; **nist;
nistic; nistically; nize**
com-mū′nĭtў, *n.,* people
living together
com-mūte′, *v.,* change,
substitute; **tation; ta-
tive; mutable; mutabil-
ity**
com-mūt′êr, *n.,* one who
travels daily to job
com-păct′, *v.,* pack; *a.,*
close; **-ness; -ly**
com-păn′ĭon, *n.,* friend,
associate; **-able; -abil-
ity; -ably; -ship**
com′pá-nў, *n.,* group of
people, business, guest
com-pāre′, *v.,* examine for
likenesses and differ-
ences; **parison** *n.;* **parative; paratively; ra-
ble; rably; rability**
com-pärt′mĕnt, *n.,* division; **-al; -alize; -aliza-
tion**
com′pass, *n.,* range, device for making circles,
device for showing di-
rection; *v.,* go around
com-pát′ĭ-blĕ, *a.,* getting
along together; **ibility;
-ness; bly**
com-pā′trĭ-ŏt, *n.,* fellow
citizen; **-ism**
com-pĕl′, *v.,* force; **-ler;
-lable**
com-pĕn′dĭ-ŭm, *n.,* summary; **dious**
com′pĕn-sāte, *v.,* make
up for, pay; **tor; tion;
tive; tory**
com-pēte′, *v.,* enter into
rivalry, vie; **petitor, ti-**
tion; **petitive; petitory;
petively**
com′pĕ-tĕnt, *a.,* able,
tence; tency; -ly
com-plā′cĕnt, *a.,* satisfied; **cency; cence; -ly**
com-plāin′, *v.,* find fault;
-er
com-plāi′sánt, *a.,* agreeable; **sance; -ly**
com′plĕ-mĕnt, *n.,* that
which completes; **-ary;
-al; -arity**
com-plēte′, *v.,* finish; *a.,*
whole; **pletion; -ness;
-ly**
com-plĕxĭon, *n.,* nature,
facial texture
com′plĭ-cāte, *v.,* make involved; **tion; cacy; -d;
-dly**
com′plĭ-mĕnt, *n.,* praise;
-ary; -arily
com-plў′, *n.,* conform,
yield; **plier, pliance;
pliancy; pliant; pliantly**
com-pôrt′, *v.,* behave;
-ment
com-pōse′, *v.,* make up,
create, calm; **-r; sition;
-d**
com′pōte, *n.,* dish
com′pound, *n., a.,* combination of parts *v.* **(cŏm-
pound′)** combine, in-
crease
cŏm-prĕ-hĕnd′, *v.,* understand; **-hension; hen-
sive; -ible; hensible;
hensibility; hensibly**
com-prĕss′, *v.,* press together; *n.* **(cŏm′prĕss)**
wet pad; **-or; -ion; -ibil-
ity; -ible; -ive**
com-prīse′, *v.,* include;
prisal; prisable
cŏm′prŏ-mīse, *n.,* settle-
ment; *v.,* settle, adjust;
-r [of finance
com-trŏl′lêr, *n.,* director
com-pŭl′sion, *n.,* driving
force; **sive; sively; siveness; sory; sorily**
com-pŭnc′tion, *n.,* remorse
com-pūte′, *v.,* calculate;
-r; tation; putable; put-

ably
cŏm'răde, *n.,* friend;
-ship; -ly
cŏn-cāve', *a.,* curved inward; -ness; -ity; -ly
cŏn-cēal', *v.,* hide; -ment
cŏn-cēde', *v.,* yield, agree
to; -r
cŏn-cēive', *v.,* become
pregnant; think; **ceivable; ceivably; ceivability**   [-er
cŏn-cĕnt', *n.,* agreement;
cŏn'cĕn-trāte, *v.,* focus
one's mind; **tor; tion;
tive**
cŏn'cĕpt, *n.,* idea; -ual;
-ually; -ualize; -ualization
cŏn-cêrn', *n.,* business,
worry, care; *v.,* deal with;
-ment; -ed
cŏn'cĕrt, *n.,* musical program, agreement
cŏn-cĕs'sion, *n.,* yielding,
-sive
cŏnch, *n.,* spiral shell
cŏn-cīl'ĭ-āte, *v.,* win over,
pacify; **tor; tion; able;
tory; tive**
cŏn-cīse', *a.,* short and
clear; -ness; -ly; sion
cŏn-clāve', *n.,* meeting
cŏn-clūde', *v.,* end, decide; **clusion; clusive;
clusively**
cŏn-cŏct', *v.,* make, invent; -er; -ion; -ive
cŏn'cŏrd, *n.,* peace, harmony; -ance; -ant;
-antly
cŏn-crēte', *n.,* cement
mixture, *a.* real; -ness;
-ly
cŏn'cŭ-bīne, *n.,* secondary wife; **nage**
cŏn-cûr', *v.,* agree;
-rence; -rency; -rent;
-rently
cŏn-cŭs'sion, *n.,* shock,
brain injury; **sive**
cŏn-dĕmn', *v.,* disapprove, declare unfit,
convict; -er; -ation;
-atory; -able
cŏn-dĕ-scĕnd', *v.,* lower
onself; -ence; scen

sion; -ing
cŏn'dĭ-mĕnt, *n.,* relish
cŏn-dī'tion, *n.,* state, requirement; *v.,* make fit;
-al; -ality; -ally
cŏn-dō'lĕnce, *n.,* sympathy
cŏn-dŏ-mĭn'ĭŭm, *n.,* building jointly owned by tenants
cŏn-dōne', *v.,* forgive; -r;
nation; -able
cŏn'dŏr, *n.,* large vulture
cŏn'dŭct, *n.,* behavior; *v.*
(cŏn-dŭct') lead, direct;
-or; -ible, -ibility
cŏn'duĭt, *n.,* pipe, tube
cōne, *n.,* solid with round
base and pointed top;
conical
cŏn-fĕc'tion, *n.,* sweet
food; -er; -ery; -ary
cŏn-fĕd'êr-àte, *n.,* ally; *a.,*
united; *v.* **(āte)** unite;
acy; tion; tive
cŏn-fêr', *v.,* give, discuss;
-rer; -ee; -ment; -ence;
-rable; -ential; -ral
cŏn-fĕss', *v.,* admit; -or;
-ion; -ional
cŏn'fĭ-dĕnce, *n.,* trust, secret; **dent**
cŏn-fĭg-ŭ-rā'tion, *n.,* form
cŏn-fīne', *n.,* *v.,* limit;
-ment
cŏn-fĭrm', *v.,* prove, make
valid, become church
member; -and *n.;* -ation;
-atory; -able
cŏn'fĭs-cāte, *v.,* seize; **tor;
tion; tory**
cŏn-flà-grā'tion, *n.,* big
fire; **grant**
cŏn-fôrm', *v.,* agree,
adapt; -er; -ism; -ist;
-ity; -able; -ability;
-ably
cŏn-found', *v.,* puzzle; -ed
cŏn-frŏnt', *v.,* face; -ation;
-al
cŏn-fūse', *v.,* mix up; **sion;**
-d; -dly; fusing; fusingly
cŏn-fūte', *v.,* disprove; **tation; tative**
cŏn-gēal', *v.,* jell; -ment;
-able

còn-gēn'iàl, *a.*, friendly; -ity; -ly

còn-gĕn'ĭ-tàl, *a.*, since birth; -ly

còn-glŏm'êr-ate (īt),*n., a.*, cluster (ed); *v.* (āte) form mass; **tion**

còn-grăt'ů-lāte, *v.*, wish joy; **tor; tion; tory**

còn'grè-gāte, *v.*, assemble; **tor; gant** *n.;* **tive**

cŏn'grèss, *n.*, meeting, legislature; **-ional; -ion- ally**

cŏn'grŭ-ènt, *a.*, in agreement, corresponding; **-ly; ence; ency; gruity; gruous; gruously**

còn-jĕc'tŭre, *n.*, guess; **tural; turable; turally**

cŏn'jŭ-gàl, *a.*, marital; **-ly**

cŏn-jŭnc-tī'và, *n.*, eyelid part; **vitis**

còn-jŭnc'tion, *n.*, union, connecting word; **tive; tively; -al; -ally**

còn-nĕct',*v.*, join; **-or; -er; -ion; -ive; -ional**

còn-nĭp'tion, *n.*, fit of anger [**nivance**

còn-nīve', *v.*, conspire; **-r;**

còn-nōte', *v.*, suggest; **tation** [**-able**

cŏn'quêr, *v.*, defeat; **-er;**

cŏn-săn'guine, *a.*, of same blood; **-ous; guinity**

cŏn'scïence, *n.*, one's moral judgment

cŏn'scioŭs, *a.*, aware; **-ness; -ly**

cŏn'sè-crāte, *v.*, make holy, devote; **tor; tion; tory**

còn-sĕ'cŭ-tĭve, *a.*, in logical order; **tion; -ly; -ness**

cŏn'sè-quènce, *n.* result, importance; **quent; quently; quential; quentially; quentiality**

cŏn-sêr'và-tôr-ẙ, *n.*, music school

còn-sêrve', *v.*, save; **-r; vation; vational; va- tionalist; vancy**

còn-sīgn',*v.*, commit; **-or;**

-er; -ee; -ment; -ation

còn-sĭst', *v.*, contain

cŏn'sōle, *n.*, cabinet

còn-sōle', *v.*, comfort; **la- tion; solatory**

cŏn-sŏm-me' (mā),*n.*, hot or cold broth

cŏn'sò-nànce, *n.*, agreement; **cy; nant; nantly**

cŏn'sôrt, *n.*, spouse; *v.*, (còn-sôrt') associate

còn-spīc'ŭ-oŭs,*a.*, noticeable; **-ness; -ly**

còn-spīre', *v.*, join in a plot; **spirator; spiracy; spiratorial; spiratori- ally** [ficer

cŏn'stà-ble, *n.*, peace of-

cŏn'stànt, *a.*, continual; **-ly**

cŏn-stĕl-lā'tion, *n.*, group of stars; **tory**

cŏn-stêr-nā'tion,*n.*, terror

cŏn-stĭ-pā'tion, *n.*, inability to empty bowels; **pated**

cŏn'stĭ-tūte, *v.*, establish, form; **tive; tively**

cŏn-stĭ-tū'tion, *n.*, structure, fundamental laws of state, club, etc.; **-al; -alism; -alist; -ality; -ally**

còn-strāin', *v.*, hold in; **straint** *n.*

còn-strĭct', *v.*, bind, limit; **-or; -ion**

còn-strŭct', *v.*, build, devise; **-or; -er; -ion; -ional; -ionally; -ive; -ively; -iveness**

còn-strūe', *v.*, interpret; **struable**

còn-sŭlt', *v.*, ask advise; **-er; -ant** *n.;* **-ation; -ative; -atory**

còn-sūme', *v.*, destroy, use up, waste, eat; **-r** sumable

cŏn'tăct, *n.*, touching; *v.*, get in touch with

còn-tā'gioŭs, *a.*, spread by contact; **gion; -ly; -ness**

còn-tāin', *v.*, hold; **-er; -ment**

còn-tăm'ĭ-nāte, *v.*, pol-

C
D

lute; **tor; tion; tive**

còn-těm′pò-rār-ÿ, *n.*, one of same period; *a.*, modern; **porize; raneous**

còn-těmpt′,*n.*, disrespect; **-uous; -uously; -ible; -ibility; -ibleness; -ibly**

còn-těnd′, *v.*, fight, compete; **-er; tention; tentious; tentiously**

cŏn′těnt,*n.*, all that is contained; *a.* (còn-těnt′) satisfied

cŏn′těxt, *n.*, meaning; **-ure; -ual; ually**

cŏn-tĭg′ŭ-oŭs, *a.*, near; **guity**

cŏn′tĭ-něnt,*n.*, land mass; **-al; -ally**

còn-tĭn′ūe, *v.*, go on, last; **-r; uance; uation; nuity; uative; uous**

còn-tôrt′, *v.*, twist; **-ion**

còn′tôur, *n.*, *v.*, outline

cŏn′trȧ-bănd, *n.*, illegal goods; **-ist**

cŏn′trăct, *n.*, agreement; *v.*, agree formally; (còn-trăct′) get, shrink; **-or; -ion; -ible; -ibility; -ual**

còn-trăl′tō, *n.*, lowest female voice

cŏn′trăst,*n.*, difference; *v.* (còn-trăst′) compare; **-able; -ive**

còn-trĭb′ūte, *v.*, give to; **tor; tion; tive; tory**

còn-trīte′, *a.*, sorry for; **tion; -ly; -ness**

còn-trīve′, *v.*, scheme, plan; **-r; trivance; trivable**

còn-trōl′,*n.*, power; *v.*, restraint direct; **-ler; -able; -ability**

cŏn-tù-mē′lĭ-oŭs, *a.*, insulting; **-ly**

còn-tū′sion, *n.*, bruise

cŏn-vȧ-lěsce′, *v.*, gradually recover; **cence; cent** [-r

còn-vēne′, *v.*, meet, call;

còn-věn′iėnt, *a.*, handy; **ience; -ly** [nuns

còn′věnt,*n.*, community of

còn-věn′tion, *n.*, assem-

bly, custom; **-al; -ally; -ality**

còn-věrse′,*v.*, talk; **-r; sation; sationalist; sationally**

còn-vêrt′, *v.*, change; **-er; -ible; -ibility; version; versional; versionally**

cŏn-věx′, *a.*, curving outward; **-ness; -ity; -ly**

còn-vey′ (vā), *v.*, carry; **-or; -er; -ance; -able**

cŏn′vĭct, *n.*, prisoner; *v.* (còn-vĭct′) find guilty; **-ion**

còn-vĭnce′, *v.*, persuade; **-r; cing; cible**

còn-vōke′,*v.*, convene

cŏn′voy (voi),*n.*, *v.*, escort

còn-vŭlse′, *v.*, have a spasm; **sion; sive; sively; siveness**

cōōk′ĭe, *n.*, small sweet cake [calm

cōōl, *a.*, moderately cold,

cōōp,*n.*, small cage

cōōp′êr,*n.*, barrel maker

cōpe,*v.*, deal with

cō′pĭ-oŭs, *a.*, plentiful; **-ness; -ly**

cŏp′pêr,*n.*, reddish-brown metal [ous snake

cŏp′pêr-hěad, *n.*, poison-

cŏpse, *n.*, thicket

cŏp′ū-lāte,*v.*, have sexual intercourse; **tion; tive; tory**

cŏp′ÿ, *n.*, thing made like another, one of many like books, etc; *v.*, imitate; **copier**

cŏp′ÿ-rĭght, *n.*, exclusive legal right to book, song, etc.; **-er; -able**

cŏr′ȧl, *n.*, stony mass of sea animal skeleton

côrd,*n.*, thick string, wood measurement; **-age; -less**

côr′dial (jĭl), *a.*, friendly; **-ness; -ity; -ly**

côrd′īte,*n.*, gunpowder

côr′dò-vȧn,*n.*, leather

côr′dù-roy (roi),*n.*, ribbed cotton fabric

côrk, *n.*, bark of oak tree, stopper; *v.*, stop; **-er; -y** *a.*

côr'nē-à, *n.,* eyeball's covering

côr'nĕr, *n.,* angle where lines or planes meet, *v.,* put in tight position

côr-nĕt', *n.,* trumpetlike horn

côr'nĭce, *n.,* wall molding

côr-nŭ-cō'pĭ-à, *n.,* horn of plenty

cŏr-rŏl'là, *n.,* flower's petals; **-ceous**

côr'ól-lār-ў, *n.,* deduction

cò-rō'nà, *n.,* crown; **-tion**

côr'ó-nār-ў, *a.,* of the heart

côr'ó-nêr, *n.,* official investigator of deaths

côr'pö-ràl, *n.,* noncommissioned military officer; *a.,* of the body

côr-pò-rā'tion, *n.,* chartered organization to act as one; **râte** *a.;* **tive**

côrps, *n.,* organized group

côrpse, *n.,* dead body

côr'pū-lĕnt, *a.,* fat; **lence**

côr-răl', *n.,* fenced area for animals

cór-rĕct', *v., a.* (make) right; **-or; -ion; -ness; -able; -ive; -ively; -ly; -ness**

côr'rĭ-dör, *n.,* hall

cór-rŏb'ó-râte, *v.,* confirm; **tor; tion; tive; rant**

cór-rōde', *v.,* wear away; **rodible; rosion; rosive; rosively; rosiveness**

côr'rŭ-gāte, *v.,* make ridged; **tion; -d**

cór-rŭpt', *v., a.* (make) dishonest; **-er; -or; -ion; -ness; -ly; -ionist; -ive; -ively; -ible; -ibility; -ibly**

côr-sàge' (sàz), *n.,* flowers worn by a woman

côr'sĕt, *n.,* tight undergarment for torso; **-ry**

côr-tĕge', *n.,* funeral procession [cal

côr'tĕx, *n.,* outer layer; **ti-**

côr'tĭ-sōne, *n.,* drug

cŏs-mĕt'ĭc, *n., a.* (preparation) to improve appearance; **tology; tolo-**

gist

cŏs'mòs, *n.,* universe; **mic; mically; mology**

cŏst, *n.* price, loss

cŏs'tūme, *n.,* style of dress

cŏt, *n.,* folding bed

cō-tĭl'lión, *n.,* formal ball

cŏt'tòn, *n.,* natural fiber, fabric

cŏt'tòn-tāil, *n.,* rabbit

coù'gàr, *n.,* wild cat

cough (câuf), *n.,* loud air burst from lungs

coŭn'cĭl, *n.,* advisory or legislative group; **-lor; -lorship**

coŭn'sĕl, *n.,* advice, lawyer; *v.,* advise; **-or; -lor; -orship; -lorship**

coŭnt, *n.,* total number; nobleman; *v.,* name numbers in order, have value; **-er; -able**

coŭn'tĕr, *n.,* long table or cabinet top; *a., adv.* opposite

coŭn'tĕr-feĭt, *a.,* false

coŭnt'ĕss, *n.,* noblewoman

coŭn'trў, *n.,* nation, rural area; **trified**

coŭn'tў, *n.,* administrative unit of a state [move

coŭp, *n.,* blow, brilliant

coŭpe, *n.,* two-door car

coŭ'ple, *n.,* two things, pair; *v.,* join

coŭ'pŏn, *n.,* paper to redeem cash or merchandise

coûr'àge, *n.,* bravery; **-ous; -ousness; -ously**

coû'rĭ-êr, *n.,* messenger

côurse, *n.,* path, series, part of meal, study program

côurt, *n.,* enclosed yard, king's family, etc., judicial assembly; *v.,* seek, woo

côur'tĕ-sàn, *n.,* court lady

côurt'lў, *a.,* elegant

coûth, *a.,* civilized

coū-tūre' (tôr), *n.,* work of designing fashion; **rier**

cōve, *n.,* small bay

cŏv'ė-nànt, *n.,* agreement;

-or; -er; -ee; -al

cŏv'êr, v., place something over; hide\, protect; **-er; -age**

cŏv'êrt, a., secret; **-ness; -ly**

cŏv'ĕt, v., envy; **-er; -ous; -ousness; -ously**

cow, n., female animal— cattle, whale, etc; v., frighten

cow'ård, n., who lacks courage; **-ice; -ly**

cowl, n., monk's hood

cow'lĭck, n., unruly piece of hair

cŏx'å, n., hip; **-l**

cŏx'swāin, n., one who steers a boat

coy (coï) a., seemingly shy; **-ness; -ly**

cō'zў, a., comfortable, snug; **ziness; zily**

crăb, n., shellfish, complainer

crăb'bў, a., cross

crăck, n., v., break, split; n., sharp noise, (coll.) try; **-er** [cuit

crăck'êr, n., thin crisp biscrā'dle, n., rocking baby bed

crăft, n., skill, art, boat

crăft'ў, a., sly, artful; **iness; ily**

crăm, v., pack full; **-mer**

crămp, n., painful spasm

crāne, n., large wading bird, lifting machine

crā'nĭ-ŭm, n., skull; **nial; nially; niology**

crănk, n., machine arm for turning, irritable person

crăps, n. pl., dice game

crăss, a., coarse; **-iness; -ly**

crāte, n., large shipping case [pit

crā'têr, n., bowl-shaped

crå-văt', n., necktie

crāve, v., long for; **-r**

crăwl, v., go on hands and knees, move slowly n., swimming stroke

cray'fĭsh, n., freshwater shellfish

cray'ŏn, n., colored wax

drawing stick

crāze, n., fad

crĕam, n., fatty part of milk, cosmetic paste; **-y** a.

crēase, n., v., fold

crĕ-āte', v., originate, cause; **tor; tion**

crĕa'tûre, n., living being

crĕ'dênce, n., belief; **dent**

crĕ-dĕn'zà, n., buffet

crĕd'ĭt, n., trust, honor, financial reputation, college study unit; **-or; -able; -ably; -ableness; -ability**

crēed, n., statement of belief; **-al**

crēek, n., small stream

crēel, n., basket for fish

crēep, n., v., crawl; **-er; -age**

crĕ'māte, v., burn dead body; **tor; tion**

crepe (crāp), n., thin wrinkled cloth

crĕ-pŭs'cûle, n., twilight; **lar**

crĕ-scĕn'dō, a., adv., musically increasing in loudness

crĕs'cĕnt, n., shape of quarter moon; **-ic**

crĕst, n., top, tuft on animal's head

crĕ'tĭn, n., idiot; **-ism**

crĕv'ĭce, n., crack, split

crĕw, n., group of workers

crĕw'ĕl, n., embroidery

crĭb, n., baby's bed; v., cheat at school work

crĭck'ĕt, n., insect, ball game

crime, n., act violating law

crĭmp, v., pleat, make wavy; **-y** a.

crĭm'sŏn, n., a., deep red

crĭn'ò-lĭne, n., stiff petticoat

crĭp'ple, n., lame person; v., make lame or unable; **-r** [emergency

crī'sĭs, n., turning point,

crĭsp, n., brittle, fresh; **-ness; -y** a.; **-ly**

crī-tĕr'ĭ-ŏn, n., standard

crĭt'ĭc, n., judge of arts, fault finder

cro-chet′ (shā), n., kind of needle work; **-er**

crock, n., earthenware pot

croc′o-dile, n., large reptile

cro′cus, n., flowering plant

crook, n., v., bend; n. (coll.) dishonest person

croon, v., sing softly; **-er**

crop, n., farm product. group; v., cut off ends; **-per**

cro-quet′(kā), n., outdoor game with ball and mallet   [ball

cro-quette′, n., fried food

cross, n., X mark, Christian symbol; v., oppose, intersect; a., cranky

crotch, n., place where legs fork

crouch, v., stoop

croup, n., respiratory disease

crow, n., black bird, rooster's cry; v., boast

crow′bar, n., long metal bar for prying

crowd, n., large group of people; v., push together

crown, n., jeweled headdress, top, head; v., honor, enthrone

cru′cial, a., very important; **-ly**

cru′ci-fix, n., figure of Christ on cross

cru′ci-fy, v., kill by nailing on a cross; **fier**

crude, a., raw, unrefined; **-ly; -ness; dity**

cru′el, a., causing pain; **-ness; -ly; -ty**

cruise, n., boat trip; v., travel; **-er**

crumb, n., small bit, bad person; **-y** a.

cru-sade′, n., church expedition, campaign

crush, v., press into bits, subdue   [**-y** a.

crust, n., outer covering;

crus-ta′cean, n., shellfish

crutch, n., cripple's staff, support

crux, n., essense

crypt, n., underground burial place

crys′tal, n., mineral formation. watch face. glassware: **-line** a.; **-lize; -lization; -lography**

cub, n., young bear, lion, etc.

cube, n., solid with six equal square sides; **bic; bical**

cub′ism, n., form of abstract art; **cubist; bistic**

cud, n., food chewed again

cud′dle, v., hold lovingly; **dly**

cudg′el, n., short thick club

cue, n., signal, billiard stick   [pants end

cuff, n., band at sleeve or

cui-sine′, n., cooking style

cu-lotte′, n., women's knee length full pants

cul′prit, n., villain, guilty person

cult, n., system of religious worship, sect

cul′ti-vate, v., raise, grow, develop, refine; **tor; tion; vable; -d**

cul′ture, n., development, way of life; **ral; rally**

cul′vert, n., drain

cum′ber-some, a., hard to handle

cu′mu-late, v., gather together; **tion; tive; tively**

cu′mu-lus, n., cloud type

cun′ning, a., sly, clever; **-ness; -ly**

cup′board, n., storage place

cu′po-la, n., small dome

cur, n., mongrel, mean person; **-rish; -rishly**

cu-ra′tor, n., museum manager

curb, n., street's edge; v., restrain

curd, n., soured milk; **-y** a.

cure, v., make well, heal; **-r; curable; curability**

cu′ri-o, n., rare article

cu′ri-ous, a., eager to learn: **riosity; -ly; -ness**

curl, n., coil (of hair); v., roll up; **-er; -y** a.

curl′i-cue, n., fancy curve

cûr′rànt, *n.,* small berry

cûr′rén-cȳ, *n.,* money, general use

cûr′rènt, *n.,* flow; *a.,* now happening; **-ly**

cûr-rĭc′ū-lŭm, *n.,* course of study; **lar**

cûr′rȳ, *n.,* seasoning; *v.,* clean animal's coat

cûrse, *v.,* make evil oath, swear [writing

cûr′sĭve, *n.,* flowing hand-

cûr′só-rȳ, *a.,* hastily done

cûrt, *a.,* blunt

cûr′taĭn, *n.,* cloth window covering

cûrt′sȳ, *n.,* respectful bend of body, bow

cûrve, *n.,* bending line; *v.,* bend, twist; **vature; vy** *a.* [ease shock

cŭsh′ĭon, *n.,* pillow; *v.,*

cŭsp, *n.,* pointed end

cŭss, *n., v.,* curse, swear

cŭs′tàrd, *n.,* pudding of milk, eggs and sugar

cŭs′tó-dȳ, *n.,* in care of; **dial**

cŭs′tóm, *n.,* usual practice; **-ary; -arily**

cŭs′tóm-ér, *n.,* buyer

cŭs′tóms, *n. pl.,* import tax

cūte, *a.,* clever, pretty; **-ness; -ly**

cŭt′ĭ-cle, *n.,* skin around fingernail

cŭt′làss, *n.,* curved sword

cŭt-lêr-ȳ, *n.,* cutting tools

cŭt′têr, *n.,* small fast ship

cŭt′thrŏat, *n.,* murderer; *a.,* ruthless

cŭt′tle-fĭsh, *n.,* sea animal

cŭt′wŏrm, *n.,* caterpillar feeding on farm crop

cȳ′à-nĭde, *n.,* poisonous substance

cȳ-bêr-nĕt′ics, *n. pl.,* science of brain and computers; **ic**

cȳ′cle, *n.,* recurring time period; **clic; clical; clically** [storm

cȳ′clŏne, *n.,* violent wind

cȳ-clò-rä′mà, *n.,* series of pictures on large round wall

cȳl′ĭn-dêr, *n.,* tubelike

solid with flat ends; **dri-cal; dricality; drically**

cȳm′bàl, *n.,* brass plate struck for musical sound

cȳn′ic, *n.,* sarcastic person; **-al; -ally; -ism**

cȳ′prĕss, *n.,* tree

cȳst, *n.,* sac in animal tissue; **-ic**

cȳ-tŏl′ó-gȳ, *n.,* study of cells; **gist; logic; logical; logically**

czâr, *n.,* Russian emperor; **-dom; -ism**

D

dăb, *v.,* light tap on

dăb′ble, *v.,* do superficially; **-r** [dog

dăchs′hŭnd, *n.,* long short

dā′crŏn, *n.,* synthetic fiber

dăf′fò-dĭl, *n.,* flower

dăft, *a.,* silly, crazy; **-ness; -ly** [stabbing

dăg′gêr, *n.,* short knife for

dăhl′ià, *n.,* flower

dāi′lȳ, *a., adv.,* every day

dāin′tȳ, *a.,* delicate; **ti-ness; tily**

dāir′ȳ, *n.,* place to make milk, butter, etc.

dā′ĭs, *n.,* raised platform

dāi′sȳ, *n.,* flower

dăl′lȳ, *v.,* flirt, loiter; **lier; liance** [dog

dăl-mä′tiàn, *n.,* spotted

dăm, *n.,* water barrier

dăm′àge, *n.,* injury; *v.,* injure; **-able**

dăm′àsk, *n.,* printed fabric of linen or silk

dămn, *v.,* condemn, curse; **-ation; -atory; -ed; -able; -ably**

dămp, *n.,* moisture; **-en** *v.;* **-ness; -ish; -ly**

dăm′sél, *n.,* maiden

dăm′sòn, *n.,* type of plum

dăn′dè-lī̈on, *n.,* lawn weed

dăn′dêr, *n.,* temper

dăn′drŭff, *n.,* flaking skin of scalp

dăn′dȳ, *n.,* vain man; *a.,* (coll.) good; **-ism; dify; dification; -ish**

dăn′gêr, *n.,* possible

harm; **-ous; -ousness;
-ously** [**-r**
dăn'gle, v., hang loosely;
dăp'pêr, a., smart, trim;
-ness; -ly
dăp'ple, a., spotted
dāre, v., challenge, risk;
-r; ing
dârk, a., without light,
shaded, gloomy; **-ness;
-en** v.; **-ish; -ly**
dâr'lĭng, n., loved one; a.,
beloved, cute
dârn, v., mend by sewing;
-er
dârt, n., small pointed missile; v., throw or move
quickly; **-er**
dăsh, n., little bit, sprint,
mark (—); v., spatter,
rush; **-er**
dăsh'bôard, n., car panel
dăs'tàrd, n., sneaky person; **-ly; -liness**
dā'tà, n. pl., facts, information
dāte, n., time period, appointment, fruit; v., set a
time; **-r; -able; -less**
dāte'line, n., newspaper's
date
dăv'ĕn-pôrt, n., sofa
daw'dle (dău), v., waste
time; **-r** [gin
dāwn, n., daybreak; v., be-
dāy, n., 24 hour period,
hours of sunlight, era
dāy'drēam, v., imagine
while awake
dāy'time, n., time from
sunrise to sunset
dāze, n., bewilderment;
-dly
dăz'zle, v., overpower with
brilliance; **-ment; -ingly**
dēa'cón, n., church officer; **-ess**
dĕad, a., not living, life-
less, dull, complete; **-en**
v.; **-ly**
dĕad'bēat, n., lazy person
dĕad-līne, n., time limit
dĕad-lŏck, n., stalemate
dĕaf-mūte, n., one who
cannot hear or speak
dēal, v., distribute, is con-
cerned with; **-er; -ing** n.;

-ership
dēan, n., church or college
officer, oldest member;
-ship; -ery
dēar, a., adv., loved, es-
teemed; costly; **-ness;
-ly**
dêarth, n., scarcity
dēath, n., end of life; **-ful;
-ly**
dēath'trăp, n., dangerous
place
dė-bă'cle, n., defeat
dė-bâr', v., exclude; **-ment**
dė-bârk', v., land; **-ation**
dė-bāse', v., lower; **-r;
-ment**
dė-bāte', v., argue formally; **-r; batable**
dė-bäuch', n., orgy; v.,
corrupt; **-er; -ee; -ment;
-ery; -edly***
dė-bĭl'ĭ-tÿ, n., weakness;
tate; tation
dĕb'ĭt, n., account entry of
money owed
dĕb-ò-nāir', a., charming
dė-bris' (brē), n., rubble,
litter [**-or**
dĕbt, n., something owed;
dė-but' (bū), n., first public
appearance, introduc-
tion to society
dĕc'āde, n., ten years
dė-cănt'êr, n., fancy glass
wine bottle
dė-căp'ĭ-tāte, v., cut off
head; **tor; tion**
dė-căth'lŏn, n., athletic
contest with ten events
dė-cāy', v., rot, waste away
dė-cēive', v., fool; **-r; ceivable; ceivingly**
dē-cĕl'êr-āte, v., reduce
speed; **tor; tion**
dē'cĕnt, n., proper;
cency; -ly
dė-cĕp'tion, n., fraud, misleading; **tive; tiveness;
tively**
dė-cīde', v., make up one's
mind; **-r; cidable; -d**
dĕc'ĭ-màl, n., a., (fraction)
of or based on ten; **-ly**
dĕc'ĭ-māte, v., destroy;
tor; tion
dė-ci'phêr, v., decode;

-ment; -able

dè-cī'sion, *n.,* judgment; **-al; sive; siveness; sively**

deck, *n.,* ship's floor, pack of playing cards; *v.,* adorn

dè-clāre', *v.,* state openly; **-r; ration; claratory; clarative**

dè-clěn'sion, *n.,* descent, grammatical case

dè-clīne', *v.,* slope downward, refuse; **-r; nation**

dè-cóm-pōse', *v.,* decay; **sition; posable**

děc'ò-rāte, *v.,* make attractive, adorn; **tor; tion; tive; tiveness; tively**

dè-cô'rŭm, *n.,* dignity; **rous; rousness; rously**

dè-crēase', *v.,* lesson

dè-crēe', *n., v.,* order

děc'rè-mént, *n.,* loss

dè-crěp'ĭt, *a.,* worn out; **-ly; -ude** *n.*

děd'ĭ-cāte, *v.,* give oneself, inscribe; **tor; tion; tory; tive**

dè-dūce', *v.,* draw conclusion; **ducible**

dè-dŭct', *v.,* subtract; **-ion; -ive; -ively; -ible; ibility**

dēed, *n.,* act, title of ownership

dēem, *v.,* think, regard

dēep, *a., adv.,* far down, intense, of low pitch; **-en; -ly; -ness**

dēer, *n.,* antlered animal

dè-fāce', *v.,* mar; **-r; -ment**

dè-făl'cāte, *v.,* embezzle; **tor; tion**

dè-fāme', *v.,* slander; **-r; mation; famatory**

dè-fâult', *n.,* failure to do; **-er**

dè-fēat', *v.,* conquer, win

děf'ė-cāte, *v.,* excrete waste; **tor; tion**

dè-fĕnd', *v.,* protect; **-er; -able; -ant** *n., a.*

dè-fěnse', *n.,* protection; **-less; -lessness; -lessly; sible; sibility; sibly; sive; siveness; sively**

dè-fêr', *v.,* put off; **-rer; -ment; -red**

dè-fī'ciènt, *a.,* lacking; **-ly; ciency**

dè-fīle', *v.,* make dirty

dè-fīne', *v.,* explain, state meaning; **-r; nition; nitional; finable**

děf'ĭ-nĭte, *a.,* exact; **-ly**

dè-flāte', *v.,* let out air, make less important; **tor; tion; tionary**

dè-flěct', *v.,* turn aside; **-or; -ion; -ive**

dè-fôrm', *v.,* disfigure; **-ation; -ity; -ed**

dè-frâud', *v.,* cheat; **-er; -ation** [-al

dè-frāy', *v.,* pay; **-ment;**

děft, *a.,* quick, skillful; **-ness; -ly**

dè-fŭnct', *a.,* dead

dè-fȳ', *v., oppose;* **fier; fiance; fiant; fiantly**

dè-gěn'êr-āte, *v.,* rot, decline; *a.,* **(āte)** depraved; **tion; tive; -ness; -ly**

dè-grāde', *v.,* lower in rank or value; **-r; -able**

dè-grēe', *n.,* stage, amount, rank, unit of measure for temperature

dē-hȳ'drāte, *v.,* remove water from; **tor; tion**

dē'ī-fȳ, *v.,* make a god, idolize; **fication; fic**

deign (dān), *v.,* condescend, grant

dē'īsm, *n.,* belief in God's existence; **deist; deistic**

dè-jěct', *v.,* depress; **-ion; -ed**

dē-lăm'ĭ-nāte, *v.,* separate into layers; **tion**

dè-lāy', *v.,* postpone; **-er**

dè-lěc'tȧ-ble, *a.,* very pleasing; **bility; bly**

děl'ė-gāte, *n.,* representative; *v.,* **(gāt)** appoint, entrust; **gacy; gation**

dè-lēte', *v.,* erase; **tion**

děl-è-tē'rī-oŭs, *a.,* harmful; **-ness; -ly**

dè-lĭb'êr-āte, *v.,* think; **tion; tive; tively**

dè-lĭb'êr-ȧte, *a.,* done on

purpose; **-ness; -ly**

dĕl'ĭ-cáte, *a.*, fine, frail, proper; **cacy; -ness; -ly**

dè-lĭ'cioùs, *a.*, pleasing; **-ly; -ness**

dè-līght', *n.*, pleasure; *v.*, rejoice; **-ed; -ful; -fully; -ness** [**-ative**

dè-lĭm'ĭt, *v.*, define; **-ation;**

dè-lĭn'ė-āte, *v.*, draw, describe; **tor; tion; tive**

dè-lĭn'quĕnt, *a.*, neglecting duty; overdue; **-ly; quency**

dè-lĭr'ĭ-ŭm, *n.*, wild excitement; **ious; iously; iousness**

dĕll, *n.*, small valley

dĕl'tà, *n.*, Greek letter, soil deposit at river's mouth

dè-lūde', *v.*, fool, mislead; **lusion; lusive; lusively; siveness**

dĕl'ūge, *n.*, *v.*, flood

dè-lŭxe', *a.*, elegant

dĕlve, *v.*, search; **-r**

dĕm'à-gŏgue, *n.*, leader who stirs up emotion; **gogy; gogism; gogic; gogical**

dē-mâr-cā'tion, *n.*, limit

dè-mēan', *v.*, degrade, behave

dè-ment'ĕd, *a.*, insane

dĕm'ĭ-gŏd, *n.*, minor god

dè-mīse', *n.*, death

dè-mĭt', *v.*, resign; **mission** [fee cup

dĕm'ĭ-tăsse, *n.*, small cof-

dè-mŏc'rà-cў, *n.*, government of, by and for the people

dè-mŏl'ĭsh, *v.*, destroy; **-er; -ment; lition**

dē'món, *n.*, devil; **-ic; -ically**

dè-môr'àl-īze, *v.*, corrupt, weaken morals; **-r; zation** [tion

dè-mōte', *v.*, lower rank;

dè-mûr', *v.*, object; **-ral**

dè-mūre', *a.*, shy; **-ly**

dè-nī'àl, *n.*, refusal

dĕn'ĭ-grāte, *v.*, blacken; **tor; tion; tory**

dĕn'ĭm, *n.*, coarse cotton cloth

dĕn'ĭ-zĕn, *n.*, inhabitant

dè-nŏm-ĭ-nā'tion, *n.*, name, kind, religious sect; **tive**

dè-nŏm'ĭ-nā-tor, *n.*, bottom number of fraction

dè-nōte', *v.*, refer to, mean; **tation; tative; tatively; notable**

dè-noŭnce', *v.*, condemn; **-r; -ment**

dĕnse, *a.*, crowded together; **sity; -ness; -ly**

dĕnt, *n.*, hollow in surface

dĕn'tàl, *a.*, of teeth; **-ly**

dĕn'tĭst, *n.*, tooth doctor; **-ry**

dĕn'tûre, *n.*, false teeth

dè-nūde', *v.*, strip

dè-nŭn'cĭ-āte, *v.*, condemn; **tor; tion; tive; tory** [nier

dè-nў', *v.* declare untrue;

dē-ō'dòr-ànt, *n.*, odor destroyer; **dorize; dorizer; dorization**

dè-pârt', *v.*, leave, go; **-ed; -ure** *n.*

dè-pârt'mént, *n.*, division; **-al; -alize; -alization**

dè-pĕnd', *v.*, rely; **-ence; -ency; -ent; -ently; -able; -ably; -ability; -ableness**

dè-pĭct', *v.*, represent; **-or; -ion**

dè-pĭl'à-tô-rў, *n.*, hair removing cosmetic

dè-plēte', *v.*, use up, empty; **tion; tive**

dè-plôre', *v.*, be sorry about; **-r; plorable; plorably**

dè-ploy' (plŏi), *v.*, extend out; **-ment**

dè-pôrt', *v.*, send away; **-ation; -able**

dè-pôrt'mént, *n.*, behavior

dè-pōse', *v.*, remove from office; **sition; posal** *n.*; **posable**

dè-pŏs'ĭt, *n.*, *v.* (thing) set down, store; **-or; -ory** *n.*

dē'pot (pō), *n.*, storehouse, train station

dè-prāve', *v.*, corrupt; **-r; pravity; -d; -dly**

děp′rê-cāte, v., ‿ disapprove; **tor; tion; cat-ingly**

dė-prē′cĭ-āte, v., lessen; **tor; tion; tory; tive**

děp-rė-dā′tion, n., looting

dė-prěss′, v., push down, lower, sadden; **-or; -ion; -ible; -ive; -ively; -iveness**

dė-prīve′, v., take or keep from; **vation; prival; privable; -d**

depth, n., deepness

dė-pūte′, v., appoint

děp′ū-tÿ, n., assistant; **tize**

dė-rāil′, v., go off the track; **-ment**

dė-rānge′, v., upset; make insane; **-ment; -d**

děr′ė-lĭct, a., deserted, neglectful; **-ion**

dė-rīde′, v., make fun of; **-r; rision; risive; risively; risiveness**

dė-rīve′, v., originate; **-r; vation; vational; rivative**

děr′má, n., skin; **-l; -tology; -tologist; -tological**

dė-rŏg′á-tô-rÿ, a., insulting; **tive; rily**

děr′rĭck, n., lifting machine

děs′cănt, n., varied melody

dė-scěnd′, v., come down, lower; **-er; -ible; scent** n.

dė-scrībe′, v., tell or write about; **-r; scribable; scribably**

dė-scrÿ′, v., see

děs′ė-crāte, v., make unholy; **-r; tor; tion**

děs′ėrt, n., dry sandy area, waste

dė-sêrt′, v., abandon, leave; **-er; -ion**

dė-sêrve′, v., merit; **-d; -dly; serving**

děs′ĭc-cāte, v., dry completely; **tion; tive**

dė-sīgn′, n., v., plan, pattern; **-er; -ee; -edly**

děs′ĭg-nāte, v., point out; **tor; tion; tive**

dė-sīre′, n., v., wish, want; **sirable; sirability; sirableness; sirably; sirous**

dė-sĭst′, v., stop; **-ance**

děsk, n., writing table

děs′ó-lāte, v., lay waste; a. (lĭt) deserted; **-r; tor; tion; -ly; -ness**

děs-pêr-á′dō, n., outlaw

děs′pêr-āte, a., hopeless, serious, reckless; **tion; -ly; -ness**

dė-spīse′, v., hate; **picable; picableness; picably** [-fully

dė-spīte′, n., malice; **-ful;**

dė-spīte′, prep., even so

dė-spŏnd′, v., lose hope **-ency; -ence; -ent; -ently**

děs′pŏt, n., absolute ruler; **-ism; -ic; -ical; -ically**

děs-sêrt′, n., sweet dish ending meal

děs′tĭne, v., intend; **-d**

děs′tĭ-nÿ, n., fate

děs′tĭ-tūte, a., very poor; **tion** [molish

dė-strōy′ (ŏĭ), v., ruin, de-

děs′uė-tūde, n., disuse

děs′ŭl-tô-rÿ, a., random; **riness; rily**

dė-tăch′, v., separate; **-able; -ability; -ment**

dė-tăch′mént, n., group for special service

dė-tāil′, n., item; tell each part; **-ed** [-ment

dė-tāin′, v., hold back; **-er;**

dė-těct′, v., discover; **-or; -ion; -ive; -able; -ible**

dė-těc′tĭve, n., crime investigator

de-tente′ (dā-tŏnt), n., lessening of international hostility

dė-těn′tion, n., holding in custody

dė-têr′, v., try to stop; **-ment; -rence; -rent**

dė-têr′gént, n., cleaning substance

dė-têr′mĭne, v., decide; **-r; -d; nation; native; nate** a.; **nately; nable; nability; nably**

dė-tĕst', v., hate; -er; -ation; -able; -ability; -ableness; -ably

dĕt'ȯ-nāte, v., explode; tor; tion

dė-tôur', n., alternate way

dė-trăct', v., take away from; -or; -ion; -ive

dĕt'rĭ-mėnt, n., harm, disadvantage; -al; -ally

deūce, n., playing card of two, tennis score, devil

dĕv'ȧs-tāte, v., destroy; tor; tion; tatingly

dė-vĕl'ȯp, v., grow, expand; -er; -ment; -mental; -mentally; -able

dė'vĭ-āte, v., turn from; tor; tion; ant n., a.; ance; ancy; vious; viously, viousness

dė-vīce, n., scheme, mechanical invention

dĕv'ĭl, n., evil spirit or person; -ment; -ry; -ish; ishly

dė-vīse', v., plan

dė-vŏlve', v., pass on to; -ment

dė-vōte', v., dedicate; -ee; tion; -ment; -d; -dness; -dly

dė-vŏur', v., eat; -er

dė-vŏut', a., pious, sincere; -ness; -ly

dew, n., atmospheric moisture; -y a.; -iness; -ily

dĕx-tĕr'ĭ-tў, n., skill; terous; terousness; terously

dĕx'trōse, n., sugar

dī-ȧ-bē'tĕs, n., disease of excess sugar in urine; betic [-ally

dī-ȧ-bŏl'ĭc, a., wicked; -al;

dī-ȧ-crĭt'ĭ-cȧl, a., distinguishing; -ly

dī'ȧ-dĕm, n., crown

dī'ȧg-nōse, v., find the cause; sis n.; nostician; n.; nostic; nostically

dī-ȧg'ȯ-nȧl, a., slanting between corners; -ly

dī'ȧ-grăm, n., drawing, chart; -matic; -matical; -matically

dī'ȧl, n., face of device indicating measurement, ex. watchface, compass; v., call on telephone

dī'ȧ-lĕct, n., speech of a certain region; -al; -ally; -ology; -ologist; -ological

dī-ȧ-lĕc'tĭc, n., logical argumentation; -al

dī'ȧ-lŏgue, n., conversation [circle

dī-ăm'ė-tėr, n., width of

dī-ȧ-mĕt'rĭ-cȧl, a., opposed; -ly

dī'a-mȯnd, n., carbon crystal, gem, rectangular shape

dī'ȧ-phrăgm (frăm), n., muscles between chest and abdomen

dī-ȧr-rhē'ȧ, n., looseness of bowel movements; -l

dice, n. pl., spotted cubes used in games, v., cut into cubes

dī-chŏt'ȯ-mў (kŏt), n., division of two opposing parts; mize; mization; mous; mously

dī-chrō-măt'ĭc (krō), a., having two colors

dĭck'êr, v., bargain, haggle

dĭck'ēy, n., false shirt front

dĭc'tāte, v., say for another to write, order; tion

dĭc'tā-tȯr, n., ruler with total power; -ship; -ial; -ially [manner

dĭc'tion, n., speaking

dĭc'tŭm, n., pronouncement

dĭd'dle, v. (coll.) cheat, waste time

die, n., tool for molding, stamping, etc.; v., stop living

die'hârd, a., very stubborn

dī'ėt, n., food eaten; v., to eat to lose weight; -etic; -ary

dĭf'fêr, v., be unlike, disagree; -ent; -ence; -entness; -ently

dĭf-fêr-ĕn'tĭ-āte, v., distinguish between; tion; al;

ally; able; ability

dĭf'fĭ-cŭlt, *a.*, hard; **-y; -ly**

dĭf'fĭ-dĕnce, *n.*, shyness; **dent; dently**

dĭf-frăct', *v.*, break into parts; **-ion; -ive; -ively**

dĭf-fūse' (fūz), *v.*, spread-out; **-r; sor; sion; sive; sively; siveness**

dĭg, *v.*, turn up as soil; **-ger**

dĭ'gest, *v.*, absorb as food into body, summarize; **-er; -ion; -ive; -ible; -ibility; -ibly**

dĭg'ĭt, *n.*, finger or toe, numerals 0 to 9; **-al; -ally**

dĭg'nĭ-tār-ў, *n.*, person in high office

dī'grăph, *n.*, two letters with one simple sound

dĭke, *n.*, embankment to hold back flood

dĭ-lăp'ĭ-dāt-ĕd, *a.*, broken down

dĭ-lāte', *v.*, expand; **tor; tion; tive; latability; latable**

dĭl'ă-tô-rў, *a.*, delaying

dĭ-lĕm'mă, *n.*, difficult choice

dĭl-ét-tănte', *n.*, follower of arts; **-ism; tantish**

dĭll, *n.*, herb

dĭ-lūte', *v.*, weaken, thin down; **-r; tor; tion; -ness**

dĭm, *v.*, darken; *a.*, not bright or clear; **-mer; -ness; -ly**

dĭme, *n.*, coin for ten cents

dĭ-mĕn'sion, *n.*, measurement- **-al; -ally**

dĭ-mĭn'ĭsh, *v.*, decrease; **-able**

dĭm'ple, *n.*, small hollow on body

dĭn, *n.*, steady noise

dĭne, *v.*, eat dinner; **-r**

dĭn'ĕr, *n.*, small restaurant

dĭnghў (gў), *n.*, small boat

dĭn'gō, *n.*, Australian dog

dĭn'gў (jў), *a.*, shabby, dirty [meal

dĭn'nĕr, *n.*, main daily

dĭ'nō-saur (sôr), *n.*, large extinct reptile

dĭ'ō-cése, *n.*, religious district

dĭ-ō-ră'mă, *n.*, miniature three dimensional scene

dĭp, *n.*, slope, plunge; *v.*, put quickly into liquid; **-per**

dĭph-thē'rĭă, *n.*, infectious disease; **ritic**

dĭph'thŏng, *n.*, sound of two joined vowels

dĭ-plō'mă, *n.*, certificate of college degree or honor

dĭ-plō'mă-cў, *n.*, relations between nations, tact; **mat** *n.*; **matic; matically**

dĭp'pêr, *n.*, ladle

dîre, *a.*, extreme; **-ness; -ly**

dĭ-rĕct', *v.*, command, guide; **-or; -ion; -ive; -ional**

dĭ-rĕc'tō-rў, *n.*, book of names, addresses, etc.

dîrge, *n.*, funeral hymn

dĭr'ĭ-gĭ-ble, *n.*, manned balloon

dîrk, *n.*, dagger

dîrn'dl, *n.*, full skirt with gathered waist

dîrt, *n.*, soil, gossip; **-y** *a.*; **-iness; -ily**

dĭs-ā'ble, *v.*, be handicapped; incapable; **bil-ity; -ment; -d**

dĭs-ăf-fĭl'ĭ-āte, *v.*, end association; **tion**

dĭs-ăl-lōw, *v.*, reject; **-ance** [**-ance**

dĭs-ăp-pēar', *v.*, vanish;

dĭs-ăp-pōint', *v.*, spoil the hopes of; **-ment; -ed**

dĭs-ăp-prove' (prōov), *v.*, consider wrong; **proval** *n.*; **provingly**

dĭs-ăr-rānge', *v.*, undo order of; **-ment**

dĭs-ăs-sō'cĭ-āte, *v.*, sever relations with; **tion**

dĭs-ăs'têr, *n.*, serious misfortune; **trous; trously**

dĭs-bănd', *v.*, break up; **-ment**

dĭs-bâr', *v.*, exclude from law practice; **-ment**

dĭs-bûrse', *v.*, pay out; **-r; -ment; bursable**

dĭsc, *n.*, disk, phonograph record

dĭs-cârd′, v., throw away

dĭs-cêrn′, v., distinguish; **-er; -ment; -ible; -ibly; -ing; -ingly**

dĭs-chârge′, v., release, shoot; **-r; -able**

dĭs-cī′ple, n., follower

dĭs′cĭ-plĭne, n., training, conduct; v., punish; **-r; plinable; plinal**

dĭs-cŏl′ör, v., change color, fade; **-ation**

dĭs-cŏm-bŏb′ū-lāte, v., confuse [**-ure**

dĭs-cŏm′fĭt, v., frustrate;

dĭs-cŏn-tĕnt′, a., restless; **-ment; -ed; -edness; -edly**

dĭs-cŏn-tĭn′ūe, v., stop; **uation; uance**

dĭs′cŏ-phĭle, n., expert of phonograph records

dĭs′côrd, n., conflict; v., clash; **-ant; -ance; -ancy; -antly**

dĭs′cŏ-thèque (tĕk), n., nightclub for dancing

dĭs′cŏunt, n., price reduction; v., **(dĭs-cŏunt′)** take for less value

dĭs-coûr′åge, v., try to prevent; **-ment**

dĭs′côurse, n., speech, talk

dĭs-cŏv′êr, v., find out; **-er; -y; -able**

dĭs-crĕd′ĭt, v., disbelieve

dĭs-crēet′, a., careful; **-ness; -ly**

dĭs-crĕp′ån-cȳ, n., inconsistency, mistake; **ant; antly**

dĭs-crē′tion, n., tactful judgment; **-ary; -al**

dĭs-crĭm′ĭ-nāte, v., see a difference; **tion; tory; nable**

dĭs′cŭs, n., metal disk thrown as track event

dĭs-cŭss′, v., talk about; **-ion; -able; -ible**

dĭs-dāin′, n., v., scorn; **-ful; -fulness; -fully**

dĭs-ēase′, n., illness

dĭs-ĕn-chằnt′, v., free from magic; **-ment**

dĭs-ĕn-cŭm′bêr, v., relieve a burden

dĭs-ĕn-gãge′, v., unfasten; **-ment; -d**

dĭs-fã′vör, n., dislike

dĭs-fĭg′ûre, v., ruin appearance; **-ment; ration**

dĭs-frăn′chĭse, v., deprive of rights; **-ment**

dĭs-grằce′, n., v., dishonor; **-ful; -fulness; -fully**

dĭs-grŭn′tle, v., displease; **-ment**

dĭs-guĭse′, v., hide the real nature; **-ment**

dĭs-gŭst′, n., distaste; v., sicken; **-ing; -ingly; -ed; -edly**

dĭs-heârt′ĕn, v., discourage; **-ing; -ingly; -ment**

dĭ-shĕv′ĕl, v., become untidy; **-ed; -led; -ment**

dĭs-ĭl-lū′sion, v., disappoint; **-ment**

dĭs-ĭn-fĕst′, v., remove pest; **-ation**

dĭs-ĭn′tĕ-grāte, v., break up; **tor; tion; tive**

disk, n., flat, circular thing

dĭs′lō-cāte, v., displace; **tion**

dĭs′mål, a., gloomy; **-ly**

dĭs-măn′tle, v., strip, take apart; **-ment**

dĭs-mãy′, n., loss of courage; v., appall

dĭs-mĕm′bêr, v., cut into pieces; **-ment**

dĭs-ōwn′, v., deny ownership

dĭs-pâr′åge, v., belittle; **-ment; aging; agingly**

dĭs-pàs′sion-åte, a., fair, unemotional; **ly**

dĭs-pătch′, n., message; v., send; **-er**

dĭs-pĕl′, v., drive away

dĭs-pĕn′så-rÿ, n., place for medical treatment

dĭs-pĕnse′, v., give out, exempt; **-r; sation; sational; sable; sability**

dĭs-pêrse′, v., scatter; **-r; sion; sal** n.; **persible; sive**

dĭs-plằce′, v., remove from; **-ment**

dĭs-plāy', *v.*, show

dĭs-pōse', *v.*, arrange, settle; -r

dĭs-pō-sĭ'tion, *n.*, frame of mind, arrangement

dĭs-pós-sĕss', *v.*, expel, oust; -or; -ion

dĭs-prōve', *v.*, show to be false

dĭs-pūte', *n.*, argument; *v.*, discuss; **tation; tatious; tative; table; tably; tant** *n.*

dĭs-qual'ĭ-fȳ (kwal), *v.*, make ineligible; **fication**

dĭs-quī'ĕt (kwi), *v.*, disturb, worry; **-ude** *n.*

dĭs-rė-gârd', *v.*, neglect; -ful

dĭs-rōbe', *v.*, undress

dĭs-rŭpt', *v.*, break up; -er; -or; -ion; -ive; -ively

dĭs-săt'ĭs-fȳ, *v.*, displease; **faction; factory; fied**

dĭs-sĕct', *v.*, cut apart, examine; -or; -ion

dĭs-sĕnt', *v.*, disagree; -er; **sension; -ient; -ious; -ing**

dĭs-sėr-tā'tion, *n.*, written thesis

dĭs-sĭm'ŭ-lāte, *v.*, pretend; **tor; tion**

dĭs'sĭ-pāte, *v.*, scatter, waste; -r; tor; tion; tive; -d

dĭs'sò-lūte, *a.*, immoral; -ness; -ly

dĭs-sōlve', *v.*, melt, end; **lution, solvable; solvent**

dĭs'sò-nánce, *n.*, lack of harmony or agreement; **nant; nantly**

dĭs'tăff, *n.*, *a.*, female

dĭs-tāste', *n.*, *v.*, dislike; -ful   [disease

dĭs-tĕm'pêr, *n.*, animal

dĭs-tĕnd', *v.*, expand; **tention; tension; tensible**

dĭs-tĭll', *v.*, purify by condensing vapor; -er; -ery; -ation

dĭs-tĭn'guĭsh, *v.*, see or show a difference; -able; -ably

dĭs-tĭn'guĭshed, *a.*, famous

dĭs-tôrt', *v.*, make out of shape, pervert; -er; -ion

dĭs-trăct', *v.*, draw away from, confuse; -ion; -ible

dĭs-trĕss', *n.*, *v.*, pain, worry; -ing; -ed; -ful

dĭs-trĭ'būte, *v.*, give out for; **tion; tive; tively; table**

dĭs-tûrb', *v.*, upset, interrupt; -er; -ance

dĭs-ūse', *v.*, stop using

dĭtch, *n.*, channel dug in earth

dĭth'êr, *n.*, confused state

dĭt'tō, *n.*, *v.*, copy

dĭt'tȳ, *n.*, simple song

dī-ûr'nàl, *a.*, every day; -ly

dī'và, *n.*, leading woman singer

dīve, *v.*, plunge head first; -r

dī-vêrge', *v.*, branch off, differ; -nce; -ncy; -nt; -ntly

dī-vêr'sĭ-fȳ, *v.*, vary; **sity**

dī-vêr'sion, *n.*, distraction; -ist; -ary *a.*

di-vĕst', *v.*, strip; -itûre

dī-vīde', *v.*, split into parts; -r; **vision; visible**

dī-vīne', *a.*, holy, great; **nize; -ly**

dī-vĭn'ĭ-tȳ, *n.*, god, study of religion

dī-vôrce', *n.*, legal end of marriage; *v.*, separate

dī-vŭlge', *v.*, make known; -nce; -ment

dĭz'zȳ, *a.*, unsteady, confused; **ziness; zily**

dŏc'īle, *a.*, tame, easy to handle; **cility; -ly**

dŏck, *n.*, place to unload ship, truck, etc. *v.*, deduct part

dŏck'ėt, *n.*, court agenda

dŏc'tör, *n.*, physician, one with college's highest degree

dŏc'trĭne, *n.*, belief, teachings; **nal; nally**

dŏc'ū-mėnt, *n.*, written record; *v.*, **(mĕnt)** prove; -ation; -ary

dŏdge, v., move aside quickly, avoid; **-r**

dŏe, n., female deer

dŏff, v., take off

dŏg'ēar, v., turn down page's corner

dŏg'gĕd, a., stubborn; **-ness; -ly**

dŏg'gêr-ĕl, n., jingle

dŏg-măt'ĭc, a., dictorial; **-ally** [tree

dŏg'wōōd, n., flowering

dŏī'lӯ, n., small lace mat

dŏl'drŭm, n., low spirit

dŏle, n., relief to needy; v., give out [**-ly**

dōle'fŭl, a., sad; **-ness;**

dŏll, n., toy like human

dŏl'lăr, n., U.S. money system, 100 cents

dŏl'lӯ, n., doll; cart for moving heavy objects

dō'lŏ-mīte, n., kind of rock

dō'lŏr-oŭs, a., sad; **-ly**

dŏl'phĭn, n., sea mammal

dōlt, n., stupid person; **-ish; -ishness; -ishly**

dō-māin', n., area of control

dōme, n., large rounded roof; **domical**

dŏ-mĕs'tĭc, n., house servant; a., of the home, tame; **-ity; -ate; -ation; -ly**

dŏm'ĭ-nāte, v., control; **tor; tion; nance; nant; nantly**

dŏ-mĭn'ion, n., power controlled region

dŏm'ĭ-nō, n., mask; tile; **oes** n., pl., game of matching dotted tiles

dŏn, n., dress

dō'nāte, v., give as to charity; **tor; tion**

dŏn'kēy, n., horselike animal

dō'nŏr, n., one who gives

dōōm, n., tragic fate; v., condemn

dôor, n., movable panel at entrance

dōpe, n., stupid person, drug; **-y; piness**

dôr'mănt, a., asleep, still; **mancy**

dôr'mêr, n., window on sloped roof

dôr'mĭ-tô-ry, n., building to sleep many

dôr'săl, a., of the back

dōse, n., medicine taken at one time; **dosage**

dŏs'sĭ-er (ā), n., data on one subject

dŏt'âge, n., senility

dōte, v., be fond; **-r; doting; dotingly**

doŭ'ble, a., adv., twofold, twice as much; v., duplicate, fold; **-y** a.

doŭ-ble-crôss', v., betray

doubt (doŭt), n., uncertainty; v., question; **-er; -ful; -fulness; -fully; -able; -less**

doŭche (dūsh), n., water jet to cleanse body

dough, n., flour mixture for baking; (coll.) money; **-y** a.

doŭr, a., gloomy; **-ness; -ly**

doŭse, v., pour liquid over

dŏve, n., kind of pigeon

dŏve'tāil, v., fit together

dŏw'ă-gĕr, n., wealthy widow

dŏw'ĕl, n., peg

dŏwn, n., descent, soft hair; adv., to lower place or state; a., lower, sad

dŏwn'căst, a., sad

dŏwn'făll, n., sudden fall, ruin [spirits

dŏwn-heârt'ĕd, a., in low

dŏwn'pôur, n., heavy rain

dŏwn'right, a., plain; adv., utterly [tic

dŏwn-tŏ-êarth', a., realis-

dŏw'rӯ, n., property bride brings to husband

dŏwse, v., search for water

dōze, n., v., nap; **dozy**

dŏz'ĕn, n., set of twelve

drăb, a., dull; **-ness; -ly**

drăft, n., drink, air current, outline, bank check; compulsory service; v., take into service

drăfts'măn, n., one who draws plans

drăg, n., hindrance; v., pull

along; pass slowly

drăg'nĕt, *n.,* system for criminal investigations

drăg'ŏn, *n.,* mythical beast

drăg'ŏn-flỹ, *n.,* insect

drāin, *n.,* pipe *v.,* let out liquid slowly, empty; **-age**

drāke, *n.,* male duck

drăm, *n.,* ⅛ ounce, small amount

drà'mà, *n.,* play, art of theater; **-tics; -tist; -tize; -tization**

drāpe, *v.,* hang loosely

drăs'tĭc, *a.,* extreme; **-ally**

dräw, *n.,* stalemate, attraction; *v.,* pull, attract, inhale, get, make pictures

drăw'băck, *n.,* disadvantage

drăw'brĭdge, *n.,* bridge that can be raised

drawer (drôr), *n.,* sliding box in chest; *pl.,* underpants

drăwl, *v..* speak slowly

drăwn, *a.,* haggard

drāy, *n.,* cart; **-age**

drĕad, *n., v.,* fear; **-ful; -fulness; -fully**

drēar'ỹ, *a.,* gloomy; **iness; ily**

drĕdge, *n., v.,* (boat, device to) scoop from water's bottom

drĕgs, *n., pl.,* particles at bottom of liquid

drĕnch, *v.,* soak with liquid

drĕss, *n.,* clothing, woman's garment with skirt; *v.,* put on clothes, prepare

drĕss'êr, *n.,* one who dresses, chest of drawers

drĕss'ĭng, *n.,* bandage, sauce for food, meat stuffing   [stress

drĕss'măk-êr, *n.,* seam-

drĭft, *n.,* tendency, general meaning, pile of sand, etc.; *v.,* move along by current

drĭll, *n., v.,* (tool to) bore holes, practice

drĭp, *v.,* fall in drops; **-py**

a.   [fee pot

drĭp'ò-lā-tŏr, *n.,* drip cof-

drīve, *n.,* motor trip, road campaign; *v.,* force to go, operate a vehicle; **-r**

drĭv'ĕl, *n.,* silly talk; **-er**

drĭv'ĕn, *a.,* forced

drĭz'zle, *n.,* fine misty rain; **-zly** *a.*

drŏit, *n.,* legal right

drŏll, *a.,* funny; **-ery**

drōne, *n.,* male bee; *v.,* hum, talk monotonously

drōōl, *v.,* drip saliva

drōōp, *v.,* hand down, weaken; **-y** *a.;* **-iness; -ily**

drŏp, *n.,* tiny liquid mass, bit, descent; *v.,* let fall, utter; **-per**

drŏp'ōut, *n.,* student who does not finish school

drŏp'sỹ, *n.,* excess body fluid

drŏss, *n.,* rubbish

drōught, *n.,* very dry weather, no rain

drōve, *n.,* animal herd

drōwn, *v.,* die in water

drōwse, *v.,* sleep lightly; **-y** *a.*

drŭdge, *n.,* one who works hard; **-ry**   [cotic

drŭg, *n.,* medicine, nar-

drŭg'gĭst, *n.,* filler of medical prescriptions

drŭg'stôre, *n.,* store selling medicine

drŭm, *n., v.,* hollow musical instrument that is beaten; **-mer**

drŭnk, *a.,* intoxicated; **-ard** *n.;* **-en** *a.*

drỹ, *a.,* not wet, not sweet; **-er; -ness**

drỹ'-clēan, *v.,* clean with waterless substance; **-er**

dū'ăd, *n.,* couple

dū'ăl, *a.,* of two, double; **-ity; -ly; -ize**

dŭb, *v.,* give nickname

dū'bĭ-oŭs, *a.,* doubtful, uncertain; **-ness; -ly; osity; bitable; bitably**

dŭch'ĕss, *n.,* duke's wife

dŭck, *n.,* small swimming

C
D

bird, cloth; v., dip under water, avoid

dŭct, n., tube, channel

dŭc'tĭle, a., easily molded; **tility**

dŭde, n., dandy, fob

dŭds, n., clothes

dŭe, a., owed, proper, expected; adv., exactly

dŭ'ĕl, n., fight between two persons [fee

dŭes, n., pl., membership

dŭ'ĕt, n., music for two performers

dŭg'out, n., shelter

dŭke, n., nobleman; **-dom**

dŭl'cĕt, a., melodious; **-ly**

dŭll, a., mentally slow, sluggish, boring, blunt; **-ish**; **-ness**; **-y** adv.

dŭmb, a., unable to talk, (coll.) stupid; **-ness**; **-ly**

dŭmb'bĕll, n., weight lifted as exercise

dŭm'mȳ, n., imitation, unreal model, stupid one

dŭmp, n., rubbish pile; v., unload, throw away

dŭmp'lĭng, n., ball of dough

dŭn, n., demand for payment

dŭnce, n., dull person

dŭne, n., hill of sand

dŭng, n., animal excrement

dŭn-gȧ-rees', n., pl., denim work pants

dŭn'geòn, n., underground prison

dŭnk, v., dip in liquid

dŭ'ō, n., pair, two

dŭpe, v., cheat

dŭ'plĕx, n., two-family house

dŭ'plĭ-cāte, v., copy; a. (cĭt) double; **tion; cable; catable**

dû-rā'tion, n., time of existence

dû-rĕss', n., pressure

dŭsk, n., start of evening darkness, dim; **-y** a.; **-iness**; **-ily**

dŭst, n., powdery dirt; v., sprinkle powder, clean; **-er**; **-y** a.; **-less**

dū'tȳ, n., obligation, task; **tiful; tifully**

dū'tȳ, n., tax; **tiable**

dwärf, n., being smaller than normal; **-ish**; **-ishness**

dwĭn'dle, v., decrease

dȳ'ăd, n., pair; **-ic**

dȳe, n., v., (substance to) change color; **-r**

dȳ'nȧ-mĭte, n., powerful explosive; **-r**

dȳ'nȧs-tȳ, n., family of successive rulers; **tic; tical; tically**

dȳs'ĕn-tēr-ȳ, n., intestinal disease; **teric**

dȳs-fūnc'tion, n., incomplete functioning; **-al**

dȳs-lĕx'ĭ-ȧ, n., reading impairment; **lexic**

dȳs-pĕp'sĭ-ȧ, n., impaired digestion; **peptic**

dȳs'trȯ-phȳ, n., faulty development

E

ēa'gêr, a., keenly desiring; **-ness**; **-ly**

ēa'gle, n., bird of prey

ēa'gle-eȳed, a., sharp in vision

ēar'drŭm, n., thin membrane in ear

êarl, n., nobleman

ēar'mârk, v., identify

êarn, v., work for wages or profit, deserve

êar'nĕst, a., serious, sincere; **-ness**; **-ly**

ēar'shŏt, n., hearing range

êarth, n., planet we live on, land, soil; **-ly; -liness**

êarth'ĕn-wāre, n., baked clay dishes

êarth'quāke, n., trembling of earth's crust

êarth'shāk-ĭng, a., very important [soil

êarth'wŏrm, n., worm in

ēar'wĭg, n., insect

ēase, n., comfort, natural manner v., lessen, move carefully; **-ful; -fully**

ēa'sĕl, n., artist's stand for picture

ēast, *n.,* direction of sunrise; *a.,* of the east; **-erly; -ern** *a.;* **-erner**

ēas'ÿ-gō-ĭng, *a.,* relaxed

ēaves, *n., pl.,* roof's edge

ēaves'drŏp, *v.,* listen secretly

ĕbb, *n.,* fallen tide *v.,* recede, lessen

ĕb'on-ÿ, *n.,* tree; *a.,* dark, black

ė-bŭl'lĭėnt, *a.,* bubbling exuberant: **lience; li-tion; liency; -ly**

ėc-cĕn'trĭc, *a.,* strange: **-ity; -ally**

ĕc-clē'sĭ-às-tĭ-càl, *a.,* of church and clergy; **-ly; cism** [mation

ĕch'ė-lŏn, *n.,* steplike for-

ėch'ō (ĕk), *n.,* repeated sound [pastry

e-clàir' (ā-). *n.,* long filled

ĕc-lĕc'tĭc, *a.,* selective from many ideas; **-ally; -ism**

ė-clĭpse', *n.,* obscuring of sun by moon or moon by earth's shadow

ė-cŏl'ŏ-gÿ, *n.,* science of man's environment; **gist; logical; logically**

ė-cŏn'ŏ-mÿ, *n.,* money and wealth management, thrift, country's prosperity; **nomics; mist; nomic** [beige

ĕc'rū, *n., a.,* light tan,

ĕc'stà-sÿ, *n.,* great delight; **static; statically**

ĕc'ū-mèn-ĭsm, *n.,* interreligious cooperation, **menic, menical; menically**

ĕc'zė-mà, *n.,* skin disease

ĕd'dÿ, *n.,* little whirlpool

ė-dē'mà, *n.,* excess body fluid; **-tous**

ė-dĕn'tàte, *a.,* toothless

ĕdge, *n.,* border, verge

ĕd'ĭ-ble, *a.,* eatable; **bility; -ness**

ē'dĭct, *n.,* public order

ĕd'ĭ-fĭce, *n.,* building

ĕd'ĭ-fÿ, *v.,* instruct or improve morally; **fication**

ė-dĭ'tion, *n.,* published form of book, issue of newspaper

ĕd'ū-cāte, *v.,* teach; **tor; tion; tional; tionally; cable; tive**

ė-dūce', *v.,* extract, draw out; **duct** *n.;* **duction; ducible**

ēel, *n.,* snakelike fish

ēe'rĭė, *a.,* weird; **riness, rily**

ĕf-fĕct', *n., v.,* result, influence; *n., pl.,* belongings; **-er; -ive; -iveness; -ively; -ual; -uate**

ĕf-fĕm'ĭ-nàte, *a.,* of female traits; **nacy; -ly**

ĕf'fĕr-ėnt, *a.,* carrying away

ĕf-fĕr-vĕsce', *v.,* bubble: **cent; cense; cently**

ĕf-fēte', *a.,* exhausted; **-ness; -ly**

ĕf-fĭ'cĭėnt, *a.,* competent; **ciency; -ly**

ĕf'fĭ-gÿ, *n.,* statue or crude image of person

ĕf'flū-ėnt, *n., a.,* (thing) flowing out; **ence**

ĕf-frŏn'tĕr-ÿ, *n.,* unashamed boldness

ĕf-fŭl'gėnce, *n.,* great brightness; **ent**

ègg, *n.,* female reproductive cell, oval body laid by bird, fish, etc

ègg'hĕad, *n.,* intellectual

ègg'nŏg, *n.,* thick drink of eggs and milk

ē'gō, *n.,* self, conceit; **-ism, -ist; -istic**

ē'gŏ-tĭsm, *n.,* selfishness; conceitedness; **tĭst; tis-tic; tistical; tistically**

ė-grē'gioŭs, *a.,* very bad; **-ness; -ly**

ē'grĕss, *n.,* exit

ė-jàc'ū-lāte, *v.,* discharge, exclaim; **tor; tion; tory**

ė-jĕct', *v.,* throw out; **-or; -ion; -ive; -able**

ēke, *v.,* barely make do

ė-làb'ŏ-rāte, *v.,* develop in detail; *a.,* (ĭt) complicated; **tor; tion; tive; -ness; -ly**

e-làn', *n.,* (ā) dash

è-lăpse', v., pass by

è-lāte', v., make happy; tion; -ness; -ly

ĕl'bōw, n., joint between lower and upper arm

ĕld'êr, n., older person; a., senior; -ly; -liness

è-lĕct', v., vote, choose; tor; tion; tive; tively

è-lĕc'tör-àte, n., all qualified voters

è-lĕc-trĭ'ciàn, n., workman for electric apparatus

è-lĕc-trĭc'ĭ-tў, n., form of energy

è-lĕc-trō-câr'dĭ-ò-grăph, n., instrument to record heartbeat; -ic

è-lĕc'trò-cūte, v., kill with electricity; tion

è-lĕc'trōde, n., conductor of electricity

è-lĕc'trŏn, n., atom's negatively charged particle; -ic; -ics; -ically

ĕl'è-gànt, n., refined, luxurious; gance; gancy; -ly

ĕl'è-gў, n., mournful poem; giac; gist

ĕl'è-mènt, n., basic part, environment, basic chemical substance; -al; -ally

ĕl'è-vā-tör, n., lifting machine

ĕlf, n., tiny fairy, small child; -ish; -ishness; -ishly [-ation

è-lĭc'ĭt, v., bring forth; -or;

ĕl'ĭ-gĭ-ble, a., qualified; bility; bly

è-lĭm'ĭ-nāte, v., remove, excrete; tor; tion; tive

è-līte', n., best group, typewriter type

è-lĭx'îr, n., medicine

ĕll, n., right angle wing of building

ĕl-lĭpse', n., oval figure; liptic; liptical; liptically

ĕl-ò-cū'tion, n., manner of speaking; -ist; -ary

è-lŏn'gāte, v., make longer, extend; tion

è-lōpe', v., run away to marry; -ment

ĕl'ò-quènt, a., expressive; quence; -ly

è-lū'cĭ-dāte, v., explain; tor; tion; tive

è-lūde', v., avoid, escape; lusion; lusive

è-lū'vĭ-ŭm, n., rock and soil debris; vial

ĕm, n., printer's measure

è-mā'cĭ-āte, v., become too thin; tion

è-măn'cĭ-pāte, v., free; tor; tion; tive; tory

è-măs'cū-lāte, v., deprive, castrate; tion; tory; tive

ĕm-bălm', v., preserve a dead body; -er; -ment

ĕm-bănk'mènt, n., protective wall or mound

ĕm-bâr'gō, n., legal restriction on trade

ĕm-bârk', v., go aboard, begin; -ment; -ation

ĕm-băr'ràss, v., feel self-conscious; -ment

ĕm'bàs-sў, n., ambassador's official residence

ĕm-băt'tle, v., prepare to fight

ĕm-bĕl'lĭsh, v., decorate, elaborate; -ment

ĕm'bêr, n., glowing coal or wood from fire

ĕm-bĕz'zle, v., steal money entrusted; -r; -ment

ĕm-bĭt'têr, v., make angry; -ment

ĕm-blā'zòn, v., decorate celebrate; -ment

ĕm'blèm, n., symbol, sign; -atic; -atical; -atically

ĕm-bŏd'ў, v., give form to, include; bodiment

ĕm'bò-lĭsm, n., obstruction of a blood vessel

ĕm-bŏss', v., make raised design; -er; -ment

ĕm'brō-cāte, v., rub with salve, oil, etc

ĕm-broĭ'dêr, v., decorate with needlework, embellish; -er; -y

ĕm-broĭl', v., involve in fight; -ment

ĕm'brў-ō, n., organism in early stage; -nic; -logy;

-logist

ĕm′êr·ăld, *n.*, green jewel

é·mêrge′, *v.*, come forth; **gency; gent**

è·mêr′gĕn·cÿ, *n.*, sudden action needing action

è·mĕr′ĭ·tŭs, *a.*, retired with honorary title

ĕm′êr·ÿ, *n.*, an abrasive

è·mĕt′ĭc, *a.*, causing vomiting

ĕm′ĭ·grāte, *v.*, leave one's country for another; **tion;** grant *n., a.*

ĕm′ĭ·nĕnt, *a.*, high, famous; **nence; nency; -ly** [on mission

ĕm′ĭs·sār·ÿ, *n.*, agent sent

è·mĭt′, *v.*, discharge, transmit; **-ter; mission; missive**

è·mŏl′li·ĕnt, *a.*, softening

è·mŏl′ū·mĕnt, *n.*, salary

è·mō′tion, *n.*, feeling; **-al; -ality**

èm·pā′thÿ, *n.*, understanding of another's situation; **thize; thetic**

ĕm′pêr·ör, *n.*, ruler; **press**

ĕm′phá·sĭs, *n.*, stress, importance; **size; phatic**

ĕm·ploy′ (plŏĭ), *v.*, use, hire; **-er; -ee; -ment; -able**

ĕm·pô′rĭ·ŭm, *n.*, trading center, department store

ĕm·pÿr′ē·ăl, *a.*, heavenly

ē′mū, *n.*, flightless Australian bird

ĕm′ū·lāte, *v.*, imitate to equal or surpass; **tor; tion; tive; tively; lous**

è·mŭl′sion, *n.*, oil suspended in watery liquid; **sive; sify; sification; sifiable**

èn·ăm′ĕl, *n.*, glossy coating or paint; **-er**

èn·ăm′ör, *v.*, charm

èn·cāge′, *v.*, confine

èn·căp′sù·lāte, *v.*, put in capsule, condense; **tion**

ĕn·cĕph·á·lī′tĭs, *n.*, brain inflammation; **tic**

èn·chănt′, *v.*, bewitch, delight; **-er; -ment; -ing**

èn·clôse′, *v.*, fence in, insert; **sure**

èn·cō′mĭ·ŭm, *n.*, tribute, praise; **miast** *n.;* **miastic**

en′côre (ăn), audience's demand for more; *int.,* more!

èn·coun′têr, *n.*, battle, chance meeting; *v.*, meet

èn·crōach′, *v.*, intrude, trespass; **-ment**

èn·cŭm′bêr, *v.*, burden, hinder; **brance**

èn·cÿ·clô·pē′dĭ·á, *n.*, book or books with information; **dic; dically**

èn·dēar′, *v.*, cause to like; **-ment; -ing**

èn·dĕav′ör, *n., v.*, try

ĕn·dĕm′ĭc, *a.*, native to region; **-al; -ity; demism**

ĕn′dīve, *n.*, leafy salad green

ĕnd′lĕss, *a.*, eternal, continual; **-ly; -ness**

ĕn′dô·crīne, *n.*, any body gland producing internal secretion; **nology**

èn·dôrse′, *v.*, sign a check, approve; **-r; -ment; dorsable**

èn·dōw′, *v.*, give money or gift, provide with; **-ment**

èn·dūre′, *v.*, last, continue; **durance, durable; durably; during**

ĕn′è·má, *n.*, fluid injected into rectum

ĕn′è·mÿ, *n.*, one against another, opponent, foe

ĕn′êr·gÿ, *n.*, vigor, power to do work; **getic; getically; gize; getics**

ĕn′êr·vāte, *v.*, weaken; **tion**

èn·fôrce′, *v.*, urge, make obey law; **-r; -ment; -able**

èn·frăn′chīse, *v.*, free, give right to vote; **-ment**

èn·gāge′, *v.*, pledge to marry, hire, involve, enter in battle; **-d; -ment**

èn·gĕn′dêr, *v.*, cause

ĕn′gĭne, *n.*, machine using energy, locomotive; **-er**

ĕn·gĭ·nēer′ĭng, *n.*, use of

science in industry

ėn-gôrge', v., eat greedily; **-ment**

ėn-gräve', v., etch letters or design in metal, impress; **-r; ing** n.

ėn-hănce', v., make greater; **-er; -ment**

ė-nĭg'mà, n., mystery; **-tic; -tical; -tically** [bid

ėn-jŏĭn', v., command, for-

ėn-lârge', v., increase size; **-r; -ment**

ėn-lĭst', v., join the military, get; **-ment**

ėn-lĭv'ėn, v., make active

ėn'mĭ-tў, n., hostility

ėn-nō'ble, v., dignify

en'nui (àn'wē), n., boredom [mity

ė-nôr'moŭs, a., huge;

ė-nough' (nŭf), a., adv., as much as necessary

ėn-räge', v., anger

ėn-răp'tŭre, v., enchant

ėn-rĭch', v., make rich, add vitamins; **-ment**

ėn-rŏll', v., sign up for; **-ment** [snugly

ėn-scŏnce', v., place

en-sem'ble (än-säm), n., whole costume, company of actors, musical band

ėn-shrĭne', v., hold sacred

ėn-sĭgn', n., flag, badge, U.S. naval officer

ėn-snäre', v., trap

ėn-snârl', v., tangle

ėn-sūe', v., follow

ėn-tāil', v., require; **-ment**

ėn-tăn'gle, v., confuse, trap; **-ment**

en-tente' (än-tänt), n., agreement between nations

ėn'têr-prĭse, n., project, venture

ėn-thräll', v., fascinate

ėn-tĭce', v., attract

ėn-tĭre', a., whole; **-ness; -ty; -ly**

ėn'tĭ-tў, n., anything real

ėn-tò-mŏl'ò-gў, n., study of insects; **gist**

ėn'trāils, n., intestines

ėn'trànce, n., place for en-

tering

ėn-trănce', v., put into trance, entrapture; **-ment**

ėn-trēat', v., beg, request; **-ment; -y; -ingly**

en'tree (än-trā), n., freedom to enter, meal's main course

ėn-trĕnch', v., establish

en-trė-prė-neûr' (än), n., one running own business

ėn-twĭne', v., wrap around

ė-nü'mêr-āte, v., count, list; **tor; tion; tive**

ė-nŭn'cĭ-āte, v., state, speak clearly; **tor; tion; tive; ciable**

ėn-vĕl'ŏp, v., cover; **-ment**

ĕn'vė-lōpe, n., paper container for letters

ėn-vĭ'ròn-mėnt, n., surroundings; **-al; -ally**

ėn-vĭ'sion, v., imagine

ĕn'voy (vŏĭ), n., diplomatic agent

ĕn'vў, n., jealousy; v., begrudge; **vious; viously; viable; viably**

ĕn'zўme, n., substance causing chemical reactions in body; **mology**

ė'ŏn, n., long period

ĕp'àu-lĕt, n., shoulder decoration

ė-phĕm'êr-àl, a., short lived; **-ly**

ĕp'ĭc, n., long poem; a., grand, heroic; **-al; -ally**

ĕp'ĭ-cūre, n., one who enjoys fine foods, wines, etc., gourmet; **rean** a.; **curism**

ĕp-ĭ-dĕm'ĭc, n., widespread disease; **-ally; miology**

ĕp-ĭ-dêr'mĭs, n., outer layer of skin; **mal; mic**

ĕp'ĭ-grăm, n., witty saying; **-matic; -matical; -matically**

ĕp'ĭ-grăph, n., building inscription, motto; **-ic; -ical; -ically**

ĕp'ĭlĕp-sў, n., disease marked by convulsive

fits; **leptic** *n., a.;* **leptic-**
ally [part
ep′i-logue, *n.,* concluding
è-pĭs′cò-pàl, *a.,* of or by
bishops; **-ly**
ĕp′ĭ-sōde, *n.,* incident;
sodic; sodical; sodic-
ally [lary
è-pĭs′tle, *n.,* letter, **-r; to-**
ĕp′ĭ-tăph, *n.,* tombstone
inscription; **-ic; -ial**
ĕp′ĭ-thĕt, *n.,* descriptive
name ex. Philip the Fair;
-ic; -ical
è-pĭt′ò-mē, *n.,* typical example, summary; **mize**
ĕp′óch (ók),*n.,* period; **-al;**
-ally [bility
ĕq′uà-ble, *a.,* steady; **bly;**
ē′quàl, *a.,* same, alike; **-ly;**
-ity; -ize; quate
è-quā′tion,*n.,* mathematic
expression of equal
quantities; **-al**
è-quā′tŏr, *n.,* imaginary
circle dividing earth
equally in half; **-ial**
è-quĕs′trĭ-àn,*n., a.,* (one)
horseback riding; **-ism**
ē-quĭ-lĭb′rĭ-ŭm, *n.,* balance
ē′quine, *n.,* horse
ē′quĭ-nŏx, *n.,* time when
sun crosses the equator;
noctial
ĕq′uĭ-tà-ble, *a.,* fair, just;
-ness; bly
è-quĭv′ò-cāte,*v.,* mislead,
lie; **tor; tion; cal; cally;**
calness; cality
ê′rà, *n.,* period of time
è-răd′ĭ-cāte, *v.,* get rid of;
tor; tion; tive; cable
è-rāse′,*v.,* rub out; **-r; sure**
è-rĕct′, *v.,* build; *a.,* upright; **-or; -ion**
ĕr′è-mĭte, *n.,* hermit;
mitical [work
êrg, *n.,* unit of energy or
êr′mĭne, *n.,* weasel with
expensive white fur
è-rōde′,*v.,* wear away; **ro-**
sion; rosive
è-rŏt′ĭc, *a.,* arousing sexual feelings and desires;
êrr, *v.,* be wrong [-ly
ĕr′rànd, *n.,* trip for a pur-

pose
êr′rànt, *a.,* wandering; **-ly**
êr-răt′ĭc,*a.,* irregular; **-ally**
êr′sätz, *a.,* artificial
ĕr′ū-dīte, *a.,* learned; **-ly**
è-rŭpt′,*v.,* burst forth; **-ion;**
-ive; -ible
ĕs′cà-lāte,*v.,* increase, go
up [stairs
ĕs′cà-lā-tŏr, *n.,* moving
ĕs′cà-pāde, *n.,* reckless
adventure
ĕs-câr-gōt′ (gō),*n.,* edible
snail
ĕs′cà-rōle, *n.,* endive
ĕs-cheẅ′, *v.,* avoid; **-al** *n.*
ĕs′côrt, *n.,* one who goes
with another; *v.,*
(ès-côrt) accompany
ĕs′crōw, *n.,* legal agreement held until condi-
tions are met
ĕs′cū-lènt, *a.,* fit for food
è-sŏph′à-gŭs, *n.,* food
tube to stomach
ĕs′pĭ-ò-nàge,*n.,* spying
ès-pŏuse′, *v.,* marry;
pousal *n.*
ès-pȳ′,*v.,* see
ĕs-quîre′,*n.,* courtesy title
ĕs′sāy, *n.,* short written
article; *v.,* **(ès-sāy)** try
ĕs′sènce,*n.,* basic nature
ès-tăb′lĭsh, *v.,* settle, set
up, prove; **-er; -ment**
ès-tāte′, *n.,* one's possessions, property
ès-tēem′, *n., v.,* regard
highly
ĕs′tĭ-màte, *n.,* approxi-
mate calculation; *v.*
(māt) judge, guess; **tor;**
tion; tive
ĕs-trānge′, *v.,* make unfriendly; **-ment**
ĕs′trò-gèn, *n.,* female sex
hormone; **-ic**
ĕs′tū-âr-ȳ, *n.,* river mouth;
arial
ĕtch,*v.,* put design on with
acid; **-er**
è-têr′nàl, *a.,* everlasting,
continual; **nity; -ly;**
-ness
è-thē′rē-àl, *a.,* heavenly;
-ity; -ness; -ly
ĕth′ĭcs, *n., pl.,* study of

E
F

conduct and moral judgment; **ical, cist**

ĕth'nĭc, *a.*, of a particular group of people, cultural; **-ity; -al; -ally; nology**

ē-tĭ-ŏl'ō-gȳ, *n.*, study of causes; **logic; logical; logically**

ĕt'ĭ-quĕtte, *n.*, manners, proper behavior

e'tüde (ā), *n.*, music for one instrument

ĕt-ȳ-mŏl'ō-gȳ, *n.*, study of word origins; **gist; logical; logically**

eū-gĕn'ĭcs, *n.*, study of improving human qualities; **ic; cist**

eū'lō-gȳ, *n.*, praise (a dead person); **gize; gizer**

eū'nŭch (nŭk), *n.*, castrated man

eū'phe-mĭsm, *n.*, nice word replacing offensive one; **mist; mize; mistic; mistically**

eū'phō-nȳ, *n.*, pleasant sound

eū-thĕn'ĭcs, *n.*, *pl.*, science of improving man through environmental changes

ė-văc'ū-āte, *v.*, remove; **tor; tion; tive; ant**

ė-vāde', *v.*, avoid, escape; **-r; vasion; vasive; vasiveness; vasively**

ė-văl'ū-āte, *v.*, find value of; **tion; tive**

ė-văn'gĕl-ĭsm, *n.*, preaching of New Testament; **gelist; gelical; gelistic; gelistically**

ē'vĕn, *v.*, equalize; *a.*, level, uniform, calm, divisible by two; *adv.*, exactly, while

ė-vĕnt', *n.*, happening, contest

ĕv'êr-grēen, *n.*, *a.*, (plant that) having green leaves all year [**-ly**

ĕv-êr-lăst'ĭng, *a.*, forever;

ē-vêrt', *v.*, turn inside out; **-or; version**

ĕv'êr-ȳ-bŏd-ȳ, *pro.*, every

person [things

ĕv'êr-ȳ-thĭng, *pro.*, all

ĕv'êr-ȳ-whĕre, *adv.*, all places

ė-vĭct', *v.*, put out; **-ion**

ĕv'ĭ-dĕnt, *a.*, easy to see, clear; **-ly**

ė-vĭnce', *v.*, show plainly; **vincible**

ė-vĭs'cė-rāte, *v.*, remove, insides, deprive; **tion**

ė-vōke', *v.*, call forth; **ocator; ocation; vocative**

ĕv-ō-lū'tion, *n.*, gradual development, process; **-al; -ally; -ary**

ewe, *n.*, female sheep

ew'êr, *n.*, water pitcher

ė-xăct', *v.*, demand; **-er; -ion; -able**

ėx-ăct', *a.*, correct, perfect; **-ness; -ly; -itude** *n.*

ėx-ăg'gė-rāte, *v.*, overstate; **tor; tion; tive**

ėx-ălt', *v.*, raise, praise, fill with joy; **-er; -ation**

ėx-ăm'ĭne, *v.*, look at or into, investigate; **-r; nation; nable**

ėx-ăm'ple, *n.*, sample, typical instance, model

ėx-ăs'pêr-āte, *v.*, anger, irritate; **tion**

ėx'că-vāte, *v.*, dig out, unearth; **tor; tion**

ėx-cĕl', *v.*, do greater than, surpass; **-lence; -lent; -lently**

ėx'cĕl-lĕn-cȳ, *n.*, title of honor [shavings

ėx-cĕl'sĭ-ōr, *n.*, wood

ėx-cĕpt', *v.*, leave out; *prep.*, *conj.*, other than, but

ėx-cĕss', *n.*, lack of moderation; *a.*, (**ĕx'cĕss**) extra; **-ive; -iveness; -ively**

ėx-chānge', *n.*, *v.*, trade; **-r; -able; -ability**

ėx-cīte', *v.*, stir up, provoke; **-r; -ment; citable; -d**

ėx-clāim', *v.*, suddenly cry out; **-er; clamation; clamatory**

ėx-clūde', *v.*, keep or shut

out; **-r; -able; clusion; clusionary**

ĕx-cŏm-mū′nĭ-cāte, *v.,* exclude from church; **tor; tion; tive; tory**

ĕx-crēte′, *v.,* eliminate from body; **tion; tory**

ĕx-cru′cĭ-āt-ĭng, *a.,* very painful; **-ly**

ĕx′cŭl-pāte, *v.,* prove guiltless; **tion; tory; pable**

ĕx-cûr′sion, *n.,* short trip

ĕx-cūse′, *n.,* explanation; *v.,* (c'uz) apologize, forgive, let leave; **cusable; cusatory**

ĕx′ē-crāte, *v.,* hate, curse; **tor; tive; tory; crable; crably**

ĕx′ē-cūte, *v.,* carry out, do, kill legally; **tion**

ĕx-ĕc′ū-tĭve, *n.,* administrator; **tory**

ĕx-ĕc′ū-tŏr, *n.,* one who carries out a will

ĕx-ē-gē′sĭs, *n.,* biblical interpretation; **getic; getics; getical; getically**

ĕx-ĕm′plâr, *n.,* model, sample; **-y** *a.,* **-iness; -ily**

ĕx-ĕmpt′, *v.,* free from, excuse; **-ion; -ible**

ĕx′ēr-cīse, *n.,* active use, bodily exertion, (pl.) formal program; *v.,* use, drill; **-r**

ĕx-êrt′, *v.,* use actively; **-ion; -ive**

ĕx-hāle′, *v.,* breathe out; **lation** [fumes

ĕx-häust′, *n.,* engine

ĕx-häust′, *v.,* use up, tire; **-ion; -ive; -ible; -ibility; -less**

ĕx-hĭb′ĭt, *n., v.,* show; **-or; -ion; -ive; -ory**

ĕx-hĭl′à-rāte, *v.,* make lively; **tion; tive**

ĕx-hôrt′, *v.,* urge; **-ation; -atory; -ative**

ĕx-hūme′, *v.,* remove from ground; **mation**

ĕx′ĭ-gĕn-cȳ, *n.,* emergency, need; **gent; gently**

ĕx′īle, *n.,* one forced to leave country; *v.,* banish

ĕx′ŏ-dŭs, *n.,* departure

ĕx-ŏn′ē-rāte, *v.,* free from blame; **tor; tion; tive**

ĕx-ôr′bĭ-tànt, *a.,* extreme; **tance; tancy; -ly**

ĕx′ôr-cise, *v.,* drive out evil spirit; **cism; cist**

ĕx-pănd′, *v.,* spread out, enlarge; **pansion; pansive; -able**

ĕx-pā′trĭ-āte, *v.,* exile; **tion**

ĕx-pĕc′tŏ-rāte, *v.,* spit; **tion**

ĕx-pē′dĭ-ėnt, *a.,* useful, convenient; **ency; ence; -ly**

ĕx-pė-dĭ′tion, *n.,* journey for a purpose; **-ary; tious; tiously**

ĕx-pĕl′, *v.,* force out; **-ler; -lee; -lable; -lant**

ĕx-pĕnse′, *n.,* cost

ĕx-pē′rĭ-ĕnce, *n.,* anything lived through, knowledge gained; *v.,* meet with; **-d; ential; entially**

ĕx-pĕr′ĭ-mėnt, *n., v.,* test to prove something; **-ation; -al; -ally**

ĕx′pĭ-āte, *v.,* be sorry for; **tor; tion; able**

ĕx-pire′, *v.,* end, die, to breathe out; **ration**

ĕx′plė-tĭve, *n.,* unneeded word or phrase; **tory**

ĕx-plĭc′ĭt, *a.,* clearly stated; **-ly; -ness**

ĕx-plōde′, *v.,* burst noisily; **-r; plodable; plosion; plosive**

ĕx-plôre′, *v.,* look into, discover; **-r; ration; ploratory; plorative**

ĕx-pôrt′, *v.,* send goods to other countries; **-er; -able; -ation**

ĕx-pōse′, *v.,* show. make known; **sûre**

ĕx-pŏs′tū-lāte, *v.,* object; **tor; tion; tory**

ĕx-prĕss′, *n.,* direct method for transporting

ĕx-prĕss′, *v.,* squeeze, symbolize, say; **-ion;**

E
F

-ive
ĕx-prō′prĭ-āte, *v.*, take from; **tor; tion**
ĕx-pŭl′sion, *n.*, forcing out; **sive**
ĕx-pŭnge′, *v.*, erase
ĕx′pûr-gāte, *v.*, delete; **-ion**
ĕx′quĭ-sĭte, *a.*, delicately beautiful; **-ness; -ly**
ĕx-tĕm-pŏ-rā′nē-oŭs, *a.*, unplanned; **-ly**
ĕx-tĕnd′, *v.*, expand, offer; **-er; -ible; tension; ten-sive; tensible**
ĕx-tĕn′ū-āte, *v.*, give excuse; **tor; ting**
ĕx-tē′rĭ-ör, *n.*, outside; **-ity**
ĕx-têr′mĭ-nāte, *v.*, kill, destroy; **tor; tion; tory**
ĕx-têr′nȧl, *a.*, outer; **-ity; -ize; -ization; -ly**
ĕx-tĭn′guĭsh, *v.*, put out; **-ment; -able**
ĕx′tĭr-pāte, *v.*, root out, destroy; **tor; tion; tive**
ĕx-tōl′, *v.*, praise; **-ler; -ment**
ĕx-tôrt′, *v.*, get money by threats; **-er; -ion; -ive**
ex-tract, *v.*, pull out, select; **-or; -ion; -able**
ĕx′trȧ-dĭte, *v.*, turn over prisoner to another state; **tion**
ĕx-trā′nē-oŭs, *a.*, not belonging; **-ness; -ly**
ĕx-trăv′ȧ-gȧnt, *a.*, excessive, wasteful; **gance; gancy; -ly**
ĕx′trĭ-cāte, *v.*, release; **tion; cable; cability**
ĕx-trĭn′sĭc, *a.*, unessential; **-ally**
ĕx-trūde′, *v.*, push out, **-r; trusion; trusive**
ĕx-ū′bêr-ȧnt, *a.*, healthy, high spirited; **ance; ancy; -ly**
ĕx-ūde′, *v.*, ooze in drops
ĕx-ŭlt′, *v.*, rejoice; **-ation; -ancy; -ant; -antly**
eye′sôre, *n.*, thing unpleasant to look at
eye′tōoth, *n.*, pointed upper tooth
eye-wĭt′nĕss, *n.*, person who saw the incident

F

fā′ble, *n.*, story teaching a moral lesson
făb′rĭc, *n.*, cloth, material
făb′rĭ-cāte, *v.*, make, lie; **tor; tion** [-ly
făb′ū-loŭs, *a.*, imaginary, hard to believe; **-ness;**
fȧ-cäde′, *n.*, building front, appearance
fāce, *n.*, front of head, surface; *v.*, meet; **facial**
făc′ĕt, *n.*, surface of cut gem; aspect
fȧ-cē′tioŭs, *a.*, witty; **-ness; -ly** [cility
făc′īle, *a.*, easy; **-ness; -ly;**
făc-sĭm′ĭ-lē, *n.*, copy
făct, *n.*, truth, real happening; **-ual; -ually**
făc′tion, *n.*, group with similar beliefs; **-al; -ally; tious; tiousness; tiously**
făc-tĭ′tioŭs, *a.*, not natural; **-ness; -ly**
făc′tör, *n.*, agent, causal element, multiplier; **-ial**
făc′ŭl-tў, *n.*, ability to do, talent, teaching staff
făd, *n.*, passing fashion; **-dish; -dishly; -dish-ness; -dism**
fāde, *v.*, lose color, die out
făg, *n.*, become tired
făg′ŏt, *n.*, bundle of sticks
fāil, *v.*, fall short, unable to do, neglect; **-ūre; -ing** *n.*
fāint, *v.*, loose consiousness; *a.*, weak; **-ness; -ly**
fāir, *n.*, carnival, exhibition; *a.*, blond, just, average, clear and sunny
fāir′lў, *adv.*, justly, moderately, clearly
fāith, *n.*, unquestioning belief; **-ful; -fully; -less**
fāke, *n., a.*, (anything) not genuine, false; *v.*, deceive; **-r; -ry**
făl′cȯn, *n.*, hunting hawk
făl′dȧ-räl, *n.*, nonsense
fäll, *n.*, descending, capture; *v.*, come down, lower, lose power; **-en** *a.*

făl′là-c̆y, *n.*, misleading idea; **cious; ciousness; ciously**

făl′lĭ-ble, *a.*, liable to error; **-ness; bly; bility**

fäll′out, *n.*, radioactive particles after nuclear explosion [active

făl′lōw, *a.*, unplanted, in-

fälse, *a.*, not true, dishonest; **-ness; -ly; -hood**

fäl′tĕr, *v.*, stumble, hesitate [utation; **-d**

fāme, *n.*, well-known rep-

făm′ĭ-lў, *n.*, parents and children, relatives; **milial** [shortage

făm′ĭne, *n.*, acute food

făm′ĭsh, *v.*, be hungry; **-ment**

făn, *n.*, device to circulate air, supporter

făn′c̆y, *n.*, imagination, notion; *v.*, imagine, like; *a.*, elaborate, decorated; **ciness; cily; ciless; ciful**

făn′fāre, *n.*, trumpet blast, showy display

făng, *n.*, long pointed tooth

făn′tà-sў, *n.* illusion, dream; **size**

fârce, *n.*, exaggerated comedy; **cical, cicality, cically**

fāre, *n.*, fee to travel, food; *v.*, go

fāre′wĕll, *n.*, going away, *int.*, goodbye [ated

fâr′fĕtched, *a.*, exagger-

fà-rĭ′nà, *n.*, cooked cereal

fârm, *n.*, land for raising crops or animals; *v.*, raise crops, rent out; **-er**

fâr-rēach′ĭng, *a.*, wide effort

fâr′thĕr, *a.*, *adv.*, more distant than [distant

fâr′thĕst, *a.*, *adv.*, most

făs′cĭ-nāte, *v.*, attract, charm; **tor; tion; nating**

făs′cĭsm, *n.*, government by dictatorship; **cist**

făsh′iòn, *n.*, current style, manner; *v.*, form; **-able; -ably** [ing

făst, *v.*, abstain from eat-

făst, *a.*, quick, firm, loyal; *adv.*, firmly, quickly; **-ness**

făs′tĕn, *v.*, connect, fix in place, tie; **-er; -ing** *n.*

făs-tĭd′ĭ-oŭs, *a.*, very particular; **-ness; -ly**

făt, *n.*, *a.*, (animal tissue that is) oily and greasy; *a.*, plump, fleshy; **-ness; -ten; -ty** *a.*

fāte, *n.*, one's lot, destiny; **-ful; -d**

făth′ŏm, *n.*, six feet deep; *v.*, understand; **-able**

fà-tīgues′, *n.*, *pl.*, military work clothes

făt′ū-oŭs, *a.*, silly; **tuity; -ness; -ly**

fäu′cĕt, *n.*, device to adjust water flow

fäult, *n.*, defect, error, blame; **-less; -y** *a.*

fäu′nà, *n.*, animals of an area; **-l**

fā′vör, *n.*, kind act, small gift; *v.*, like, resemble; **-able; -ably; -ed**

fā′vör-ĭte, *n.*, *a.*, (one) highly preferred; **itism**

fäwn, *n.*, young deer; *v.*, show friendliness

fāze, *v.*, bother

fēar, *n.*, feeling of danger; *v.*, be afraid of; **-ful; -fulness; -fully; -less**

fēa′sĭ-ble, *a.*, possible; **bility; bly; -ness**

fēast, *n.*, rich elaborate meal, celebration

fēat, *n.*, remarkable deed

fēath′êr, *n.*, outgrowth of a bird's body; **-y** *a.*

fēath′êr-weight (wāt), *n.*, boxing weight less than 126 pounds

fēa′tûre, *n.*, facial part, special item; *v.*, give prominence

fē′brĭle, *a.*, feverish

fē′cēs, *n.*, *pl.*, excrement; **-cal** [-ness; -ly

fĕck′lĕss, *a.*, careless;

fē′cŭnd, *a.*, productive; **-ity; -ate**

fĕd′êr-àl, *a.*, of central government; **-ly; -ism;**

-ist
fĕ-dô'rà, *n.,* felt hat
fĕe, *n.,* charge for service, payment [bly
fĕe'ble, *a.,* weak; **-ness;**
fĕed, *v.,* give food to, supply; **-er**
fĕel, *n.,* instinctive ability; *v.,* touch, be aware of, believe; **-er; -ing** *n.*
feign (fān), *v.,* pretend
feint (fānt), *n.,* false attempt [relsome
feist'ў, *a.,* excited, quar-
fĕ-lĭc'ĭ-toŭs, *a.,* fitting; -ly
fĕ-lĭc'ĭ-tў, *n.,* happiness; **cĭfic** [cat family
fĕ'līne, *n., a.,* (any cat) of
fĕll, *v.,* cut down
fĕl'lōw, *n.,* a male, companion; **-ship**
fĕl'òn, *n.,* criminal; **-y**
fĕ'māle, *n., a.,* (one) of sex that bears children
fĕm'ĭ-nĭsm, *n.,* belief that women need equal rights; **nist**
fĕnce, *n.,* barrier, enclosure, one who deals in stolen goods; *v.,* fight with swords
fĕnc'ing, *n.,* art of sword fighting
fĕnd, *v.,* resist; **-er**
fêr-mĕnt', *v.,* change chemically, excite; **-ation; -ative; -able**
fêrn, *n.,* nonflowering plant
fĕ-rō'cioŭs, *a.,* wild; **city; -ly; -ness**
fĕr'rĕt, *v.,* search
fĕr'rĭc, *a.,* of iron; **rous**
fĕr'rў, *n., v.,* (boat to) cross a river
fêr'tĭle, *a.,* productive, able to produce young; **-ly; -ness; tility; lize**
fêr'vòr, *n.,* intensely warm feeling, zeal; **vent; vency; vid** *a.*
fĕs'cūe, *n.,* type of grass
fĕs'têr, *v.,* become infected
fĕs'tĭ-vàl, *n.,* celebration
fĕt'à, *n.,* soft white cheese
fĕtch, *v.,* get, bring
fete (fāt), *n.,* celebration

fĕt'ĭd, *a.,* bad smelling; **-ness; -ly**
fĕt'ĭsh, *n.,* symbol of magical power
fĕt'têr, *n.,* angle chain; *v.,* restrain, hamper
fĕt'tle, *n.,* condition
fē'tŭs, *n.,* unborn young; **tal**
feŭd, *n.,* bitter argument; *v.,* quarrel; **-al; -ality**
fē'vêr, *n.,* high body temperature; **-ish**
fĭ-àn-ce' (cā), *n.,* engaged man [gaged woman
fĭ-àn-cee' (cā), *n.,* en-
fĭ-às'cō, *n.,* failure
fĭ'àt, *n.,* decree
fĭ'bêr, *n.,* fabric thread, muscle tissue, quality; **brous**
fĭck'le, *a.,* changeable
fĭc'tion, *n.,* imaginary happening, story; **-al; -ally; titious, titiously**
fĭ-dĕl'ĭ-tў, *n.,* faithfulness
fĭdg'ĕt, *v.,* more about restlessly; **-y** *a.*
fiĕf, *n.,* lord's land under feudalism
fiĕld, *n.,* piece of land, area of knowledge
fiĕnd, *n.,* cruel person, addict; **-ish** [-ly; -ness
fiêrce, *a.,* violent, intense;
fĭ-ĕs'tà, *n.,* holiday
fife, *n.,* flutelike instrument
fĭg, *n.,* fruit [-er
fĭght, *n., v.,* battle, conflict;
fĭg'mĕnt, *n.,* thing imagined [-ly
fĭg'ūr-à-tĭve, *a.,* not exact;
fĭg'ūre, *n.,* form, person drawing, design, number: *v.,* consider, form, compute
fĭg-ū-rĭne', *n.,* small statue
fĭl'bêrt, *n.,* nut of hazel tree
file, *n.,* line of people, container, tool for smoothing and grinding; *v.,* arrange in order, register
fĭl'ĭ-bŭs-têr, *n.,* excessive talk to delay legislation
fĭl'ĭ-grēe, *n.,* ornamental lace work in metal
fĭl'let (lā), *n.,* boneless

piece of meat, fish, etc.

fil'ly, *n.,* young female horse

film, *n.,* thin coating; **-y** *a.*

film, *n.,* plasticlike material used in photography; *v.,* make a motion picture; **-ic**

fil'ter, *n., v.,* (device to) strain or purify; **-able**

filth, *n.,* dirt, garbage; **-y** *a.* [**-ization; -ly**

fi'nal, *a.,* last; **-ity; -ize;**

fi-nance', *n.,* study of money management; *v.,* supply money; **cial; cially; cier**

finch, *n.,* small songbird

find, *v.,* come upon, discover, learn, locate; **-er; -ing** *n.*

fine, *n.,* money paid as penalty; *a.,* excellent, delicate, sharp

fi-nesse', *n.,* subtle skill

fin'ger-print, *n.,* impression skin markings on finger tip

fin'ick-y, *a.,* too particular; fussy; **ical; icality; ically**

fi'nite, *a.,* limited; **tude** *n.*

fir, *n.,* evergreen tree

fire'arm, *n.,* gun, rifle

fire'bird, *n.,* brightly colored bird

fire'fly, *n.,* winged beetle with glowing abdomen

fire'trap, *n.,* unsafe building in case of fire

fire'works, *n., pl.,* explosive devices that display light

firm, *n.,* business; *a.,* hard, stable, steady; **-ness; -ly**

fir'ma-ment, *n.,* sky

first-aid, *a.,* of temporary medical care

first-class', *a.,* of best kind

fis'cal, *a.,* financial; **-ly**

fish'mon-ger, *n.,* one who sells fish

fis'sion, *n.,* division into parts; **-able**

fis'sure, *n.,* crack, cleft

fist, *n.,* clenched hand

fit, *n.,* sudden outburst, convulsion; *v.,* suit, be or make to right size, equip [**-ly**

fit'ful, *a.,* restless; **-ness;**

fix, *n.,* (coll.) predicament

fix, *v.,* set firmly, repair, cook; **-er**

fix-a'tion, *n.,* obsession

fix'ture, *n.,* thing firmly in place ex. furniture

fizz, *v.,* hiss and bubble; **-y** *a.*

flab, *n.,* (coll.) sagging flesh; **-by** *a.;* **-biness**

flab'ber-gast, *v.,* surprise

flac'cid, *a.,* soft and limp

flag, *n.,* cloth symbol, banner

flag'el-late, *v.,* beat, whip; **tor; tion; tory**

fla-gi'tious, *a.,* shamefully wicked; **-ness; -ly**

flag'on, *n.,* kind of pitcher

fla'grant, *a.,* evil, notorious; **grancy; -ly**

flag'stone, *n.,* paving stone

flail, *n.,* tool to thresh grain, *v.,* use a flail, beat

flair, *n.,* natural talent

flake, *n.,* thin slice; **flaky** *a.*

flam, *n.,* trick, lie

flam-boy'ant (boi), *a.,* showy; **ance; ancy; -ly**

flame, *n.,* light of fire, blaze; **flaming**

flam'ma-ble, *a.,* easily set on fire; **bility**

flank, *n.,* side; *v.,* be at or put to side

flan'nel, *n.,* soft wool cloth

flap, *n.,* flat loose piece; *v.,* wave up and down; **-py** *a.*

flare, *n.,* sudden burst of fire, signal light; *v.,* blaze

flare'-up, *n.,* outburst

flash, *n.,* sudden light, moment, sudden news report; *v.,* sparkle, move quickly [**isode**

flash'back, *n.,* earlier episode

flash'light, *n.,* battery powered hand lantern

flask, *n.,* small bottle**

flăt, *a.,* level, spread out smoothly, broad and thin, dull; **-ten; -ly; -ness**

flăt'tĕr, *v.,* praise too much; please; **-er; -y**

flăt'ŭ-lĕnt, *a.,* having stomach gas, boastful; **ence; ency; -ly**

flăunt, *v.,* show off

flā'vŏr, *n.,* taste; *v.,* add seasoning; **-ing** *n.;* **-ful**

flăx, *n.,* linen plant and its fiber [sect

flēa, *n.,* small wingless in-

flĕck, *n.,* spot, particle

flĕdg'lĭng, *n.,* young bird

flēe, *v.,* run away, escape

flēece, *n.,* sheep's wool; **-y** *a.*

flēece, *v.,* swindle; **-r**

flēet, *n.,* group of ships

flēet, *v.,* move quickly; *a.,* swift; **-ing; -ness; -ly**

flĕsh, *n.,* body tissue, meat, fruit or vegetable pulp; **-y** *a.*

flĕx, *v.,* bend, contract muscle; **-ûre; -ible; -ibil-ity; -ibly**

flĭck'ĕr, *v.,* flutter, burn unsteadily [of stairs

flĭght, *n.,* flying, fleeing, set

flĭm'sў, *a.,* weak, made poorly; **sily; siness**

flĭnch, *v.,* draw back from

flĭp, *n.,* somersault; *v.,* move or turn with a jerk

flĭp, *a.,* disrespectful; **-pant; -pantly; -pancy**

flĭp'pêr, *n.,* broad flat limp of seal, whale, etc. for swimming

flĭt, *v.,* flutter, dart

flōat, *n.,* decorated vehicle for parade; *v.,* stay on top of liquid

flŏck, *n.,* group; *v.,* gather together

flŏg, *v.,* beat with whip

flŏod, *n.,* overflowing of water; *v.,* overflow, fill

flŏod'lĭght, *n.,* very bright light

flŏor, *n.,* bottom surface of room, ocean, etc., build-ing level, (coll.) surprise

flŏp, *n.,* (coll.) failure; *v.,* drop noisily

flŏr'ȧl, *a.,* of flowers, **-ly; -lst; -istic**

flŏr'ĭd, *a.,* rosy, showy; **-ity; -ness; -ly** [-y *a.*

flŏss, *n.,* soft silky fibers;

flō-tā'tion, *n.,* floating

flŏunce, *n.,* ruffle; *v.,* jerk

flŏun'dĕr, *n.,* flatfish; *v.,* struggle awkwardly

flŏur, *n.,* fine powdery sub-stance ground from grain; **-y** *a.*

flŏur'ĭsh, *v.,* succeed, thrive; **-er; -ing**

flōw, *v.,* move smoothly, as water; **-age; -ingly**

flōw'êr, *n.,* plant's repro-ductive organ, blossom; *v.,* bloom; **-y** *a.;* **-ing**

flŭc'tū-āte, *v.,* change ir-regularly; **ant; tion**

flŭe, *n.,* chimney shaft

flū'ĭd, *n.,* liquid; *a.,* able to flow; **-ity; -ness; -ly**

flūke, *n.,* stroke of luck; **-y** *a.* [school

flŭnk, *v.,* (coll.) fail in

flū-ŏ-rĕs'cĕnce, *n.,* emis-sion of reflected light when exposed to radia-tion; **cent**

flū'ŏrīne, *n.,* gaseous chemical element

flûr'rў, *n.,* gust, sudden confusion; *v.,* confuse

flŭsh, *n.,* sudden feeling of heat; *v.,* blush, wash out with water; *a.,* wealthy

flŭs'têr, *v.,* confuse

flūte, *n.,* woodwind instru-ment

flŭt'têr, *v.,* flap or vibrate rapidly, tremble; **-er; -y** *a.*

flŭx, *n.,* constant change

flȳ, *n.,* insect, opening of pants

flȳ, *v.,* move through air, move swiftly, flee; **flier; -able**

flȳ'whēel, *n.,* wheel regu-lating machine's speed

fōal, *n.,* very young horse

fōam, *n.,* white bubbly mass; **-y** *a.;* **-less**

fŏb, *n.*, pocket watch chain

fō′cŭs, *n.*, point where light rays meet, adjustment for clear image, central point; **cal; cally; calize**

fŏd′dêr, *n.*, food for horses, cattle, etc.

fŏg, *n.*, thick mist, confusion; **-gy** *a.*; **-giness**

fŏi′ble, *n.*, small weakness

fŏil, *n.*, thin metal sheet, fencing sword; *v.*, frustrate

fŏist, *v.*, deceive by fraud

fōld, *n.*, sheep pen, group; *v.*, bend over itself

fō′lĭ-āge, *n.*, mass of leaves; **aceous**

fō′lĭ-ō, *n.*, large book

fōlk (fōk), *n.*, ethnic group; (*pl.*), family; *a.*, of the common people

fŏl′lĭ-cle, *n.*, small body sac, cavity or gland

fŏl′lōw, *v.*, come or go after, happen, support; **-er**

fŏl′lў, *n.*, foolishness

fō′mĕnt, *v.*, incite; **-ation**

fŏn′dle, *v.*, caress; **-r**

fŏn-tà-nĕl′, *n.*, soft boneless area of baby's skull

fōod, *n.*, substance eaten, nourishment

fōol, *n.*, silly person; *v.*, joke, trick; **-ery**

fōot′hōld, *n.*, secure place for foot when climbing

fōot′lights, *n.*, *pl.*, lights on floor of stage front

fōot′nōte, *n.*, extra comment at bottom of page

fŏp, *n.*, vain man, dandy; **-pish; -pishness; -pishly**

fôr′àge, *n.*, fodder; *v.*, search for food; **-r**

fôr′āy, *n.*, *v.*, raid, attack

fôr′beăr, *v.*, restrain; **-er; -ance; -ingly**

fôr′bĭd, *v.*, not permit; **-dance; -den** *a.*; **-ding**

fôrce, *n.*, power, violence, united group; *v.*, use power, compel; **-d; -ful; -fully; -fulness; cible; cibly** [pinchers

fôr′cĕps, *n.*, surgical

fôrd, *n.*, shallow place in river; *v.*, cross water; **-able**

fôre-bōde′, *v.*, predict something bad; **boding; bodingly**

fōre′căst, *v.*, estimate in advance, ex. weather; **-er**

fôre-clōse′, *v.*, deny the right to redeem mortgage; **sure; closable**

fôre′hĕad, *n.*, part of face above eyebrows

fŏr′eĭgn, *a.*, of or from another country, strange; **-ness; -er**

fôre′màn, *n.*, man in charge of workers, jury chairman; **-ship**

fŏ-rĕn′sĭc, *a.*, of law courts or debate; **-ally**

fôre′rŭn-nêr, *n.*, person or thing foretelling another

fôre-sēe′, *v.*, know in advance; **-r; -able**

fôre′skĭn, *n.*, skin over end of penis

fŏr′ĕst, *n.*, land with thick growth of trees; **-er; -ry**

fôre-stăll′, *v.*, anticipate; **-er; -ment**

fôre′thought, *n.*, previous consideration; **-ful; -fully** [always

fôr-ĕv′êr, *adv.*, for all time,

fôre′wörd, *n.*, introduction

fôr′feĭt, *n.*, penalty; *v.*, give up; **-er; -ûre; -able**

fôrge, *n.*, furnace to heat metal; *v.*, counterfeit, move ahead slowly; **-r**

fôr-gĕt′, *v.*, be unable to remember, neglect, overlook; **-ful; -fulness; -fully**

fôr-gĭve′, *v.*, stop being angry with, pardon; **-er; -ness; givable; giving**

fôrk, *n.*, pronged eating utensil; place of branching; **-ed** [sad

fôr-lŏrn′, *a.*, miserable,

fôrm, *n.*, shape, outline, style, type; *v.*, make, develop; **-ation; -ative**

fôr′màl, *a.*, according to

custom, elaborate; **-ity; -ize; -ly**

fôr'mĭ-dà-ble, a., causing fear, powerful; **bility; -ness; bly**

fôr'mŭ-là, n., fixed rule, prescription; **-te; -tor; -tion**

fôr'nĭ-cāte, v., commit illicite sexual intercourse; **tion**

fôrt, n., military place of defense; **-ress**

fôrth, adv., onward

fôr'tĭ-fȳ, v., strengthen; **fier; fication; fiable**

fôr'tĭ-tūde, n., courage; **tudinous** [-ly

fôrt'nīght, n., two weeks;

fôr'tūne (chun), n., luck, chance; **-less; nàte** a.; **nately**

fô'rŭm, n., place for public discussion

fŏs'sĭl, n., rocklike remains of previous animal and plant life; **-ize; -ization**

fôs'tēr, v., help, cherish, rear; a., sharing in the care

fŏŭl, v., dishonor; break game rules; a., disgusting, filthy, unfair, stormy, obscene; **-ness**

fŏŭnd, v., base, establish; **-er; -ation; -ational**

fŏŭnd'êr, v., stumble, fall, sink [metal

fŏŭnd'rȳ, n., place to cast

fŏŭn'taĭn, n., spring or jet of water

fŏwl, n., bird, domestic bird

fŏx, n., wild doglike animal; v., trick craftily

frà'càs, n., brawl

frăc'tion, n., part of a whole; small portion; **-al; -ally**

frăc'tūre, n., break in a bone; v., break; **tural**

frăg'ĭle, a., easily broken, delicate; **gility**

frăg'mênt, n., broken part; **-ary; -ate; -ation**

frāil, a., weak; **-ly; -ness; -ty** n.

frāme, n., basic structure border; v., make, build, enclose in border, falsify; **-r**

frăn'chĭse, n., right to vote or operate

frănk, a., honest and open; **-ness; -ly**

frăn'tĭc, a., wild with worry; **-ally**

frà-têr'nàl, a., brotherly; **-ism; -ly; nity; nize; nization**

frăught, a., filled

frāy, n., battle; v., become ragged

frăz'zle, v., become tired

frēak, a., abnormal, odd; **-y** a.; **-ish; -ishly; -ishness**

frĕck'le, n., small brown spot on skin; **ly**

frēe, v., release; a., not restricted, open, no cost; **-ly; -dom**

frēe-thĭnk'êr, n., one with unorthodox views

frēeze, v., form into ice, harden; **-r; freezable**

freight (frāt), n., good transported; **-er; -age**

frĕn'zȳ, n., wild excitement

frĕs'cō, n., painting on wet plaster

frĕsh, a., new, clean; **-ness; -ly; -en**

frĕt, n., v., worry; **-ful; -fully; -fulness**

frĭc'tion, n., a rubbing together, conflict; **-less; -al**

friĕnd, n., person one knows and likes; **-ship; -ly; -liness**

frīght, n., sudden fear; **-en; -eningly; -ful; -fully**

frĭg'ĭd, a., very cold, stiff; **-ness; -ly**

frĭll, n., ruffle, unnecessary ornament; **-y** a.

frĭnge, n., decorative edge, border; **-y** a.

frĭsk, v., search quickly

frĭt'têr, n., small cake of fried batter; v., waste

frĭv'ò-loŭs, a., trivial, silly; **-ness; -ly; volity**

frŏck, n., monk's robe, garment

frŏnd, n., fern or palm leaf

frŏnt, n., forward or first part; v., face; **-al**

frŏn'tiēr, n., nation's border, undeveloped region; **-sman** n.

frŏst, n., frozen dew; **-y** a.

frŏst'ĭng, n., sugar mixture for covering cake

frōwn, v., wrinkle eye brows, look with disapproval

frō'zėn, a., turned into ice

frū'găl, a., thrifty; **-ity; -ly**

frūit, n., edible plant product, result; **-ful; -fully; -fulness; -less; -y** a.

frū-i'tion, n., fulfillment

frŭs'trāte, v., block, disappoint; **tration**

frȳ, n., child; v., cook in hot fat or oil; **-er**

fūch'siȧ, n., flowering plant

fŭdge, n., soft chocolate candy; v., cheat

fū'ėl, n., material burned for heat or power

fūgue, n., musical form

fŭll, a., all that can be held, ample, complete; **-ness; -y** adv.

fŭl'mĭ-nāte, v., explode with violence; **tor, tion; tory**

fŭm'ble, v., handle clumsily; **-r; blingly**

fūme, n., offensive smoke or vapor; v., give off fumes, show anger

fūm'ĭ-gāte, v., disinfect; **tor; tion**

fŭnc'tion, n., purpose, duty; **-al**

fŭnd, n., pool of money; v., give money to [**-ly**

fŭn-dȧ-měn'tȧl, a., basic;

fū'nêr-ȧl, n., burial rites

fŭn'gŭs, n., a parasitic plant, ex. mold, mushroom

fŭn'nėl, n., inverted hollow cone with hole at neck

fûr, n., animal's soft thick hair; **-ry** a.; **-riness**

fûr'lōugh, n., military vacation [ing chamber

fûr'nȧce, n., heat produc-

fûr'nĭ-tûre, n., tables, chairs, beds etc. in room

fū'rôr, n., rage

fûr'rōw, n., groove made by plow

fûr'thêr, v., promote; a., additional; adv., moreover [**-ness**

fûr'tĭve, a., secretive; **-ly;**

fū'rÿ, n., violent anger

fūse, n., wick of an explosive; safety device in an electrical circuit

fūse, v., melt together; **fusion; fusible; fusibility**

fū'sė-lȧge, n., body of airplane [**-y** a.

fŭss, n., v., bother, worry;

fū'tĭle, a., hopeless; **-ly; -ness; tility**

fū'tûre, n., time to come

G

găb, n., v., chatter; **-ber; -by** a.

gā-ble, n., triangular wall under roof's edge

găd, v., wander; **-der**

gădg'ét, n., small device

găff, n., large hook

gāi'ė-tÿ, n., cheerfulness

gāin, n., increase; v., get, earn, reach; **-er; -ful; -less**

gāit, n., way of walking

gā'lȧ, n., festive occasion

găl'ăx-ÿ, n., huge group of stars

gāle, n., strong wind

găll, n. bile, boldness; v., annoy

găl'lȧnt, a., brave and noble, polite; **-ly; -ry**

găl'lėr-ÿ, n., balcony, place for art exhibits

găl'lĭ-vănt, v., search for amusement

găl'lòn, n., liquid measure, four quarts

găl'lòp, n., horse's fast gait; v., hurry; **-er**

găl'lōws, n., structure for hanging people

gà-lŏsh′, *n.,* overshoe

găl′và-nīze, *v.,* shock electrically, coat metal with zinc; **zation; nism; ic; ical; ically**

găm′bĭt, *n.,* chess move

găm′ble, *n., v.,* risk, bet; **-r**

găme, *n.,* competitive sport, amusement, hunted animals; *a.,* ready, courageous

găm′ŭt, *n.,* whole range

găn′dêr, *n.,* male goose

găn′glĭng, *a.,* tall and awkward; **gly**

găn′glĭ-ŏn, *n.,* group of nerve cells

găn′grēne, *n.,* decay of body tissue

găng′stêr, *n.,* member of a criminal gang; **-ism**

găp, *n.,* opening, separation

gāpe, *v.,* look, stare

gà′râge, *n.,* automobile shelter or repair shop

gârb, *n.,* style of dress

gâr′ble, *v.,* confuse

gâr′dén, *n.,* ground for growing plants; **-er**

gâr′gle, *v.,* rinse the throat with liquid

gâr′goyle (gŏĭl),*n.,* carved creature projecting from gutter of building

gâr′ĭsh, *a.,* gaudy; **-ness; -ly** [flowers

gâr′lånd, *n.,* wreath of

gâr′lĭc, *n.,* plant bulb used as strong seasoning; **-ky** *a.*

gâr′nĭsh, *v.,* decorate. trim; **-er; -ment**

gâr′rét, *n.,* attic

gâr′rŭ-loŭs, *a.,* talking much; **lity; -ness; -ly**

gâr′têr, *n.,* stocking supporter

găs, *n.,* vapor, substance like air; **-eous**

găsh, *n.,* long deep cut

găs-ȯ-līne′, *n.,* liquid fuel for engines

găsp, *v.,* catch one's breath [stomach

găs′trĭc, *a.,* relating to

găs-trŏn′ȯ-mÿ, *n.,* art of eating; **mist; mer; nomic; nomical; nomically**

găth′ér, *v.,* bring together, collect, meet; **-er; -ing** *n.*

gauche (gōsh),*a.,* lacking social grace; **-ness; -ly**

gäud′y, *a.,* showy in bad taste, flashy

gäuge, *n.,* measurement

gäunt, *a.,* very thin; **-ness; -ly**

gäuze, *n.,* loosely woven fabric; **gauzy** *a.*

găv′él, *n.,* mallet for presiding officer

gäwk, *v.,* stare stupidly

gāy, *a.,* happy, lively, bright; **-ness**

gà-zē′bō,*n.,* free-standing covered porch

gà-zĕlle′, *n.,* small antelope

gà-zĕtte′,*n.,* newspaper

găz-ét-tēer′,*n.,* dictionary of geographical names

gēar, *n.,* equipment, toothed wheel; *v.,* connect by gears

gĕl, *n.,* jellylike substance

gĕld′ĭng, *n.,* castrated male horse

gĕm, *n.,* precious stone

gĕn′dêr, *n.,* classification of word by sex

gēne, *n.,* unit of heredity on chromosome

gē-nē-ăl′ȯ-gÿ, *n.,* study of one's ancestry; **gist; logical; logically**

gĕn′êr-ål, *a.,* for or of all, common, usual; **-ly**

gĕn-êr-ăl′ĭ-tÿ, *n.,* vague statement; **alize; alization** [tor; tion

gĕn′êr-āte, *v.,* produce;

gĕn-êr-ā′tion, *n.,* people of same era; **tive**

gȅ-nêr′ĭc, *a.,* common; **-ally**

gĕn′êr-oŭs, *a.,* giving freely, ample; **osity; -ly**

gĕn′ė-sĭs, *n.,* origin

gē′niål, *a.,* friendly, kind; **-ity; -ly**

gĕn'ĭ-tȧl, *n.*, sex organ

gĕn'ĭŭs, *n.*, one with great mental talent

gĕn'ŏ-cīde, *n.*, killing of whole ethnic group; **dal**

gĕn-tēel', *a.*, polite, refined; **-ness; -ly**

gĕn'tĭle, *n.*, *a.*, (one) not a Jew [**-ness; tly**

gĕn'tle, *a.*, soft, kind;

gĕn'ū-īne, *a.*, real; **-ly**

gē'nŭs, *n.*, class, type

gē-ŏg'rȧ-phÿ, *n.*, science of earth's surface; **pher; graphic; graphical**

gē-ŏl'ȯ-gÿ, *n.*, study of earth structure; **gist; gize; logic; logical; logically**

gē-ŏm'ė-trÿ, *n.*, mathematics of points, lines, surfaces; **ric; rical; rically; trize**

gĕr-ĭ-ăt'rĭcs, *n.*, study of human old age; **ric**

gĕrm, *n.*, microscopic organism, seed

gĕr-māne', *n.*, related to

gĕr'mĭ-nāte, *v.*, start growing; **tion; tive**

gĕs'tāte, *v.*, carry in uterus; **tion**

gĕs'tûre, *n.*, body movement of expression; **-r; ral**

geÿ'sêr, *n.*, spouting hot spring

ghȧst'lÿ (gȧst), *a.*, horrible

ghêr'kĭn (gêr), *n.*, immature cucumber

ghĕt'tō (gĕt), *n.*, section of city restricted to a minority group; **-ize**

ghōst (gōst), *n.*, spirit; **-like** *a.*; **-ly**

gī'ȧnt, *n.*, *a.*, (one) of great size

gĭb'bȯn, *n.*, small ape

gibe, *v.*, mock, taunt

gĭb'lĕt, *n.*, fowl's edible internal part

gift, *n.*, something given

gĭft'ĕd, *a.*, talented

gĭg'gle, *v.*, laugh foolishly; **-r; gly** *a.* [**-ing** *n.*

gĭld, *v.*, coat with gold; **-er;**

gĭll, *n.*, fish's breathing organ

gĭm'mĭck, *n.*, clever gadget, trick; **-y** *a.*

gĭn, *n.*, alcoholic liquor, device to separate cotton from its seeds, card game

gĭn'gêr, *n.*, spice

gĭng'hȧm, *n.*, cotton cloth woven in checks or stripes

gîrd, *v.*, encircle, prepare

gîr'dle, *n.*, undergarment for abdominal support; *v.*, surround

gîrth, *n.*, horse's saddle band around belly; *v.* encircle

gĭst, *n.*, main point

gĭz'zȧrd, *n.*, bird's second stomach

glā'ciêr, *n.*, large mass of ice; **ciate; cial; cially**

glāde, *n.*, forest clearing

glăm'oûr, *n.*, bewitching charm; **orize; orous**

glănce, *n.*, quick look; *v.*, flash

glănd, *n.*, secreting body organ; **-ular** *a.*

glāre, *n.*, angry stare, brilliant light; *v.*, look, shine

glăss, *n.*, hard brittle transparent substance, drinking cup; **-y** *a.*

glȧu-cō'mȧ, *n.*, eye disease; **-tous**

glēam, *n.*, beam of light

glēan, *v.*, collect bit by bit as grain

glēe, *n.*, lively joy; **-ful**

glĕn, *n.*, secluded valley

glĭb, *a.*, in easy manner; **-ness; -ly**

glīde, *v.*, move smoothly

glĭm'mêr, *n.*, faint light

glĭmpse, *n.*, brief view

glĭs'tĕn, *n.*, *v.*, sparkle

glōat, *v.*, show malicious pleasure

glōbe, *n.*, round model of the world, ball; **global; globular** *a.*

glŏss, *n.*, shiny polished surface; **-y** *a.*

glŏs'sȧ-rÿ, *n.*, alphabetical list of terms

G
H

glŏve, *n.,* hand covering

glōw, *n.,* brightness; *v.,* shine warmly; **-ingly**

glow'êr, *v.,* frown; **-ingly**

glū'cōse, *n.,* type of sugar

glūe, *n.,* sticky liquid; *v.* stick or join with glue; **-y** *a.* [**-ness**

glŭm, *a.,* unhappy; **-ly;**

glŭt, *n.,* excess; *v.,* feed or supply too much

glŭt'ton, *n.,* one who does things in excess; **-ous; -y; -ously**

glyc'êr-ĭn, *n.,* colorless syrupy liquid [**-ed**

gnârl, *n.,* knot; *v.,* twist;

gnăsh, *v.,* grind the teeth

gnăt, *n.,* insect

gnōme, *n.,* dwarf

gnū, *n.,* large antelope

gōal, *n.,* end, aim, purpose

gōat'ēe, *n.,* pointed beard

gŏb'ble, *n.,* turkey sound; *v.,* eat greedily, snatch

gŏb'lĕt, *n.,* stemmed glass

gŏb'lĭn, *n.,* evil spirit

gŏd, *n.,* deity, thing or person worshipped, idol; **-hood; -like; -ly**

Gŏd, *n.,* divine being, creator of universe

gŏd'sĕnd, *n.,* something unexpected and needed

gŏg'gles, *n.,* *pl.,* large protective glasses

gōld, *n.,* yellow metal, money; *a.,* deep yellow; **-en** *a.*

gŏlf, *n.,* outdoor sport with ball and clubs

gŏn-ŏr-rhē'à, *n.,* venereal disease; **-l**

gŏŏd, *a.,* favorable, real, pleasant, able, honest, correct, considerable; **-ness**

gŏŏds, *n.,* *pl.,* merchandise, fabric

gŏŏd'y̆, *n.,* (coll.) something good to eat; *int.* Yea! [silly person

gōose, *n.,* large water bird,

gō'phêr, *n.,* burrowing rodent

gôre, *n.,* clotted blood; *v.,* pierce with horn; **gory** *a.*

gôrge, *n.,* deep narrow pass; *v.* eat greedily

gôr'geoŭs, *a.,* splendid, beautiful; **-ly; -ness**

gŏs'pĕl, *n.,* Jesus's teaching

gŏs'sà-mêr, *a.,* filmy, thin

gŏs'sĭp, *n.,* idle talk; *v.,* spread rumors; **-y** *a.*

gouge, *n.,* chisel, groove; *v.,* make grooves, cheat

gôur'met (mā), *n.,* excellent judge of food and wine

gout, *n.,* painful swelling of the joints; **-y** *a.*

gŏv'êrn, *v.,* rule, guide, regulate; **-or; -ment; -mental; -mentally; -able; -orship** [dress

gown, *n.,* woman's elegant

grāce, *n.,* beauty, favor, decency; prayer before eating; **-ful; -less**

grāde, *n.,* step, degree, slope, division in school system, test rating; *v.,* classify, rate; **-r; dation**

grā'dĭ-ĕnt, *n.,* slope

grăft, *n.,* skin or plant transplant, political dishonesty; **-er; -age**

grāin, *n.,* seed or fruit of cereal plant, particle

grăm, *n.,* unit of weight

grăm'mâr, *n.,* structure and usage of language; **matical; matically**

grănd, *a.,* splendid, great; **-ly; -ness**

grăn'dĭ-ōse, *a.,* impressive, important; **osity; -ly**

grănd'stănd, *n.,* seating structure in stadium

grăn'īte, *n.,* very hard rock

grănt, *v.,* give, bestow an honor, admit; **-er; -able**

grăn'ūle, *n.,* small grain; **late; lator; lation; lative; lar** *a.;* **larity; larly**

grăph, *n.,* drawing showing change in value; **-ic; -ics** [**-al; -ally**

grăph'ĭc, *a.,* vivid; written;

grăph'īte, *n.,* soft, black carbon for pencils

grasp, v., take hold, understand; **-er; -able**

grass, n., green lawn plant; **-y** a.; **-iness**

grate, n., framework of bars; v., grind, rub, irritate

grate'ful, a., thankful; **-ly; -ness**

gra'tis, a., adv., free

grat'i-tude, n., thankfulness

gra-tu'i-ty, n., tip, gift

grave, n., burial place

grave, a., serious; **-ness; -ly; gravity**

grav'el, n., bits of rocks

grav'i-ty, n., force causing thing toward another

gra'vy, n., meat sauce

gray, n., color of black and white mixture; a., dull, old, of gray [lightly

graze, v., eat grass, touch

grease, n., melted animal fat, oily substance; **greasy**

great, a., large, above average, wonderful; **-en; -ness; -ly**

greed, n., great desire; **-y** a., **-ily; -iness**

green, n., color of grass, yellow and blue mixture; a., of green

greet, v., welcome, meet; **-er; -ing** n.

gre-gar'i-ous, a., fond of people; **-ness; -ly**

gre-nade', n., hand bomb

grid'dle, n., flat metal pan

grid'i-ron, n., grill, football field

griev'ance, n., complaint

grieve, v., feel sad; **-r; grievously**

grill, n., framework of metal bars; v., broil on grill

grim, a., harsh, fierce; **-ly; -ness** [face

grim-ace', n., distorted

grime, n., dirt; **grimy** a.

grin, n., v., smile

grind, n., hard work; v., crush by rubbing

grip, v., hold tightly; **-per**

gris'ly, a., horrible; **liness**

gris'tle, n., meat cartilage

grit, n., sand particles, courage; v., grind teeth; **-ty** a.; **-tily; -tiness**

griz'zly, a., grayish

gro'cer, n., food dealer; **-y**

groom, n., man tending horses, bridegroom; v., make neat, train

groove, n., long narrow slit, routine [blindly

grope, v., feel, search

gross, n., total, twelve dozen; a., large, vulgar; **-ly; -ness**

grouch, n., complainer; **-y** a.; **-ily; -iness**

ground, n., land, basis

group, n., people or things together [complain

grouse, n., game bird; v.,

grove, n., group of trees

grov'el, v., crawl, beg; **-er**

grow, v., enlarge, mature, raise crops; **-er**

growl, n., rumbling throat sound

growth, n., process of growing, development

grub, n., wormlike insect larva; v., dig

grudge, n., ill will

gru'el-ing, a., exhausting

grue'some, a., horrible; **-ly; -ness** [**-ness**

gruff, a., rough, rude; **-ly;**

grum'ble, v., complain, mumble; **bler; bly**

grunt, n., deep sound from throat; **-er**

guard, n., protector; v., keep from harm, defend

gu-ber-na-to'ri-al, a., of a governor

guer-ril'la, n., irregular soldier usually undercover

guess, n., v., estimate, judge by chance

guest, n., visitor

guide, v., lead, train, direct; **guidance**

guild, n., association

guile, n., deceit; **-ful; -fully; -less; -lessness**

guilt, n., feeling of shame

G
H

or remorse; **-y** a.; **-less;**
-ily; -iness
guise, n., appearance
guĭ-târ′, n., stringed musical instrument; **-ist**
gŭlf, n., large arm of ocean,
gap ⁌
gŭl′lĕt, n., esophagus
gŭl′lĭy, n., deep ditch
gŭlp, v., swallow deeply
gŭm, n., flesh around teeth,
sticky substance; **-my** a.
gŭn, n., device for shooting, firearm; **-ner; -nery**
gûr′gle, n., bubbling
sound   [in Hinduism
gū′rū, n., spiritual advisor
gŭsh, v., pour out; **-er; -y**
a.
gŭst, n., burst of air; **-y** a.
gŭs′tō, n., taste, zest
gŭt, n., cord from intestine;
v., destroy
gŭt′têr, n., channel to run
water off roof   [throat
gŭt′tûr-ăl, a., deep in the
gŭz′zle, v., drink greedily
gўm-nā′sĭ-ŭm, n., place
for physical training and
sports
gўm-năs′tĭcs, n., exercises for body develop-
ment; **tic; tically**
gўn-ė-cŏl′ó-gў, n., medical science of women;
gist
gўp, n., v., cheat; **-ster**
gўp′sŭm, n., chalky mineral   [group
gўp′sў, n., wanderer ot a
gў′rāte, v., spin, rotate;
tor; tion; tory; ral

H

hăb′êr-dăsh-êr, n., dealer
in men's clothing; **-y**
hăb′ĭt, n., automatic practice, costume; **-ual;**
-ually
hăb′ĭ-tăt, n., one's natural
environment; **-ion**
hăck, n., cutting tool; v.,
chop, cough
hăck′nĕyed, a., trite
hăft, n., tool handle
hăg, n., ugly old woman;

-gish; -gishly
hăg′gård, a., worn out; **-ly;**
-ness   [price; **-r**
hăg′gle, v., argue over
hāil, n., frozen raindrops;
v., greet, pour down hail
hāir, n., threadlike out-
growths from skin; **-y** a.;
-less
hāir′brĕadth, n., a.,
(space that is) very nar-
row
hāir′splĭt-tĭng, a., quib-
bling   [peaceful
hăl′cў-ón, a., calm,
hāle, a., healthy; v., drag
hălf, n., a. (one) of two
equal parts
hălf-heârt′ĕd, a., with little
interest or enthusiasm
hălf′-wĭt, n., fool; **-ted**
hăll, n., large public room,
passageway
hăl-lė-lū′jáh (yá), int.,
praise the Lord!
hăll′mârk, n., mark of
genuineness   [-ed
hăl′lōw, v., honor as holy;
hál-lū′cĭ-nāte, v., imagine
unreal thing; **tion; tory**
hā′lō, n., ring of light
hălt, n., v., stop, pause
hăm, n., meat from pig's
thigh   [beef patty
hăm′bûrg-êr, n., ground
hăm′lĕt, n., small village
hăm′mêr, n., tool for
pounding
hăm′mŏck, n., swinging
canvas or rope bed
hăm′pêr, n., large covered
basket; v., hinder
hănd′băg, n., woman's
purse   [structions
hănd′bōok, n., book of in-
hănd′cŭff, n., locked
bracelet to restrain
hănd′ĭ-căp, n., difficulty,
disadvantage; **-ped**
hănd′kêr-chĭef, n., cloth
for wiping nose, etc.
hăn′dle, n., part of tool to
be held; v., touch, use,
manage; **-r**
hănd′ў, a., convenient,
clever with hands; **han-
dily; handiness**

hăng, v., suspend, let swing at one end; **-er; -ing**

hăng'ár, n., aircraft shelter

hăng'ō-vêr, n., after effects of too much liquor

hănk'êr, v., crave

hăn'sóm, n., two-wheeled covered carriage

hăp, n., luck; **-less; -lessly; -lessness**

hăp'pén, v., take place; **-ing** [**pily; piness**

hăp'py̆, a., joyous, glad;

hà-răngue', n., noisy, scolding speech; **-r**

hàr-ăss', v., constantly bother, worry; **-er; -ment**

hàr'bĭn-gêr, n., one who announces another

hård, a., solid, difficult, unfeeling; adv., with strength, fully, firmly; **-ness; -en; -ened; -ener; -ening**

hård'ly̆, adv., barely

hård'wāre, n., metal tools equipment and devices

hāre, n., rabbit

hā'rém, n., place for women in Moslem household

hârk, v., listen

hâr'lē-quĭn, n., clown

hăr'lŏt, n., prostitute

hârm, n., v., hurt, injure; **-er; -ful; -fulness; -fully; -less; -lessly; -lessness** [organ

hâr-mŏn'ĭ-cá, n., mouth

hâr'mó-ny̆, n., friendly relations, pleasing arrangement (of music); **nize; nic; nically; nious; niously**

hâr'nĕss, n., straps to hitch horse to vehicle

hârp, n., stringed musical instrument; v., persist

hâr-pōōn', n., spear

hârp'sĭ-chórd, n., piano-like musical instrument; **-ist**

hăr'rŏw, n., machine to break up plowed ground; v., torment; **-ing**

hăr'ry̆, v., torment, harass

hârsh, a., unpleasant, cruel; **-ly; -ness**

hâr'vĕst, n., gathering of matured crop; v., reap; **-er**

hăsh, n., mixture, chopped vegetables and meat dish

hăsp, n., hinged fastener

hăs'sóck, n., padded footstool [**hasty** a.

hăste, n., hurry, speed; **-n;**

hătch, n., door, opening on ship's deck; v., bring forth from egg, plan

hătch'ét, n., small ax

hāte, v., dislike greatly; **hatred** n.; **-able; -ful; -fully; -fulness**

hăugh'ty̆, a., arrogant; **tily; tiness**

hăul, v., pull; **-er; -age**

hăunch, n., rump and upper thigh of body

hăunt, v., visit often

hā'vén, n., safe place

hăv'óc, n., v., ruin

hăwk, n., bird of prey, advocate of war

hăwk'êr, n., peddler

hăw'thôrn, n., thorny shrub [for animal feed

hāy, n., grass cut and dried

hăz'árd, n., danger, chance; **-ous; -ously**

hāze, n., mist, slight confusion; **hazy** a.

hĕad'ĭng, n., title, caption

hĕad'līne, n., newspaper title [rashly

hĕad'lŏng, adv., headfirst;

hĕad'quar-têrs (quôr), n. pl., main office

hĕad'strŏng, a., stubborn

hĕad'wāy, n., progress

hĕad'y̆, a., intoxicating; **headily; headiness**

hēal, v., cure; **-er**

hĕalth, n., physical and mental condition

hēap, n., v., pile

hēar, v., receive sounds through ear, listen; **-ing** n. [sip

hēar'sāy, n., rumor, gos-

hêarse, n., funeral vehicle for corpse

heârt, *n.,* blood-pumping body organ, main part, humane feeling

heârt'āche, *n.,* grief

heârt'ĕn, *v.,* encourage

heârth, *n.,* fireplace floor

heârt'lĕss, *a.,* unkind

heârt'y̆, *a.,* friendly, strong, plentiful; **heart-ily**

hēat, *n.,* hotness, strong feeling, excitement; *v.,* make warm; **-edly**

hēath, *n.,* wasteland

hēa'thĕn, *n.,* irreligious person, pagan

hēave, *v.,* lift and throw with effort, rise and fall rhythmically

hĕav'ĕn, *n.,* sky, place of God, happy state; **-ly**

hĕav'y̆, *a.,* weighing much, difficult, intense; **heavily**

hĕck'le, *v.,* annoy; **-r**

hĕc'tĭc, *a.,* confusing, wild; **-ally** [*v.,* avoid

hĕdge, *n.,* row of shrubs;

hē'dòn-īsm, *n.,* devotion to pleasure

hēed, *n.,* close attention; *v.,* notice, **-ful; -fully; -less; -lessly; -lessness**

hēel, *n.,* back part of foot, shoe part, (coll.) cad; *v.,* follow closely, lean

hĕif'êr, *n.,* young cow

height, *n.,* highest point, tallness; **-en**

hei'noŭs (hā) *a.,* outrageous; **-ly; -ness**

hĕir, *n.,* one who inherits; **-ess**

hĕir'lōom, *n.,* inherited personal property

hĕl'ĭ-cŏp-têr, *n.,* aircraft that can hover [ment

hē'lĭ-ŭm, *n.,* gaseous ele-

hĕll, *n.,* place of the damned, torrent; **-ish**

hĕl'mĕt, *n.,* hard protective head covering

hĕlp, *n.,* aid, remedy, hired helper; *v.,* assist, aid, remedy, avoid; **-er; -ful; -fully; -fulness; -less;**

-lessly; -lessness

hĕm, *n.,* garment's border; *v.,* surround

hē-mȧ-tŏl'ò-gy̆, *n.,* study of blood; **gist; logic; logical**

hĕm'ī-sphēre, *n.,* half a globe; **spheric; spherical**

hĕm'lŏck, *n.,* poisonous plant, evergreen tree

hē'mò-glō-bĭn, *n.,* red pigment of blood; **-ic; -ous**

hē-mò-phĭl'ī-ȧ, *n.,* disease of prolonged bleeding

hĕm'ŏr-rhȧge, *n.,* heavy bleeding

hĕmp, *n.,* fibrous plant used to make rope

hĕn, *n.,* female fowl

hĕnch'mȧn, *n.,* trusted helper

hĕn'pĕck, *v.,* nag; **-ed**

hĕp-ȧ-tī'tĭs, *n.,* inflammation of liver

hĕr'ȧld, *n.,* messenger; *v.,* announce

hêrb, *n.,* plant used for seasoning; **-al; -age; -y** *a.*

hêrd, *n.,* group of animals; *v.,* group together

hēre-ȧf'têr, *n.,* life after death; *adv.,* from now on

hē-rĕd'ī-ty̆, *n.,* passing on of traits to offspring; **tary** *a.;* **tarily; tariness**

hĕr'ė-sy̆, *n.,* belief opposed to church doctrine; **etic** *n.;* **etical**

hĕr'mĭt, *n.,* one who lives secluded life; **-age**

hêr'nĭ-ȧ, *n.,* protrusion or rupture of body organ **-te; -tion**

hē'rō, *n.,* brave noble man, central man in story; **-ic; -ism**

hĕr'ò-in, *n.,* narcotic

hĕr'òn, *n.,* large wading bird [fish

hĕr'rĭng, *n.,* small edible

hĕs'ī-tāte, *v.,* pause, feel unsure; **ter; tor; tion; tive; tively; tancy; tant; tantly**

hĕt-êr-ò-gē'nē-oŭs, *a.,*

varied, dissimilar; **neity; -ly; -ness**

hĕx′å-gŏn, *n.*, six-sided figure; **-al; -ally**

hi′bĕr-nāte, *v.*, sleep all winter; **tor; tion**

hĭc′cŭp, *n.*, throat spasm causing sound

hĭde, *n.*, animal skin; *v.*, keep out of sight

hĭd′ē-oůs, *a.*, very ugly; **-ly; -ness**

hĭe, *v.*, hurry

hĭ′ĕr-ârch- y̆ (ärk), *n.*, system of rank; **chism; chical; chically**

hĭgh, *a.*, tall, far up, superior, costly, shrill, excited; **-ly; -ness**

hĭgh′băll, *n.*, liquor and mixer

hĭgh′boy (bŏi), *n.*, tall chest of drawers

hĭgh′brōw, *n.*, *a.*, intellectual

hĭgh-hănd′ĕd, *a.*, arbitrary

hĭgh-mĭnd′ĕd, *a.*, proud, moral; **-ly; -ness**

hĭgh-strŭng′, *a.*, nervous, tense

hĭ′jăck, *v.*, steal by force; ex. airplane; **-er**

hĭke, *n.*, long vigorous walk; *v.*, pull up; **-r**

hĭ-lār′ĭ-oůs, *a.*, funny, merry; **ity; -ly; -ness**

hĭll, *n.*, raised, rounded land; **-y** *a.* [mountains

hĭll′bĭl-ly̆, *n.*, person from

hĭll′ŏck, *n.*, small hill

hĭlt, *n.*, handle, entirety

hĭnd, *a.*, back, rear

hĭn′dĕr, *v.*, keep from doing, stop; **drance**

hĭnd′sĭght, *n.*, judgment after event

hĭnge, *n.*, moving metal joint for door

hĭnt, *n.*, suggestion, trace; *v.*, suggest; **-er**

hĭp, *n.*, body part between waist and upper thigh

hĭre, *v.*, pay for service, give job to; **-r; -able**

hĭr′sůte, *a.*, hairy; **-ness**

hĭs-tŏl′ȯ-gy̆, *n.*, study of plant and animal tissues

hĭs′tȯ-ry̆, *n.*, study or record of past events; **rian** *n.*; **toric; torical; torically** [**-ally; -s**

hĭs-trĭ-ŏn′ĭc, *a.*, theatrical;

hĭt, *n.*, blow, something successful; *v.*, strike; **-ter** [fasten

hĭtch, *n.*, obstacle; *v.*, jerk,

hĭtch′hĭke, *v.*, travel by asking for auto rides

hĭve, *n.*, shelter for bees

hôard, *n.*, hidden supply; *v.*, collect and store away

hôarse, *a.*, sounding husky and rough; **-ly; -ness; -n**

hôar′y̆, *a.*, grayish-white, old; **hoariness**

hōax, *n.*, trick; *v.*, cheat

hŏb′ble, *v.*, limp; **-r**

hŏb′nŏb, *v.*, associate with

hō′bō, *n.*, tramp

hŏck, *n.*, animal leg joint; *v.*, pawn

hŏck′ēy, *n.*, team sport played on field or ice

hŏdge′pŏdge, *n.*, jumble

hōe, *n.*, garden tool

hōld, *n.*, grip; *v.*, keep in hand or place, have, grasp, contain; **-er**

hōle, *n.*, hollow place, opening

hŏl′ĭ-dāy, *n.*, religious festival, work-free day

hŏl′lêr, *n.*, *v.*, shout, yell

hŏl′lōw, *a.*, empty within, worthless; **-ness; -ly**

hŏl′ly̆, *n.*, evergreen shrub

hŏl′stêr, *n.*, pistol case

hō′ly̆, *a.*, sacred, saintly, of religion; **liness; lily**

hŏm′åge, *n.*, respect, honor [hat

hŏm′bûrg, *n.*, man's felt

hōme, *n.*, place where one lives, family life; **-less**

hōme′ly̆, *a.*, of home, of family, plain

hōme′māk-êr, *n.*, one who manages household

hōme′y̆, *a.*, cozy, familiar; **-ness**

hŏm′ĭ-cīde, *n.*, killing of a person; **dal; dally**

G
H

hŏm'ĭ-lȳ, *n.*, sermon; **list**
hŏm'ĭ-nȳ, *n.*, ground dry corn
hȯ-mŏg'ė-nīze, *v.*, blend (milk); **tion**
hŏm'ȯ-nȳm, *n.*, word pronounced as another but defined and spelled differently
hō-mȯ-sĕx'ū-ȧl, *n.*, *a.*, (one) desiring person of same sex; **-ity; -ly**
hōne, *v.*, sharpen
hŏn'ėst, *a.*, truthful, sincere; **-y; -ly**
hȯn'ēy, *n.*, sweet substance made by bees, sweet one
hȯn'ēy-dew, *n.*, melon
hȯn'ēy-sŭck-le, *n.*, vine with fragrant flowers
hŏn'ŏr, *n.*, high regard, dignity, high moral ideals; *v.*, respect greatly; **-able; -ably; -ability; -ableness**
ho͝od'lŭm, *n.*, gangster, lawless person
ho͝od'wĭnk, *v.*, cheat, trick
ho͝of, *n.*, horny bottom on feet of cattle, deer, etc.
ho͝ok, *n.*, curved pointed device; *v.*, catch or fasten with hook
ho͞op, *n.*, large band or ring
hōpe, *n.*, expected desire; *v.*, want and expect; **-ful; -fully; -fulness; -less; -lessly; -lessness**
hôrde, *n.*, crowd
hȯ-rī'zȯn, *n.*, line where sky seems to meet earth; **-tal; -tally**
hôr'mōne, *n.*, stimulating chemical made by gland; **monal; monic**
hôrn, *n.*, bony growth on animal's head, blown musical instrument
hôrn'ȳ, *a.*, hard; **horniness**
hô-rŏl'ȯ-gȳ, *n.*, science of measuring time; **gist; logical**
hôr'ȯ-scōpe, *n.*, pattern of heavens used to predict future; **scopic**

hôr'rŏr, *n.*, strong fear, terrible dislike; **rible; ribly; rific; rify; rification**
hôrse, *n.*, large domesticated animal
hôrse-läugh, *n.*, loud laugh
hôrse-pow-êr, *n.*, unit of power for motors
hôrse'răd-ĭsh, *n.*, pungent-tasting white fleshy root
hōse, *n.*, garment for foot, ankle and leg, water tube
hŏs'pĭ-tȧl, *n.*, place for medical treatment; **-ize; -ization**
hōst, *n.*, one who entertains guests, crowd; **-ess**
hŏs'tȧge, *n.*, one held as a pledge
hŏs'tėl, *n.*, inn; **-er; -ry**
hŏs'tĭle, *n.*, unfriendly; **tility; -ly**
hō-tĕl', *n.*, large place with rooms for travellers
hŏt'hĕad, *n.*, rash person; **-ed; -edness; -edly**
ho͝und, *n.*, hunting dog; *v.*, continue pursuing
ho͝use, *n.*, place to live in, family, building, business, legislative body; *v.*, **(ho͝uz)** reside, lodge; **-ful** [ter
hȯv'ėl, *n.*, small poor shel-
hȯv'êr, *v.*, linger anxiously
ho͝w-ĕv'êr, *adv.*, in whatever way, yet; *conj.*, although [non
ho͝w'ĭtz-ĕr, *n.*, small can-
ho͝wl, *n.*, long mournful cry; **-er; -ing**
hŭb, *n.*, center
hŭb'bŭb, *n.*, noise
hŭck'stêr, *n.*, peddler
hŭd'dle, *v.*, crowd together, hunch oneself up
hŭff, *n.*, fit of anger; *v.*, puff up; **-y** *a.*; **-ish; -iness**
hŭg, *n.*, embrace; *v.*, put arms around, hold closely [**-ness; -ly**
hūge, *a.*, very large;
hŭlk, *n.*, big clumsy person or thing; **-ing**

hŭll, *n.,* seed covering, ship's frame

hū′mån, *n.,* person; *a.,* of mankind; **-ness; -ity; -ism; -ize**

hū-māne′, *a.,* kind; **-ness; -ly**

hū-măn-ĭ-tār′ĭ-ån, *n.,* one who thinks of others; **-ism** [**-ness; -r**

hŭm′ble, *a.,* modest; **bly;**

hŭm′bŭg, *n.,* fraud, impostor

hŭm′drŭm, *a.,* dull

hū′mĭd, *a.,* damp; **-ity; -ify; -ification; -ifier; -ly**

hū-mĭl′ĭ-tÿ, *n.,* modesty, humbleness [bird

hŭm′mĭng-bîrd, *n.,* tiny

hū′mör, *n.,* mood, quality of seeming funny; *v.,* indulge

hŭmp, *n.,* mound, bump; *v.,* arch; **-y** *a.*

hū-′mŭs, *n.,* dark soil from partially decayed matter

hŭnch, *n.,* suspicion; *v.,* arch into hump

hŭn′gêr, *n.,* need for food, desire; *v.,* crave; **gry** *a.;* **grily; griness**

hŭnt, *n., v.,* search; **-er; -ing** *n.*

hûr′dle, *n.,* obstacle; *v.,* jump over; **-r** [**-er**

hûrl, *v.,* throw with force;

hûr-räh′, *int., n.,* shout of joy [storm

hûr′rĭ-cāne, *n.,* violent

hûr′rÿ, *n.,* rush; *v.,* move quickly; **ried; riedly**

hûrt, *n., v.,* harm, wound; **-ful; -fully; -fulness**

hûr′tle, *v.,* move swiftly

hŭs′bånd-rÿ, *n.,* farming

hŭsh, *n., v., a.,* quiet

hŭsk, *n.,* dry covering of fruit

hŭsk′ÿ, *a.,* dry in throat, big and strong; **huskiness; huskily**

hŭs′tle, *v.,* move roughly, work with energy; **-r**

hŭt, *n.,* crude little house

hŭtch, *n.,* china cabinet, animal cage

hÿ′brĭd, *n.,* mixed breed; **-ize; -ization; -ity; -ism**

hÿ-dräu′lĭc, *a.,* of moving liquid; **-s; -ally**

hÿ-drȯ-ė-lĕc′trĭc, *a.,* of electricity by water power; **-ity**

hÿ′drȯ-gėn, *n.,* gaseous chemical element; **-ous; dric; -ate**

hÿ-ē′nȧ, *n.,* wolflike animal

hÿ′giêne, *n.,* science of health, cleanliness; **enic; enically; enist**

hÿmn, *n.,* song of praise, religious song; **-ist; -ology**

hÿ-pêr-ăc′tĭve, *a.,* very active; **tivity**

hÿ-pêr′bȯ-lē, *n.,* exaggeration; **bolic; bolical; bolically**

hÿ-pêr-tĕn′sion, *n.,* abnormally high blood pressure; **sive**

hÿ′phėn, *n.,* punctuation mark (-); **-ate**

hÿp-nō′sĭs, *n.,* sleeplike state when one can respond to suggestion; **notic; notically; notism; notist; notize; nology**

hÿ-pȯ-chŏn′drĭ-ȧ, *n.,* abnormal fear of illness; **-c** *n.*

hÿp′ȯ-crĭte, *n.,* one who pretends to be what he is not; **critical; critically; risy** *n.*

hÿ-pȯ-dêr′mĭc, *n., a.,* (injection) under skin

hÿ-pŏt′ė-nūse, *n.,* side of triangle opposite right angle

hÿ-pŏth′ė-sĭs, *n.,* theory; **size; thetical; thetically**

hÿs-têr-ĕc′tȯ-mÿ, *n.,* surgical removal of uterus

hÿs-tē′rĭ-ȧ, *n.,* uncontrolled emotional outburst; **rical**

I

I, *pro.,* person speaking or writing

ī′bĕx, *n.,* wild goat

ĭ'bĭs, *n.*, large wading bird

īce, *n.*, frozen water, cold-ness; *v.*, freeze, cool, frost a cake; **icy** *a.*

īce'bêrg, *n.*, great ice mass afloat in sea

īce crēam, *n.*, creamy fro-zen dessert

ĭch-thў-ŏl'ô-gў, *n.*, sci-ence of fish; **gist; logical**

ĭ'cĭ-cle, *n.*, hanging stick of ice

ĭc'ĭng, *n.*, frosting [-ic

ĭ'cŏn, *n.*, sacred image;

ĭ-cŏn'ô-clăst, *n.*, attacker of conventional ideas; **clasm** [psyche

ĭd, *n.*, unconscious part of

ĭ-dē'â, *n.*, thought, belief, plan, notion; **-l**

ĭ-dē'âl, *n.*, perfect model; imaginary concept; **-ism; -ist; -istic; -isti-cally; -ity; -ize; -ization; -izer**

ĭ-děn'tĭ-câl, *a.*, same; **-ly**

ĭ-děn'tĭ-fў, *v.*, recognize as similar, associate; **fica-tion; fier; fiable**

ĭ-děn'tĭ-tў, *n.*, sameness, individuality

ĭ-dē-ŏl'ô-gў, *n.*, system of beliefs; **gist; gize; logi-cal; logically**

ĭd'ĭ-ôm, *n.*, accepted phrase or expression; **-atic; -atically**

ĭd-ĭ-ô-sўn'crâ-sў, *n.*, per-sonal peculiarity; **cratic; cratically**

ĭd'ĭ-ôt, *n.*, mentally re-tarded person; **ocy; -ic; -ically**

ĭ'dle, *a.*, useless, not busy, lazy; **dly; -ness; -r**

ĭ'dŏl, *n.*, worshipped ob-ject; **-ater; -atry; -atrize; -atrous; -atrously**

ĭ'dŏl-ĭze, *v.*, worship, adore; **zation**

ĭ'dўll, *n.*, short poem; **-ic; -ically; -ist** [whether

ĭf, *conj.*, in case that,

ĭf'fў, *a.*, (coll.) doubtful

ĭg'lōō, *n.*, Eskimo house of ice

ĭg'nē-oŭs, *a.*, fiery

ĭg-nīte', *v.*, set fire to; **ter; tor; tion; nitable**

ĭg-nō'ble, *a.*, not noble, low; **bly; -ness**

ĭg'nô-mĭ-nў, *n.*, disgrace, shame; **minous; min-ously; minousness**

ĭg-nô-rā'mŭs, *n.*, stupid person

ĭg'nô-rânt, *a.*, lacking knowledge, unaware; **-ly; rance** [tion to; -r

ĭg-nôre', *v.*, pay no atten-

ĭ-guā'nâ, *n.*, lizard

ĭlk, *n.*, *a.*, same, type

ĭll, *a.*, bad, sick; **-ness**

ĭl-lē'gâl, *a.*, against the law; **-ity; -ly**

ĭl-lĕg'ĭ-ble, *a.*, impossible to read; **bility; bly**

ĭl-lē-gĭt'ĭ-mâte, *a.*, born of unwed parents, unlaw-ful; **macy; -ly** [-ness

ĭl-lĭc'ĭt, *a.*, improper; **-ly;**

ĭl-lĭt'êr-âte, *a.*, unable to read or write; **acy; -ly**

ĭl-lŏg'ĭ-câl, *a.*, not logical; **-ity; -ly**

ĭl-lū'mĭ-nāte, *v.*, light up, explain; **tor; tion; tive; nant**

ĭl-lū'sion, *n.*, false idea or look; **-al; -ary; -ist; sive; sively; siveness; sory**

ĭl'lŭs-trāte, *v.*, explain, make picture; **tor; tion; tive; tively**

ĭl-lŭs'trĭ-oŭs, *a.*, bright, fa-mous; **-ly; -ness**

ĭm'âge, *n.*, mental picture, likeness, reflection

ĭ-măg'ĭn-ār-ў, *a.*, unreal; **narily; nariness**

ĭ-măg'ĭne, *v.*, conceive in the mind, think; **nation; native; natively; na-tiveness; inable**

ĭm-bĕ-cīle, *n.*, mentally re-tarded person, fool; **cility** [sorb;-r

ĭm-bībe', *v.*, drink, ab-

ĭm-būe', *v.*, inspire

ĭm'ĭ-tāte, *v.*, act like, copy; **tor; tion; tive; table**

ĭm-măc'ū-lâte, *a.*, per-fectly clean, sinless;

ĭacy; -ness; -ly

ĭm-mē′dĭ-āte, a., closest, at once; -ly; acy

ĭm-mė-mô′rĭ-ål, a., ancient; -ly

ĭm-mĕnse′, a., enormous; sity; -ly; -ness

ĭm-mêrse′, v., dip into liquid; sion; -d; mersible

ĭm′mĭ-grāte, v., come to live in new country; tion; grant

ĭm′mĭ-nėnt, a., about to happen; nence; -ly

ĭm-mūne′, a., free from disease, exempt from; munity; nize; nization

ĭm-mūre′, v., confine to prison; -ment

ĭm-mū′tȧ-ble, a., unchangeable; bility; -ness; bly

ĭmp, n., mischievous child; -ish; -ishly; -ishness

ĭm′păct, n., collision, shock; v., (ĭm-păct′) press together; -ed; -ion

ĭm-pāir′, v., injure; -ment

ĭm-pāle′, v., fix on something pointed; -ment

ĭm-păl′pȧ-ble, a., not to be felt or understood; bility; bly

ĭm-pȧrt′, v., give, tell; -er; -ation; -able

ĭm-pȧr′tial, a., fair; -ity; -ly

ĭm-pȧsse′, n., deadlock

ĭm-păs′sion, v., arouse emotionally; -ed; -edly

ĭm-păs′sĭve, a., unemotional, calm; sivity; -ly

ĭm-pēach′, v., accuse public official of wrong doing; -ment; -able; -ability

ĭm-pĕc′cȧ-ble, a., flawless; bility; bly

ĭm-pė-cū′nĭ-oŭs, a., poor; osity; -ness; -ly

ĭm-pēde′, v., hinder; -r

ĭm-pĕd′ĭ-mėnt, n., obstacle [-ler; -lent

ĭm-pĕl′, v., drive, push;

ĭm-pĕnd′, v., occur soon; -ent; -ence; -ency

ĭm-pĕr′ȧ-tĭve, a., urgent; -ly; -ness

ĭm-pē′rĭ-ål, a., of an empire; -ism; -istic; -istically; -ly [-ment

ĭm-pĕr′ĭl, v., put in danger;

ĭm-pē′rĭ-oŭs, a., domineering; -ly; -ness

ĭm-pêr′sŏn-āte, v., imitate, pretend; tor; tion

ĭm-pêr′tĭ-nėnt, a., irrelevant, rude; nence; nency; -ly

ĭm-pêr′vĭ-oŭs, a., impenetrable; -ly; -ness

ĭm-pĕt′ū-oŭs, a., impulsive, sudden; -ly; -ness

ĭm′pė-tŭs, n., force of movement, stimulus

ĭm-pĭnge′, v., touch, encroach; -r; -ment

ĭm-plănt′, v., plant firmly; -ation

ĭm′plė-mėnt, n., tool; v., (ĭm-plė-mėnt′) fulfill, do; -ation; -al

ĭm′plĭ-cāte, v., infer, involve; tion; tive; tively

ĭm-plĭc′ĭt, a., suggested; absolute; -ly; -ness

ĭm-plōde′, v., burst inward; plosion; plosive; plosively [plied

ĭm-plȳ′, v., hint, suggest;

ĭm′pôrt, n., imported good, meaning; v., (ĭm-pôrt′) bring goods into country; -er; -ation; -able

ĭm-pôr′tȧnt, a., having value; tance; -ly

ĭm-pôr-tūne′, v., urge, beg; nity; tunåte a.; -ly; -ness

ĭm-pōse′, v., force on another; position

ĭm-pŏs′tör, n., pretender; tūre

ĭm′pȯ-tėnt, a., ineffective, sterile; ence; ency; -ly

ĭm-pound′, v., seize by law; -ment

ĭm-prĕg′nȧ-ble, a., unyielding; bility; bly

ĭm-prĕg′nāte, v., fertilize, make pregnant; tor; tion

ĭm-prĕss′, v., stamp, affect strongly; -ion; -ional; -ionable; -ible; -ibly

ĭm-prĕs′sion-ĭsm, n.,

I
K

school of art; **ist; istic;
istically** [ing; **-ing** n.
ĭm-prĭnt′, v., mark by print-
ĭm-prĭs′ŏn, v., put in jail;
-ment
ĭm-prŏmp′tū, a., adv.,
without preparation
ĭm-prove′ (prūv), v., make
better; **-r; -ment; provable**
ĭm′prȯ-vīse, v., do without
preparation; **-r; sor; sation; sational**
ĭm′pū-dĕnt, a., disre-
spectful; **ence; ency;
-ly**
ĭm-pūgn′, v., oppose ver-
bally; **-er; -ation; -able**
ĭm′pŭlse, n., sudden force;
**sion; sive; sively; sive-
ness**
ĭm-pū′nĭ-tӯ, n., freedom
from punishment
ĭm-pūte′, v., attribute,
charge; **tation; tative;
putable; putability;
putably**
ĭn, prep., contained by,
during, having, concern-
ing, using; adv., to in-
side
ĭn-ăl′ĭĕn-à-ble, a., that
cannot be taken away;
bility; bly
ĭn-āne′, a., foolish; **-ly**
ĭn-às-mŭch′, conj., since
ĭn-äu-gu-rate, v., begin,
install in public office;
tor; tion; ral
ĭn′bôrn, a., natural
ĭn′brĕd, a., innate
ĭn-cán-dĕs′cĕnt, a., glowing with heat, bright;
cence; -ly
ĭn-cán-tā′tion, n., magical
spell; **-al; tory**
ĭn-câr′cêr-āte, v., im-
prison; **tor; tion**
ĭn-câr′năte, v., make real;
a., (năte) in human form;
tion
ĭn′cĕnse, n., substance
burned for pleasant
odor; v., (ĭn-cĕnse′)
make angry
ĭn-cĕn′tĭve, n., motive; a.,
encouraging

ĭn-cĕp′tion, n., beginning;
tive; tively
ĭn-cĕs′sánt, a., continual;
sancy; -ness; -ly
ĭn′cĕst, n., sexual relations
with close relatives;
**-uous; -uously; -uous-
ness**
ĭn-chō′àte (kō), a., just be-
gun, incomplete; **tion;
-ness; -ly**
ĭn′cĭ-dĕnce, n., range of
occurrence
ĭn′cĭ-dĕnt, n., occurrence
ĭn-cĭ-dĕn′tàl, a., liable to
happen; casual; **-ly**
ĭn-cĭn′êr-āte, v., burn; **tor;
tion**
ĭn-cĭp′ĭ-ėnt, a., beginning;
ence; ency; -ly
ĭn-cĭ′sion, n., cut
ĭn-cĭ′sĭve, a., sharp, keen;
-ly; -ness
ĭn-cĭ′sör, n., cutting tooth
ĭn-cīte′, v., urge to act;
-ment; tation
ĭn′clīne, n., slope; v.,
(ĭn-clīne′) slope, have a
tendency; **-r; nation;
national; clinable**
ĭn-clŭde′, v., contain;
**cludable; clusion; clu-
sive; clusively**
ĭn-cŏg-nĭ′tō, a., adv., hidden, disguised
ĭn′come (cŭm), n., money
one earns
ĭn-côr′pȯ-rāte, v., com-
bine, merge, form into
corporation; **tor; tion;
tive; -d**
ĭn-côr′rĭ-gĭ-ble, a., unable
to change; **bility; bly;
-ness**
ĭn′crēase, n., growth; v.,
(ĭn-crēase′) become
greater; **-r; creasable;
creasingly**
ĭn-crĕd′ĭ-ble, a., too unusual, unbelievable; **bility; bly**
ĭn-crĕd′ŭ-loŭs, a., doubt-
ing; **lity; -ly** [gain; **-al**
ĭn′crė-mĕnt, n., increase,
ĭn-crĭm′ĭ-nāte, v., accuse,
involve in crime; **tion;
tory**

ĭn-crŭst′, v., cover with crust or hard coat; **-ation**

ĭn′cū-bāte, v., hatch eggs, develop; **tor; tion; tional; tive**

ĭn-cŭl′cāte, v., teach by drill; **tor; tion**

ĭn-cŭm′bĕnt, a., currently in office; **bency**

ĭn-cûr′, v., bring upon one-self; **-rence** [**-ness**

ĭn-dĕbt′ĕd, a., owing;

ĭn-dēed′, adv., truly; int., exclamation of surprise

ĭn-dĕl′ĭ-ble, a., permanent; **bility; bly**

ĭn-dĕm′nĭ-fȳ, v., protect, repay for loss; **fier; nity; nification**

ĭn-dĕnt′, v., notch, cut into, make dent; **-ation**

ĭn-dĕn′tûre, n., contract (of service)

ĭn-dē-pĕnd′ĕnt, a., not controlled by another, free; **ence; ency; -ly**

ĭn′dĕx, n., pointer, indica-tion, alphabetical list of topics in book; **-er**

ĭn′dĭ-cāte, v., show, point out; **tor; tion; tive; tively; cant**

ĭn-dict′ (dīt), v., accuse of crime; **-er; -or; -ment; -able**

ĭn-dĭf′fĕr-ĕnt, a., neutral, unconcerned; **ence; -ly**

ĭn-dĭg′ė-noŭs, a., native inherent; **-ly; -ness**

ĭn′dĭ-gĕnt, a., poor, in pov-erty; **ence; ency; -ly**

ĭn-dĭ-gĕs′tion, n., difficulty in digesting food; **tive**

ĭn-dĭg′nȧnt, a., angry; **na-tion; -ly**

ĭn-dĭg′nĭ-tȳ, n., insult

ĭn-dĭs-pōsed′, a., sick; **si-tion**

ĭn-dĭ-vĭd′ū-ȧl, n., single being or thing; a., char-acteristic, distinct; **-ity; -ize; -ization; -ly**

ĭn-dŏc′trĭ-nāte, v., teach beliefs, drill into; **tor; tion** [**lence; -ly**

ĭn′dȯ-lĕnt, a., lazy, idle;

ĭn-dŏm′ĭ-tȧ-ble, a., uncon-querable; **bility; bly; -ness** [**building**

ĭn′dôor, a., of inside of a

ĭn-dū′bĭ-tȧ-ble, a., un-questionable; **bly**

ĭn-dūce′, v., persuade, cause; **-r; -ment; ducible** [**-ee; -ion**

ĭn-dŭct′, v., install, initiate;

ŭn-dŭc′tĭve, a., conclusive from facts; **tion**

ĭn-dŭlge′, v., yield; **-r; -nce; -nt; -ntly**

ĭn-dŭs′trĭ-oŭs, a., busy; **-ly; -ness**

ĭn′dŭs-trȳ, n., business, manufacturing, hard work; **trial; trialist; tri-alism; trialize; trializa-tion**

ĭn-ē′brī-ȧte, n., a., drunk; v., (āte) make drunk; **tion; -d**

ĭn-ĕf′fȧble, a., too awe-some to be spoken; **bil-ity; bly; -ness**

ĭn-ĕpt′, a., unfit, awkward; **-itude; -ly; -ness**

ĭn-êrt′, a., inactive; **-ly; -ness**

ĭn-êr′tĭȧ, n., tendency of matter to stay in rest or motion

ĭn-ĕv′ĭ-tȧ-ble, a., sure to happen; **bility; bly**

ĭn-ĕx′ȯ-rȧ-ble, a., inflexi-ble; **bility; bly**

ĭn-ĕx′plĭ-cȧ-ble, a., mys-terious; **bility; bly**

ĭn′fȧ-mȳ, n., bad reputa-tion, disgrace; **mous; mously**

ĭn′fȧnt, n., very young child; **fancy**

ĭn′fȧn-tĭle, a., babyish im-mature; **lism**

ĭn′fȧn-trȳ, n., foot soldiers; **-man,** n.

ĭn-fȧt-ū-ā′tion, n., foolish love; **ated**

ĭn-fĕct′, v., make dis-eased; **-or; -ion; -ious; -iously; -iousness**

ĭn-fêr′, v., conclude by rea-soning; **-rer; -ence; -able**

ĭn-fē′rĭ-ôr, a., lower, poor

I
K

in quality; **-ity**
ĭn-fêr′nål, a., of hell; **-ly**
ĭn-fĕst′, v., overrun; **-er;
-ation**
ĭn′fĭ-dĕl, n., disbeliever
ĭn-fĭl′trāte, v., join secretly, penetrate; **tor; tion; tive**
ĭn′fĭ-nīte, a., endless, vast; **nity; -ly; -ness**
ĭn-fĭrm′, a., weak, feeble; **-ity; -ly; -ness**
ĭn-fĭr′må-rȳ, n., hospital
ĭn-flāme′, v., set on fire, excite, become red and sore; **flammation; flammable**
ĭn-flāte′, v., blow up, swell; **-r; flatable; -d**
ĭn-flā′tion, n., fall in money value with rise in prices; **-ary**
ĭn-flĕct′, v., change tone in voice; **-ion; -ive**
ĭn-flĭct′, v., cause pain, impose; **-er; -or; -ion; -ive**
ĭn′flu-ĕnce, n., power, authority, prestige; v., have an effect on; **ential; entially**   [disease
ĭn-flŭ-ĕn′zå, n., infectious
ĭn′flŭx, n., flowing in
ĭn-fôrm′, v., give knowledge; **-er**   [**-ly**
ĭn-fôr′mål, a., casual; **-ity;**
ĭn-fôr-mā′tion, n., facts; **tive; tively**
ĭn-frăc′tion, n., violation
ĭn-frå-rĕd′, a., of invisible rays outside spectrum
ĭn-frĭnge′, v., violate; **-ment**   [**tion; atingly**
ĭn-fū′rĭ-āte, v., enrage;
ĭn-fūse′, v., pour into, instill; **sion; sible; sive**
ĭn-gēn′ioŭs, a., clever; **ity; -ly; -ness**
ĭn-gĕn′ū-oŭs, a., frank, naive; **-ly; -ness**
ĭn-gĕst′, v., take food into body; **-ion; -ive**
ĭn′gŏt, n., metal bar
ĭn-grāined′, a., firmly fixed
ĭn′grāte, n., thankless person
ĭn-grā′tĭ-āte (shĭ), v., seek one's favor; **tion; ating; atingly**   [of mixture

ĭn-grē′dĭ-ĕnt, n., element
ĭn-hăb′ĭt, v., live in; **-er; -ation; -able; -ancy; -ant** n.   [**halation**
ĭn-hāle′, v., breathe in; **-r;**
ĭn-hĕr′ĕnt, a., natural, inborn; **ence; ency**
ĭn-hĕr′ĭt, v., receive (traits, possessions, etc.) from ancestor; **-or; -ress; -ance; -able**
ĭn-hĭb′ĭt, v., keep from doing, restrain; **-or; -ion; -ive; -ory**
ĭn-ĭm′ĭ-cål, a., hostile, unfriendly; **-ly**
ĭn-ĭq′uĭ-tȳ, n., wickedness; **tous; tously; tousness**
ĭn-ĭ′tĭål, n., capital letter; a., first; **-ly**
ĭn-ĭ′tĭ-āte (shĭ), v., begin; **tor; tion**
ĭn-ĭ′tĭ-å-tĭve (shĭ), n., first step, ability to take lead
ĭn-jĕct′, v., push fluid into, insert; **-or; -ion; -able**
ĭn-jŭnc′tion, n., court order; **tive**
ĭn′jûre, v., harm physically; **-r; jury; jurious; juriously; juriousness**
ĭnk, n., colored liquid for writing; **-y** a.
ĭnk′lĭng, n., notion, hint
ĭn′lånd, a., adv., away from sea; **-er**
ĭn-lăw′, n., relative by marriage   [**laid** a.
ĭn′lāy, v., set into surface;
ĭn′lĕt, n., narrow strip of water
ĭn-′māte, n., prisoner
ĭnn, n., place providing food and/or bed for travellers
ĭn′nårds, n., pl., (coll.) inner organs of body
ĭn-nāte′, a., existing from birth, inborn; **-ly; -ness**
ĭn′nêr, a., interior
ĭn′nŏ-cĕnt, a., without evil, naive; **cence; -ly**
ĭn-nŏc′ū-oŭs, a., harmless, dull; **-ly; -ness**
ĭn′nŏ-vāte, v., start something new; **tor; tion; tive**
ĭn-nū-ĕn′dō, n., hint, sly

remark

ĭn-nū'mêr-à-ble, *a.,* very many; **bility; bly; -ness**

ĭn-ŏc'ŭ-lāte, *v.,* inject serum to prevent disease; **tor; tion; tive**

ĭn-ôr'dĭ-nàte, *a.,* too great; **-ly; -ness** [tigation

ĭn'quĕst, *n.,* judicial inves-

ĭn-quīre', *v.,* ask; **-r; quiry; quisition**

ĭn-quĭs'ĭ-tĭve, *a.,* asking many questions, curious; **-ly; -ness**

ĭn-scrĭbe', *v.,* write words; **scription; scriptive**

ĭn-scrŭ'tà-ble, *a.,* mysterious; **bility; bly**

ĭn'sĕct, *n.,* tiny animal with six legs

ĭn-sĕm'ĭ-nāte, *v.,* sow seeds, implant; **tion**

ĭn-sêrt', *n., v.,* (something) put in; **-ion**

ĭn-sīde, *n., a.,* interior; *adv.,* indoors; *prep.,* within [**-ness**

ĭn-sĭd'ĭ-oŭs, *a.,* sly; **-ly;**

ĭn'sīght, *n.,* understanding

ĭn-sĭg'nĭ-à, *n.,* badge or mark of rank, office, etc.

ĭn-sĭn'ū-āte, *v.,* imply, hint; **tor; tion; tive**

ĭn-sĭp'ĭd, *a.,* tasteless, dull; **-ity; -ly**

ĭn-sĭst', *v.,* demand strongly; **-ence; -ent; -ently**

ĭn'só-lĕnt, *a.,* insulting, disrespectful; **ence; -ly**

ĭn-sŏm'nĭ-à, *n.,* inability to sleep; **-c**

ĭn-sō-mŭch', *adv.,* to such an extent

ĭn-soŭ'cĭ-ànt, *a.,* calm, carefree; **ance; -ly**

ĭn-spĕct', *v.,* look at carefully; **-tor; -tion**

ĭn-spīre', *v.,* stimulate, arouse thought or emotion; **-r; spiration; spirational; spirable**

ĭn-stăll', *v.,* put in (office formally); **-er; -ation**

ĭn-stăll'mĕnt, *n.,* one of several parts

ĭn'stánce, *n.,* example

ĭn'stánt, *n.,* moment; *a.,* immediate; **stancy; -ly**

ĭn-stántā'nē-oŭs, *a.,* immediate; **-ly; -ness**

ĭn-stĕad', *adv.,* as an alternative

ĭn'stĕp, *n.,* arched part of top of foot

ĭn'stĭ-gāte, *v.,* incite; **tor; tion; tive**

ĭn-stĭll', *v.,* teach gradually; **-er; -ation; -ment**

ĭn'stĭnct, *n.,* natural tendency; **-ive; -ively; -ual**

ĭn'stĭ-tūte, *n.,* organization to promote art, science, etc.; *v.,* establish, start; **-r; tor; tion; tional; tionally; tionalize; tive**

ĭn-strŭct', *v.,* teach, command; **-or; -ion; -ional; -ive; -ively**

ĭn'strŭ-mĕnt, *n.,* tool, device producing music; **-al; -ally; -ality**

ĭn-sŭb-ôr'dĭ-nāte, *n., a.,* (one who is) disobedient; **-ly; tion**

ĭn'sŭ-làr, *a.,* of an island

ĭn'sŭ-lāte, *v.,* set apart, protect from heat loss; **tor; tion**

ĭn'sŭ-lĭn, *n.,* hormone regulating use of sugar

ĭn'sŭlt, *n.,* indignity; *v.,* **(ĭn-sŭlt')** hurt one's pride; **-er; -ing; -ingly**

ĭn-sŭr'ánce, *n.,* contract to pay for loss.

ĭn-sūre', *v.,* make sure, protect; **-r; surable; surability**

ĭn-sûr'gĕnt, *a.,* rebellious; **gence; gency; -ly**

ĭn-sûr-rĕc'tion, *n.,* rebellion; **-ist; -al; -ary**

ĭn-tăct', *a.,* kept whole

ĭn-tăn'gĭ-ble, *a.,* vague, not material; **bility; bly**

ĭn'tė-gêr, *n.,* whole number [entire

ĭn'tė-gràl, *a.,* essentially,

ĭn'tė-grāte, *v.,* join together, end racial segregation; **tion; tive; tional; tionist**

ĭn-tĕg'rĭ-tÿ, *n.,* wholeness,

honesty

in'tel-lect, *n.,* ability to reason, superior mind; **-ual; -uality; -ually; -ive**

in-tel'li-gence, *n.,* ability to learn, information

in-tel'li-gent, *a.,* having an alert mind; **-ly**

in-tel'li-gi-ble, *a.,* clear, understandable; **bly; bility**

in-tend', *v.,* have in mind, plan; **tention; -ed**

in-tense', *a.,* very strong, strenuous; **sity; -ly; -ness; sive; sively**

in-ten'si-fy, *v.,* strengthen

in-tent', *n.,* purpose; *a.,* firmly fixed; **-ly; -ness**

in-ter', *v.,* bury; **-ment**

in-ter-act', *v.,* act on each other; **-ion; -ive**

in-ter-cede', *v.,* plead for another; **cessor; cession**

in-ter-cept', *v.,* stop, interrupt; **-or; -ion; -ive**

in-ter-change', *v.,* exchange; **-able; -ably**

in'ter-course, *n.,* dealings between others, sexual union

in-ter-de-pend'ence, *n.,* mutual dependence; **ency; ent; ently**

in-ter-dict', *v.,* prohibit; **tor; tion; tive; tory**

in'ter-est, *n.,* concern, fee paid to use one's money; *v.,* show concern; **-ed; -ing**

in-ter-fere', *v.,* come between, meddle; **-nce**

in-ter,fuse', *v.,* combine; **sion** [*a.,* temporary

in'ter-im, *n.,* time between;

in-te'ri-or, *n.,* inside; *a.,* situated within

in-ter-ject', *v.,* insert; **-or; -ion; -ional** [gether

in-ter-lock', *v.,* lock to-

in-ter-lo-cu'tion, *n.,* conversation; **tor; tory**

in-ter-lope', *v.,* intrude; **-r**

in'ter-lude, *n.,* period between

in-ter-mar'ry, *v.,* marry

one of different race; **riage**

in-ter-me'di-ate, *n.,* a go-between; *a.,* in the middle

in-ter'mi-na-ble, *a.,* without, end; **bly**

in-ter-mis'sion, *n.,* period between acts

in-ter-mit'tent, *a.,* periodic, from time to time; **-ly**

in'tern, *n.,* doctor training in hospital; *v.,* **(in-tern')** confine; **-ship**

in-ter'nal, *a.,* inside; **-ize; -ization; -ity; -ly**

in-ter-na'tion-al, *a.,* among nations; **-ize; -ization; -ity; -ly**

in'ter-nist, *n.,* doctor of internal medicine

in-ter-per'son-al, *a.,* between persons; **-ly**

in'ter-play, *n.,* interaction

in-ter'po-late, *v.,* alter by inserting new words; **-r; tor; tion; tive**

in-ter-pose', *v.,* place between; **-r; sition; posal**

in-ter'pret, *v.,* explain meaning, translate; **-er; -ation; -ive; -able**

in-ter'ro-gate, *v.,* question formally; **tor; tion; tive; tively; tory**

in-ter-rupt', *v.,* break into the continuity; **-er; -ion; -ive**

in-ter-sect', *v.,* divide, cross; **-ion; -ional**

in-ter-sperse', *v.,* scatter

in'ter-state, *a.,* among states [between

in'ter-val, *n.,* space or time

in-ter-vene', *v.,* come or be between; **vention**

in'ter-view, *n., v.* (meeting to) ask questions; **-er; -ee** [will; **tacy**

in-tes'tate, *a.,* having no

in-tes'tine, *n.,* tube extending from stomach to anus; **tinal; tinally**

in'ti-mate, *v.,* hint; **tion**

in'ti-mate, *a.,* personal, private; **macy; -ly; -ness**

In-tĭm′ĭ-dāte, v., make afraid; tor; tion

In′to (tü), prep., inside, to the form of, toward

In-tȯ-nā′tion, n., voice pitch

In-tōne′, v., chant

In-tŏx′ĭ-cāte, v., make drunk; tion; cant n., a.

In-trȧ-mū′rȧl, a., among school's members; -ly

In-trăn′sĭ-gėnt, a., refusing to compromise; gence; gency; -ly

In-trȧ-stāte′, a., within the state [vein; -ly

In-trȧ-vē′noŭs, a., in a

In-trĕp′ĭd, a., brave; -ity; -ness; -ly

In′trĭ-cȧte, a., very complex; cacy; -ly; -ness

In-trīgue′, n., secret plot or love affair

In-trĭn′sĭc, a., innate, essential; -ally; -ness

In-trȯ-dūce′, v., bring into, present, begin; -r; duction; ductory

In′trȯ-vêrt, n., shy person; version; versive

In-trūde′, v., force oneself when not welcome; -r; trusion; trusive

In-tū-ĭ′tion, n., instinctive understanding; -al; -ally; tive; tively

In′ŭn-dāte, v., flood, overwhelm; tor; tion

In-ūre′, v., become used to, accustom; -ment

In-vāde′, v., enter forcibly; -r; vasion; vasive

In′vȧ-lĭd, n., chronically ill person [tack

In-vĕc′tĭve, n., verbal attack

In-vēi′gle, v., deceive, lure; -r; -ment

In-vĕnt′, v., create, make new thing; -or; -ion; -ive

In′vėn-tȯ-rÿ, n., itemized list; rial; rially [site

In-vêrse′, n., direct opposite

In-vêrt′, v., turn upside down, reverse; version

In-vĕst′, v., put money into, install; -ment

In-vĕs′tĭ-gāte, v., examine in detail; tor; tion; tive

In-vĕt′êr-ȧte, a., habitual; acy; -ly

In-vĭd′ĭ-oŭs, a., offensive, harmful; -ly; -ness

In-vĭg′ȯr-āte, v., fill with vigor; tor; tion; tive

In-vĭn′cĭ-ble, a., unconquerable; bility; bly; -ness

In-vīte′, v., ask one to attend, tempt; tation

In′vȯice, n., list of shipped merchandise

In-vōke′, v., call on God in prayer; -r; vocation

In′vȯ-lūte, a., complicated, curled in spiral; tion

In-vŏlve′, v., include, complicate, occupy, draw into; -ment; -d

In′wȧrd, adj., inside; -ly; -ness

I′ȯ-dīne, n., chemical element, antiseptic; dize; dous

I′ȯn, n., electrically charged atom; -ize; -ic

i-ō′tȧ, n., Greek letter, small quantity

i-rāte′, a., angry; -ly; -ness

īre, n., anger; -ful; -fully; -fulness

ĭr-ĭ-dĕs′cėnt, a., showing shining colors; cence; -ly [part of eye

ī′rĭs, n., flower, colored

îrk, v., annoy; -some

ī′ron (êrn), n., strong metal, pressing device, strength; v., press cloths

ī′ron-clăd (êrn), a., fixed

ī′rȯ-nÿ, n., the opposite of what is said, done or expected; ronical; ronically

ĭr-rā′dĭ-āte, v., light up, make clear; tor; tion; tive

ĭr′rĭ-gāte, v., supply with water by ditches; tor; tion; tive; gable

ĭr′rĭ-tȧ-ble, a., easily annoyed; bly; -ness; bility

ĭr′rĭ-tāte, v., annoy, anger, make sore; tion; tive

I
K

ĭr-rŭpt', v., burst violently -ion; -ive

is'lănd (ī), n., land mass surrounded by water; -er

isle (īl), n., small island

is'lĕt (ī), n., very small island [theory, system

ism (ĭzĕm), n., doctrine,

ĭ'so-lāte, v., keep apart; tor; tion; lable

ĭ-so-môr'phĭsm, n., similarity of different things or beings; phic

ĭs'sūe (ĭsh), n., result, offspring, disputed point; v., emerge, give out, publish; suance; suable; suably

ĭsth'mŭs, n., narrow land strip joining two land masses

ĭt, pro., animal or thing being referred to

ĭ-tăl'ĭc, a., of slanted type; -s; -ize; -ization

ĭtch, n., skin irritation, restless desire; -y a.; -iness; -ily

ĭ'tĕm, n., specific thing; -ize; -ization

ĭt'ĕr-āte, v., repeat; tion; tive; ant [ancy; -ly

ĭ-tĭn'ĕr-ănt, a., travelling;

ĭ-tĭn'ĕr-ār-ў, n., trip route

ĭ'vŏ-rў, n., elephant tusk, creamy white

ĭ'vў, n., climbing vine

J

jăb, v. poke, punch

jăb'bĕr, n., v., chatter; -er

jăck, n., lifting device, playing card of page boy, electrical plug; v., raise

jăck'ăss, n., male donkey, fool

jăck'ĕt, n., short coat

jăck'knife, n., large pocket knife [sional

jăck'lĕg, a., unprofes-

jăck'-ŏ'-lăn-tĕrn, n., hollow pumpkin with face cut out [stakes

jăck'pŏt, n., cumulative

jāde, n., green stone; v.,

tire; a., green

jăg, n., spree

jăg'uăr, n., large spottec cat

jăl'ŏu-siē, n., window or door with movable slats

jăm, n., fruit spread, (coll.) predicament, crowding; v., squeeze, crush

jămb, n., side frame o: doorway [tior

jăm-bŏ-rēe', n., celebra-

jăn'gle, n., harsh sound, quarrel [taker

jăn'ĭ-tŏr, n., building care

jâr, n., cylindrical container, jolt, grating sound; v., shock, shake

jâr'gŏn, n., incoherent speech, dialect; -ize

jăun'dĭce, n., liver disease, yellowing of skin

jäunt, n., short trip

jăv'e-lĭn, n., light spear

jăzz, n., strong rhythmic music; -y a.

jĕal'oŭs, a., resentfully suspicious, envy; -y; -ly; -ness [twilled cotton

jēans, n., pl., pants of

jēep, n., small, rugged automotive vehicle

jēer, n., v., mock, ridicule

jĕ-jūne', a., dull; -ly; -ness

jĕl'lў, n., coagulated fruit syrup [creature

jĕl'lў-fĭsh, n., jellylike sea

jĕop'ărd-īze, v., risk; ardy a.

jêrk, n., abrupt movement; v., pull suddenly; -y a.

jêr'sĕy, n., soft, knitted cloth

jĕt, n., powerful spray, jet-propelled airplane; a., black

jĕt'tĭ-sŏn, v., lighten load

jĕt'tў, n., wall or pier in water

jew'ĕl, n., gem, precious thing or person; -er; -ry

jībe, v., shift course, agree

jĭg'gle, v., shake slightly; gly

jĭlt, v., reject a lover

jĭnx, n., (coll.) bad luck

jĭt'tĕr, v., be nervous; -y a.;

teriness

jŏb′bêr, *n.,* distributor of goods, middleman

jŏck′ĕy, *n.,* race horse rider; *v.,* maneuver

jŏc′ū-lȧr, *a.,* joking; **-ity; -ly**

jŏc′ŭnd, *a.,* merry; **-ity; -ly**

jŏdh′pûr, *n., pl.,* riding pants

jŏg, *n.,* notched part; *v.,* nudge, go at slow steady pace; **-ger**

jŏin, *v.,* connect, unite, become a part of; **-er**

jŏint, *n.,* place where two parts connect; *a.,* shared; **-ly**

jŏist, *n.,* beams holding up floor planks

jōke, *n.,* funny thing; *v.,* make fun; **-r**

jŏl′lў, *a.,* gay; **lity; lify; liness; lily**

jŏlt, *n., v.,* jerk, shake; **-er; -y** *a.;* **-ingly**

jŏs′tle, *v.,* shove; **-r**

jŏunce, *v.,* shake; **jouncy** *a.*

joûr′nȧl, *n.,* diary, record of happenings, periodical; **-ize**

joûr′nȧl-ĭsm, *n.,* occupation of news media; **nalist; nalistic; nalistically**

joûr′nĕy, *n.,* trip; *v.,* travel

jŏust, *n., v.,* fight with lances on horseback

joy (jŏi), *n.,* happiness; **-ful; -fully; -fulness; -ous; -ously; -ousness; -less; -lessly; -lessness**

jū′bĭ-lȧnt, *a.,* elated; **lance; late; lation; -ly**

jŭdge, *n., v.,* (one who is designated to) hear and decide law cases; **-ship**

jū-dĭ′ciȧl, *a.,* of judge or law court; **-ly**

jŭg, *n.,* liquid container

jŭg′gle, *v.,* perform skillful tricks; **-r; -ry**

jŭg′ū-lȧr, *a.,* of neck

jūice, *n.,* liquid of fruit or vegetable; **juicy** *a.*

jŭm′ble, *v.,* mix, confuse

jŭmp, *v.,* leap, move suddenly; **-er; -y** *a.*

jŭmp′ĕr, *n.,* sleeveless dress [ing

jŭnc′tion, *n.,* place of join-

jŭn′gle, *n.,* tropical forest

jŭnk, *n.,* worthless stuff, trash, Chinese boat; *v.,* throw away

jŭn′kĕt, *n.,* pleasure trip, milky dessert

jŭn′tȧ, *n.,* council

jû-rĭs-dĭc′tion, *n.,* authority; **-al; -ally**

jû-rĭs-prŭ′dĕnce, *n.,* science of law; **dential; dentially**

jŭst, *a.,* upright, fair, correct; *adv.,* exactly, only, nearly; **-ly; -ness**

jŭs′tĭ-fў, *v.,* show to be fair, make excuse for; **fier; fication; fiable; fiability; fiably**

jŭt, *v.,* stick out

jūte, *n.,* strong fiber

jū′vĕn-ile, *n.,* child; *a.,* young, of youth; **nility**

jŭx-tȧ-pōse′, *v.,* put side by side; **position**

K

kai′sêr, *n.,* emperor

kāle, *n.,* cabbagelike vegetable

kȧ-leī′dȯ-scōpe, *n.,* tube showing changing designs of colored glass

kăn-gȧ-rōo, *n.,* leaping animal [like insect

kā′tў-dĭd, *n.,* grasshopper-

kaў′ăk, *n.,* Eskimo canoe

kē′ȧ, *n.,* parrot

kēēn, *a.,* sharp, eager, strong; **-ly; -ness**

kēēp, *n.,* food and shelter; *v.,* adhere to, protect, mantain, hold, continue; **-er; -ing** *n.*

kēēp′sāke, *n.,* memento

kĕg, *n.,* small barrel

kĕlp, *n.,* seaweed

kĕn, *n.,* knowledge

kêr′chĭef, *n.,* scarf

kêr′nĕl, *n.,* a grain, core

kĕr'ó-sēne, *n.,* oil from petroleum

kĕtch'ŭp, *n.,* tomato sauce

kĕt'tle, *n.,* cooking pot

kĕt'tle-drŭm, *n.,* large copper drum

kēy, *n.,* device to work a lock, lever, explanation, low island, musical tone; *a.,* essential

kēy'nōte, *n.,* basic note of musical scale; *a.,* main

kēy'stōne, *n.,* top stone of arch, main part

khä'kĭ, *n., a.,* dull yellowish-brown, tan

kĭck, *n., v.,* strike with foot, recoil; **-er**

kĭck'băck, *n.,* sudden reaction, illegal return of money

kĭd'năp, *v.,* seize and hold person for ransom; **-per**

kĭd'nĕy, *n.,* organ that excretes urine

kĭll, *v.,* make die, destroy; **-er; -ing** *n.*

kĭln, *n.,* pottery oven

kĭl'ó-grăm, *n.,* 1000 grams, 2.2 pounds

kĭ-lŏ'mĕ-têr, *n.,* 1000 meters, ⅝ mile

kĭl'ó-wätt, *n.,* 1000 watts

kĭlt, *n.,* pleated skirt

kĭl'têr, *n.,* (coll.) proper order

kĭ-mō'nó, *n.,* loose robe

kĭn, *n.,* relatives, family; **-ship**

kĭnd, *n.,* sort, type, class

kĭnd, *a.,* gentle, good; **-ly; -ness; -less**

kĭn'dêr-gâr-tĕn, *n.,* class for preschool children

kĭn'dlĭng, *n.,* bits of wood to start fire

kĭn-ĕs-thĕt'ĭc, *a.,* of muscular activity

kĭng, *n.,* male ruler; **-dom; -ly**

kĭng'lĕt, *n.,* songbird

kĭnk, *n.,* curl, twist; **-y** *a.*

kĭ'ŏsk, *n.,* small open building   [imal hide

kĭp, *n.,* small untanned an-

kĭp'pêr, *n.,* smoked herring

kĭss, *n., v.,* caress with lips; **-er**

kĭt, *n.,* carrying case, set of tools, equipment

kĭtch'ĕn, *n.,* room for cooking; **-er**

kīte, *n.,* paper-covered frame flown in wind

kĭt'tÿ, *n.,* kitten, pooled money, poker stakes

kĭ'wĭ, *n.,* flightless bird

klätch, *n.,* (coll.) informal gathering

klĕp-tò-mā'nĭ-à, *n.,* impulse to steal; **-c** *n.*

knăck, *n.,* ability

knăp'săck, *n.,* bag carried on back   [**knavish**

knāve, *n.,* rascal; **-ry;**

knēad, *v.,* squeeze and press

knēel, *v.,* bend on knee

knĭck'êrs, *n.,* pants ending and gathered below knee

knīfe, *n.,* cutting or stabbing blade with handle

knight, *n.,* medieval soldier, honorary rank; **-hood; -ly**

knĭt, *v.,* loop yarn with needles, unit; **-ter; -ting** *n.*   [*a.*

knŏb, *n.,* round handle, **-by**

knŏck, *n., v.,* hit, rap, (make) pounding noise

knŏck'à-bout, *n.,* sailboat; *a.,* boisterous

knŏt, *n.,* tangled thread; *v.,* intertwine, tie, unite; **-ter; -ted**

knōw, *v.,* be sure of, aware of or acquainted with; **-er; -ing** *a.;* **-able**

knōw'hŏw, *n.,* skill

knŏwl'ĕdge, *n.,* information, awareness; **-able; -ability; -ably; -ableness**

knŭck'le, *n.,* finger joint

knûrl, *n., v.,* knot; **-ed; -y** *a.*

kō-à'là, *n.,* small bear

kō'dĭ-ăk, *n.,* very large brown bear

kō'shêr, *a.,* edible by Jewish dietary laws

kōw'tōw', *v.,* show submissive respect

krýp'tŏn, *n.,* gaseous element   [citrus fruit

kŭm'quăt,*n.,* small orange

L

lā'bĕl, *n.,* descriptive tag, or word, title; *v.,* mark, tag, call; **-er**

lā'bĭ-ŭm, *n.,* lip; **bial**

lā'bŏr, *n.,* job, all worker, childbirth; *v.,* work; **-er**

lăb'o-rȧ-tô-rȳ,*n.,* place for scientific work

lăb'ȳ-rĭnth,*n.,* maze

lāce,*n.,* string to tie shoe, fancy open work fabric; **lacing** *n.;* **lacy** *a.*

lăc'êr-āte, *v.,* tear jaggedly, hurt; **tion; erable**

lāce'wĭng,*n.,* insect

lăch'rȳ-môse, *a.,* tearful, sad; **mal**

lăck-ȧ-dāī'sĭ-cȧl, *a.,* lacking vigor; **-ly**

lăck'ēy, *n.,* low servant, follower

lȧ-cŏn'ĭc, *a.,* brief; **-ally**

lăc'quêr, *n.,* varnish, polished finish

lȧ-crŏss', *n.,* sport with webbed sticks and ball

lăc'tĭc, *a.,* of milk

lād'dêr, *n.,* climbing device with rungs for stepping

lād'ĭng,*n.,* cargo

lā'dle, *n.,* cuplike spoon

lā'dȳ, *n.,* woman, polite woman; **-like** *a.*   [tle

lā'dȳ-bŭg,*n.,* spotted bee-

lăg, *v.,* fall behind

lăg'gȧrd, *n.,* slow person

lȧ-gōon', *n.,* shallow lake or pond, water inside atoll

lāir, *n.,* animal's den

lā'ĭ-tȳ, *n.,* laymen as a group   [water

lāke, *n.,* enclosed body of

lā'mȧ, *n.,* Buddhist monk

lāme, *a.,* crippled, weak; **-ly; -ness**

lȧ-mĕnt', *v.,* mourn, grieve; **-ed; -ation; -able; -ably**

lăm'ĭ-nāte, *v.,* form into or cover with thin layers; **tor; tion; -d**

lămp, *n.,* device for producing light

lăm'pōon, *n.,* satire; *v.,* mock   [mal

lăm'prēy, *n.,* eellike ani-

lănce,*n.,* long spear; **-r**

lănd,*n.,* solid part of earth, soil, ground; *v.,* go on shore, catch; **-ed**

lăn'dȧu, *n.,* carriage

lănd'lôrd, *n.,* property leaser

lănd'scāpe, *n.,* natural scenery; *v.,* plant lawns and gardens

lănd'slīde, *n.,* sliding down of land, great victory   [road

lāne, *n.,* narrow path or

lăn'guȧge, *n.,* means of communication, speech

lăn'guĭsh, *v.,* become weak, suffer; **-er; -ment**

lănk, *a.,* tall and lean; **-y** *a.;* **-ly; -ness**

lăn'o-lĭn, *n.,* oil from wool as ointment base

lăn'têrn, *n.,* portable case for light

lăn'yȧrd, *n.,* rope, cord

lȧ-pĕl', *n.,* folded part of coat's front

lăp'ĭ-dār-ȳ,*n.,* gem expert

lăpse, *n.,* fault, passing of time; *v.,* backslide, fall end; **-r; lapsable**

lâr'cė-nȳ,*n.,* theft

lârch,*n.,* pine tree

lârd,*n.,* melted hog fat

lârd'êr, *n.,* pantry, food supplies

lârge-mĭnd-ĕd,*a.,* tolerant

lâr-gĕss', *n.,* generous giving   [at end

lăr'ĭ-ȧt, *n.,* rope with loop

lârk, *n.,* songbird, fun

lâr'vȧ, *n.,* immature insect

lâr'ȳnx, *n.,* voice organ at top of windpipe; **yngeal; yngitis**

lȧs-cĭv'ĭ-oŭs, *a.,* lustful; **-ly; -ness**

lā'sêr, *n.,* device emitting intense light

L
M

lăsh, *n.,* whip, whip stroke; *v.,* strike, tie with rope; **-ing** *n.*

lăs'sĭ-tūde, *n.,* tiredness

lăst, *n.,* end; *v.,* continue; *a.,* most recent, final; **-ly**

lătch, *n.,* door fastener of bar fitting into notch

lā'tènt, *a.,* undeveloped, hidden; **tency; -ly**

lăt'êr-ál, *a.,* sideways; **-ly**

lā'tĕx, *n.,* milky plant or tree liquid

lāthe, *n.,* machine for shaping wood, metal, etc.

lăth'êr, *n., v.,* foam; **-y** *a.*

lăt'ĭ-tūde, *n.,* distance in degrees from equator, scope, freedom; **dinal; dinally**

lăt-ĭ-tū-dĭ-nār'ĭ-án, *a.,* very tolerant; **-ism**

là-trīne', *n.,* toilet

lăt'tĭce, *n.,* criss-crossed wooden bars

lăud, *n., v.,* praise; **-ation; -atory; -able; -ability; -ably**

lăugh, *v.,* express merriment orally; **-able; -ably**

lăunch, *v.,* send off, start; **-er**

lăun'dêr, *v.,* wash and iron (clothes); **-er; dress; dry**

lău'rē-àte, *n.,* one honored

lâu'rèl, *n.,* flowering evergreen, *(pl.)* fame

lăv'à-tô-rў, *n.,* wash room

lăv'ĭsh, *v.,* spend freely; *a.,* more than enough; **-ly; -ness**

lăw, *n.,* rules of conduct, obedience, legal profession; **-ful; -fully; -fulness; -less, -lessly; -lessness**

lăwn, *n.,* grass-covered land

lăx'à-tĭve, *n.,* substance to loosen bowels

lāy, *v.,* put down, place, produce eggs

lāy, *a.,* not professional; **laic; -man**

lāy'êr, *n.,* single thickness

lāy-ĕtte', *n.,* infant's full outfit

lāy'ŏff, *n.,* temporary discharge of workers

lā'zў, *a.* not eager to work, sluggish; **lazily; laziness**

lēa, *n.,* meadow

lēad, *n.,* first place, clue, main role; *v.,* guide, be first, spend; **-er; -ership; -ing** *n., a.*

lĕad, *n.,* metallic element, bullets, graphite

lēaf, *n.,* flat, green outgrowth of plant stem, page; **-age; -y** *a.*

lēague, *n.,* association, three miles

lēan, *v.,* incline, slant, rely, tend; **-er; -ing** *n.*

lēan, *a.,* with little fat, meager; **-ness; -ly**

lēap, *v.,* spring through air, jump; **-er**

lēarn, *v.,* get knowledge of; **-er; -ing** *n.;* **-ed; -able**

lēase, *n.,* rental contract; *v.,* rent, hire

lēash, *n.,* line to hold animal, ex. dog

lēath'êr, *n.,* tanned animal skin; **-y** *a.*

lēave, *n.,* permission; *v.,* remain, entrust, go

lĕav'én, *n.,* fermented dough, yeast; **-ing** *n.*

lĕch'êr, *n.,* lewd man; **-y; -ous; -ously; -ousness**

lĕc'têrn, *n.,* reading stand

lĕc'tûre, *n.,* informative talk, speech, scolding; **-r** [shelf

lĕdge, *n.,* narrow edge,

lĕdg'êr, *n.,* account book

lēe, *n.,* shelter from wind

lēech, *n.,* bloodsucking worm, parasite [ble

lēek, *n.,* onionlike vegeta-

lēer, *n.,* malicious look

lēe'wăy, *n.,* additional time or space

lĕg'à-cў, *n.,* inheritance

lē'găl, *a.,* of law or lawyers, permitted; **-ity; -Ize; -ization; -ly**

lè-gā'tion, *n.,* envoy and

staff and residence

lĕg′énd, *n.,* traditional tale, map key; **-ary**

lĕg′ĭ-ble, *a.,* that can be read; **bility; bly**

lē′gĭon, *n.,* military division, large number; **-ary**

lĕg′ĭs-lāte, *v.,* make laws; **tor; tion; tive; tively**

lė-gĭt′ĭ-máte, *a.,* lawful, born of a married couple; **macy; tion; mize; -ly** [pods; **minous**

lĕg′ūme, *n.,* plant with

lēi′sûre, *n.,* free time; *a.,* idle; **-ly** [rus fruit

lĕm′ón, *n.,* sour yellow cit-

lĕngth, *n.,* measure from end to end, distance, duration; **-en; -y** *a.*

lē′nĭ-ėnt, *a.,* kind, merciful; **ency; ence; -ly**

lĕns, *n.,* curved glass for adjusting light rays, focusing part of eye

lĕop′árd, *n.,* large spotted wild cat

lē′ò-târd, *n.,* one-piece, tight garment

lĕp′rė-chaun (kön), *n.,* elf in form of old man

lĕp′rò-sỹ, *n.,* disease of skin and nerves; **leper; rous**

lē′sion, *n.,* bodily injury

lĕs′sòn, *n.,* something learned, instruction

lĕst, *conj.,* in case

lĕt, *v.,* allow, rent, cause, leave [ment

lĕt′doˉwn, *n.,* disappoint-

lē′thàl, *a.,* deadly; **-ity; -ly**

lĕth′ár-gỹ, *n.,* lack of energy; **gic; gize**

lĕt′tèr, *n.,* written message, character of alphabet

leū-kē′mĭ-á, *n.,* cancer of the blood; **mic** [bank

lĕv′ēe, *n.,* built-up river

lĕv′ėl, *n.,* device for determining plane's evenness, horizontal plane, rank; *a.,* even, flat; **-ness; -ly**

lĕv′êr, *n.,* bar on support used to lift, **-age** [huge

lė-vī′á-thán, *n.,* anything

lĕv′ĭ-tāte, *v.,* rise or float in air; **tor; tion**

lĕv′ĭ-tỹ, *n.,* improper gaiety

lĕv′ÿ, *n.,* tax; *v.,* impose and collect (tax); **leviable** [**-ly**

leˉwd, *a.,* obscene; **-ness;**

lĕx′ĭ-còn, *n.,* dictionary

lī′á-ble, *a.,* legally responsible, likely; **bility**

lī′ài-sòn, *n.,* connection for coordination

lī′ár, *n.,* one who tells lies

lī′bél, *n.,* malicious statement written to harm one's reputation; **-er; -ee; -ous; -ously**

lĭb′êr-ál, *a.,* generous, large, tolerant, for reform; **-ity; -ly; -ness; -ism; -ize; -izer; -ization**

lĭb′êr-āte, *v.,* set free; **tor; tion** [person

lĭb′êr-tĭne, *n.,* immoral

lĭb′êr-tỹ, *n.,* freedom, particular right, familiarity

lī′brār-ỹ, *n.,* book collection; **brarian** [era; **tist**

lĭ-brĕt′tō, *n.,* words of op-

lī′cénse, *n.,* legal permit, freedom from rules; **-r; -e**

lī′chen (kén), *n.,* mosslike plant; **-ous**

lĭc′ĭt, *a.,* legal; **-ly; -ness**

lĭck, *v.,* pass tongue over, (coll.) defeat; **-ing** *n.*

lĭc′ò-rĭce (rĭsh), *n.,* black, sweet flavoring

lĭd, *n.,* movable top

līe, *n.,* false statement; *v.,* tell falsehood, rest in flat position

lieū-tĕn′ànt, *n.,* officer

life, *n.,* existence, vigor, activity [ship

life′bōat, *n.,* small boat on

life′guârd, *n.,* swimming supervisor

lĭft, *v.,* raise, (coll.) steal; **-er** [necting bones

lĭg′á-mėnt, *n.,* tissue con-

light, *n.,* energy that stimulates sight, brightness, light source, knowledge; *v.,* brighten, set fire; *a.,* bright, fair; **-er; -en; -ness**

light, *a.*, not heavy, mild, gay, dizzy; **-en; -ly; -ness**

light-heârt'èd, *a.*, gay; **-ly; -ness** [to guide ships

light'hoŭse, *n.*, light tower

light'ning, *n.*, flash of electricity in sky

lig'nē-oŭs, *a.*, woody

like, *a.*, similar; *prep.*, similar to, for example; *con.*, as; **-n; -ness**

like, *v.*, be fond of, wish

like'lÿ, *a.*, probable; *adv.*, probably

li'lâc, *n.*, flowering shrub, pale purple

lilt, *n.*, light, swingy rhythm

lim'bêr, *a.*, easy to bend

lim'bō, *n.*, place of oblivion

lime, *n.*, sour green citrus fruit, substance from limestone [position

lime'light, *n.*, prominent

lim'êr-ick, *n.*, nonsense poem of five lines

lime'stóne, *n.*, rock of calcium carbonate

lim'it, *n.*, end place or point; *v.*, restrict; **-er; -ation; -ative; -ary; -ed; -less**

lim'ou-sine, *n.*, large luxury automobile

limp, *v.*, walk lamely; **-er**

limp'ét, *n.*, mollusk

lim'pïd, *a.*, clear; **-ity; -ness; -ly**

line, *n.*, rope, wire, etc., long thin mark, border, series, path, stock of goods; **-ar** *a.*

lin'ē-àge, *n.*, ancestry; **eal; eality; eally**

lin'én, *n.*, fabric of flax

lin'gêr, *v.*, stay; **-er; -ing; -ingly**

lin-ge-rie' (làn-zē-rā'), *n.*, lady's underwear

lin'gō, *n.*, jargon

lin-guis'tic, *a.*, of language; **guist; -s; -ally**

lin'ï-mént, *n.*, medicated liquid for skin

lin'ïng, *n.*, inside covering

link, *n.*, loop of chain, connection; *v.*, join; **-age**

lin'nèt, *n.*, songbird

li-nō'lē-ŭm. *n.*, floor covering

lin'sēed, *n.*, seed of flax

lint, *n.*, cotton fiber, thread bits [brave

li'ón-heârt-èd, *a.*, very

lip'stïck, *n.*, small stick of paste to color lips

liq'uė-fÿ, *v.*, change to liquid; **fier; fiable**

li-queûr', *n.*, sweet alcoholic beverage

liq'uïd (wïd), *n.*, *a.*, (substance) that flows easily

liq'uï-dāte, *v.*, settle debt, convert to cash; **tor; tion**

liq'uŏr, *n.*, alcoholic drink

list, *n.*, series of items; *v.*, set forth list, tilt, lean

lis'tén, *v.*, hear, pay attention; **-er** [-ness

list'lèss, *a.*, spiritless; **-ly;**

li'têr, *n.*, metric measure of volume [-ity; -ly

lit'êr-àl, *a.*, exact, factual;

lit'êr-à-tûre, *n.*, writings, books; **ary**

lithe, *a.*, limber; **-ness; -ly**

lith'ï-ŭm, *n.*, metallic element

li-thŏg'rà-phÿ, *n.*, printing process; **graph** *n.*, *v.*; **pher; graphic; graphically**

li-thŏl'ó-gÿ, *n.*, study of rocks; **logic; logical; logically**

lit-ï-gā'tion, *n.*, lawsuit; **gable; gious; giously**

lit'ur-gÿ, *n.*, religious ritual for worship; **gist; gical; gically**

live, *v.*, have life, endure, reside; **livable**

live'lï-hóod, *n.*, way of supporting life, work

live'lÿ, *a.*, full of life, energetic, gay, vivid

liv'êr, *n.*, glandular organ secreting bile

liv'êr-ÿ, *n.*, care of horses for a fee. [animals

live'stóck, *n.*, domestic

liv'ïd, *a.*, bruised, pale,

(coll.) furious; **-ity; -ness**

lōad, n., amount carried, burden; v., fill, add to; **-er; -ing** n.; **-ed**

lōaf, n., mass of baked bread

lōaf, v., waste time; **-er**

lōaf'êr, n., moccasinlike shoe

lōam, n., rich soil

lōan, n., something lent; v., lend

lōathe, v., hate; **-r; ing** n.

lŏb'bў, n., entrance hall

lŏb'bў, n., group influencing legislator; **-ist**

lōbe, n., rounded projection

lŏb'stêr, n., sea animal with large claws

lō'căl, n., organization chapter; a., of a particular place; **-ity; -ize; -ization; -ly**

lō'cāte, v., find, establish, place; **-r; tion**

lŏck, n., fastening device, canal section, hair curl v., fasten, jam

lŏck'jäw, n., tetanus

lō-cȯ-mō'tion, n., movement; **tive** [gine

lō-cȯ-mō'tĭve, n., train engine

lō'cŭst, n., grasshopperlike insect, tree

lŏdge, n., small house or hotel, local chapter; v., house, be placed; **-r**

lŏft, n., atticlike space

lŏg, n., tree section, record of journey

lōge, n., theater box

lŏg'ĭc, n., reasoning, science of reasoning; **-al; -ally**

lŏĭn, n., back from ribs to hips [**-er**

lŏĭ'têr, v., spend time idly;

lŏll, v., lounge, hang down

lōne, a., by oneself; **-ly** a.

lŏng, v., wish; **-ing** n.

lŏng, a., having great length, too much time

lŏn'gĭ-tūde, n., east or west distance across earth; **dinal; dinally**

lŏng'shôre-măn, n., dock worker

lōōk'ōut, n., careful watching, sentry

lōōm, n., weaving machine v., come into sight

lōōp, n., line, string, etc. that curves back over itself

lōōp'hōle, n., means of evasion or escape

lōōt, n., stolen goods; v., steal; **-er**

lŏp, v., cut off; **-per** [**-r**

lōpe, n., long easy stride;

lŏp'sĭd-ėd, a., unbalanced; **-ly; -ness**

lō-quā'cioŭs, a., talkative; **city; -ness; -ly**

lôrd, n., master, nobleman, (Lord) God; **-ly; -ship**

lôre, n., knowledge

lose (lūs), v., become unable to find, fail to keep or win; **-r; losable**

lŏss, n., defeat, ruin, failure to keep, waste

lŏt, n., fate, chance decision, share, piece of land, great number

lō'tion, n., liquid for skin

lŏt'têr-ў, n., game of selling chances on prizes

lō'tŭs, n., water lily

lōŭd'spēak-êr, n., device to amplify sound

lōŭnge, n., v., (place to) rest or relax

lōŭs'ў, a., having lice, (coll.) dirty, poor; **lousily lousiness**

lōŭ'vêr, n., slanted boards in opening for air

lŏve, n., great fondness for, devotion; v., show love, delight in; **-r; lovable; lovably; loving; lovingly**

lōw'êr, v., put down, make less; a., below another, inferior, less

lōw'lў, a., of low rank, humble, softly; **liness**

loy'ăl (lŏĭ), a., faithful; **-ty; -ly**

lū'brĭ-cāte, v., make smooth, apply oil or grease; **tor; tion; tive;**

cant *n.* [-ness; -ly
lū′cĭd, *a.*, sane, clear; **-ity;**
lŭck, *n.*, good fortune; **-y**
a.; -ity; -iness; -less
lū′crá-tĭve, *a.*, profitable;
-ly; -ness
lū′cŭ-brāte, *v.*, write or
study laboriously; **tion**
lū′dĭ-croŭs, *a.*, absurd; -ly;
-ness
lŭg′gáge, *n.*, suitcases,
trunks, etc.
lū-gū′brĭ-oŭs, *a.*, mournful; -ly; -ness
lŭll, *n.*, short quiet period;
v., soothe, calm
lŭm′bêr, *n.*, building
wood; *v.*, move heavily
lŭ-mĭ-nĕs′cênce, *n.*, giving off light; **cent**
lŭmp, *n.*, solid mass,
swelling; *v.*, group together; -y *a.;* -iness
lū′nár, *a.*, of the moon
lū′ná-tĭc, *n.*, *a.*, (person
who is) insane; **nacy**
lŭng, *n.*, body organ for
breathing
lŭnge, *n.*, sudden thrust
lûrch, *n.*, danger; *v.*, sway
suddenly
lū′rĭd, *a.*, shocking, horrible -ly; -ness
lûrk, *v.*, stay hidden ready
to attack [-ly; -ness
lŭs′cioŭs, *a.*, delicious;
lŭst, *n.*, strong craving,
sexual desire; **-ful;**
-fully; -fulness; -y *a.;*
-ily -iness
lŭs′têr, *n.*, brightness,
frame; **trous; trously;**
trousness [ment
lūte, *n.*, guitarlike instru-
lŭx′ū-rŷ, *n.*, costly comfort
or pleasure; **rious;**
riously; riousness
lŷe, *n.*, strong alkali
lŷmph, *n.*, clear, yellowish
body fluid; **-atic**
lŷnch, *v.*, kill by mob; **-er;**
-ing *n.*
lŷnx, *n.*, wildcat
lŷre, *n.*, small harplike instrument
lŷr′ĭ-cĭst, *n.*, writer of words
in song

M

má-cá′brė, *a.*, gruesome
mác-ăd′ám, *n.*, road made
of crushed stone; **-ize**
măc-á-rō′nĭ, *n.*, tubular
noodles
má-cãw′, *n.*, large parrot
māce, *n.*, official staff,
spice
măc′êr-āte, *v.*, soften and
break down; **tor; tion**
măch-ĭ-nā′tion (măk), *n.*,
evil scheme
má-chīne′, *n.*, device with
moving parts to do work;
chinist; -ry
măck′êr-ėl, *n.*, edible fish
măc′rá-me (mā), *n.*, art of
knotting thread into
designs [verse; -ic
măc′ró-cŏsm, *n.*, uni-
măc-ró-scŏp′ĭc, *a.*, visible
to naked eye
măd, *a.*, insane, frantic,
foolish, angry; **-ness;**
-den; -ly [woman
măd′ám, *n.*, polite title for
măd′căp, *n.*, reckless
person [cloth
măd′rás, *n.*, fine cotton
măd′rĭ-gál, *n.*, song with
many singing parts
maes′trō (mīs), *n.*, composer, orchestra conductor
măg-á-zīne′, *n.*, periodical
publication, storage
place [plish-red
má-gĕn′tá, *n.*, *a.*, pur-
măg′gŏt, *n.*, wormlike insect larva
măg′ĭc, *n.*, use of charms,
spells, tricks of illusion;
-ian *n.;* **-al; -ally**
măg′ĭs-trāte, *n.*, judge;
tracy; tratical
măg′má, *n.*, liquid or molten rock
măg-năn′ĭ-moŭs, *a.*, generous; **nimity; -ly**
măg′nāte, *n.*, influential
person [very metal
măg-nē′sĭ-ŭm, *n.*, light silver-
măg′nėt, *n.*, iron or steel
that attracts iron or steel;
-ism; -ize; -ic; -ically

măg-nĭf'ĭ-cĕnt, *a.,* splendid; **cence; -ly**

măg'nĭ-fÿ, *v.,* make larger; **fier; fication**

măg'nĭ-tūde, *n.,* greatness of size or influence

măg-nō'lĭ-à, *n.,* flowering tree

măg'pĭe, *n.,* kind of crow

mà-hŏg'à-nÿ, *n.,* tree, dark, heavy wood

māid, *n.,* young woman, female servant

māil, *n.,* letters, packages, etc., postal system; *v.,* send by mail; **-man; -er; -ing** *n.;* **-able; -ability**

māil, *n.,* metal mesh armor

māim, *v.,* cripple, disable; **-er** [portant; **-ly**

māin, *a.,* chief, most im-

māin-tāin', *v.,* continue, keep in repair, support; **tenance**

māize, *n.,* corn, yellow

māj'ĕs-tÿ, *n.,* dignity, grandeur, ruler's title; **tic; tical, tically**

mā'jŏr, *n.,* military officer, main subject; *a.,* main, greater [half

mà-jŏr'ĭ-tÿ, *n.,* more than

māke, *n.,* brand; style; *v.,* bring into being, cause to be, amount to, earn, perform, force; **-r; ing** *n.*

māke'shĭft, *a.,* temporary

māke'-ŭp, *n.,* construction, nature, cosmetics

măl-à-drŏit', *a.,* awkward; **-ly; -ness**

măl'à-dÿ, *n.,* disease

măl'à-prŏp, *n.,* ludicrous misuse of words; **-ism**

mà-lār'ĭ-à, *n.,* infectious disease; **-l; ious**

măl'cŏn-tĕnt, *a.,* dissatisfied

mà-lĕf'ĭ-cĕnt, *a.,* harmful; **cence**

mà-lĕv'ò-lĕnt, *a.,* wishing evil; **lence; -ly**

măl-fēa'sànce, *n.,* wrongdoing; **sant**

măl'ĭce, *n.,* desire to harm; **cious; ciously; ciousness**

mà-līgn', *v.,* speak evil of; *a.,* evil; **-er**

mà-lĭg'nànt, *a.,* harmful; likely to cause death; **nancy; -ly**

mà-lĭn'gêr, *v.,* fake illness to escape work; **-er**

măll, *n.,* shaded public walk, shopping center

măl'làrd, *n.,* duck

măl'lē-à-ble, *a.,* can be reshaped; **bility; -ness**

măl'lĕt, *n.,* wooden hammer

măl-nū-trĭ'tion, *n.,* faulty diet [improper practice

măl-prăc'tĭce, *n.,* doctor's

mălt, *n.,* barley used in brewing; **-y; -iness**

măm'màl, *n.,* class of animals who feed on milk from breast

măm'mā-rÿ, *a.,* of breast

măm'mòn, *n.,* riches

măm'mŏth, *n.,* extinct elephant; *a.,* huge

măn, *n.,* human being, adult male, human race; *v.,* supply people; **-hood; -ly**

măn'à-cle, *n.,* handcuff

măn'àge, *v.,* control, conduct, operate; **-r; -ment; -able; -ability; -ableness; -ably**

măn'dāte, *n.,* order, people's will; **tory; tary**

măn'dò-lĭn, *n.,* stringed instrument [hair

māne, *n.,* animal long neck

mà-neŭ'vêr, *n.,* planned military movement; *v.,* scheme; **-ability; -able**

măn'gà-nēse, *n.,* grayish metallic element

măn'gêr, *n.,* trough to hold hay

măn'gle, *v.,* disfigure; **-r**

măn'gō, *n.,* tropical fruit

măn'gÿ, *a.,* shabby; **gily; giness**

măn'ĭ-cūre, *n.,* care of fingernails; **curist**

măn'ĭ-fĕst, *n.,* cargo list; *v.,* make clear; *a.,* obvious; **-ation; -able; -ly**

măn-ĭ-fĕs'tō, *n.,* public

L M

declaration

măn'ĭ-fōld, v., multiply; a., many; **-er; -ness; -ly**

mȧ-nĭp'ū-lāte, v., handle, control; **tor; tion; lable; tive; tory**

măn'nê-quĭn, n., model of human body

măn'nêr, n., way, style, behavior, (pl.) social customs; **-less; -ly**

măn'ör, n., large estate

măn'pŏw-êr, n., human strength   [dence

măn'sion, n., large resi-

măn'slaugh-têr, n., accidental killing of person

măn'těl, n., shelf above fireplace

măn'tĭs, n., insect

măn'tle, n., cloak, cover

măn'ū-ȧl, n., handbook; a., of or by hand; **-ly**

măn-ū-făc'tûre, v., make by machinery; **-r**

mȧ-nūre', n., animal waste as fertilizer

măn'ū-scrĭpt, n., author's written composition; a., written by hand

măp, n., drawing of earth's surface or sky; v., make a map, plan

mā'ple, n., tree for wood, sap and shade

mâr, v., damage, spoil

mär'ȧ-boū, n., large stork

mär'ȧ-thŏn, n., foot race, endurance contest

mȧ-räud'êr, n., raider

mär'ble, n., hard ornamental limestone

märch, n., steady advance, progress; v., walk at steady pace; **-er**

māre, n., female horse, sea

mär'gȧ-rĭne, n., butter substitute

mär'gĭn, n., edge, limit, amount in reserve; **-al; -ality; -ally**

mȧ-rĭ-jua'nȧ (wȧ), n., plant, drug

mȧ-rī'nȧ, n., yacht harbor

mär-ĭ-nāde', n., tasty solution to soak food in before cooking; **nate**

mȧ-rīne', n., member of Marine Corps; a., of sea, ships, etc.

mär-ĭ-ȯ-nĕtte', n., puppet operated by strings

mär'ĭ-tȧl, a., of marriage; **-ly**

mâr'jȯ-rȧm, n., spice

mârk, n., visible impression, sign, grade, target; v., make a mark, rate; **-er**

mâr'kĕt, n., place to buy and sell goods; v., sell; **-ing** n.; **-able; -ability**

mârks'mȧn, n., one who shoots well; **-ship**

mär'lĭn, n., deep-sea fish

mȧ-rōon', n., a., brownish red; v., abandon, leave

mär'rōw, n., soft core inside bones

mär'rў, v., join a man and woman legally; **riage; ried; riageable**

mârsh, n., low, wet, soft land; **-y** a.   [official

mâr'shȧl, n., high ranking

mâr-sū'pĭ-ȧl, n., mammal with pouch for young

märt, n., market

mâr'tĕn, n., weasellike animal with valuable fur

mär'tiȧl, a., of war, military; **-ist; -ism; -ly**

mär'tўr, n., one who suffers for beliefs; **-dom; -ize; -ization**

mär'vĕl, n., wonderful thing; v., be amazed; **-ous; -ously; -ousness**

măs-că'rȧ, n., cosmetic to color eyelashes

măs'cŏt, n., thing or animal kept for good luck

măs'cū-lĭne, a., male; **lin-ity; -ly**

măsk, n., covering for face

măs'ŏch-ĭsm, n., pleasure from suffering; **ochist; ochistic; ochistically**

mā'sȯn, n., worker in stone or brick; **-ry**

măs-quêr-āde', n., costume party; **-r**

măss, n., large quantity, lump of matter

măs'sȧ-cre (kêr), n.,

slaughter of many people

măs-săge', *n.,* rubbing or kneading body; **seur** *n.;* **seuse** *n.*

măst, *n.,* pole for ship's sail

măs-tĕc'tō-mȳ, *n.,* surgical removal of breast

măs'tĕr, *n.,* man who rules others, owner, expert; **-ful; -fully; -fulness**

măs'tĕr-pīece, *n.,* great work of art

măs'tĭ-căte, *v.,* chew; **tor; tion; tory**

măs'tŭr-bā-tion, *n.,* sexual self-stimulation; **bate; tor**

măt, *n.* small rug, pad, border around picture

măt'à-dôr, *n.,* bullfighter

mătch, *n.,* small stick that ignites, like thing, contest, marriage; *v.,* mate, be equal

māte, *n.,* one of pair, spouse, ship's officer

mà-tē'rĭ-ȧl, *n.,* what thing is made of, fabric; *a.,* of matter, physical, essential; **-ity; -ize; -ization; -ly**

mà-tĕr'nȧl, *a.,* of or like mother; **nity; -ly**

măt-ĭ-nee' (nā), *n.,* afternoon performance

mā'trĭ-ârch, *n.,* woman as head of family; **-y; -al; -ic** [college; **tion**

mà-trĭc'ū-lāte, *v.,* enroll in

măt'rĭ-mō-nȳ, *n.,* marriage; **nial; nially**

mā'trĭx, *n.,* mold

mā'trȯn, *n.,* married woman, woman supervisor; **-ly; -liness**

măt'tĕr, *n.,* physical substance of thing, importance, trouble

măt'tȯck, *n.,* garden tool

măt'trĕss, *n.,* cloth case used on bed

mà-tūre, *v.,* develop fully; *a.,* full grown, ripe; **ra-tion; rity; -ly; -ness**

măud'lĭn, *a.,* sentimental

māul, *n.,* large hammer; *v.,* beat; **-er** [tomb

māu-sȯ-lē'ŭm, *n.,* large

māuve, *n., a.,* pale purple

măx'ĭm, *n.,* concise principle

măx'ĭ-mŭm, *n.,* upper limit, greatest amount; **mize; mal**

māy-ȯn-nāise', *n.,* creamy salad dressing [**-al**

māy'ȯr, *n.,* head of city;

māze, *n.,* intricate network of paths

mĕad'ōw, *n.,* field of grass

mēa'gêr, *a.,* thin, of poor quality; **-ly; -ness**

mēal, *n.,* time for eating, coarsely ground grain

mēan, *v.,* have in mind, intend; **-ing** *n.;* **-ingful; -ingfully; -ingless; -inglessly; -inglessness**

mēan, *a.,* poor, low, cruel, difficult; **-ness; -ly**

mēan, *n.,* average (*pl.* wealth, resources

mē'ȧn-dêr, *v.,* roam; **drous**

mēa'slĕs, *n.,* contagious disease with red spots; **sly**

mĕas'ûre, *n.,* size, amount, system of dimensions, step, law; *v.,* determine extent of, judge; **-ment; -d**

mēat, *n.,* animal flesh as food, meaning; **-y** *a.;* **-iness; -less**

mȇ-chăn'ĭ-cȧl (kăn), *a.,* of machines; **-ly; nize; nizer; nization**

mĕd'ȧl, *n.,* metal piece as an award; **-ist**

mĕd'dle, *v.,* interfere; **-r**

mē'dĭ-ȧn, *n.,* midpoint; **al; ally**

mē'dĭ-āte, *v.,* settle a dispute; **tor; tion; tive; tory**

mĕd'ĭ-cīne, *n.,* science of disease and health, drug for treatment; **cate; cation; cal; cally; nal; nally**

mȇ-dĭ-ē'vȧl, *a.,* of period (700–1400 A.D.)

L
M

mĕ-dĭ-ō'cre (cêr), *a.*, ordinary, average; **rity**

mĕd'ĭ-tāte, *v.*, think about; **tor; tion; tive**

mē'dĭ-ŭm,*n.*, middle state, culture, agency; *a.*, average [things

mĕd'lĕy, *n.*, mixture of

mēek, *a.*, mild, humble; **-ly; -ness**

mēet, *v.*, come together with, see arrival of, deal with; **-ing** *n.*

mĕg-à-lō-mā'nĭ-à,*n.*, passion for grandeur

mĕg-à-lŏp'ò-lĭs, *n.*, large dense urban area

mĕl'àn-chŏl-ÿ (kŏl), *n.*, sadness; **cholic; choli-cally**

mĕl'iò-rāte, *v.*, improve; **tor; tion; tive; rable**

mĕl'lōw,*a.*, ripe, full, rich

mĕl'ò-drà-mà, *n.*, sensational stage play; **-tist; -tic; -tics; -tically**

mĕl'ò-dÿ, *n.*, tune, song; **dize; lodic; lodically; dious; diously; dious-ness**

mĕl'òn, *n.*, large, juicy, thick-skinned fruit

mĕlt,*v.*, change from solid to liquid, heat, soften; **-age**

mĕm'bêr,*n.*, part of whole, one who officially belongs; **-ship**

mĕm'brāne, *n.*, thin, soft skin layer; **nous; nously**

mė-mĕn'tō, *n.*, souvenir

mĕm-ò-rà-bĭl'ĭ-à, *n.*, things worth remembering [to remind

mĕm-ò-răn'dŭm, *n.*, note

mè-mô'rĭ-àl, *n.*, thing to help one remember; **-ize**

mĕm'ò-rÿ, *n.*, mental power to retain past things

mė-nàg'êr-iē, *n.*, collection of animals

mĕnd, *v.*, repair, improve; **-er; -able**

mĕn-dā'cioŭs, *a.*, not truthful; **dacity; -ly; -ness**

mĕn'dĭ-cànt, *n.*, beggar

mē'nĭ-àl, *a.*, servile, low; **-ly**

mĕn-ĭn-gī'tĭs, *n.*, inflammation of brain tissue

mĕn-strū-ā'tion, *n.*, monthly blood discharge from uterus; **strate; strual**

mĕn-sŭ-rā'tion, *n.*, act of measuring; **able; ability; ral; tive**

mĕn'tàl, *a.*, of the mind, mentally ill; **-ity; -ly**

mĕn'thōl, *n.*, mint derivative

mĕn'tion, *n.*, brief reference; *v.*, speak about; **-able**

mêr'càn-tĭle, *a.*, of merchant or trade

mêr'cè-nār-ÿ, *a.*, interested in money only, greedy

mêr'chàn-dīse, *n.*, goods bought and sold; **-r**

mêr'cŭ-rÿ, *n.*, heavy metallic element; **rial; rially; rialness; ric; rous**

mêr'cÿ, *n.*, kindness, forgiveness; **ciful; cifully; cifulness; ciless; cilessly; cilessness**

mēre, *a.*, only; **-ly**

mêrge, *v.*, combine, mix; **-nce**

mė-rĭd'ĭ-àn, *n.*, highest point, circle through earth's poles

mė-ringue' (răng'), *n.*, beaten eggs and sugar baked

mêr'ĭt, *n.*, worth, honor; *v.*, deserve; **-orious; -oriously; -oriousness; -less**

mêr'māid, *n.*, imaginary creature of half woman and fish

mĕsh,*n.*, net; *v.*, entangle, interlock; **-y** *a.*

mĕs'mêr-īze, *v.*, hypnotize; **-r; zation; ism**

mĕss,*n.*, communal meal, jumble, untidy state; *v.*, make dirty, meddle; **-y** *a.* [cation, idea

měs′såge, *n.*, communi-

mė-tăb′ȯ-lĭsm, *n.*, conversion of food to energy; **lize; bolic**

mět′ål, *n.*, shiny, solid malleable chemical element; **-ist; -ize; -lic; -li-cally**

mět′ål-lûr-gў, *n.*, science of metals; **gist; gic; gi-cal; gically**

mět-å-môr′phȯ-sĭs, *n.*, change in form

mět′å-phôr, *n.*, term or phrase of one meaning applied to another; **-ic; -ical; -ically**

mět-å-phýs′ĭcs, *n.*, philosophy of abstract principles; **ical; ically**

mēte, *v.*, apportion

mē′tē-ör, *n.*, flash of heavenly body entering earth's atmosphere

mē-tē-ör-ŏl′ȯ-gў, *n.*, study of weather and climate; **gist; logical; logically**

mē′têr, *n.*, verse or musical rhythm, unit of length, measuring device; **tric; trical; trically**

měth′āne, *n.*, gas

měth′ȯd, *n.*, orderly procedure; **-ology; ologist; -ical; -ically**

mė-tĭc′ū-loŭs, *a.*, very careful; **losity; -ly; -ness** [city; **itan** *a.*

mė-trŏp′ȯ-lĭs, *n.*, large

mět′tle, *n.*, courage

měz′zå-nīne, *n.*, floor between two main floors

mez′zō (met), *a.*, musical middle [layer

mi′cå, *n.*, mineral of thin

mi′crȯ-cŏsm, *n.*, world in miniature; **-ic; -ically**

mi′crȯ-fĭlm, *n.*, film that copies records in reduced size

mi-crŏm′ė-têr, *n.*, device for measuring tiny distances

mi′crȯ-phōne, *n.*, device that transmits sounds; **phonic**

mi′crȯ-scōpe, *n.*, device

that enlarges tiny objects

mĭd′dle, *a.*, halfway between two things

mĭd′dle-măn, *n.*, trader who buys from producer and sells to retailer

mĭdge, *n.*, gnatlike insect

mĭdg′ėt, *n.*, very small person; *a.*, miniature

mĭd′rĭff, *n.*, body part between chest and abdomen

mĭd′shĭp-mån, *n.*, student at U.S. Naval Academy

mĭd′wĭfe, *n.*, woman who helps another in childbirth; **-ry**

miēn, *n.*, one's manner

mĭght, *n.*, strength; **-y** *a.*; **-ily; -iness**

mi′grāine, *n.*, intense headache

mi′grāte, *v.*, move from one place to another; **tion; tory; ant**

mĭl, *n.*, one thousandth of an inch

mĭld, *a.*, soft, gentle, moderate; **-ly; -ness**

mĭl′dew, *n.*, fungus on things caused by dampness

mile, *n.*, unit of length, 5,280 feet [event

mile′stōne, *n.*, important

mi-lieū′, *n.*, environment

mĭl′ĭ-tånt, *a.*, aggressive; **tancy; -ly**

mĭl′ĭ-tār-ў, *a.*, of or by soldiers or war; **tarily; rism; rist; rize**

mĭlk, *n.*, white liquid from female mammals; **-y** *a.*

mĭll, *n.*, grinding machine, factory; *v.*, process in mill, move aimlessly

mĭl-lěn′nĭ-ŭm, *n.*, 1,000 years, period of peace; **nial**

mĭl′lėt, *n.*, cereal grain

mĭl′lĭ-mē-têr, *n.*, one thousandth of a meter

mĭl′lĭ-nĕr-ў, *n.*, women's hats [chanic

mĭll′wrĭght, *n.*, mill me-

mĭm′ē-ȯ-grăph, *n.*, *v.*,

(machine to) stencil many copies

mĭm′ĭc, *n.,* one who copies; *v.,* imitate; **-ry; -ker**

mĭnce, *v.,* chop up, weaken; **-r**

mĭnd, *n.,* organ that thinks, intelligence; *v.,* obey, care for, object

mĭne, *n.,* excavation to get minerals, gems, etc, large supply, explosive hidden under enemy; *v.,* dig in mine; **-r; mining**

mĭn′ếr-ál, *n.,* substance found in earth; **-ize; -izer; -ization; -ogy**

mĭn′gle, *v.,* mix; **-r**

mĭn′ĭ-mŭm, *a.,* smallest possible; **mize; mizer; mization; mal; mally**

mĭn′ĭs-tếr, *n.,* person acting for another, diplomat, clergyman; **try; tration; trative; -ial; -ially**

mĭnk, *n.,* brown weasel with valuable fur

mĭn′nŏw, *n.,* small fish

mī′nŏr, *a.,* lesser, under legal age; **-ity**

mĭn′strél, *n.,* performer

mĭnt, *n.,* government place where money is made, **-age**

mĭnt, *n.,* aromatic plant

mī′nŭs, *a.,* negative; *prep.,* less

mī-nūte′, *a.,* tiny; **-ly; -ness**

mĭr′à-cle, *n.,* event that seems to go against scientific fact; **raculous; raculously; raculousness** [sion

mĭ-râge′, *n.,* optical illu-

mĭr′rŏr, *n.,* glass that reflects image

mîrth, *n.,* gaiety with laughter; **-ful; -fully; -fulness; -less; -lessly; -lessness**

mĭs′án-thrōpe, *n.,* hater of all people; **thropy; thropic; thropical; thropically**

mĭs-căr′rў, *v.,* go wrong, lose a fetus before full

term; **riage**

mĭs-cél-lā′nē-oŭs, *a.,* varied, mixed; **ny; -ly; -ness**

mĭs′chĭef, *n.,* harm, prank, teasing; **chievous; chievously; chievousness** [ancy

mĭs′crē-ánt, *n.,* villain;

mĭs-dē-mēan′ŏr, *n.,* minor legal offense [-ly

mī′sếr, *n.,* stingy person;

mĭs′ếr-ў, *n.,* suffering, wretchedness; **erable; erably; erableness**

mĭs-nō′mếr, *n.,* name wrongly applied

mĭs′sĭle, *n.,* object thrown or shot

mĭs′sion, *n.,* special task, delegation, religious errand

mĭs′sión-ār-ў, *n.,* church person sent to make converts

mĭs′sĭve, *n.,* letter

mĭst, *n.,* water vapor, thin fog; **-y** *a.;* **-ily; -iness**

mĭs′tle-tōe, *n.,* evergreen plant with white berries

mĭs′trếss, *n.,* female in control, unmarried woman living with man

mĭte, *n.,* tiny parasite

mī′tếr, *n.,* angled joint, bishop's hat

mĭt′ĭ-gāte, *v.,* lessen; **tor; tion; tive, tory; gable**

mī-tō′sĭs, *n.,* simple cell division; **totic totically**

mĭtt, *n.,* baseball glove

mĭx′-ŭp, *n.,* confusion

mōan, *n.,* low, mournful sound; *v.,* bewail, complain

mōat, *n.,* deep ditch around castle

mŏb, *n.,* disorderly crowd; *v.,* crowd around

mō′bĭ-līze, *v.,* put into use; **-r; zation; lizable**

mŏc′cà-sĭn, *n.,* soft heelless leather shoe

mŏck, *v.,* ridicule, mimic; *a.,* false; **-er; -ery; -ingly**

mōde, *n.,* fashion, method

mŏd′él, *n.,* small copy, one

to imitate, style, artist's subject; v., form, display clothing; **-er**

mŏd'êr-āte, v., preside make calm; **tor**

mŏd'ĕr-ȧte,n., a. (person) avoiding excesses; **tion**

mŏd'êrn, a., of present times, new; **-ly; -ness**

mŏd'ĕst, a., shy, humble, decent; **-y; -ly**

mŏd'ūle, n., architectural unit of measurement; **lar** a.

mō'hāir,n., goat hair cloth

moĭst, a., slightly wet, damp; **-en; -ener; -ure; -ly; -ness**

mō'lȧr,n., large back tooth

mȯ-lăs'sȧs, n., thick dark syrup

mōld,n., v., pattern, shape, influence; **-er; -able**

mōld,n., fungus growth on organic matter; **-y** a.

mōld'ĭng, n., decorative strip of wood

mōle,n., dark spot on skin, small burrowing mammal

mŏl'ė-cūle, n., smallest whole part of an element; **lar**   [**-er; -ion**

mȯ-lĕst', v., annoy, harm;

mŏl'lĭ-fy̆, v., pacify, soothe; **fier; fication**

mŏl'lŭsk, n., soft-bodied animal enclosed in shell

mōlt, v., shed hair, skin, etc. before getting new growth

mō'mȧnt, n., very brief time, importance; **-ary; -arily; -ly**

mō-mĕn'tŭm, n., force of moving object

mŏn'ârch, n., sole ruler; **-y; -al; -ally; -ical; -ically; -ism; -ist**

mŏn'ȧs-tĕr-y̆, n., monks' residence; **tic; tical; tically**

mŏn'ė-tār-y̆, a., of money, financial; **tarily**

mŏn'ēy,n., medium of exchange or value, wealth; **-ed; -less**

mŏn'gêr,n., dealer, trader

mŏn'grȧl,n., a. (animal or plant) of mixed breed

mŏn'ĭ-tōr,n., v. (person or thing that can) watch, check, warn

mŏnk, n., male religious recluse

mŏn-ȯ-chrō-măt'ĭc, a., of one color; **-ally**

mŏn'ȯ-cle, n., single eyeglass

mȯ-nŏg'ȧ-my̆, n., marriage to one person at a time; **mist; mous; gamic**

mŏn'ȯ-grăm,n., initials of one's name in design

mŏn'ȯ-grăph,n., scholarly writing on one subject; **-ic**   [block; **-ic**

mŏn'ȯ-līth,n., single stone

mŏn'ȯ-lŏgue, n., dramatic act for one; **loguist**

mȯ-nŏp'ȯ-ly̆, n., exclusive control of commodity; **list; lize; lizer; lization**

mŏn'ȯ-thē-ĭsm, n., belief in one god; **ist; istic; istical; istically**

mȯ-nŏt'ȯ-ny̆, n., lack of variety, boredom; **nous; nously; nousness**

mŏn-sōon', n., seasonal wind; **-al**

mŏn'stêr, n., abnormal thing, imaginary creature

mŏn'ū-mȧnt, n., memorial structure; **-al; -ally; -alize**

mōod, n., state of mind

mōon,n., planet's satellite

mōon'shīne, n., moon's light, nonsense, unlawful whiskey

môor,n., open wasteland; v., hold in place

mōot, a., debatable

mŏp, n., bunch of yarn on handle to wash floors, thick mass; v., wipe clean

mōpe,v., be gloomy; **-y** a.; **mopish; mopishly**

môr'ȧl,n., a., (standard) of right and wrong; a., virtuous, good; **-ity; -ist; -ize; -ly**

mȯ-răle', *n.*, mental condition, ex. courage, zeal

mȯ-răss', *n.*, swamp

môr'bĭd, *a.*, diseased, gruesome; **-ity; -ly; -ness**

môre-ō'vêr, *adv.*, besides

mō'rēs, *n.*, customs

môrgue, *n.*, place for unidentified bodies

mō'rŏn, *n.*, person with low intelligence; **-ic**

mȯ-rōse', *a.*, gloomy; **-ly; -ness**   [pain

môr'phĭne, *n.*, drug for

mor'rōw (mâr), *n.*, next day   [food

môr'sĕl, *n.*, small bit, as

môr'tăl, *a.*, that must die, deadly, fatal; **-ity; -ly**

môr'tår, *n.*, bowl with pestle, cannon, plaster between bricks

mort'gage (môr), *n.*, pledge of property for security on debt; **-e; -r**

môr-tĭ'ciàn, *n.*, undertaker

môr'tĭ-fy̆, *v.*, humiliate, shame; **fier; fication**

môr'tū-ār-y̆, *n.*, place to hold dead bodies

mō-sā'ĭc, *n.*, inlaid design of stone, glass, etc.

mȯs-quï'tō, *n.*, small blood-sucking insect

môss, *n.*, tiny green plant on rock; **-y** *a.*; **-iness**

mō-tĕl', *n.*, hotel for motorists   [sect

môth, *n.*, four-winged in-

mō-tĭf', *n.*, main theme

mō'tion, *n.*, movement, gesture, proposal; **-al; -less; -lessly; -lessness**

mō'tĭve, *n.*, reason for action; **vate; vator; vation; vational; vative**

mŏt'lĕy, *a.*, varied

mō'tör, *n.*, engine that produces motion; *v.*, go by auto; **-ist; -ize**

mŏt'tle, *v.*, blotch

mŏt'tō, *n.*, saying

mōund, *n.*, small hill

mŏun'taĭn, *n.*, very high land rise; **-ous; -ously**

môurn, *v.*, grieve; **-er; -ing** *n.*; **-ful; -fully; -fulness**

move (mōōv), *v.*, change place, set in motion, arouse, propose; **-r; -ment**   [-er

mōw, *v.*, cut down (grass);

mū'cĭ-làge, *n.*, glue; **laginous**   [-y *a.*

mŭck, *n.*, filth, black dirt;

mū'cŭs, *n.*, slimy body secretion; **cous**   [-dy *a.*

mŭd, *n.*, wet sticky earth;

mŭd'dle, *v.*, confuse

mŭff, *n.*, cylindrical fur covering for hand

mŭf'fĭn, *n.*, small round bread

mŭf'flêr, *n.*, warm neck scarf, device to silence noise

mŭg, *n.*, drinking cup; *v.*, assault; **-ger**

mŭg'gy̆, *a.*, hot and damp; **giness**

mŭlch, *n.*, rotted matter to protect plants

mūle, *n.*, offspring of donkey and horse, stubborn person; **mulish**

mŭll, *v.*, ponder

mŭl'lĕt, *n.*, edible fish

mŭl'tĭ-ple, *a.*, of many parts

mŭl'tĭ-ply̆, *v.*, increase, add a number so many times; **plier; plication; plicative; pliable**

mŭl'tĭ-tūde, *n.*, large number, crowd; **tudinous; tudinously**

mŭm'ble, *v.*, say indistinctly; **-r; blingly**

mŭm'my̆, *n.*, ancient embalmed body

mŭmps, *n.*, disease of glandular swelling

mŭn-dāne', *a.*, of the world, ordinary; **-ly**

mū-nĭc'ĭ-pål, *a.*, of local government; **-ity**

mū-nĭf'ĭ-cĕnt, *a.*, very generous; **cence; -ly**

mū-nĭ'tions, *n. pl.*, war supplies

mū'ràl, *n., a.* (large picture painted) on wall

mûrk'ÿ, *a.,* dark, gloomy

mûr'mûr, *n.,* soft steady sound; **-er; -ous**

mŭs'cle, *n.,* fibrous tissue that moves body, strength; **cular** *a.;* **cularly**

mūse, *v.,* ponder

mū-sē'ŭm, *n.,* place for showing art

mŭsh, *n.,* boiled corn meal; **-y** *a.*

mū'sĭc, *n.,* rhythmic vocal and/or instrumental sounds; **-al; -ally; -ology**

mŭs'kėt, *n.,* long gun

mŭs'lĭn, *n.,* sheer simple cotton cloth

mŭs'sėl, *n.,* mollusk

mŭst, *n.,* necessity; *v.,* have to, be sure to

mŭs'têr, *v.,* gather

mŭs'tÿ, *a.,* stale, smelly **tily; tiness**

mū'tāte, *v.,* undergo change; **tion; tional; tionally; table; tability; tably; tableness**

mūte, *n.,* silent person; *a.,* voiceless; **-ly; -ness**

mū'tĭ-lāte, *v.,* maim, cut off, damage; **tor; tion; tive**

mū'tĭ-nÿ, *n.,* revolt against authority; **nous; nously; nousness**

mŭt'tòn, *n.,* sheep meat

mū'tū-ȧl, *a.,* interchangeable, shared jointly; **-ity; -ly**

mŭz'zle, *n.,* snout, straps to keep mouth closed, gun's front end

mÿ-ō'pĭ-ȧ, *n.,* nearsightedness; **opic; opically**

mÿr'ĭ-ȧd, *n.,* great number; *a.,* countless

myr'tle (mîr), *n.,* evergreen

mÿs'têr-ÿ, *n.,* unexplained matter, secret; **rious; riously; riousness**

mÿs'tĭc, *n., a.* (believer) of magic power; **-al; -ally; -alness; -ism**

mÿth, *n.,* traditional story explaining phenomena; **-ical, -ically; -ology**

N

năb, *v.,* catch

nȧ-cĕlle', *n.,* enclosed part of airplane

nā'dĭr, *n.,* lowest point

năg, *n.,* inferior horse; *v.,* urge or scold constantly

nāil, *n.,* thin horny end of fingers and toes, pointed metal piece to hold wood

nȧ-ïve', *a.,* innocent, unsophisticated; **-té** *n.;* **-ly**

nā'kėd, *a.,* without clothes, uncovered; **-ly; -ness**

nāme, *n.,* word for person, place or thing, reputation; **-less**   [say

nāme'lÿ, *adv.,* that is to

nāme'sāke, *n.,* person named for another

năp, *n.,* short sleep, hairy surface of cloth; *v.,* doze

nā'pȧlm, *n.,* substance in bomb

nāpe, *n.,* back of neck

năph'thȧ, *n.,* oily liquid used as solvent, fuel

năp'kĭn, *n.,* cloth used on lap at mealtimes

nȧ-pō'lē-òn, *n.,* old French coin, pastry

nâr'cĭs-sĭsm, *n.,* self-love

nâr-cĭs'sŭs, *n.,* bulbous plant

nâr-cŏt'ĭc, *n.,* drug for pain or sleep   [**tion**

năr'rāte, *v.,* tell story; **tor;**

năr'rȧ-tĭve, *n.,* story

năr'rōw, *a.,* thin in width, limited, biased

nā'sȧl, *a.,* of nose; **-ity; -ly**

năs'cént, *a.,* beginning; **cence; cency**

nȧ-stûr'tiŭm, *n.,* flower

năs'tÿ, *a.,* filthy, offensive; **tily; tiness**

nā'tȧl, *a.,* of birth

nā'tion, *n.,* people organized as state; **-al; -ally**

nȧ'tion-ȧl-ĭsm, *n.,* devotion to nation; **ist; istic;**

N O

istically [quality
nă-tion-ăl'ĭ-tў, n., national
nā'tĭve, a., inborn, of place
of origin, natural; -ly;
-ness
nâ-tĭv'ĭ-tў, n., birth
năt'ŭ-răl, a., of nature, innate, normal. at ease; -ly
năt'ŭ-răl-īze, v., make a
citizen of; ization
nā'tûre, n., basic quality,
type, sort, physical uni-
verse; turalist
năught, n., zero, nothing
năugh-tў, a., mischievous;
bad; tily; tiness
nău'sē-à, n., sick feeling
in stomach; -te; -nt;
seous; seously;
seousness; -tinely
nău'tĭ-căl, a., of sailors,
ships, navigation; -ly
nāve, n., main long part of
church
nā'vĕl, n., small depres-
sion in abdomen
năv'ĭ-gāte, v., steer ship
or plane, travel; tor;
tion; tional; tionally;
gable; gability; gably
nā'vў, n., nation's war-
ships, dark blue; val
nāy, n., vote of "no"
nēap, a., low as tide
nēar, v., approach; a.,
adv., close, almost;
prep., at short distance
nēar'bў', a., adv., close at
hand
nēar'lў, adv., almost
nēar-sight'ĕd, a., seeing
items nearby well; -ly;
-ness
nēat, a., clean and orderly;
-en; -ly; -ness
nĕb'ŭ-là, n., star cluster
nĕb'ŭ-loŭs, a., vague; losity; -ly; -ness
nĕc'ĕs-sār-ў, a., needed,
required, essential; sity;
sitate; sitation; sarily
nĕ-cĕs'sĭ-toŭs, a., in great
need, urgent; -ly; -ness
nĕck, n., part joining head
to body, narrow part; v.,
caress [scarf
nĕck'ĕr-chĭef, n., neck

nĕck'lâce, n., ornament
worn around neck
nĕck'weâr, n., articles
worn around neck
nĕ-crŏl'ŏ-gў, n., death notice
nĕc'târ, n., delicious beverage, liquid of flowers
nĕc-târ-īne', n., fruit
nēē, a., indicating
woman's maiden name,
born
nēed, n., thing required,
want, poverty; v., re-
quire; -er; -y a.; -ness;
-ful; -fully; -fulness;
-less; -lessly; -less-
ness
nēe'dle, n., slender
pointed metal piece for
sewing, injections,
phonograph, etc.
nēe'dle-wŏrk, n., fancy
sewing, embroidery
nĕ-fār'ĭ-oŭs, a., very
wicked; -ly; -ness
nĕ-gāte', v., deny; tor;
tion
nĕg'à-tĭve, n., denial, a.,
saying "no," denying,
less than zero; tivity; -ly;
-ness; tivism
nĕg-lĕct', n., lack of proper
care; v., fail to do or care
for; -er; -ful; -fully;
-fulness
nĕg-lĭ-gee' (gā), n.,
woman's dressing gown
nĕg'lĭ-geṅt, a., habitually
careless; gence; -ly
nĕg'lĭ-gĭ-ble, a., trifle;
gibility; gibly
nĕ-gō'tĭ-āte, v., discuss to
reach agreement, sell or
transfer; tor; tion; able;
ability
neigh (nā), n., horse's cry
neigh'bŏr (nā), n., person
living near another;
-hood; -ing; -ly; -liness
nēi'thêr, a., pro., conj., not
either
nĕm'ĕ-sĭs, n., retribution
nĕ-ŏ-līth'ĭc, a., of late
stone age
nē'ŏn, n., inert gaseous
element [fant

nē'ȯ-nāte, *n.,* newborn in-
nē'ȯ-phȳte, *n.,* new convert, amateur
nē-ȯ-tĕr'ĭc, *n.,* modern
person; *a.,* new; **-ally**
nĕ-phŏl'ȯ-gȳ, *n.,* study of
clouds; **gist; logical**
nĕ-phrī'tĭs, *n.,* kidney disease; **phritic**
nĕp'ȯ-tĭsm, *n.,* favoring
relatives in politics; **tist;
tistic**
nêrve, *n.,* cordlike fiber
sending impulse to and
from brain, courage
nêrve'lĕss, *a.,* without
courage, weak; **-ly;
-ness**
nêrv'oŭs, *a.,* of nerves,
restless, tense; **vosity;
-ness**
nĕs'ci'ȇnt, *a.,* ignorant;
ence
nĕst, *n.,* place for birds,
fish to raise young; **-er;
-able** [snug; **-r**
nĕs'tle, *v.,* lie close and
nĕt, *n.,* meshed fabric; *v.,*
snare, clear as profit; *a.,*
final
nĕth'êr, *a.,* lower
nĕt'tle, *n.,* weed; *v.,* irritate, **-r; -some** *a.*
nĕt'wŏrk, *n.,* group of connected things
neŭ'rȧl, *a.,* of a nerve
neŭ-rȧl'giȧ, *n.,* pain along
nerve; **gic**
neŭ-rī'tĭs, *n.,* inflammation
of nerves; **ritic**
neŭ-rŏl'ȯ-gȳ, *n.,* study of
nervous system; **gist;
logical, logically**
neŭ-rō'sĭs, *n.,* emotional
disorder; **rotic; roti-
cally; roticism**
neŭ'têr, *a.,* neither male
nor female
neŭ'tral, *a.,* of neither side,
impartial; **-ity; -ism;
-ize; -izer; -ization; -ly**
neŭ'trŏn, *n.,* uncharged
particle of atom
nĕv'êr, *adv.,* at no time
nĕv-êr-môre', *adv.,* never
again [however
nĕv-êr-thȇ-lĕss', *adv.,*

nēw, *a.,* of first time, unfamiliar, recent; **-ly;
-ness** [rival
nēw'cȯm-êr, *n.,* recent ar-
nēw'făn-glĕd, *a.,* new,
novel
nēw'lȳ-wĕd, *n.,* recently
married person
nēws, *n.,* new information,
report of recent events;
-y *a.*
nēws'căst, *n.,* news
broadcast; **-er; -ing** *n.*
nēws'lĕt-têr, *n.,* regularly
issued bulletin
nēws'pā-pêr, *n.,* news
publication
nēws'rēel, *n.,* short motion
picture of news
nēwt, *n.,* small salamander
nĕxt, *a., adv.,* nearest;
prep., beside
nĕxt'dôor', *a.,* in or at
nearest building or
house
nĕx'ŭs, *n.,* connection
nĭb, *n.,* point, as pen
nĭb'ble, *v.,* take small bites
nīce, *a.,* pleasant, agreeable, good, delicate, re-
fined; **-ty; -ly; -ness**
nīche, *n.,* wall recess
nĭck, *n.,* small cut
nĭck'ĕl, *n.,* hard metallic
element, five cent coin;
-ic; -ous [piano
nĭck-ĕl-ō'dē-ȯn, *n.,* player
nĭck'nāme, *n.,* short substitute name
nĭc'ȯ-tīne, *n.,* poisonous
liquid in tobacco; **tinic**
nĭc'ti-tāte, *v.,* wink rapidly;
tion
nĭg'gȧrd, *a.,* stingy; **-ly;
-liness** [near
nĭgh, *v., a., adv., prep.,*
nĭght, *n.,* darkness after
sunset [tertainment
nĭght'clŭb, *n.,* place of en-
nĭght'fȧll, *n.,* close of day,
dusk [gown
nĭght'gōwn, *n.,* sleeping
nĭght'ĭn-gāle, *n.,* thrush
nĭght'lȳ, *a., adv.,* every
night
nĭght'māre, *n.,* frightening
dream; **marish**

**N
O**

ni'hïl-ïsm, *n.,* denial of law, religion, etc.; **ist; istic**

nïl, *n.,* nothing

nïm'ble, *a.,* agile, quick; **bly; -ness** [cloud

nïm'bŭs, *n.,* saint's halo,

nïn'nў, *n.,* fool

ni-ō'bï-ŭm, *n.,* metallic element

nïp, *n., v.,* pinch, bite; *n.,* small drink of liquor

nïp'ple, *n.,* breast part giving milk, nipplelike thing

nïp'pў, *a.,* cold; **piness**

nït, *n.,* egg or larva of a louse

nït'pïck-ïng, *a.,* petty

ni'trāte, *n.,* salt of nitric acid; *v.,* make into nitrate; **tion**

ni'trŏ-gĕn, *n.,* gaseous element essential to life; **-ize; trify; trifier; trification; tric; -ous**

ni-trŏ-glўc'ẽr-ïn, *n.,* explosive oil

nït'wït, *n.,* stupid person

nō, *n.,* denial; *a.,* not any; *adv.,* not at all

nō-bïl'ï-tў, *n.,* titled class

nō'ble, *n., a.,* (one) of high rank; *a.,* famous, highly moral, splendid; **bly; -ness**

nō'bŏd-ў, *n., pro.,* no one

nŏck, *n.,* nock in bow or arrow [**-ly**

nŏc-tûr'nàl, *a.,* of night;

nŏc'tûrne, *n.,* dreamy night music [**-ness**

nŏc'ū-oŭs, *a.,* harmful; **-ly;**

nŏd, *v.,* tilt head forward; **-der** [**nodal**

nōde, *n.,* knot, swelling;

nŏd'ūle, *n.,* small lump; **lar** *a.;* **lose** *a.;* **lous**

nŏg'gïn, *n.,* (coll.) head

noïse, *n.,* loud unpleasant sound; **-less; noisy** *a.*

nō'măd, *n.,* wanderer; **-ism; -ic; -ically**

nō'mén-clā-tûre, *n.,* system of names

nŏm'ï-nàl, *a.,* in name only, very small; **-ly**

nŏm'ï-nāte, *v.,* appoint, select as candidate; **tor;** nee; tion; tive

nŏn-, *prefix,* not

nŏn'àge, *n.,* state of being legally under age

nŏn-à-gė-nār'ï-àn, *n.,* one ninety years old

nŏn-chà-lànt', *a.,* cool, indifferent; **lance; -ly**

nŏn-dė-scrïpt', *a.,* hard to describe

none (nŭn), *n., a.,* not any; *adv.,* not at all; *pro.,* no one [tant person

nŏn-ĕn'tï-tў, *n.,* unimpor-

none-thė-lèss (nŭn), *adv.,* in spite of that

nŏn-môr'àl, *a.,* not moral or immoral

nōok, *n.,* corner

nōose, *n.,* rope loop, trap

nôr, *conj.,* not either

nôrm, *n.,* standard, average; **-ative; -atively**

nôr'màl, *a.,* usual, natural; **-cy; -ity; -ize; -ly**

nôrth, *n.,* direction to right when facing sunset; *a., adv.,* in or of the north; **-erly; -ward, -wardly** *a., adv.;* **-ern** *a.*

nôrth-ēast', *n.,* direction between north and east; **-erly, -ward, -wardly** *a., adv.;* **-ern** *a.*

nôrth-wĕst', *n.,* direction between north and west; **-erly, -ward, -wardly** *a., adv.;* **-ern** *a.*

nōse, *n.,* facial feature with openings for breathing and smelling; *v.,* find by smell, meddle

nōse'gāy, *n.,* small bouquet

nŏs-tăl'già, *n.,* longing for something; **gic; gically**

nŏs'trïl, *n.,* nose opening

nŏs'trŭm, *n.,* remedy

nōs'ў, *a.,* curious, prying; **nosily; nosiness**

nŏt, *adv.,* in no way

nō'tà-ble, *n., a.,* (one who is) famous; **bly; bility**

nō'tà-rīze, *v.,* certify; **zation**

nō-tā'tion, *n.,* system of signs, note; **-al**

nŏtch, *n.,* V-shaped cut

nōte, *n.,* importance, mark, short writing, musical tone; *v.,* observe, indicate   [**-ness**

nōt'ĕd, *a.,* famous; **-ly**

nōte'wŏr-thy̆, *a.,* outstanding; **thily; thiness**

nŏth'ĭng, *n.,* not anything, zero; **-ness**

nō'tĭce, *n.,* announcement, attention, *v.,* observe; **-able; -ably**

nō'tĭ-fy̆, *v.,* inform; **fier; fication; fiable** ·

nō'tion, *n.,* idea, small useful article; **-al**

nō-tô'rĭ-oŭs, *a.,* widely but unfavorably known; **riety; -ly; -ness**

nŏt-wĭth-stănd'ĭng, *adv., prep., conj.,* in spite of

nou'găt, *n.,* chewy candy with nuts

noŭn, *n.,* name of person, place or thing

nouʼr'ĭsh, *v.,* feed, develop; **-er; -ment; -ing; -ingly**

nŏv'ĕl, *n.,* long fictional story; **-ist; -ize; -ization**

nŏv'ĕl, *a.,* new, unusual; **-ty**   [ateur

nŏv'ĭce, *n.,* beginner, amnŏẅ, *adv.,* at present, then; *conj.,* since

now'ă-dāys, *n., adv.,* these days, at present

nō'whĕre, *n., adv.,* not in any place   [**-ness**

nŏx'ioŭs, *a.,* harmful; **-ly;**

nŏz'zle, *n.,* hose spout

nu'ănce, *n.,* slight difference

nu'bĭle, *a.,* marriageable; **bility**

nu'clē-ŭs, *n.,* central part ex. cell; **clear** *a.*

nūde, *a.,* unclothed; **nudity; -ly; -ness**

nŭdge, *v.,* push gently; **-r**

nu'gă-tô-ry̆, *a.,* worthless

nŭg'gĕt, *n.,* lump of gold ore   [inconvenience

nūi'sănce, *n.,* annoyance,

nŭll, *a.,* not valid; **-ity; -ify; -ifier; -ification**

nŭmb, *a.,* not able to feel; **-ly; -ness**

nŭm'bêr, *n.,* symbol or word for how many, total; *v.,* count, limit

nŭm'bêr-lĕss, *a.,* countless   [ble

nu'mêr-ă-ble, *a.,* counta-

nu'mêr-ăl, *n.,* symbol for a number

nu'mêr-ā-tŏr, *n.,* counter, top part of fraction

nu-mĕr'ĭ-căl, *a.,* of number; **-ly**   [**-ness**

nu'mêr-oŭs, *a.,* many; **-ly;**

nu-mĭs-măt'ĭcs, *n.,* study or collection of money; **tist; ic**   [son

nŭm'skŭll, *n.,* stupid per-

nŭn, *n.,* religious woman living in convent

nŭn'nêr-y̆, *n.,* convent

nŭp'tiăl, *n., pl.,* wedding; *a.,* of marriage

nûrse, *n., v.,* (person trained to) care for sick or young

nûrs'êr-y̆, *n.,* room for children, place to raise plants, trees, etc.

nûr'tûre, *v.,* feed, train, raise; **-r; tural**

nŭt, *n.,* hard-shelled fruit, metal block with threaded hole for bolt; *pl.,* (coll.) crazy; **-ty** *a.*

nŭt'hătch, *n.,* bird

nŭt'mĕg, *n.,* spice

nu'trĭ-ĕnt, *a.,* nourishing

nu'trĭ-mĕnt, *n.,* food; **-al**

nu-trĭ'tion, *n.,* assimilation of food, study of proper diet; **-ist; tious; -al; -ally**

nŭz'zle, *v.,* rub nose against, snuggle; **-r**

nȳ'lŏn, *n.,* synthetic material   [maiden

ny̆mph, *n.,* goddess,

O

ōaf, *n.,* clumsy person

ōak, *n.,* tree; **-en** *a.*

ôar, *n.,* rowing implement

ō-ā'sĭs, *n.,* place with water in desert

ōat, *n.,* cereal grain; **-en**

N O

a. [tion, curse
ōath, *n.*, formal declara-
ŏb'dū-râte, *a.*, inflexible,
stubborn; **racy; -ly**
ō-bei'sȧnce (bā), *n.*,
showing of respect; **sant**
ŏb'ė-lĭsk,*n.*, tall four-sided
pillar with pointed top
ō-bēse', *n.*, very fat; **sity**
ō-bey' (bā), *v.*, follow or-
ders; **-er**
ŏb'fŭs-cāte, *v.*, confuse;
tion [tice
ō-bĭt'ū-ār-ȳ, *n.*, death no-
ŏb'jĕct, *n.*, tangible thing,
recipient of action or
feeling, purpose; **-ive**
ŏb-jĕct', *v.*, oppose; **-ion**;
-ionable
ŏb-jĕc'tĭve, *n.*, goal; *a.*,
real, without bias, fair;
tivity; -ly; -ness
ŏb'jûr-gāte, *v.*, scold, ber-
ate; **tor; tion; tory**
ŏb'lĭ-gāte,*v.*, bind by legal
or moral tie; **tion; tional;**
tory [**-r; bliging**
ō-blīge', *v.*, do a favor for;
ŏb-līque', *a.*, slanting, indirect; **uity; -ly; -ness**
ŏb-lĭt'êr-āte,*v.*, erase; **tor;**
tion; tive
ŏb-lĭv'ĭ-oŭs, *a.*, forgetful,
unmindful; **ion; -ly;**
-ness [broad
ŏb'lŏng, *a.*, longer than
ŏb'lȯ-quȳ, *n.*, disgrace
from public blame
ŏb-nŏx'ioŭs, *a.*, unpleasant, offensive; **-ly; -ness**
ō'bōe, *n.*, woodwind musical instrument
ŏb-scēne', *a.*, immoral,
lewd; **scenity; -ly**
ŏb-scūre', *a.*, dark, not
clear, hidden; **rity; -ly;**
-ness [**-ly; -ness**
ŏb-sē'quĭ-oŭs, *a.*, servile;
ŏb-sêrv'ȧ-tô-rȳ, *n.*, building for scientific obser-
vation
ŏb-sêrve', *v.*, celebrate,
adhere to law, duty, etc.;
-r; servance; servant;
servantly
ŏb-sĕss', *v.*, dwell in mind
persistently; **-ion; -ive;**

-ional; -ively; -iveness
ŏb-sȯ-lĕs'cėnt, *a.*, going
out of use; **cence; -ly**
ŏb-sȯ-lēte', *a.*, out of date,
old; **-ly; -ness**
ŏb'stȧ-cle, *n.*, hindrance
ŏb-stĕt'rĭcs, *n.*, medicine
of childbirth; **ic; cian** *n.*
ŏb'stĭ-nȧte, *a.*, stubborn;
nacy; -ly; -ness
ŏb-strĕp'ėr-oŭs, *a.*, noisy,
unruly; **-ly; -ness**
ŏb-strŭct', *v.*, block,
hinder; **-er; -or; -ion;**
-ive; -ively; -iveness
ŏb-tāin', *v.*, get posses-
sion of; **-er; -ment; -able**
ŏb-trūde', *v.*, force oneself
upon; **-r; trusion; tru-**
sive; trusively;
trusiveness [**-ness**
ŏb-tūse', *a.*, dull; **sity; -ly;**
ŏb'vĭ-āte,*v.*, make unnecessary; **tion**
ŏb'vĭ-oŭs, *a.*, easy to understand; **-ly; -ness**
ȯc-cās'sion, *n.*, happening, opportunity; *v.*,
cause
ȯc-clūde', *v.*, stop up,
close; **clusion; clusive;**
-nt
ȯc-cŭlt', *a.*, secret, mysti-
cal; **-ism; -ist; -ly; -ness**
ŏc-cū-pā'tion, *n.*, control
of area, one's work; **-al;**
-ally
ŏc'cū-pȳ, *v.*, possess, live
in, fill; **pier; pancy; pant**
n.
ȯc-cûr', *v.*, come to mind;
happen; **-rence**
ō'cėan (shėn), *n.*, great
body of salt water; **-ic;**
-ology; -ologist [cat
ō'cė-lŏt, *n.*, large spotted
ō'chêr (kêr), *n.*, clay with
iron ore, dark yellow
ŏc'tȧ-gŏn, *n.*, eight-sided
plane; **-al; -ally**
ŏc'tāne, *n.*, gasoline
measure [tones; **val**
ŏc'tȧve, *n.*, eight musical
ŏc-tĕt', *n.*, group of eight
ŏc'tȯ-pŭs, *n.*, eight-armed
sea animal
ŏc'ū-lȧr, *a.*, of the eye; **-ly**

ŏc′ū-lĭst, *n.,* eye doctor

ŏdd, *a.,* left over, not even, strange; **-ity; -ly; -ness**

ŏdds, *n.,* advantage, betting ratio

ōde, *n.,* poem of praise

ō′dĭ-oŭs, *a.,* disgusting; **-ly; -ness**

ō′dŏr, *n.,* smell; **-ous; -ously; -ousness; -less**

ôf′fȧl, *n.,* garbage

ȯf-fĕnd′, *v.,* anger, displease, commit crime; **-er; fense; fensive; fensively; fensiveness**

ôf′fêr, *n.,* something offered; *v.,* present, propose, bid; **-er; -ing** *n.*

ŏff′hănd′, *a., adv.,* without preparation

ȯf′fĭce, *n.,* position, place of business; **ciate; ciator; ciation**

ȯf′fĭ-cêr, *n.,* person of authority, policeman

ȯf-fĭ′cioŭs, *a.,* meddlesome, domineering; **-ly; -ness**

ôff′sĕt, *n.,* compensation, type of printing; *v.* **(ôff-sĕt′)** balance

ôff′sprĭng, *n.,* child

ō′gle, *n., v.,* stare; **-r**

ō′gre (gêr), *n.,* fictitious monster

ŏil, *n.,* greasy combustile liquid; *v.,* lubricate; **-y** *a.*

ŏĭnt′mėnt, *n.,* oily cream to soothe

ō′krȧ, *n.,* vegetable of sticky green pods

ōld, *a.,* existed for a long time, former, shabby; **-ster; -ish** [shrub

ō′lĕ-ăn-dêr, *n.,* flowering

ō-lĕ-ō-mâr′gȧ-rĭne, *n.,* butter substitute

ŏl-făc′tȯ-rȳ, *a.,* of the sense of smell

ŏl′ĭ-gâr-chȳ, *n.,* rule of a few [fruit

ŏl′ĭve, *n.,* tree, oval green

ŏm′e-lĕt, *n.,* egg dish

ō′mĕn, *n.,* sign

ŏm′ĭ-noŭs, *a.,* threatening; **-ly; -ness**

ō-mĭt′, *v.,* leave out, neg-

lect; **-ter; mission; missive; missively; missible** [bus

ŏm′nĭ-bŭs, *n.,* collection,

ŏm-nĭp′ȯ-tĕnt, *a.,* all-powerful; **tence; -ly**

ŏm-nĭs′ciĕnt, *a.,* knowing all things; **cience; -ly**

ŏm-nĭv′ȯ-roŭs, *a.,* devouring everything; **-ly; -ness**

once (wŭns), *adv.,* one time, long ago

ŏn′êr-oŭs, *a.,* troublesome; **-ly; -ness**

ȯn′iȯn, *n.,* edible bulb with strong taste

ŏn′lōok-êr, *n.,* spectator

ōn′lȳ, *a.,* alone, best; *adv.,* just, merely; *con.,* but

ŏn′sĕt, *n.,* attack, start

ŏn′slȧught, *n.,* violent attack

ō′nŭs, *n.,* blame, burden

ŏn′ȳx, *n.,* semiprecious stone

ōoze, *n.,* slime; *v.,* leak slowly; **oozy** *a.* [stone

ō′pȧl, *n.,* semiprecious

ō-pāque′, *n.,* impermeable to light; **pacity; -ly; -ness**

ō′pĕn, *v.,* unfasten, expose, begin, be or make liberal; *a.,* not shut, unrestricted, free, frank; **-er; -ly; -ness**

ō-pĕn-hănd′ėd, *a.,* generous; **-ly; -ness**

ō-pĕn-heârt′ėd, *a.,* frank, generous; **-ly; -ness**

ō-pĕn-mĭnd′ėd, *a.,* free from bias; **-ly; -ness**

ō′pĕn-wȯrk, *n.,* ornamental designs with openings in it

ŏp′êr-ȧ, *n.,* musical drama; **-tic; -tically**

ŏp′êr-āte, *v.,* function, manage, perform surgery; **tor; tion; tional; tive; tively; able; ability; ably**

ŏp-êr-ĕt′tȧ, *n.,* light opera

ŏph-thăl-mŏl′ȯ-gȳ, *n.,* medicine of the eyes; **gist; logical**

N O

ō'pĭ-áte, *n.,* narcotic drug with opium

ȯ-pĭn'ĭȯn, *n.,* one's judgment, belief; **-ative; -atively; -ativeness**

ȯ-pĭn'ĭȯn-ăt-ĕd, *a.,* holding opinion stubbornly; **-ly; -ness**

ō'pĭ-ŭm, *n.,* narcotic drug

ȯ-pŏs'sŭm, *n.,* nocturnal tree-dwelling animal

ȯp-pō'nĕnt, *n.,* one against

ŏp-pȯr-tū'nĭ-tÿ, *n.,* chance

ȯp-pōse', *v.,* be against; **-r; position**

ŏp'pȯ-sĭte, *a.,* radically different, facing; **-ly; -ness**

ȯp-prĕss', *v.,* worry, rule harshiy; **-or; -ion; -ive; -ively; -iveness**

ŏpt, *v.,* choose; **-ion; -ional**

ŏp'tĭc, *a.,* of eye; **-al; -ally**

ŏp-tĭ'cián, *n.,* maker of eyeglasses

ŏp'tĭ-mĭsm, *n.,* cheerful view of life; **mist; mistic; mistically**

ŏp'tĭ-mŭm, *n.,* best possible result; **mize; mization; mal; mally**

ŏp-tŏm'ĕ-trÿ, *n.,* examination of eyes; **trist; rical** [ency; -ly

ŏp'ū-lĕnt, *a.,* rich; **ence;**

ō'pŭs, *n.,* work, composition

ôr'à-cle, *n.,* prophet, prophesy; **racular** *a.;* **racularity; racularly**

ô'rál, *a.,* of mouth, spoken; **-ly**

ŏr'ánge, *n.,* edible citrus fruit, reddish yellow

ȯ-răng'ŭ-tăn, *n.,* ape

ȯ-rá'tion, *n.,* speech; **tor**

ôr'à-tôr-ÿ, *n.,* skill in public speaking; **torical; torically**

ôrb, *n.,* sphere, eye

ôr'bĭt, *n.,* eye socket, path of a heavenly body; **-er; -al** [trees

ôr'chárd, *n.,* land with fruit

ôr'chĕs-trá (kĕs), *n.,* many

musicians playing together; **-l**

ôr'chĕs-tràte, *v.,* arrange music; **tor; tion**

ôr'chĭd (kĭd), *n.,* decorative flower, pale purple; **-ology**

ôr-dāin', *v.,* decree, admit to ministry; **-er; -ment; dination** [perience

ôr-dēal', *n.,* difficult ex-

ôr'dêr, *n.,* position, system proper state, request; *v.,* command, arrange

ôr'dêr-lÿ, *n.,* attendant; *a.,* proper, methodical

ôr'dĭ'nál, *n.,* number indicating order ex. third

ôr'dĭ-nánce, *n.,* law

ôr'dĭ-nār-ÿ, *a.,* usual, common; **narily; nariness**

ôrd'nánce, *n.,* weapons, military equipment

ôre, *n.,* natural substance of minerals and/or elements

ȯ-rĕg'à-nō, *n.,* seasoning

ôr'găn, *n.,* large musical instrument, body part with special function

ôr'găn-dÿ, *n.,* sheer fabric

ôr-găn'ĭc, *a.,* of body organ, of life, inborn, systematic; **-ally**

ôr'găn-ĭsm, *n.,* living thing

ôr'găn-īze, *v.,* arrange systematically, unite; **-r; zation** [max; **-ic**

ôr'găsm, *n.,* sexual cli-

ôr'gÿ, *n.,* wild party

ôr'ĭ-ĕnt, *n.,* Asia; *v.,* adjust, adapt; **-ation**

ôr'ĭ-fīce, *n.,* opening; **cial**

ȯ-rĭ-gá'mĭ, *n.,* art of folding paper

ŏr'ĭ-gĭn, *n.,* beginning; **-ate; -ator; -ation**

ȯ-rĭg'ĭ-nál, *a.,* first, new, inventive; **-ity; -ly**

ôr'nà-mĕnt, *n.,* decoration; *v.,* adorn; **-er; -al; -ation** [-ness

ôr-nāte', *a.,* fancy; **-ly;**

ôr'nêr-ÿ, *n.,* obstinate

ôr-nĭ-thŏl'ȯ-gÿ, *n.,* science of birds; **gist; logical**

ôr'phản, *n.*, child without parents; **-hood; -age**

ôr-thỏ-dŏn'tĭcs, *n.*, corrective dentistry; **tist; tic**

ôr'thỏ-dŏx, *a.*, conforming to established practices; **-y**

ôr-thỏ-pē'dĭcs, *n.*, bone surgery; **dist; dic**

ỏ'rỳx, *n.*, antelope

ŏs'cĭl-lāte, *v.*, swing, waver; **tor; tion; tory**

ŏs'cū-lāte, *v.*, kiss; **tion; tory**

ŏs-mō'sĭs, *n.*, passage of fluid through thin membrane

ŏs'sē-oŭs, *a.*, of bone

ŏs'sĭ-fȳ, *v.*, change to bone; **fication**

ŏs-tĕn'sĭ-ble, *a.*, apparent; **bly; sive; sively**

ŏs-tĕn-tā'tion, *n.*, showy display; **tious; tiously; tiousness**

ŏs-tē-ŏp'ȧ-thȳ, *n.*, medicine of treating disease by massage; **path** *n.*; **pathic; pathically**

ŏs'trȧ-cĭze, *v.*, banish; **ism**

ŏs'trĭch, *n.*, large bird

ỏ-tŏl'ỏ-gȳ, *n.*, medicine of ear; **gist; logical**

ŏt'tẽr, *n.*, weasellike animal

cŭght, *v.*, be required to

oŭst, *v.*, force out; **-er**

oŭt, *a.*, external, away from; *adv.*, away from, outdoors, fully

oŭt-bĭd', *v.*, offer more

oŭt'bôard, *a., adv.*, outside main body of ship

oŭt'breāk, *n.*, sudden occurrence

oŭt'bŭrst, *n.*, sudden release of feeling, energy, etc.   [rejected

oŭt'cǎst, *n., a.*, (person)

cŭt'cỏme, *n.*, result

oŭt'crȳ, *n.*, protest

oŭt'do (dū), *v.*, surpass

oŭt'dôor, *a.*, in the open

oŭt'dôors, *n., adv.*, (place) outside of building

oŭt'ẽr, *a.*, external

oŭt'fĭt, *n.*, equipment, en-

semble, unit of people; *v.*, furnish

oŭt-fŏŏt', *v.*, go faster than

oŭt'gỏ-ĭng, *a.*, leaving, sociable

oŭt'grŏwth, *n.*, result

oŭt'hoŭse, *n.*, outside toilet   [cursion

oŭt'ĭng, *n.*, pleasant ex-

oŭt-lǎnd'ĭsh, *a.*, strange; **-ly; -ness**

oŭt'lǎw, *n.*, criminal; *v.*, declare illegal

oŭt'lāy, *n.*, money spent

oŭt'lĕt, *n.*, way out, market, place to plug in to electricity   [mary

oŭt'līne, *n.*, sketch, sum-

oŭt'lŏŏk, *n.*, viewpoint, prospect

oŭt'lȳ-ĭng, *a.*, remote

oŭt-mŏd'ĕd, *a.*, obsolete

oŭt'pŏst, *n.*, remote post

oŭt'pŭt, *n.*, amount done

oŭt'rāge, *n.*, violent act, great insult or anger; *v.*, offend greatly; **-ous; -ously; -ousness**

oŭt'rĭght, *a.*, straight forward; *adv.*, fully, openly

oŭt'sīde, *n.*, exterior; *a.*, outer, from another place, slight; **-er**

oŭt'skĭrt, *n.*, remote part of city   [by cleverness

oŭt-smȧrt', *n.*, overcome

oŭt'spŏ'kĕn, *a.*, frank; **-ly; -ness**   [prominent; **-ly**

oŭt-stǎnd'ĭng, *a.*, unpaid,

oŭt'strĭp, *v.*, surpass

oŭt'wȧrd, *a.*, outer, visible; **-ly; -ness**

oŭt-weigh' (wā), *v.*, be more valuable

oŭt-wĭt', *v.*, outsmart

ō'vȧl, *a.*, egg-shaped; **-ly; -ness**

ō'vȧ-rȳ, *n.*, female reproductive gland; **varian** *a.*

ō-vā'tion, *n.*, great applause   [baking

ŏv'ĕn, *n.*, compartment for

ō'vẽr, *a.*, finished; *adv.*, above, in excess, on other side, again; *prep.*, above, upon, across

ō'vẽr-ǎlls, *n., pl.*, work

pants with bib

ō-vêr-beãr'ĭng, a., arrogant; -ly; -ness

ō'vêr-bôard, adv., over ship's side, to extremes

ō'vêr-căst, a., cloudy, dark

ō-vêr-còme', v., master, conquer, defeat

ō'vêr-drăft, n., withdrawal of money in excess of that in account

ō-vêr-dūe', a., late

ō-vêr-flōw', v., flood

ō-vêr-häul', v., repair

ō-vêr-hēar', v., hear without speaker knowing

ō'vêr-lănd, n., on land

ō-vêr-lăp', v., cover, extend over

ō'vêr-lў, adv., too

ō'vêr-păss, n., bridge over road; v., outdo, overlook

ō-vêr-pow'êr, v., subdue

ō-vêr-rīde', v., nullify

ō-vêr-rūle', v., reverse

ō-vêr-rŭn', v., spread rapidly

ō-vêr-sēe', v., watch over, manage; -r

ō'vêr-shoe (shū), n., protective boot worn over shoe

ō-vêrt', a., open, public; -ly [with

ō-vêr-tāke', v., catch up

ō-vêr-thrōw', v., defeat

ō'vêr-tōne, n., musical tone heard with another, implication

ō'vêr-tûre, n., musical introduction

ō-vêr-tûrn', v., turn over

ō'vêr-vieẃ, n., survey

ō-vêr-whĕlm', n., crush, overpower; -ing; -ingly

ō-vêr-wrôught', a., emotionally distressed

ō'vū-lāte, v., produce and discharge ovum; tion

ō'vŭm, n., female reproductive cell

ōwe, v., be obliged to pay

ōwl, n., night bird of prey; -like; -ish; -ishly; -ishness

ōwn, v., possess, admit;

-er; -ership; -erless

ŏx, n., castrated bull

ŏx'fôrd, n., shoe, cotton cloth

ŏx'īde, n., compound of oxygen and an element

ŏx'ī-dīze, v., unite with oxygen; -r; dizable

ŏx'ў-gên, n., gaseous element; -ate; -ic; -ous

oys'têr (ŏis), n., edible mollusk

ō'zōne, n., form of oxygen

P

păb'ū-lŭm, n., food

pă'cả, n., rodent

pāce, n., walking step, rate; v., walk; -r

păch'ў-dêrm, n., large thick-skinned animal; -al; -ic; -atous; -atously

păc'ī-fў, v., make calm; fier; fiable; fic

păck, n., bundle, group; v., put together, fill; -er; -ing

păct, n., agreement

păd, n., cushion, stacked and attached paper sheets; v., walk softly; -ding n.

păd'dle, n., flat blade with handle for canoeing, stirring, etc.; v., canoe, beat; -r

păd'dòck, n., small enclosed field [lock

păd'lòck, n., removable

paē'ản, n., song of joy

pā'gản, n., heathen; -ize

pāge, n., leaf of a book, boy attendant; v., call name out [show; -ry

păg'ềant, n., elaborate

pả-gō'dản, n., oriental towerlike temple

pâil, n., bucket; -ful

pāin, n., hurt felt in body, (pl.) great care; -ful; -fully; -fulness; -less; -lessly; -lessness

pāint, n., colored pigment; v., cover or draw with paint; -er; -ing n.

pả-jă'mảs, n., pl., pants

and shirt for sleeping

pal′ace, *n.,* royal residence; **latial; latially**

pal′at-a-ble, *n.,* pleasant tasting; **bility; bly; -ness**

pal′ate, *n.,* roof of mouth

pa-lav′er, *n., v.,* talk

pale, *n.,* white, colorless

pa-le-o-lith′ic, *a.,* of Stone Age   [artist's paint

pal′ette, *n.,* thin board for

pal′let, *n.,* straw bed

pal′li-ate, *v.,* excuse, ease, lessen; **tor; tion; tive**

pal′lid, *a.,* pale; **-ly; -ness**

pal′lor, *n.,* lack of color

palm, *n.,* tall tropical tree, inside surface of hand

palm′is-try, *n.,* fortune telling from reading palm; **ist**   [ored horse

pal-o-mi′no, *n.,* light col-

pal′pa-ble, *a.,* that can be felt, obvious; **bility; bly**

pal′pi-tate, *v.,* throb; **tion**

pal′sy, *n.,* paralysis

pam′per, *v.,* spoil, indulge

pam′phlet, *n.,* unbound booklet

pan, *n.,* broad container for cooking; *v.,* (coll.) criticize

pan-a-ce′a, *n.,* cure-all

pan′cre-as, *n.,* gland aiding digestion; **atic**

pan′da, *n.,* bearlike mammal   [confusion

pan-de-mo′ni-um, *n.,* wild

pane, *n.,* sheet of glass

pan-e-gyr′ic, *n.,* speech of praise; **gyrist; gyrize; -al; -ally**

pan′el, *n.,* wall section, group that judges, discusses, etc.; **-ing** *n.*

pan′ic, *n.,* hysterical fear; **-ky** *a.,* **-ally**

pan-o-ra′ma, *n.,* wide view, extended picture; **ramic; ramically**

pant, *v.,* breathe rapidly

pan-ta-loons′, *n., pl.,* trousers

pan′to-mime, *n.,* acting without talking; **mimist; mimic**

pan′try, *n.,* storeroom or closet for food

pa′pa-cy, *n.,* authority of Pope; **pal; pally**

pa-pa′ya, *n.,* tree with edible fruit

pa′per, *n.,* thin sheet for writing; **-y** *a.*   [ing

pap′ri-ka, *n.,* red season-

pa-py′rus, *n.,* water plant, ancient paper

par, *n.,* value, average

par′a-ble, *n.,* story with moral; **bolic; bolical; bolically**

par′a-chute, *n.,* umbrellalike device to descend through air; **chutist**

pa-rade′, *n., v.,* march in public   [place

par′a-dise, *n.,* heavenly

par′a-dox, *n.,* contrary statement; **-ical; -ically; -icalness**

par′af-fin, *n.,* waxy substance   [cellence

par′a-gon, *n.,* model of ex-

par′a-graph, *n.,* related sentences placed together

par′a-keet, *n.,* small parrot

par′al-lel, *a.,* in same direction and distance apart

pa-ral′y-sis, *n.,* loss of power to move body; **lyze; lyzation**

par′a-mount, *a.,* supreme; **-cy** *n.;* **-ly**

par′a-noid, *a.,* oversuspicious   [wall

par′a-pet, *n.,* protective

par-a-pher-na′li-a, *n.,* belongings, equipment

par-a-ple′gi-a, *n.,* paralysis from waist down; **gic** *n., a.*

par′a-site, *n.,* one that lives off another; **sitic; sitical; sitically**

par′a-sol, *n.,* woman's decorative umbrella

par′cel, *n.,* wrapped bundle; *v.,* divide

parch, *v.,* make dry and thirsty

parch′ment, *n.,* animal skin used to write on

pâr′dŏn, v., absolve, forgive, release; **-able; -ably**

pāre, v., peel, lessen

pâr-faĭt′ (fā), n., ice cream dessert in tall glass

păr′ĭsh, n., church district; **-ioner**

păr′ĭ-tў, n., equality

pârk, n., land for recreation; v., leave (car) temporarily

pâr′kă, n., hooded jacket

pâr′lāy, v., bet winnings

pâr′lēy, n., discussion

pâr′liă-mĕnt, n., legislative body; **-ary**

pâr′lŏr, n., living room

pâr′loŭs, a., dangerous, clever

pà-rō′chĭ-ăl (kĭ), a., of parish, restricted; **-ly**

păr′ŏ-dў, n., funny imitation; **dist**

pà-rōle′, n. release from jail ending full term

pâr′rў, v., deflect, evade

pâr-sĭ-mō′nĭ-oŭs, a., stingy; **mony; -ly; -ness**

pârs′lēy, n., leafy plant for garnishing food

pârs′nĭp, n., white vegetable root [**-age**

pâr′sŏn, n., clergyman;

pârt, n., portion, segment; v., divide; **-ing** n.; **-ible**

pâr-tāke′, v., share, participate

pâr-tĭc′ĭ-pāte, v., take a part, do; **tor; tant** n.; **tion; pance; tive; tory**

pâr′tĭ-cĭ-ple, n., verbal adjective [piece

pâr′tĭ-cle, n., very small

pâr-tĭc′ŭ-lăr, a., special, hard to please; **-ity; -ize; -ly**

pâr′tĭ-săn, n., supporter of one side, guerrilla

pâr-tĭ′tion, n., separation, divider; **-er; -ed**

pârt′nêr, n., one who shares, teammate; **-ship**

pâr′trĭdge, n., game bird

pâr′tў, n., political group, social gathering, person

păss, n., free ticket, mountain gap; v., go forward or by, occur, decide

păs′săge, n., movement, journey, part of reading matter, hallway

păs′sĕn-gêr, n., traveler

păs′sion, n., strong emotion; **-āte** a.; **ately; -less; -lessly**

păs′sĭve, a., inactive, yielding; **sivity; -ly; -ness**

păss′pôrt, n., document of citizenship for travel abroad [aroni, etc.

păs′tă, n., spaghetti, mac-

pāste, n., sticky mixture of flour and water; **pasty** a.; **pastiness**

păs-tĕl′, n., a., (color that is) soft and pale

păs′têur-īze, v., kill bacteria in liquid; **-r; zation**

păs′tŏr, n., clergyman; **-al**

păs′tŏ-răl, a., rural, rustic; **-ly** [good

pās′trў, n., fancy baked

păs′tûre, n., animal's grazing ground

păt, n., gentle tap, small lump; v., tap; a., suitable; **-ter**

pătch, n., material to mend hole, small land plot, v., mend

pāte, n., top of head

păt′ĕnt, n., exclusive right to invention

păt′ĕnt, a., open, obvious; **ency; -ly**

păth, n., course followed, trail [pity; **-ally**

pà-thĕt′ĭc, a., arousing

pà-thŏl′ŏ-gў, n., medicine of the nature of disease; **gist; logical**

pā′thŏs, n., quality of arousing pity

pā′tiĕnt, n., one under doctor's care

pā′tiĕnt, a., calm, enduring; **tience; -ly**

pă′tĭ-ō, n., paved area of house [of family

pā′trĭ-ârch, n., father, head

pà-trĭ′ciăn, n., nobleman

pā′trĭ-ŏt, n., one loyal to

his country; **-ism**

pā′trȯn, *n.*, sponsor, regular customer; **-age; -ize**

păt′têrn, *n., v.,* model

păt′tў, *n.,* small fish or meat cake

pȧunch, *n.,* large belly; **-y** *a.;* **-iness**

pȧu′pêr, *n.,* poor person

pȧuse, *n.,* temporary stop; *v.,* hesitate

pȧ-vǐl′iȯn, *n.,* large tent, exhibition building

pȧwn, *n., v.,* pledge; *n.,* lowest chessman

pȧwn′brō-kêr, *n.,* one who loans money on thing left as security

pāy, *n.,* salary; *v.,* give what is due ex. money, make; **-er; -ee; -ment; -able**

pēach, *n.,* fruit, orangish yellow; **-y** *a.*

pēa′cŏck, *n.,* bird with large colorful tail

pēak, *n.,* highest point

pēak′ĕd, *a.,* sickly; **-ness**

pēal, *n.,* ringing sound

pēa′nŭt, *n.,* vine with edible seeds

pêarl, *n.,* smooth round gem found in oyster; **-y** *a.*

pĕas′ȧnt, *n.,* small farmer, ignorant person; **-ry**

pēat, *n.,* decayed plant matter [bly

pĕb′ble, *n.,* small stone;

pė-cȧn′, *n.* tree with edible nut [mal

pĕc′cȧ-rў, *n.,* piglike ani-

pĕck, *n.,* dry measure of eight quarts; *v.,* strike with beak, kiss

pė-cūl′iȧr, *a.,* out of ordinary, odd; **-ity; -ly**

pĕc′u-lāte, *v.,* embezzle; **tor; tion**

pė-cū′nĭ-ār-ў, *a.,* of money, financial; **arily**

pĕd′ȧ-gŏ-gў, *n.,* teaching profession; **gogics; gogic; gogical; gogically** [by foot

pĕd′ȧl, *n.,* lever operated

pĕd′ȧnt, *n.,* one who ov-

erstresses his learning; **-ry; -ic; -ically**

pĕd′ĕs-tȧl, *n.,* base, ex. column, statue

pė-dĕs′trĭ-ȧn, *n.,* walker; *a.,* on foot, ordinary

pė-dī-ăt′rĭcs, *n.,* medicine of children; **cian** *n.;* **ric**

pĕd′ĭ-cūre, *n.,* care of feet; **curist**

pĕd′ĭ-grēe, *n.,* ancestry

pēel, *n.,* rind; *v.,* cut or strip away

pēer, *n.,* an equal, nobleman; **-less; -lessly; -lessness**

pēer, *v.,* look closely

pēe′vĭsh, *a.,* fretful; **-ly; -ness**

peign-oir′, *n.,* (pān-wâr) woman's short robe

pĕl′ĭ-cȧn, *n.,* water bird

pĕl′lĕt, *n.,* little ball

pĕlt, *n.,* animal fur; *v.,* throw things at; **-er**

pĕl′vĭs, *n.,* body cavity of hip bones and lower backbone; **vic**

pĕn, *n.,* small enclosure for animals, writing device

pē′nȧl, *a.,* of legal punishment; **-ty; -ize; -ization; -ly** [of sin

pĕn′ȧnce, *n.,* repentance

pĕn′chȧnt, *n.,* inclination, liking

pĕnd′ȧnt, *n.,* hanging ornament, ex. locket, charm

pĕnd′ĭng, *a.,* not decided; *prep.,* during, until

pĕn′dū-lŭm (jū), *n.,* body hung to swing freely; **lous; lously; lousness**

pĕn′ė-trāte, *v.,* enter, affect; **tion; tive; trant**

pĕn′gu̇in, *n.,* flightless bird [drug

pĕn-ĭ-cǐl′lĭn, *n.,* antibiotic

pĕn-ĭn′su̇-lȧ, *n.,* land projecting into water; **-r** *a.*

pē′nĭs, *n.,* male sex organ; **nile** *a.*

pĕn′ĭ-tĕnt, *a.,* sorry for doing wrong; **tence; -ly**

pĕn-ĭ-tĕn′tiȧ-rў, *n.,* prison

pĕn′nȧnt, *n.,* long narrow

P
R

flag [**-ness**
pĕn'nĭ-lĕss, *a.*, very poor;
pĕn'sion, *n.*, regular payment for past services; **-er; -ary** *a.*; **-able**
pĕn'sĭve, *a.*, thinking deeply; **-ly; -ness**
pĕnt, *a.*, held in
pĕn'tȧ-gŏn, *n.*, five-sided figure; **-al; -ally**
pĕnt'hoūse, *n.*, rooftop apartment
pė-nū'rĭ-oŭs, *a.*, stingy; **-ly; -ness**
pĕn'ū-rȳ, *n.*, poverty
pē'ŏn, *n.*, laborer; **-age**
pēo'ple, *n.*, human beings, group members
pĕp'pėr, *n.*, spicy seasoning, vegetable; **-y** *a.*
pĕp'sĭn, *n.*, digestive enzyme; **peptic**
pêr-ăm'bū-lāte, *v.*, walk; **tor; tion; tory**
pêr-cāle', *n.*, fine cotton cloth
pêr-cēive', *v.*, grasp through senses; **-r; ceivable; ceivably**
pêr-cĕnt', *a., adv.*, out of a hundred; **-age; -ile** *n.*
pêr-cĕp'tion, *n.*, perceiving; **-al; tible; tibility; tibly; tive; tively; tiveness; tual; tually**
pêrch, *n.*, fish; *v.*, sit
pêr'cȯ-lāte, *v.*, brew coffee; **tor; tion**
pêr-dī'tion, *n.*, hell
pêr'ė-grĭ-nāte, *v.*, travel; **tor; tion**
pêr-ĕn'nĭ-ȧl, *a.*, lasting for a long time; **-ly**
pêr-fĕct', *v.*, make perfect; *a.*, (**pêr'fĕct**) complete, exact, excellent; **-er; -ion; -ness; -ible; -ibility, -ly**
pêr'fĭ-dȳ, *n.*, treachery; **fidious; fidiously**
pêr'fȯ-rāte, *v.*, make holes in; **tor; tion; tive; rable**
pêr-fôrm', *v.*, do, accomplish, act; **-er; -ance; -able** [ing liquid
pêr'fūme, *n.*, sweet smell-
pêr-fŭnc'tȯ-rȳ, *a.*, done in-

differently; **rily; riness**
pêr-fūse', *v.*, spread with liquid; **sion; sive**
pêr'il, *n.*, danger, **-oŭs; -ously; -ousness**
pė-rĭm'ė-têr, *n.*, measurement of a boundary of area
pē'rĭ-ȯd, *n.*, portion of time, punctuation mark (.)
pė-rĭph'êr-ȳ, *n.*, edge, perimeter; **eral**
pêr'ĭ-scōpe, *n.*, tube with mirrors to see above; **scopic**
pêr'īsh, *v.*, die, be ruined; **-able; -ability; -ableness**
pêr'jû-rȳ, *n.*, lying under oath; **jure** *v.*; **jurer; jurious**
pêr'mȧ-nėnt, *a.*, lasting, forever; **nence; nency; -ly**
pêr'mē-āte, *v.*, pass or spread through; **tion; tive; ance; ant; able; ability; ably**
pêr-mĭs'sion, *n.*, consent; **sive; sively; siveness**
pêr-nĭ'cious, *a.*, harmful, deadly; **-ly; -ness**
pêr-pėn-dĭc'ū-lȧr, *a.*, exactly upright; **-ity; -ly**
pêr'pė-trāte, *v.*, do evil thing; **tor; tion**
pêr-pĕt'ū-ȧl, *a.*, lasting forever; **-ity; ate; ator; ation; -ly**
pêr-plĕx', *v.*, puzzle, confuse; **-ity; -ing; -ingly**
pêr'sė-cūte, *v.*, harass, punish; **tor; tion; tive; tory**
pêr-sė-vēre', *v.*, continue despite difficulties; **-nce; -nt**
pêr'sĭst, *v.*, continue steadily; **-ence; -ent; -ently**
pêr'sȯn-ȧ-ble, *a.*, attractive; **bly; -ness**
pêr'sȯn-ȧl, *a.*, individual, private; **-ity; -ize; -ism; -ly**
pêr-sŏn'ĭ-fȳ, *v.*, represent as a person; typify; **fier;**

fication [ees
pêr-sȯn-nĕl′, *n.,* employ-
pêr-spĕc′tĭve, *n.,* appearance at a distance, pro-
portion; **-ly**
pêr-spĭc′ū-oŭs, *a.,* easily
understood; **-ly; -ness;
cuity**
pêr-spīre′, *v.,* sweat; **ration; spiratory**
pêrt, *a.,* impudent; **-ly;
-ness** [to
pêr-tāin′,*v.,* belong, relate
pêr-tĭ-nā′cioŭs, *a.,* stubborn; **nacity; -ly**
pêr′tĭ-nĕnt, *a.,* relevant;
nence; nency; -ly
pêr-tûrb′, *v.,* alarm, worry;
-er; -ation; -able; -edly
pė-rūse′, *v.,* study, read;
-r; rusal
pêr-vāde′, *v.,* spread
throughout; **vasion; va-
sive; vasively; vasive-
ness**
pêr-vêrse′, *a.,* improper,
contrary; **sion; sity;
sive; -ly; -ness**
pêr′vêrt,*n.,* perverted person; *v.,* **(pêr-vêrt′)** lead
astray, distort; **-ed;
-edly; -edness**
pêr′vĭ-oŭs, *a.,* open to influence; **-ness**
pĕs′sĭ-mĭsm, *n.,* tendency
to expect the worst;
mist; mistic; mistically
pĕst, *n.,* annoyance; **-er** *v.*
pĕs′tĭ-lĕnce, *n.,* contagious disease; **lent;
lently**
pĕs′tle, *n.,* club-shaped
tool for grinding
pĕt, *n.,* tamed animal,
cherished person; *v.,* caress; *a.,* favorite; **-ter**
pė-tī′tion, *n.,* written request; *v.,* appeal; **-er;
-ary**
pĕt′rĭ-fȳ, *v.,* change into
stone, frighten; **fied**
pė-trō′lė-ŭm,*n.,* oily liquid
found in rock layers
pĕt′tĭ-cōat, *n.,* female undergarment
pĕt′tȳ, *a.,* trivial, minor
pĕt′u-lȧnt, *a.,* impatient;

lance; lancy; -ly
pė-tū′nĭ-ȧ, *n.,* flower
pew̄, *n.,* church bench
pew̄′têr, *n.,* alloy of tin
phăl′lŭs, *n.,* image of
penis; **lic**
phâr′mȧ-cȳ, *n.,* preparing
and dispensing medi-
cine, drugstore; **cist;
cology; cological; col-
ogically; ceutics; ceut-
ical; ceutically**
phăr′ȳnx, *n.,* tube joining
mouth and esophagus
phāse,*n.,* aspect, stage of
development; **sic**
phė-nŏm′ė-nȯn, *n.,* unusual happening; **nal;
nally**
phĭ-lăn′dêr, *v.,* make love
insincerely; **-er**
phĭ-lăn′thrȯ-pȳ, *n.,* charity; generosity; **pist;
pize; thropic; thropi-
cally**
phĭ-lăt′ė-lȳ, *n.,* collecting
stamps; **list; lic;
telically** [music
phĭl-hâr-mŏn′ĭc,*a.,* loving
phĭ-lŏs′ȯ-phȳ, *n.,* study of
truths, system of princi-
ples; **pher; phize;
sophic; sophically**
phlĕgm, *n.,* secreted
mucus [cool; **-al; -ally**
phlĕg-măt′ĭc, *a.,* dull,
phō′bĭ-ȧ, *n.,* excessive
fear; **bic**
phŏn′ĭcs, *n.,* science of
sound, method of teach-
ing reading
phō′nȯ-grăph, *n.,* record
player; **-ic; -ically**
phŏs′phāte, *n.,* chemical
fertilizer; **tize; phatic**
phŏs′phô-rŭs, *n.,* white
chemical element;
phoric; rous
phȯ-tŏg′rȧ-phȳ, *n.,* art of
taking pictures with
camera; **pher; graphic;
graphically**
phrė-nĕt′ĭc, *a.,* insane
phȳ′lŭm,*n.,* division of animal kingdom
phȳs′ĭc, *n.,* laxative
phȳs′ĭ-cȧl, *a.,* of matter,

bodily, material; **-ity; -ly**

phý-sĭ'ciàn, *n.,* doctor, one who practices medicine

phýs-ĭ-ŏl'ó-gȳ, *n.,* science of function of organisms; **gist**

pĭ-ăn'ō, *n.,* large keyboard instrument; **anist**

pĭ'cà, *n.,* type size

pĭc'có-lō, *n.,* small flute

pĭck, *n.,* pointed tool, choice; *v.,* dig at, pluck, select; **-er**

pĭck'le, *n.,* food prepared in spicy vinegar solution

pĭc'nĭc, *n.,* meal eaten outdoors; **nicker**

pĭc'tûre, *n.,* visual representation, likeness, description

pĭc-tûr-ĕsque', *a.,* quaint, beautiful; **-ly; -ness**

pie, *n.,* bake pastry with filling

piēce, *n.,* part, single thing; *v.,* join

piĕd'mŏnt, *a.,* at base of mountain   [dock

piĕr, *n.,* bridge support,

piĕrce, *v.,* make a hole in, sound sharply; **-r; -ingly**

pĭ'ė-tȳ, *n.,* religious devotion, loyalty

pĭg'hĕad-ėd, *a.,* stubborn; **-ly; -ness**

pĭg'mėnt, *n.,* coloring matter; **-ation; -ize; -ary**

pĭg'tāil, *n.,* braid of hair

pīke, *n.,* freshwater fish

pīle, *n.,* heap, rug's fluffiness, heavy beam; *v.,* load accumulate

pĭl'fêr, *v.,* steal; **-er; -age**

pĭl'grĭm, *n.,* traveler to holy place; **-age**

pĭl'làge, *n., v.,* plunder; **-r**

pĭl'làr, *n.,* upright support

pī'lŏt, *n.,* person licensed to steer ship or plane

pĭ-mĕn'tō, *n.,* sweet red pepper   [swelling

pĭm'ple, *n.,* small skin

pĭn'à-fôre, *n.,* sleeveless dress

pĭn'cêrs, *n. pl.,* gripping tool, lobster or crab claw

pĭnch, *n.,* distress; *v.,*

squeeze between finger and thumb, steal

pīne, *n.,* evergreen tree; **naceous; -y** *a.*

pīne, *v.,* long for

pīne'àp-ple, *n.,* tropical fruit

pĭnk, *n., a.,* pale or light red   [point

pĭn'nà-cle, *n.,* highest

pĭ-nŏch'le, *n.,* card game

pĭn'pŏint, *v.,* locate exactly; *a.,* exact

pĭn'tō, *n.,* spotted horse

pĭn'ŭp, *n.,* sexy picture of girl   [discoverer

pĭ-ó-nēer', *n.,* early settler,

pī'oùs, *a.,* holy, religious; **osity; -ly; -ness**

pīpe, *n.,* tube through which things pass; **-ful**

pī'quànt, *a.,* pugent, stimulating; **quancy; -ness; -ly**

pīque, *n.,* resentment; *v.,* provoke, offend

pĭ-que' (quā), *n.,* cotton cloth

pĭs-tä'chĭ-ō, *n.,* edible nut, tree

pĭs'tĭl, *n.,* seed-bearing part of flower

pĭs'tòn, *n.,* movable disk in cylinder

pĭt, *n.,* stone in fruit, hole in ground, small scar; *v.,* mark with pits, compete

pĭtch, *n.,* tar, throw; *v.,* set up, toss, degree, slope

pĭtch'êr, *n.,* one who pitches, container for pouring liquid

pĭth, *n.,* inner plant tissue, main part; **-y** *a.*

pĭt'tànce, *n.,* small amount (of money)

pĭt'ȳ, *n.,* sorrow felt for another; **pitiful; pitiless**

pĭv'òt, *n.,* point on which thing turns; *v.,* turn; **-al**

plăc'àrd, *n.,* notice, sign

plā'cāte, *v.,* appease; **-r; tion; tive; tory; able; ability; ably**

plăc'ĭd, *a.,* calm; **-ity; -ly; -ness**

plā'già-rīze, *v.,* take an-

other's ideas as own; **-r;
rism**

plāgue, *n.*, fatal epidemic
disease; *v.*, annoy

plāin'tĭff, *n.*, one who
brings law suit

plāin'tĭve, *a.*, sad; **-ly;
-ness**

plāit, *n.*, braid (of hair)

plăn, *n.*, detailed method,
arrangement; *v.*, make a
plan, intend; **-ner**

plăn-ė-tār'ĭ-ŭm, *n.*, building to project heavenly
images

plănk, *n.*, long thick board

plănt, *n.*, living thing that
is stationary ex. tree,
herb, factory; *v.*, put in
soil to grow, set firmly

plăn-tā'tion, *n.*, large tropical farm

plăs'mà, *n.*, fluid part of
blood; **-tic**

plăs'têr, *n.*, pasty mixture
that hardens; **-er; -y** *a.*

plăs'tĭc, *n.*, *a.* (syntheti-
cally made compound
that is) flexible; **-ity; -ize;
-ally**

plāte, *n.*, shallow dish,
metal sheet, denture; *v.*,
coat with gold or silver

plă-teau' (tō), *n.*, high
level land

plăt'fôrm, *n.*, flat, raised
flooring, political policy

plăt'ĭ-nŭm, *n.*, grey metallic chemical; **nize; tinic**

plăt'ĭ-tūde, *n.*, trite remark;
**dinize; dinous; di-
nously**

plăt'ў-pŭs, *n.*, mammal

plău'sĭ-ble, *a.*, seemingly
true; **bility; bly; -ness**

plāy'fŭl, *a.*, full of fun; **-ly;
-ness**

plāy'ground, *n.*, outdoor
recreation area

plāy'wright, *n.*, one who
writes plays

plă'zà, *n.*, public square

plēad, *v.*, argue a law
case, beg

plēase, *v.*, be agreeable,
be kind enough of

plēas'ûre, *n.*, enjoyment,

wish; **-ful; urable; ura-
bility; urableness; ur-
ably**

plēat, *n.*, fold in cloth

plė-bī'àn, *n.*, common person; **-ism; -ly**

plĕdge, *n.*, security, oath;
v., promise; **-r**

plĕ'nà-rў, *a.*, full, attended
by membership; **rily**

plĕn'tў, *n.*, ample amount;
tiful; tifulness; tifully

plĕth'ó-rà, *n.*, excess

plĕx'ŭs, *n.*, network

plī'à-ble, *a.*, easily bent or
influenced; **bility; bly;
-ness**

plī'êrs, *n. pl.*, small gripping tool   [tion

plīght, *n.*, danger, condi-

plŏd, *v.*, move heavily;
-der; -dingly

plŏt, *n.*, small area of
ground, evil scheme

plŏw, *n.*, *v.* (farm implement to) cut and turn up
soil; **-er; -able**

ploy (plŏi), *n.*, outwitting
maneuver   [out

plŭck, *n.*, courage; *v.*, pull

plŭck'ў, *a.*, brave

plŭg, *n.*, hole stopper device to make electrical
contact; *v.*, stop up, ad-
vertise

plŭm, *n.*, tree, fruit

plŭmb, *n.*, device to find
water depth; *a.*, vertical

plŭm'mĕt, *v.*, fall, drop

plŭmp, *v.*, drop; *a.*, full and
rounded; **-per**

plŭn'dêr, *n.*, robbery, loot;
v., take by force; **-er;
-age; -ous**

plŭnge, *n.*, *v.*, dive, rush

plū-răl'ĭ-tў, *n.*, greatest
number, ex. of votes

plŭsh, *n.*, thick, velvety
fabric; *a.*, luxurious; **-y**
a.

plū-tŏc'rà-cў, *n.*, government by wealthy; **crat**

plū-tō'nĭ-ŭm, *n.*, metallic
element

plū'vĭ-àl, *a.*, of rain

plў, *n.*, single thickness;
v., bend, do work, ask,

**P
R**

travel

pneu-măt'ĭc, *a.,* filled with air; **-s; -ally**

pneu-mō'nĭ-à, *n.,* lung disease

pōach, *v.,* boil in water, hunt or fish illegally; **-er**

pŏd, *n.,* shell holding seeds or beans

pō-dī'à-trÿ, *n.,* treatment of human foot; **trist; ric**

pō'dĭ-ŭm, *n.,* raised platform

pō'ĕm, *n.,* rhythmical composition; **etry; etic; etical; etically**

pō-grŏm', *n.,* organized massacre

pōĭgn'ànt, *a.,* sharp, painful; **ancy; -ly**

pōĭnt'êr, *n.,* indicator, hint, hunting dog

pōĭnt'lĕss, *a.,* without meaning; **-ly; -ness**

pōĭse, *n.,* balance, dignity of manner

pōĭ'sòn, *n.,* substance causing death or illness; **-er; -ous; -ously; -ousness** [-r

pōke, *n., v.,* jab, search;

pōk'êr, *n.,* card game

pō-lăr'ĭ-tÿ, *n.,* magnetic attraction to pole; **ize; ization; izer**

pò-lĕm'ĭc, *a.,* controversial; **-ally**

pò-līce, *n.,* governmental law enforcement, its members; *v.,* control by police; **-man** *n.*

pŏl'ĭ-cÿ, *n.,* principle, insurance contract

pō-lĭ-ō-mÿ-è-lī'tĭs, *n.,* virus disease of spine

pŏl'ĭsh, *v.,* rub to make smooth and glossy, refine; **-er**

pò-līte', *n.,* showing good manners; **-ly; -ness**

pŏl-ĭ-tĭ'cian, *n.,* one active in government

pŏl'ĭ-tĭcs, *n.,* science of government; **cal; calize; cally**

pŏl'kà, *n.,* fast dance

pŏll, *n.,* head, counting of

votes, survey; *v.,* count

pŏl'lén, *n.,* powdery male sex cells of flower

pòl-lūte', *v.,* make dirty; **-r; tion**

pŏl'ÿ-ĕs-têr, *n.,* synthetic fiber

pò-lÿg'à-mÿ, *n.,* marriage to two or more spouses at once; **mist; mous; mously**

pŏl-ÿ-tĕch'nĭc, *a.,* of instruction in technical areas

pŏmp, *n.,* splendor

pŏm'pà-dôur, *n.,* hair style

pŏn'chō, *n.,* blanketlike cloak

pŏnd, *n.,* small lake

pŏn'dêr, *v.,* think deeply; **-er; -able; -ability**

pŏn'dêr-oŭs, *a.,* heavy; **osity; -ly; -ness**

pŏn'tĭff, *n.,* Pope, bishop

pŏn-tōon', *n.,* flat bottomed boat or float

pōol, *n.,* small garden pond, billiards, common fund

pôor, *a.,* lacking material things, inferior; **-ly**

Pōpe, *n.,* head of Catholic Church; **popish**

pŏp'lĭn, *n.,* ribbed cotton cloth

pŏp'ū-làce, *n.,* people

pŏp'ū-làr, *a.,* of common people, prevalent, well liked; **-ity; -ize; -izer; -ization** [ants

pŏp-ū-lā'tion, *n.,* inhabit-

pôr'cè-laĭn, *n.,* hard white ceramic ware; **laneous**

pôrch, *n.,* covered entrance to building

pôr'cū-pīne, *n.,* animal covered with sharp spines

pôre, *n.,* tiny opening; *v.,* study carefully, think

pôrk, *n.,* meat of pig

pôr-nŏg'rà-phÿ, *n.,* lewd writings or pictures; **pher, graphic; graphically**

pôr'ridge, *n.,* hot cereal

pôrt, *n.,* harbor, red wine,

left side of ship, opening

pôr′á-ble, *a.*, easily carried; **bility**

pôr-tĕnd′, *v.*, be an omen

pôr′tĕnt, *n.*, omen

pôr-tĕn′toŭs, *a.*, ominous, pompous; **-ly; -ness**

pôrt-fō′lĭ-ō, *n.*, small case for papers

pôr′tĭ-cō, *n.*, large porch with columns

pôrt′lỹ, *a.*, fat and stately; **liness**

pôr′traĭt, *n.*, representation of a person; **-ist; -ure**

pôr-trāy′, *v.*, make a picture, describe; **-al** *n.;* **-er; -able**

pōse, *n.*, assumed manner; *v.*, present, model, pretend

pó-sĭ′tion, *n.*, opinion, place, status, job

pŏs′ĭ-tĭve, *a.*, very sure, greater than zero; **-ly; -ness**

pós-sĕss′, *v.*, own, have, control; **-or; -ion; -ed; -ive; -ively; -iveness**

pōst, *n.*, upright piece of wood, position, military camp, mail; *v.*, put up, assign to a post, mail

pōst′áge, *n.*, fee for sending mail

pōs-tē′rĭ-ŏr, *a.*, behind, later; **-ity; -ly**

pōst′hŭ-moŭs, *a.*, occurring after death; **-ly**

pōst′mârk, *n.*, mark that cancels postage stamp

pōst-môr′tĕm, *a.*, done after death

pōst-nā′tăl, *a.*, after birth

pōst-nŭp′tĭăl, *a.*, after marriage; **-ly**

pōst-pōne′, *v.*, delay; **-r; -ment; ponable**

pōst′scrĭpt, *n.*, addition to letter

pŏs′tûre, *n.*, position of body, attitude

pō′tá-ble, *a.*, fit to drink; **bility; -ness**

pó-tăs′sĭ-ŭm, *n.*, soft metallic element [tuber

pó-tā′tó, *n.*, vegetable

pō′tĕnt, *a.*, powerful, effective; **tency; -ly**

pō′tĕn-tāte, *n.*, ruler

pó-tĕn′tĭăl, *n.*, undeveloped ability; *a.*, possible, latent; **-ity; -ly**

pō′tion, *n.*, drink

pōt-pôur′rĭ, *n.*, mixture

pŏuch, *n.*, small bag; **-y** *a.*

pōul′trỹ, *n.*, fowls raised for meat or eggs; **-man**

pŏund, *n.*, weight of 16 ounces, place of confinement; *v.*, beat

pôur, *v.*, flow freely, rain heavily; **-er**

pŏv′êr-tỹ, *n.*, being poor, need, inadequacy

pōw′dêr, *n.*, fine, dustlike particles; **-y** *a.*

pōw′êr, *n.*, ability, strength, authority; **-ful; -fully; -fulness; -less; -lessly; -lessness**

pŏx, *n.*, disease with skin eruptions

prăc′tĭce, *n.*, custom, habit, work in a profession; *v.*, do repeatedly

prăg-măt′ĭc, *a.*, practical; **tist; tism; -ally**

prai′riĕ, *n.*, level grassland

prāise, *v.*, express approval; **-r**

prănce, *v.*, strut with spirit

prănk, *n.*, mischievous trick; **-ster; -ish; -ishly; -ishness**

prāte, *n.*, *v.*, chatter; **-r**

prăwn, *n.*, shrimplike animal   [God

prāy, *v.*, implore, ask of

prēach, *v.*, give moral or religious advice; **-er; -y** *a.*   [tion

prē′ăm-ble, *n.*, introduc-

pré-cār′ĭ-oŭs, *a.*, risky; **-ly; -ness**

pré-cēde′, *v.*, come before; **-nce; cession; cessional**

prē′cĕpt, *n.*, rule of conduct; **-ive; -ively**

prē′cĭnct, *n.*, city district

prē′cioŭs, *a.*, of great value; **-ly; -ness**

P R

prė-cĭp'ĭ-tāte, v., bring on; a., (tāte) sudden; **tor; tive; -ly; -ness**

prė-cĭp-ĭ-tā'tion, n., rain, snow, etc.

prė-clūde', v., prevent; **clusion; clusive; clusively**

prė-cō'cioŭs, a., developed beyond one's years; **city; -ly; -ness**

prė-cŭr'sŏr, n., forerunner

prĕd'ȧ-tô-rỹ, a., exploiting others; **tor; rily; riness**

prė-dĭc'ȧ-mėnt, n., difficult situation; **-al**

prĕd'ĭ-cāte, v., declare, base; **tion; tive; tively**

prė-dĭct', v., tell in advance; **-or; -ion; -ive; -ively; -able; -ability; -ably** [ence

prė-dĭ-lĕc'tion, n., preference

prė-dŏm'ĭ-nāte, v., be greater, rule; **tor; tion; nant; nance; nancy; nantly**

prė-ėm'ĭ-nėnt, a., excelling others; **nence; -ly**

prēen, v., clean feathers, primp; **-er**

prė-fêr', v., like better, choose; **-rer; -ence; -ential; -able; -ability; -ableness; -ably**

prĕg'nȧnt, a., carrying fetus in womb, filled; **nancy; -ly**

prėj'ŭdĭce, n., unfair opinion, intolerance; **cial; cially**

prĕl'ȧte, n., clergyman

prĕl'ūde, n., introduction

prė-miẽr', n., prime minister of a nation; a., chief

prĕm'īse, n., basic assumption, (pl.) property

prė'mi-ŭm, n., reward, insurance payment, high value

prė-pāre', v., get ready; **ration; paratory; paratorily; -dly; -dness**

prė-pŏn'dêr-āte, v., surpass; **tion; ant; ance; ancy; antly**

pre-pŏs'têr-oŭs, a., absurd; **-ly; -ness**

prė-rŏg'ȧ-tĭve, n., privilege

prĕs'ȧge, n., warning; v., (āge) foretell; **-r**

prė'sci-ence, n., foresight

prė-scrībe', v., order, give medical advice; **-r; scription; scriptive; scriptively**

prĕs'ênce, n., attendance, appearance

prĕs'ėnt, n., something given; a., existing; v., (prės-ĕnt') introduce, give, show; **-er; -ation**

prė-sêrve', n., jam; v., save, maintain; **servable**

prĕs'ĭ-dėnt, n., highest officer; **dency; -ial; -ially**

prĕss, n., pressure, crushing machine, printing, journalists; v., squeeze, iron clothes, urge; **-er**

prĕs'sure (shûr), n., force, urgency, influence

prĕs-tīge', n., influence, earned fame; **gious**

prė-sūme', v., take for granted; **-r; sumption; sumptive**

prė-tĕnd', v., claim falsely, make believe; **-er; tense**

prė'tĕxt, n., excuse, cover-up

prĕt'tỹ, a., pleasing and dainty; adv., somewhat; **tify; tily**

prė-vȧr'ĭ-cāte, v., lie, tell falsehood; **tor; tion**

prė-vĕnt', v., keep from doing; **-er; -ion; -ive; -ively; -able**

prey (prāy), n., something hunted; v., plunder, hunt, weigh heavily; **-er**

prīce, n., v., cost, value; **-less**

prĭck, n., tiny hole made from sharp point; v., pierce; **-er**

prīde, n., self-respect; **-ful; -fully; -fulness**

prīest, n., one who leads religious rites; **-hood; -ly**

prĭg, *n.,* smug person; **-gish; -gishly; -gishness**

prī'mă-rȳ, *n.,* first, political party election; *a.,* first, basic; **rily**

prī'māte, *n.,* highest order of mammals; **-ship; tial**

prīme, *n.,* best part; *v.,* prepare; *a.,* first chief, basic

prĭm'ī-tĭve, *a.,* ancient, uncivilized, basic; **-ly; -ness**

prĭmp, *v.,* dress up fussily

prĭm'rōse, *n.,* flowering plant

prĭnce, *n.,* king's son, ruler; **-ss** *n.;* **cipality; -ly** *a.*

prĭn'cĭ-păl, *n.,* school director; money owed; *a.,* chief, first; **-ship; -ly**

prĭn'cĭ-ple, *n.,* basic truth, integrity

prĭnt, *n.,* mark made on something by pressure, photograph, copy; *v.,* mark by pressing; **-er; -ing** *n.;* **-able; -ability**

prī-ôr'ĭ-tȳ, *n.,* preference

prĭsm, *n.,* solid figure with equal and parallel sides; **-atic; -atically**

prĭs'ŏn, *n.,* jail

prī'văte, *a.,* limited to particular persons, secret; **vacy; -ly**

prĭv'ĭ-lĕge, *n.,* special right or favor

prĭv'ȳ, *n.,* outside toilet; *a.,* secret

prīze, *n.,* something won, reward; *v.,* value

prō'bāte, *v.,* validate a document

prō-bā'tion, *n.,* suspension of prison sentence, testing

prōbe, *n., v.,* (device that can) explore, investigate; **-r**

prŏb'lĕm, *n.,* perplexing question; **-atic; -atically**

prō-bŏs'cĭs, *n.,* long flexible snout, ex. elephant's trunk [*n.*

prŏ-cēed', *v.,* go on; **-ing**

prŏ-cēed'ĭngs, *n., pl.,* transaction, legal action

prŏc'ĕss, *n.,* continuing development, method

prŏ-cĕs'sion, *n.,* parade

prŏ-clĭv'ĭ-tȳ, *n.,* tendency

prŏ-crăs'tĭ-nāte, *v.,* put off doing; **tor; tion**

prŏ'crē-āte, *v.,* beget offspring; **tor; tion; tive**

prŏc'tŏr, *n.,* supervisor

prŏd, *v.,* poke with pointed stick; **-der**

prŏd'ĭ-găl, *a.,* wasteful; **-ity; -ly**

prŏ-dĭ'gioŭs, *a.,* amazing, huge; **-ly; -ness**

prŏd'ĭ-gȳ, *n.,* marvel

prō'dūce, *n.,* farm products; *v.,* **(prŏ-dūce')** bring forth, make, cause, grow; **-r; duction; ducible; ducibility**

prŏ-fāne', *a.,* irreligious, contempt for sacred things; **fanity; nation; fanatory; -ness; -ly**

prŏ-fĕs'sion, *n.,* belief, learned occupation; **-al; -ally** [teacher

prŏ-fĕs'sŏr, *n.,* college

prŏf'fêr, *n., v.,* offer

prŏ-fĭ'cĭĕnt, *a.,* skilled; **ciency; -ly**

prŏf'ĭt, *n., v.,* benefit; *n.,* business gain; **-able; -ability; -ableness; -ably; -less**

prŏ-foūnd', *a.,* deep in feelings or ideas; **fundity; -ly; -ness**

prŏ-fūse', *a.,* abundant; **fusion; -ly; -ness**

prŏg'ė-nȳ, *n.,* offspring

prŏg-nō'sĭs, *n.,* medical prediction

prō'grăm, *n., v.,* plan; *n.,* schedule of events; **-matic**

prŏg'rĕss, *n.,* moving forward; *v.,* **(prŏg-rĕss')** advance; **-ion**

prŏ-hĭb'ĭt, *v.,* forbid; **-er; -or; -ion; -ive**

prŏj'ĕct, *n.,* organized undertaking; *v.,* **(prŏj-ĕct')** propose, send forth,

P
R

stick out; **-or; -ion**
prō-lė-tăr'ĭăt, n., working
  class; **an** n., a.
prō-lĭf'ěr-āte, v., produce;
  tion [**-ally**
prō-lĭf'ĭc, a., fruitful; **-acy;**
prō'lŏgue, n., introduction
prō-lŏng', v., extend; **-er;**
  -ation [surely walk
prŏm-ė-nāde', n., lei-
prŏm'ĭ-nĕnt, a., noticeable, famous; **nence; -ly**
prō-mĭs'cū-oŭs, a., lack of
  discrimination; **cuity;**
  -ly; -nous
prŏm'ĭse, n., agreement,
  vow, cause for hope; v.,
  pledge
prō-mōte', v., advance in
  position; **-r; tion; tional**
prŏmpt, v., inspire, urge;
  a., quick; **-er; -ly; -ness**
prōne, a., lying flat; **-ly;**
  -ness [fork
prŏng, n., pointed end of
prō-noŭnce', v., declare,
  utter sounds, words,
  etc.; **-r**
prō-noŭnce'mĕnt, n., au-
  thoritative statement
prōof, n., test, conclusive
  evidence
prŏp-ȧ-găn'dȧ, n., systematic promotion of
  ideas; **dism; dist; dize;**
  distic; distically
prŏp'ȧ-gāte, v., produce
  offspring, spread; **tor;**
  tion; tive
prō-pĕl', v., drive forward
prō-pĕn'sĭ-tȳ, n., tendency
prŏp'ĕr, a., suitable, correct; **-ly**
prŏp'ĕr-tȳ, n., things
  owned, quality
prŏph'ė-cȳ, n., prediction
prŏph'ė-sȳ, v., predict
prō'phȳ-lăc-tĭc, a., protective against disease;
  laxis n.
prō-pĭn'quĭ-tȳ, n., nearness, kinship
prō-pī'tĭ-āte, v., gain favor
  of; **tor; tion; pitious; pi-**
  tiously; pitiousness;
  able
prō-pôr'tion, n., part, com-

parative relation be-
  tween things; v., bal-
  ance; **-al; -ally; -āte** n.;
  -ātely; -able
prō-pōse', v., suggest for
  consideration, offer marriage; **-r; position; po-**
  sitional; posal n.
prō-prī'ė-tŏr, n., owner; **-y**
prō-prī'ė-tȳ, n., conformity
  to proper standards
prō-sā'ĭc, a., common
  place; **-ally; -ness**
prō-scrībe', v., outlaw; **-r;**
  scription; scriptive;
  scriptively [word
prōse, n., spoken or written
prŏs'ė-cūte, v., take legal
  action against; **tor; tion;**
  cutable
prŏs'ė-lȳte, n., convert to
  another belief; **lytism;**
  lytize
prŏs'pĕct, n., outlook, an-
  ticipation, likely cus-
  tomer
prō-spĕc'tŭs, n., outline of
  proposed plan
prŏs'pĕr, v., succeed; **-ity;**
  -ous; -ously
prŏs'thė-sĭs, n., artificial
  substitute of body part;
  thetic
prŏs'tĭ-tūte, n., woman
  paid for sexual inter-
  course; **tor; tion**
prŏs'trāte, v., lay flat; a.,
  prone; **tion**
prō-tăg'ȯ-nĭst, n., main
  character in fiction
prō'tė-ge (gā), n., one
  helped by a patron in a
  career
prō'tēin, n., nitrogenous
  substance in all living
  things
prō'tĕst, n., objection; v.,
  (prō-test') oppose, assert; **-er; -or; -ation**
prō'tŏn, n., positive particle in atom's nucleus
prō'tȯ-plăsm, n., essential
  matter of all living
  things; **-ic**
prō'tȯ-tȳpe, n., original
  model; **typal; typic; typ-**
  ical

prō-tȯ-zō′ȧn, *n.*, microscopic animal; **zoic**

prō-trăct′tör, *n.*, device to draw or measure angles

prō-trūde′, *v.*, jut out; **trusion; trusive; trusively; trusiveness**

prō-tū′bêr-ȧnt, *a.*, swelling; **ance; -ly**

prŏūd, *a.*, feeling pride, stately; **-ly**

prove (prūv), *v.*, show to be true; **-r; provable; provability; provably**

prŏv′êrb, *n.*, wise saying; **-ial; -ially**

prȯ-vĭde′, *v.*, supply, prepare, require; **-r**

prŏv′ĭ-dėnt, *a.*, looking into future, economical; **dence; -ly**

prŏv′ĭnce, *n.*, geographical area, sphere

prȯ-vĭ′sion, *n.*, supplying, arrangement, requirement

prȯ-vĭ′sō, *n.*, condition; **-ry; -rily**

prȯ-vōke′, *v.*, arouse action of feeling; **-r; ocation; vocative; vocatively; vocativeness; voking; vokingly**

prŏw′ėss, *n.*, bravery

prŏwl, *v.*, wander stealthily; **-er**

prŏx′ĭ-māte, *a.*, nearest; **imity; -ly**   [to vote

prŏx′ў, *n.*, agent, authority

prūde, *a.*, one overly modest; **prudish; prudishly; prudishness**

prū′dėnt, *a.*, wisely careful; **dence; -ly; -ial; -ially**

prў, *n.*, lever; *v.*, force up, look closely   [-ist

psälm, *n.*, sacred song;

pseŭ′dȯ-nўm, *n.*, false name used by author; **-ous; -ously**

psȯ-rī′ȧ-sĭs, *n.*, skin disease   [mind

psў′chē (kē), *n.*, human

psў-chė-dėl′ĭc (kė), *a.*, of bright, vivid colors, intensification of percep-

tion; **-ally**

psў-chī′ȧ-trў (kī), *n.*, medical study of mental illness; **trist; tric; trical; trically**

psў-chō-ȧ-năl′ў-sĭs (kō), *n.*, examination of mental process; **lyst** *n.*; **lyze** *v.*; **lytic; lytical; lytically**

psў-chŏl′ȯ-gў (kol), *n.*, science of behavior; **gist; gize; logical; logically**

psў′chȯ-päth (kȯ), *n.*, one with mental disorder; **-y; -ic; -ology; -ologist; -ological**

psў-chō′sĭs (kō), *n.*, severe mental disorder; **chotic**

psў-chō-sȯ-măt′ic (kō), *a.*, having bodily symptoms from mental origin; **-ally**

ptȯ′māine (tō), *n.*, poisonous substance found in decaying food

pū′bêr-tў, *n.*, physical development when sexual maturity begins

pŭb′lĭc, *n.*, people; *a.*, of the people, known by all; **-ly**

pŭb-lĭc′ĭ-tў, *n.*, notice to the people; **cize**

pŭb′lĭsh, *v.*, make known publicly, issue written work; **-er; -able**

pŭck, *n.*, hard rubber disk for ice hockey

pŭd′dĭng, *n.*, soft cooked food

pū′êr-īle, *a.*, childish; **ilism; ility; -ly**

pŭg-nā′ciȯŭs, *a.*, quarrelsome; **nacity; -ly; -ness**

pŭl′chrĭ-tūde (krĭ), *n.*, physical beauty; **dinous**

pŭl′lėt, *n.*, young hen

pŭl′mȯ-nār-ў, *a.*, of lungs

pŭlp, *n.*, soft moist mass; **-y** *a.*   [platform

pŭl′pĭt, *n.*, church's raised

pŭlse, *n.*, beat of blood flow through arteries

pŭl′vêr-īze, *v.*, crush into powder; **-r; zation**

P
R

pū'mà, *n.,* cougar

pŭm'īce, *n.,* light porous rock; **-ous**

pŭmp, *n.,* machine that forces liquid or gas in or out, low cut shoe; **-er**

pŭmp'kĭn, *n.,* large orange gourdlike fruit [**-ster**

pŭn, *n.,* play on words;

pŭnch, *n.,* piercing tool, fruit drink; *v.,* hit with fist; **-er**

pŭnc-tĭl'ĭ-oŭs, *a.,* very exact; **-ly; -ness** [**-ness**

pŭnc'tū-ăl, *a.,* on time; **-ly;**

pŭnc'tûre, *n.,* hole made by sharp point; *v.,* pierce

pŭn'gĕnt, *a.,* sharp or strong in taste or smell; **gency; -ly**

pŭn'ĭsh, *v.,* make suffer for wrongdoing; **-er; -ment; -able; -ability**

pŭnt, *n.,* football kick, flat-bottomed boat

pū'nỹ, *a.,* inferior, weak

pū'pà, *n.,* insect in stage before adulthood

pū'pĭl, *n.,* student, dark opening in center of eye

pŭp'pĕt, *n.,* animated doll; **-eer** *n.;* **-ry**

pū-ree' (rā), *n.,* mashed, strained food

pûr-gà-tô'rỹ, *n.,* state of temporary punishment

pûrge, *v.,* cleanse, get rid of, **-r**

pū'rĭ-fỹ, *v.,* make pure; **fier; fication; ficatory**

pū-rĭ-tăn'ĭ-càl, *a.,* very strict; **-ly**

pûr'pôrt, *n.,* meaning; *v.,* imply

pûr'pòse, *n.,* aim, intension; **-ful; -fully; -fulness; -less; -lessly; -lessness; -ly**

pûr-sūe', *v.,* chase, strive for [**-ance**

pûr-vey' (vā) *v.,* supply;

pŭs, *n.,* discharge of an infection; **-sy** *a.*

pŭsh'ō-vêr, *n.,* goal easy to accomplish

pŭs'tūle, *n.,* small pimple containing pus

pū'trĭd, *a.,* rotten, bad smelling; **trefy; trefier; trefaction; -ity; -ness; -ly**

pŭtt, *v.,* tap golf ball into hole; **-er**

pŭt'tỹ, *n.,* soft plastic mixture

pŭz'zle, *n.,* very difficult problem; *v.,* confuse; **-r; -ment**

pỹg'mỹ, *n.,* very undersized person; **-ism**

pȳ'lŏn, *n.,* tall tower

pȳ-ór-rhē'à, *n.,* gum disease; **-l**

pȳre, *n.,* wood pile for burning dead

pȳ-rò-mā'nĭ-à, *n.,* compulsion to start fires; **-c** *n.,* *a.;* **-cal**

pȳ'thŏn, *n.,* large snake

Q

quăck, *n.,* fraudulent medical practitioner; **-ery; -ish; -ishly**

quàd'rànt, *n.,* quarter part of a circle; **-al**

quàd'rū-pĕd, *n.,* animal with four feet; **-al**

quàd-rū'plĕt, *n.,* any of four offspring born together

quàff, *v.,* drink deeply

quăg'mĭre, *n.,* land yielding under foot

quáil, *n.,* small game bird; *v.,* draw back in fear

quáint, *a.,* pleasingly old-fashioned, odd; **-ly; -ness**

quàl'ĭ-fỹ, *v.,* make fit, limit, characterize; **fier; fication; fied; fiedly; fiedness; fiable; -ingly**

quàl'ĭ-tỹ, *n.,* feature, nature, excellence; **tative; tatively**

quàlm, *n.,* uneasy feeling; **-ish; -ishly; -ishness**

quàn'da-rỹ, *n.,* state of uncertainty

quàn'tĭ-tỹ, *n.,* amount

quâr'àn-tĭne, *n.,* isolation for contagious disease

quär′rĕl, *n.,* *v.,* dispute verbally; **-er; -some** *a.*

quär′rÿ, *n.,* prey, place where rock is excavated

quar′ter (quôr), *n.,* fourth, city district, (pl.) lodgings

quartz (quôrtz), *n.,* bright mineral; **iferous**

quăsh, *v.,* suppress; **-er**

quä′sī, *a.,* seeming; *adv.,* in part

quä′vêr, *v.,* tremble; **-er; -y** *a.;* **-ingly**

quĕa′sÿ, *a.,* causing nausea; **sily; siness**

quĕer, *a.,* strange; **-ly; -ness** [**-er**

quĕll, *v.,* subdue, quiet;

quĕnch, *v.,* put out, satisfy; **-er; -able; -less**

quêr′ŭ-loŭs, *a.,* complaining; **-ly; -ness**

quē′rÿ, *n.,* *v.,* question

quĕst, *n.,* search

quĕs′tion, *n.,* inquiry, doubt, problem; *v.,* ask, challenge; **-er; -less**

queūe, *n.,* line of waiting people, hair braid

quĭb′ble, *n.,* minor objection; *v.,* evade; **-r**

quĭche, *n.,* custard pie

quĭck′sănd, *n.,* wet, loose sand yielding to weight

quĭck-wĭt′tĕd, *a.,* alert; **-ly; -ness** [**cence ;-ly**

quī-ĕs′cĕnt, *a.,* quiet;

quī′ĕt, *v.,* *a.,* (make) still, silent, calm; **-ude** *n.;* **-ly; -ness**

quĭll, *n.,* large feather, porcupine's spine

quĭlt, *n.,* layered bedcover; **-ing** *n.* [**malaria**

quī′nīne, *n.,* medicine for

quĭn-tĕt′, *n.,* any of five offspring born together

quĭn-tū′ple, *v.,* *a.,* make five times as much

quĭp, *n.,* witty remark; *v.,* joke; **-ster**

quĭrk, *n.,* peculiarity; **-y** *a.*

quĭt, *v.,* stop, leave; **-ter**

quīte, *adv.,* completely, really

quĭv′êr, *v.,* shake

quĭx-ŏt′ĭc, *a.,* idealistic, impractical; **-ally**

quĭz′zĭ-căl, *a.,* comical, perplexed; **-ity; -ly**

quō′rŭm, *n.,* minimum number of members to legally do business

quō′tȧ, *n.,* assigned share

quōte, *v.,* repeat words exactly, state price of; **-r; tation; quotable**

quō′tiĕnt, *n.,* resulting number from division

R

răb′bī, *n.,* Jewish clergyman; **-nic; -nical; -nically**

răb′bĭt, *n.,* long-eared rodentlike mammal

răb′ble, *n.,* *v.,* mob

răb′ĭd, *a.,* fanatical, of rabies; **-ity; -ly; -ness**

rā′biēs, *n.,* disease gotten from animal bite

rāce, *n.,* speed competition; *v.,* be in race, move swiftly

rāce, *n.,* division of mankind; **cial; cially**

răc′ĭsm, *n.,* racial discrimination; **ist**

răck, *n.,* framework for holding things, torture instrument, torment

răck′ĕt, *n.,* noise, dishonest scheme, stringed frame for tennis

răc-ön-teûr′, *n.,* story teller

răc′ÿ, *a.,* pungent, spirited; **raciness; racily**

rā′dâr, *n.,* radio detecting and ranging device

rā′dĭ-ȧnt, *a.,* shining brightly; *n.,* source of light or heat; **ance; -ly**

rā′dĭ-āte, *v.,* give forth, shine, send from center; **tion**

rā′dĭ-ā-tör, *n.,* heating device for homes

răd′ĭ-căl, *a.,* politically extreme, basic; **-ism; -ize; -ization; -ness; -ly**

rā′dĭ-ō, *n.,* device to send

P R

and receive sound by electric waves

rā-dǐ-ō-ǎc'tǐve, *a.*, giving off radiant energy; **tivity; -ly**

rā-dǐ-ǒl'ȯ-gÿ, *n.*, medical science of X-rays; **gist; logical; logically**

rǎd'ǐsh, *n.*, edible root

rā'dǐ-ŭm, *n.*, radioactive metallic element

rā'dǐ-ŭs, *n.*, line from center to edge of circle

rǎf'fle, *n.*, lottery of buying chances for prize

rǎft, *n.*, floating platform, large number

rǎft'ẽr, *n.*, roof support

rǎg, *n.*, worn piece of cloth, (pl.) old worn clothes; **-ged**

rāge, *n.*, furious anger, fad; *v.*, be uncontrolled; **ingly**

rāid, *n.*, hostile attack; **-er**

rāil, *n.*, bar across posts, track for train; *v.*, reproach

rāi'mẽnt, *n.*, clothing

rāin, *n.*, water dropping to earth; **-y** *a.*

rāin'bōw, *n.*, arc of colors formed from sun on rain

rāise, *n.*, increase; *v.*, lift, construct, increase, bring up

rāi'sǐn, *n.*, dried grape

rāke, *n.*, long-handled tool with teeth; *v.*, gather, scrape

rǎl'lÿ, *n.*, mass meeting; *v.*, gather together, revive

rǎm, *n.*, male sheep; *v.*, drive into, force; **-mer**

rǎm'ble, *v.*, roam about; **-r**

rǎm-bŭnc'tioŭs, *a.*, wild, unruly; **-ly; -ness**

rǎmp, *n.*, sloping surface

rǎm-pāge', *n.*, violent action; *v.*, rage

rǎmp'ȧnt, *a.*, widespread, wild; **ancy; -ly**

rǎm'shǎck-le, *a.*, rickety

rǎnch, *n.*, large animal farm; **-er**

rǎn'cǐd, *a.*, smelling rotten,

spoiled; **-ly; -ness**

rǎn'cör, *n.*, bitter hate; **-ous; -ously**

rǎn'dȯm, *a.*, haphazard; **-ly; -ness**

rānge, *n.*, extent, distance, open land, group of mountains, stove; *v.*, extend, roam

rǎnk, *n.*, relative position; *v.*, place in order; *a.*, extreme, rancid

rǎn'sǎck, *v.*, search, plunder; **-er**

rǎn'sȯm, *n.*, price demanded to free kidnapped person; **-er**

rǎnt, *v.*, talk wildly; **-er**

rȧ-pā'cioŭs, *a.*, greedy, plundering; **city; -ly; -ness**

rāpe, *n.*, crime of sexual intercourse by force

rǎp'ǐd, *n.*, swift current; *a.*, fast; **-ity; -ly; -ness**

rā'pǐ-êr, *n.*, sword

rǎp-port' (pôr), *n.*, close relationship

rǎpt, *a.*, engrossed

rǎp'ture, *n.*, great pleasure

rāre, *a.*, scarce, of great value, partly raw; **-ness**

rāre'lÿ, *adv.*, seldom

rǎs'cȧl, *n.*, mischievous person; **-ly** *a.*, *adv.*

rǎsh, *n.*, red spots on skin

rǎsh, *a.*, hasty; **-ly; -ness**

rǎsp, *v.*, grate, irritate; **-er; -y** *a.*; **-ingly** [son

rǎt, *n.*, rodent, sneaky per-

rāte, *n.*, relative amount, evaluate; ratable

rǎt'ǐ-fÿ, *v.*, approve officially; **fier; fication**

rā'tiō, *n.*, comparison, proportion

rā'tion, *n.*, fixed portion

rā'tion-ȧl, *a.*, able to reason; **-ity; -ize; -ization; -ly**

rȧ-tion-āle', *n.*, reason for something [wicker

rǎt-tǎn', *n.*, cane to make

rǎt'tle, *n.*, *v.*, (thing that can) make quick sharp sounds

rǎt'tle-snāke, *n.*, snake

with rattle at its tail

rău'coŭs, *a.,* loud; **-ly; -ness**

răv'åge, *n.,* violent destruction; *v.,* ruin; **-er**

rave, *v.,* talk wildly, praise greatly; **-r**

răv'ĕl, *v.,* untwist; **-er; -ment**   [black

rā'vĕn, *n.,* large crow; *a.,*

răv'ē-noŭs, *a.,* very hungry; **-ly; -ness**

răv'īsh, *v.,* carry away, enrapture; **-er; -ment**

rāw, *a.,* in natural state, sore, bleak   [hide

rāw'hīde, *n.,* untanned

rāy, *n.,* thin line of light, straight line, flat fish

rāy'ŏn, *n.,* synthetic fiber

răze, *v.,* destroy

rā'zŏr, *n.,* sharp-edged device for shaving

rēach, *v.,* extend hand, achieve, influence; **-er**

rē-ăct', *v.,* act in return, respond; **-ion; -ive; -ivity; -ively; -ivensss**

rē-ăc'tion-är-ȳ, *a.,* politically very conservative; **tionist**

rē-ăc'tŏr, *n.,* device producing atomic energy

rēad, *v.,* understand or say aloud printed words, study; **-er; -ing** *n.;* **-able; -ability; -ableness; -ably**

rĕad'ȳ, *a.,* prepared, apt, willing, prompt; **readily; readiness**   [**-ly**

rē-ăl, *a.,* true, existing; **-ity;**

rē'ål-ism, *n.,* tendency to face facts; **ist; istic; istically**

rĕalm, *n.,* kingdom, area

rē'ål-tȳ, *n.,* land and whatever is part of it; **tor**

rēam, *n.,* large amount; *v.,* enlarge   [tain; **-er**

rēap, *v.,* gather crop, obrēar,** *n.,* back part; *v.,* raise, stand on hind legs

rēa'sŏn, *n.,* explanation, cause, ability to think; *v.,* think logically; **-ing** *n.;* **-able**

rē-bāte', *n., v.,* return of part payment

rĕb'ĕl, *n.,* one who resists authority; *v.,* **(rĕb-ĕl')** revolt against; **-lion; -lious; -liously; -liousness**

rē-bŭff', *n.,* refusal, snub

rē-būke', *n., v.,* reprimand

rē'bŭs, *n.,* puzzle

rē-bŭt'tål, *n.,* argument in debate

rē-căl'cĭ-trāte, *v.,* rebel; **tion; trant; trance; trancy; trantly**

rē-căll', *v.,* call back, remember, cancel; **-able**

rē-cà-pĭt'ū-lāte, *v.,* repeat, summarize; **tion; tory**

rē-căp'tûre, *v.,* retake, remember   [diminish

rē-cēde', *v.,* move back,

rē-cēipt' (cēt), *n.,* written proof of something received

rē-cēive', *v.,* get, accept, be given; **-er; ceivable**

rē'cĕnt, *a.,* of time just past; **cency; -ness; -ly**

rē-cĕp'tà-cle, *n.,* container

rē-cĕp'tion, *n.,* receiving, greeting, response; **-ist**

rē-cĕp'tĭve, *a.,* able to receive; **tivity; -ness; -ly**

rē'cĕss, *n.,* hollow place, time of rest

rē-cĕs'sion, *n.,* withdrawal, temporary drop in business

rē-cĕs'sion-ål, *n.,* concluding music

rē-cĕs'sĭve, *a.,* of latent hereditary factor; **-ly; -ness**

rĕc'ĭ-pē, *n.,* directions for preparing food

rē-cĭp'ĭ-ĕnt, *n.,* one who receives

rē-cĭp'rŏ-cål, *a.,* done in return, mutual; **-ity; cate; cation; cator; cative; -ly**   [action

rĕc-ĭ-prŏc'ĭ-tȳ, *n.,* mutual

rē-cĭt'ål, *n.,* telling, musical program

rĕc-ĭ-tā'tion, *n.,* public

speech

rė-cīte', *v.*, speak formally from memory; **-r**

rĕck'lĕss, *a.*, careless; **-ly; -ness**

rĕck'ŏn, *v.*, count, consider, settle; **-er**

rė-clāim', *v.*, rescue, recover; **-er; claṃation; -able**   **[nation**

rė-clīne', *v.*, lie back; **-r;**

rĕc'lūse, *n.*, one living a secluded life; **sion; sive**

rĕc'ŏg-nīze, *v.*, identify, accept; **-r; nition; nitive; nitory; nizable; nizability; nizably**

rĕc-ŏm-mĕnd', *v.*, suggest, advise; **-er; -ation; -atory; -able**

rĕc'ŏm-pĕnse, *v.*, pay for

rĕc'ŏn-cile, *v.*, make friendly again, settle; **ciliation; ciliatory; cilable; cilability; cilably**

rĕc'ŏn-dīte, *a.*, obscure; **-ly; -ness**

rė-cŏn'nais-sȧnce (nȧ), *n.*, exploration, survey

rĕc'ŏrd, *n.*, account, evidence, disc of recorded sound; *a.*, best; *v.*, **(rė-côrd')** put in writing, register, put on disc; **-er**

rė-coŭp', *v.*, regain; **-ment; -able**

rė-cŏv'êr, *v.*, get back, regain health; **-y**

rĕc-rė-ā'tion, *n.*, form of amusement or relaxation; **-al**

rė-crĭm'ĭ-nāte, *v.*, accuse in return; **tion; tive; tory**

rė-crŭit', *n.*, new member; *v.*, enlist; **-er; -ment**

rĕc'tĭ-fȳ, *v.*, correct, adjust; **fier; fication; fiable**

rĕc'tĭ-tūde, *n.*, honesty

rĕc'tŏr, *n.*, clergyman; **-y**

rĕc'tŭm, *n.*, end part of large intestine; **tal**

rė-cŭm'bėnt, *a.*, lying down; **bency; -ly**

rė-cū'pêr-āte, *v.*, restore health; **tor; tion; tive; tory**

rė-cûr', *v.*, occur again; **-rence; -rent; -rently**

rĕd, *n., a.*, color of blood, communist; **-den; -dish; -dishness**

rė-dăct', *v.*, edit; **-or; -ion**

rė-dēem', *v.*, get back by paying; **-er; demption; demptive; -able**

rĕd'hănd'ĕd, *a., adv.*, in the act of a wrongdoing

rė-doŭbt', *n.*, fort

rė-drĕss', *v.*, make right; **-er; -able**

rė-dūce', *v.*, lessen, lower, change form; **-r; duction; ductive; ducability; ducible; ducibly**

rė-dŭn'dȧnt, *a.*, wordy, excess; **dancy; -ly**

rēed, *n.*, hollow grass stem; **-y** *a.*

rēef, *n.*, ridge just under water; *v.*, take in part of sail

rēek, *n.*, stench; *v.*, smell offensively

rēel, *n.*, lively dance, spool for winding thread, film, etc.; *v.*, stagger

rė-fêr', *v.*, mention, direct to; **-rer; -ral** *n.*; **-rable**

rĕf-êr-ēe', *n.*, judge

rĕf'êr-ĕnce, *n.*, regard, mention, information

rĕf-êr-ĕn'dŭm, *n.*, direct vote by people

rė'fĭll, *n.*, new supply

rė-fīne', *v.*, make pure, make elegant; **-r; -ry; -ment**

rė-flĕct', *v.*, give back an image of, result in, think; **-or; -ion; -ive; -ivity; -iveness; -ively**

rē'flĕx, *n.*, involuntary response; **-ly**

rė-flĕx'ĭve, *a.*, of verb with same subject and object; **flexivity; -ly; -ness**

rė-fôrm', *v.*, correct, change improve; **-er; -ation; -able; -ative**

rė-fôrm'ȧ-tô-rȳ, *n.*, prison for juveniles

rė-frăct', *v.*, bend light rays; **-or; -ion; -ive; -ive-**

ness; -ively

rĕ-frāin', *n*., repeated verse of song or poem; *v*., keep from doing

rĕ-frĕsh', *v*., make fresh, renew; **-er**

rĕ-frĕsh'mĕnt, *n*., light meal, food

rĕ-frĭg'ĕr-āte, *v*., make or keep cold; **tor; tion; tive**

rĕf'ūge, *n*., shelter

rē'fŭnd, *n*., repayment; *v*., **(rĕ-fŭnd')** pay back

rĕ-fûr'bĭsh, *v*., renovate; **-ment**

rĕf'ūse, *n*., trash

rĕ-fūse', *v*., decline, reject; **-r; fusal** *n*.

rĕ-fūte', *v*., prove to be wrong; **-r; tation; futable; futably**

rē'găl, *a*., royal, stately; **-ity; -ly**

rĕ-gârd', *n*., concern, esteem; *v*., look at, consider; **-less**

rĕ-gârd'ĭng, *prep*., about

rĕ-gĕn'ĕr-āte, *v*., form again; *a*., **(āte)** reborn; **tor; tion; acy; -ness; -ly**

rē'gĕnt, *n*., one ruling for a monarch; **gency**

rĕ-gīme', *n*., ruling system or period

rĕg'ĭ-mĕnt, *n*., military unit; *v*., discipline; **-ation; -al; -ally**

rē'gĭon, *n*., particular area, district; **-al; -alism; -alist; -alistic; -ally**

rĕg'ĭs-têr, *n*., list, counting device, air ventilator; *v*., list, enroll, show; **trar; trary; tration**

rĕ-grĕss', *v*., go backward; **-or; -ion; -ive; -ively**

rĕ-grĕt', *v*., feel sorry about; **-er; -ful; -fully; -fulness; -able; -ably**

rĕg'ū-làr, *a*., usual, consistent; **-ity; -ize; -ization; -ly**

rĕg'ū-lāte, *v*., control, adjust; **tor; tion; tory**

rĕ-gûr'gĭ-tāte, *v*., throw up food; **tion**

rē-hȧ-bĭl'ĭ-tāte, *v*., restore; **tion; tive**

rē-hăsh', *v*., go over again

rĕ-hêarse', *v*., perform for practice; **hearsal** *n*.

reign (rān), *n*., time of rule

rē-ĭm-bûrse', *v*., pay back; **-ment; bursable**

rein (rān), *n*., strap for guiding horse

rē-ĭn-câr-nā'tion, *n*., rebirth [deer

rein'dēer (rān), *n*., large

rē-ĭt'ĕr-āte, *v*., repeat; **tion; tive; tively**

rĕ-jĕct', *v*., throw out, deny; **-er; -or; -ion; -ive**

rĕ-joĭce', *v*., be happy; **joicing** *n*.; **joicingly**

rĕ-joĭn'dêr, *n*., answer

rĕ-lāte', *v*., tell, associate; **-r; tion; tionship; latable** [ily

rĕ-lāt'ĕd, *a*., of same fam-

rĕl'ȧ-tĭve, *n*., person in same family; *a*., having connection; **tivity; -ly; -ness**

rĕ-lăx', *v*., be at ease, lessen, **-er; -ation**

rē'lāy, *n*., fresh supply, team race; *v*., **(rĕ-lāy')** send on [public

rĕ-lēase', *v*., let go, make

rĕl'ĕ-gāte, *v*., exile, assign refer; **tion**

rĕl'ĕ-vȧnt, *a*., related to; **vance; vancy; -ly**

rē-lī'ȧ-ble, *a*., trustworthy; **ability; -ness; ably**

rĕl'ĭc, *n*., thing from past

rĕ-lieĕf', *n*., aid, thing that lessens

rĕ-lieĕve', *v*., ease, help; **-r; lievable**

rē-lĭ'gĭon, *n*., system of belief and worship; **gious; giously; giousness**

rĕ-lĭn'quĭsh, *v*., give up; **-ment**

rĕl'ĭsh, *n*., pleasing task, appetizer; *v*., enjoy

rĕ-lŭc'tȧnt, *a*., unwilling; **tance; tancy; -ly**

rĕ-lȳ', *v*., trust, depend; **liance; liant; liantly**

rĕ-māin', *v*., stay, continue

P
R

to be; **-der**

rė-mârk', *n.*, *v.*, comment

rė-mârk'á-ble, *a.*, unusual; **bly; -ness**

rĕm'ė-dy̆, *n.*, *v.*, cure; **dial; dially; diable; diableness; diably**

rė-mĕm'bêr, *v.*, think of again, keep in mind; **brance** [-er; -ful

rė-mīnd', *v.*, remember;

rĕm-ĭ-nīsce', *v.*, recall the past; **-nce; -nt; -ntly**

rė-mĭss', *a.*, careless; **-ly; -ness**

rė-mĭt', *v.*, forgive, send money, decrease; **mission; missive**

rė-mĭt'tánce, *n.*, money sent

rĕm'nánt, *n.*, remainder

rė-mŏn'strāte, *v.*, object; **tor; tion; tive; tively**

rė-môrse', *n.*, deep guilt; **-ful; -fully; -fulness; -less; -lessly; -lessness**

rė-mōte', *a.*, far off; **-ly; -ness**

rė-move' (mūv), *v.*, take, get rid of; **-r; moval; movable; movability; movably**

rĕn'áis-sánce, *n.*, rebirth, revival

rĕnd, *v.*, rip apart

rĕn'dêr, *v.*, give; **-er; -able**

rĕn-dĭ'tion, *n.*, performance

rĕn'ė-gāde, *n.*, traitor

rė-nėge', *v.*, go back on a promise

rė-nēw', *v.*, make new again by replacement; **-er; -al** *n.;* **-able; -ability**

rė-nŏunce', *v.*, give up officially; **-r; -ment**

rĕn'ȯ-vāte, *v.*, make fresh again; **tor; tion; tive**

rė-nȯwn', *n.*, great fame

rė-nŭn-ci-ā'tion, *n.*, renouncing; **tive; tory**

rė-pāir', *v.*, fix, mend; **-er; -able**

rĕp-á-rā'tion, *n.*, making amends, compensation

rĕp-ár-tēe', *n.*, witty reply

rė-păst', *n.*, meal

rė-pāy', *v.*, pay back, compensate; **-ment; -able**

rė-pēal', *v.*, abolish; **-er; -able**

rė-pēat', *v.*, say or do again; **-er; -ability; -able**

rė-pĕl', *v.*, force back, reject, disgust; **-ler; -lent; -lence; -lency; -lently**

rė-pĕnt', *v.*, be sorry for; **-er; -ance; -ant; -antly**

rė-pêr-cŭs'sion, *n.*, reaction; **sive**

rĕp'êr-toire (twâr), *n.*, works a performer is familiar with

rĕp-ė-tī'tion, *n.*, thing repeated; **tious; tiously; tiousness; tive; tively**

rė-phrāse', *v.*, phrase differently

rė-plāce', *v.*, put back, take place of; **-r; -ment; -able**

rė-plĕn'ĭsh, *v.*, supply again; **-er; -ment**

rĕp'lĭ-cá, *n.*, copy

rė-plȳ', *n.*, *v.*, answer; **plier**

rė-pôrt', *n.*, account, factual statement, rumor; *v.*, tell, present oneself; **-er; -edly** [-fully

rė-pōse', *n.*, *v.*, rest; **-ful;**

rĕp-rė-hĕnd', *v.*, find fault; **hension; hensive; hensively; hensible; hensibility; hensibly**

rĕp-rė-sĕnt', *v.*, portray, symbolize; **-ation; -ational; -ative; -atively; -ativeness**

rė-prĕss', *v.*, hold back, control too strictly; **-er; -or; -ion; -ive; -ively; -iveness; -ible**

rė-priēve', *n.*, *v.*, delay of punishment

rĕp'rĭ-mănd, *n.*, *v.*, rebuke

rė-prīs'ál, *n.*, injury done in return

rė-prōach', *n.*, shame; *v.*, accuse; **-er; -ful; -fully; -fulness; -able; -ingly**

rĕp'rȯ-bāte, *n.*, scoundrel; *v.*, condemn; *a.*, depraved; **tion; tive**

rė-prȯ-dūce', v., do again, produce offspring and copies; **-r; tion; tive; tively; tiveness; ducible**

rė-prōof', n., blame; **proval**

rė-prove' (prūv), v., criticize; **-r; provingly**

rėp'tile, n., scaly, crawling animal

rė-pŭb'lĭc, n., government by elected representatives; **-an** n., a.

rė-pŭg'nȧnt, a., distasteful; **nance; nancy; -ly**

rė-pŭlse', v., repel, reject; **sion** [**-ly; -ness**

rė-pŭl'sĭve, a., disgusting;

rėp'ū-tȧ-ble, a., respectable; **bility; bly**

rė-pūte', v., think to be; **-d; -dly**

rėp-ū-tā'tion, n., others' opinion of a person, fame   [politely ask

rė-quĕst', n., asking; v.,

rė-quire', v., demand, need; **-ment**

rĕq'uĭ-sĭte, n., a., (thing) necessary

rĕq-uĭ-sĭ'tion, n., formal order; v., demand

rė-scĭnd', v., cancel; **-er; scission; -able**

rĕs'cūe, v., save, free; **-r; cuable**

rė-sêarch', n., careful study; v., investigate; **-er; -able**   [**blance**

rė-sĕm'ble, v., be similar;

rė-sĕnt', v., be angry at, feel hurt; **-ment; -ful; -fully; -fulness**

rĕs-êr-vā'tion, n., reserving, land put aside

rė-sêrve', n., reticence, something held for later use; v., set aside, keep

rĕs'êr-voir (vwâr), n., large supply, place for storing water

rė-sīde', v., live, dwell

rĕs'ĭ-dénce, n., place where one lives; **dency; dent** n., a., **dential;**

dentially   [**ual; ually**

rĕs'ĭ-dūe, n., remainder;

rė-sīgn', v., give up, accept passively; **-ation; -ed; -edly**

rė-sĭl'ĭėnt, a., elastic; **ience; iency; -ly**

rĕs'ĭn, n., gummy substance from trees

rė-sĭst', v., oppose, fight against; **-er; -ence; -ant** n., a.; **-ive; -ively; -ivity; -ible; -ibility; -less; -lessly; -lessness**

rĕs'ȯ-lūte, a., determined; **-ly**

rĕs-ȯ-lū'tion, n., decision, formal statement

rė-sŏlve', v., decide; **-r; -nt** n., a.; **-d; -dly; solvable; solvability**

rĕs'ȯ-nȧnt, a., of returning sound; **nance; nate; nator; -ly**

rė-sôrt', n., vacation place; v., turn to

rė-sôurce'fŭl, a., capable; **-ly; -ness**

rė-spĕct', n., honor; v., regard, consider; **-ful; -fully; -fulness**

rė-spĕct'ȧ-ble, a., proper, moderate; **bility; bly**

rė-spĕc'tĭve, a., several; **-ly**

rė-spīre', v., breathe air; **rator; ration; ratory; rational**

rĕs'pĭte, n., postponement

rė-splĕnd'ėnt, a., splendid; **ence; ency; -ly**

rė-spŏnd', v., answer; **-er; sponse** n.; **-ent** n., a.; **sponsive; sponsively; sponsiveness**

rė-spŏn'sĭ-ble, a., liable for, accountable, dependable; **bility; bly; -ness**

rĕst, n., inactivity, peace, relief, remainder; v., be at ease, lie, stop

rĕs'tȧu-rȧnt, n., place to buy and eat a meal

rĕs-tĭ-tū'tion, n., making good for loss; **tive**

rė-stôre', v., give or bring

back, renew; **-r; stora-tion; storative; stora-ble**

rĕ-strāin′, v., hold back, limit; **-er; straint** n.; **-able**

rĕ-strĭct′, v., limit; **-ion; -ive; -ively; -iveness; -ed; -edly**

rĕ-sŭlt′, n., outcome, consequence; v., happen; **-ant** n., a.; **-antly**

rĕ-sūme′, v., start again; **sumption; sumable**

rĕ′sū-me′ (mā), n., summary

rĕ-sûr′gĕnt, a., rising again; **gence**

rĕs-ûr-rĕct′, v., bring back to life; **-ion; -ional**

rĕ-sŭs′cĭ-tāte, v., revive; **tor; tion; tive**

rĕ′tāil, n., sale of goods to consumer; **-er**

rĕ-tāin′, v., keep, hire, remember; **-er; -ment; -able**

rĕ-tăl′ĭ-āte, v., get even; **tion; tive; tory**

rĕ-târd′, v., delay, slow down; **-er; -ation; -ative**

rĕtch, v., strain to vomit

rĕten′tion, n., capacity to retain; **tive; tivity; tively; tiveness**

rĕt′ĭ-cĕnt, a., silent, withdrawn; **cence; cency; -ly**

rĕt′i-nà, n., eye part

rĕ-tīre′, v., go away, withdraw, go to bed, leave job because of age; **-ment** [**-ly**

rĕ-tīr′ĭng, a., shy, modest;

rĕ-tôrt′, v., reply sharply

rĕ-trāce′, v., go back over; **-able**

rĕ-trăct′, v., draw or take back; **-or; -ion; -ive; -ability; -able**

rĕ-trēat′, n., withdrawal, seclusion; v., go back

rĕ-trĕnch′, v., curtail, economize; **-ment**

rĕt-rĭ-bū′tion, n., deserved punishment or reward; **tive; tory; tively**

rĕ-triēve′, v., get back, recover; **-r; trieval** n., **trievable**

rĕt-rō-ăc′tĭve, a., effective as of a past date **tivity; -ly**

rĕ-tûrn′, n., recurrence, profit; v., go or come back, answer, restore; **-er; -ee; -able**

rē-ūn′iȯn, n., coming together again

rē-vămp′, v., make over

rĕ-vēal′, v., make known a secret, tell; **-er; -ment; -able** [waken soldiers

rĕ′vėil-lē, n., signal to

rĕv′ėl, v., make merry, delight; **-er; -ry**

rĕv-ė-lā′tion, n., disclosure, revealing; **-ist; tory**

rĕ-vĕnge′, n., v., harm in return; **-r; -ful; -fully; -fulness; vengingly**

rĕv′ė-nūe, n., income from taxes

rĕ-vêr′bêr-āte, v., return, re-echo, reflect; **tor; tion; tive; tively; tory; berant**

rĕ-vēre′, v., respect greatly; **-nce; -nt; -ntly**

rĕv′êr-iē, n., daydream

rĕ-vêrse′, v., n., (change to the) opposite; a., contrary; **-r; versal;** a.; **sion; sionary; sional; versible; versibility; versibly** [**-ible**

rĕ-vêrt′, v., go back to;

rĕ-vīle′, v., insult; **-r; -ment**

rĕ-vīse′, v., change, correct; **-r; -visal** n.; **vision; visionist; visionary; visional; visory** ‥

rĕ-vīve′, v., bring back to life or health; **-r; vival** n.; **vivable; vivability**

rĕ-vōke′, v., cancel, abolish; **ocation; ocable; ocability**

rĕ-vōlt′, n., rebellion; v., rebel, disgust; **-er**

rĕv-ȯ-lū′tion, n., cycle, complete change, rebellion; **-ist; -ize; -ary**

rė-vŏlve', v., turn in a circle, ponder

rė-vŏlv'êr, n., handgun

rė-vūe', n., musical show

rė-vŭl'sion, n., disgust

rė-ward' (wôrd), n., thing given for a deed; **-er; -able** [ing of

rė-wŏrd', v., change word-

rhăp'sò-dў, n., ecstasy, musical composition; **dize; sodic; sodically**

rhē'à, n., large non-flying bird

rhē'sŭs, n., monkey

rhĕt'ò-rĭc, n., art of effective language, eloquence; **-al; -ally**

rheü'mà-tĭsm, n., painful conditions of joints; **matic; matically**

rhīne'stōne, n., artificial gem [imal

rhĭ-nŏc'êr-òs, n., huge an-

rhī'zōme, n., rootlike stem

rhō-dò-dĕn'dròn, n., flowering shrub

rhŭ'bărb, n., edible plant, (coll.) argument

rhўme, n., same ending sound in words

rhўthm, n., regular pattern of beat or flow; **-ic; -ical; -ically; -icity**

rĭb, n., curved chest bone, ridge in cloth; **-bing** n.

rĭb'bòn, n., narrow strip of cloth [grass

rīce, n., aquatic cereal

rĭch, a., worth much, well supplied; **-en; -ly; -ness**

rĭch'ĕs, n., pl., wealth

rĭck'ĕts, n., bone disease

rĭck'ĕt-ў, n., weak; **etiness**

rĭd, v., free, relieve; **-dance**

rĭd'dle, n., puzzling problem; v., make holes in

rīde, v., be carried, move along, control; **-r; -able**

rĭdge, n., raised strip, crest

rĭd'ĭ-cūle, v., make fun of

rĭ-dĭc'ū-loŭs, a., absurd; **-ly; -ness**

rīfe, a., widespread, abundant; **-ness** [people

rĭff'răff, n., insignificant

rī'fle, n., long shoulder gun; **-r; -man** n.; **-ry**

rĭft, n., v., crack, split

rĭg, n., equipment; v., equip, arrange dishonestly; **-ger**

rĭght, n., what is right, privilege; v., make amends; a., correct, virtuous, normal, of side to east when facing north; adv., straight, properly; **-ful; -fully; -ly**

rīght'eoŭs, a., morally just; **-ly; -ness**

rīght'ĭst, n., politically conservative person

rĭg'ĭd, a., stiff, strict; **-ity; -ify; -ly; -ness**

rĭg'ŏr, n., severity, exactness; **-ous; -ously; -ousness**

rīle, v., (coll.) anger

rĭm, n., edge [skin

rīnd, n., firm outer layer,

rĭng, n., anything circular, resonant sound; v., encircle, make sound like bell; **-er**

rĭng'lĕt, n., little curl

rĭng'wŏrm, n., skin disease

rĭnk, n., skating arena

rĭnse, v., wash lightly, flush

rī'òt, n., wild public disorder, (coll.) funny person; **-er**

rĭp, v., tear, cut apart; **-per**

rīpe, a., ready to be harvested, fully grown; **-n; -ly; -ness** [ply a.

rĭp'ple, n., small waves;

rīse, n., ascent, slope, increase; v., get up, go up, increase, begin, rebel

rĭsk, n., dangerous chance; v., take the chance; **-er** [mony

rīte, n., formal act, cere-

rĭt'ū-àl, n., system of rites; a., of rite; **-ism; -ist; -istic; -istically; -ize; -ly**

rī'văl, n., competitor; **-ry**

rĭv'êr, n., large stream of flowing water [tener

rĭv'ĕt, n., metal bolt, fas-

rōad, n., way for travelling, path [-er

rōam, v., travel aimlessly;
rôar, v., loud, deep, rumbling sound; -er; -ing n.
rŏast, n., cut of meat; v., cook in oven or over fire; -er
rŏb, v., steal, take illegally; -ber; -bery   [ment
rōbe, n., long flowing garrŏb'ĭn, n., red-breasted bird   [being
rō'bŏt, n., mechanical
rō-bŭst', a., vigorous, healthy; -ious; -iously; -iousness; -ly; -ness
rŏck, n., large stone; -y a.; -iness   [forth; -er
rŏck, v., move back and
rŏck'ĕt, n., projectile propelled by combustible substance, missile; -ry
rŏd, n., straight, narrow stick, linear measure of 16½ feet   [mal
rō'dĕnt, n., gnawing mamrō'dē-ō, n., competition of cowboys skills
rōe, n., fish eggs
rōgue, n., scoundrel, fun-loving person; -ry; guish; guishly; guishness
rŏĭl, v., make cloudy, stir up; -y a.   [function
rōle, n., actor's part in play.
rōll, n., cylinder, list, small cake of bread, loud echoing sound; v., move by turning, sway, start, flatten with roller
rōll'êr, n., rolling cylinder
rŏl'lĭck-ĭng, a., lively, gay
rō'lÿ-pō'lÿ, n., pudgy
rō-māine', n., kind of lettuce
rō-mănce', n., tale of love and adventure, love affair; mantic; manticism; manticist; manticize; manticization; mantically
rŏmp, v., play boisterously
rŏmp'êrs, n., pl., loose pantlike garment for baby   [ing; -er
rōof, n., top cover of buildrŏŏk, n., crow, chess

piece; v., cheat   [ner
rŏŏk'ĭē, n., (slang) beginrōŏm, n., enough space, place enclosed by walls; -y a.; -iness; -ily
rōŏst, n., v., perch
rōŏs'têr, n., male chicken
rōŏt, n., plant part below ground, source; v., dig, (coll.) cheer; -y a.; -less
rōpe, n., strong twisted cord; v., fasten with rope; -r
rō'sȧ-rÿ, n., holy beads
rōse, n., flower, reddish pink; rosy
rōse'mār-ÿ, n., herb
rō-sē-ō'lȧ, n., rash
rŏs'ĭn, n., pine resin
rŏs'têr, n., list
rŏs'trŭm, n., speaker's platform
rŏt, n., decay; v., decompose, become sickly; -ten a.; -tenly; -tenness
rō'tȧ-rÿ, a., rotating
rō'tāte, v., turn on center point; tor; tion; tional; tive; tively
rōte, n., fixed routine
rō-tŭnd', a., round, plump; -ly; -ness
roŭge, n., reddish cosmetic for coloring cheeks
rough'ȧge (rŭf), n., coarse food   [game
roū-lĕtte', n., gambling
rŏŭnd, n., one of series, (pl.) circuit; v., make round, turn; a., circular, complete; adv., in circle or cycle; prep., about, throughout; -ish; -ly; -ness
roŭse, v., wake, excite; -r
rŏŭt, n., disorderly mob in defeat; v., conquer, dig up
roūte, n., course travelled
roū-tīne', n., regular procedure; a., customary; tinize; tinization; -ly
rōve, v., wander; -r
rōw, n., things in a line; v., propel boat with oars; -er

rŏw, *n.,* dispute, brawl

rŏw'dў, *a.,* disorderly; **-ism; -ish; dily; diness**

roy'ȧl (rōi), *a.,* of a monarch of kingdom; **-ism; -ist; -ty; -ly**

rŭb, *v.,* move back and forth with pressure; **-ber**

rŭb'bêr, *n.,* elastic substance, *(pl.)* overshoes; **-y** *a.* [sense; **-y** *a.*

rŭb'bĭsh, *n.,* trash, non-

rŭb'ble, *n.,* fragmented rock [sles

rū-bĕl'lȧ, *n.,* German mea-

rū'bў, *n.,* red gem

rŭck'ŭs, *n.,* (coll.) uproar

rŭd'dêr, *n.,* steering device

rŭd'dў, *a.,* rosy; **diness**

rūde, *a.,* rough, unmannerly; **-ly; -ness**

rū'dĭ-mėnt, *n.,* first principle; **-ary; -al; -arily**

rūe, *v.,* regret; **-ful; -fully; -fulness** [person

rŭf'fĭ-ȧn, *n.,* brutal, lawless

rŭf'fle, *n.,* pleated cloth trimming; *v.,* wrinkle, disturb

rŭg, *n.,* floor covering

rŭg'gėd, *a.,* rough, strong, harsh; **-ly; -ness**

rū'ĭn, *n.,* destruction, downfall; *v.,* destroy; **-ous; -ously; -ousness**

rūle, *n.,* set guide, law, habit; *v.,* govern, determine, mark lines; **-r**

rŭm, *n.,* alcoholic drink

rŭm'bȧ, *n.,* dance

rŭm'ble, *n.,* deep, rolling sound; **-r; blingly; bly**

rū'mĭ-nāte, *v.,* chew cud, ponder; **tor; tion; tive; tively**

rŭm'māge, *n.,* miscellaneous items; *v.,* search thoroughly; **-r**

rŭm'mў, *n.,* card game

rū'mōr, *n.,* unconfirmed report

rŭmp, *n.,* hind part

rŭm'ple, *n., v.,* wrinkle; **ply**

rŭm'pŭs, *n.,* (coll.) uproar

rŭn, *n.,* trip, race, rapid movement, course; *v.,*

go or move rapidly, race, spread, continue, operate; **-ner**

rŭn'-down', *a.,* not running, in poor state

rŭng, *n.,* crosspiece of ladder or chair

rŭn-nêr-ŭp', *n.,* second one in race

rŭnt, *n.,* undersized animal or thing

rŭn'wāy, *n.,* landing strip

rŭp'tûre, *n.,* bursting; *v.,* break apart

rū'rȧl, *a.,* of country life; **-ism; -ist; -ize; -ly**

rūse, *n.,* trick

rŭsh, *n.,* marsh plant, hurry, swift sudden attack; *v.,* move recklessly or quickly

rŭst, *n.,* russet oxidation on metal; **-y** *a.*

rŭs'tĭc, *a.,* rural, simple; **-ity; -ally**

rŭs'tle, *v.,* make soft rubbing sound, steal cattle; **-r**

rŭt, *n.,* groove, dull routine

rū-tȧ-bā'gȧ, *n.,* yellow turnip [**-ness**

rŭth'lĕss, *a.,* cruel; **-ly;**

rўe, *n.,* cereal grain, whiskey

S

Săb'bȧth, *n.,* day of rest and worship [rest

săb-băt'ĭ-cȧl, *n.,* period of

sā'bêr, *n.,* soldier's sword

săb'ȯ-tȧge, *n.,* intentional destruction; **teur** *n.*

săc'chȧ-rĭn (kȧ), *n.,* sugar substitute

să-chet' (shā), *n.,* small perfumed bag

săck, *n.,* large bag; *v.,* dismiss from job, plunder

săc'rȧ-mėnt, *n.,* Christian rite; **-al; -ally**

săc'rėd, *a.,* holy, consecrated; **-ly; -ness**

săc'rĭ-fice, *n.,* offering of something valuable, loss; **cial; cially**

săc'rĭ-lėge, *n.,* destruction

or disrespect of something holy; **gious; giously; giousness**

săd, a., unhappy, sorrowful; **-den; -ly; -ness**

săd'dle, n., rider's seat on horse

săd'ĭsm, n., pleasure from hurting another; **ĭst; distic; distically**

sà-fâ'rĭ, n., hunting expedition

sāfe, n., locked box for valuables; a., free from danger; **-ty; -ly**

sāfe-kēep'ĭng, n., protection [oil in seeds

săf'flow-êr, n., flower with

săf'fròn, n., flowering plant, dye, medicine

săg, v., hang down, droop

sà'gà, n., long heroic story

sà-gā'cioŭs, a., wise; **city; -ly; -ness** [soning

sāge, n., wise man, sea-

sāge'brŭsh, n., shrub

sāil, n., cloth that catches wind to move ship; v., travel on water; **-or; -ing** n.

sāint, n., holy or kind person; **-hood; -ly** a.; **-liness**

sāke, n., reason, benefit

sà-lā'cioŭs, a., obscene; **city; -ly; -ness**

săl'ăd, n., cold vegetable or fruit dish

săl'à-măn-dêr, n., lizard-like amphibian

sà-là'mĭ, n., spiced sausage [work

săl'à-rў, n., payment for

sāle, n., exchange of goods for money; **-sman** n.; **-able; salability**

sā'liĕnt, a., noticeable; **lience; liency; -ly**

sā'lĭne, a., salty

sà-lì'và, n., watery fluid in mouth; **-tion; -te** v.; **-ry** a.

săl'lōw, a., of sickly yellow complexion; **-ish; -ness**

săl'ĭў, n., sudden rush forth, witticism, jaunt

sà-lŏn', n., reception hall, parlor [room

sà-lōōn', n., large public

sălt, n., sodium chloride, seasoning; **-y** a.; **-iness**

sà-lūte', n., gesture to honor; v., greet; **-r; tation; tatory**

săl-vā'tion, n., saving

salve (săv), n., medicinal ointment

săm'bà, n., dance

sāme, a., alike, identical; adv., in like manner; **-ness** [tern

săm'ple, n., example, pat-

sănc'tĭ-mō-nў, n., pretended holiness; **nious; niously; niousness**

sănc'tion, n., approval; v., authorize, allow; **-able**

sănc'tĭ-tў, n., holiness

sănc'tū-ār-ў, n., holy place, shelter

sănd, n., loose grains of rock; **-y** a.; **-iness**

săn'dàl, n., open shoe with straps

sănd'pā-pêr, n., paper with sand for smoothing

sănd'pi-pêr, n., small shore bird

sănd'wĭch, n., filling, of meat, cheese, etc. between bread slices

sāne, a., mentally healthy; **-ly; -ness**

săn'guĭ-nār-ў, a., of bloodshed, bloodthirsty; **narily; nariness**

săn'guĭne, a., ruddy, cheerful; **-ly; -ness**

săn-ĭ-tār'ĭ-ŭm, n., institution to regain health

săn'ĭ-tār-ў, a., clean and healthy; **tation; tize; tarily; tariness**

săp, n., juice of plant, vigor; v., undermine, weaken; **-py** a. [-ly

sā'pĭ-ĕnt, n., wise; **ence;**

săp'lĭng, n., young tree

săp'phīre, n., blue gem

sär'căsm, n., cutting ironical remark; **castic; castically** [fish

sär-dīne', n., small ocean

sär-dŏn'ĭc, a., bitterly sarcastic; **-ally**

sar-sa-på-rĭl′là (săs), *n.*, soft drink

săsh, *n.*, band for waist or shoulder, frame for glass window   [a.

săss, *n.*, impudent talk; **-y**

sā-tăn′ĭc, *a.*, devilish, evil; **-al; -ally**   [case

sătch′ĕl, *n.*, small carrying

sāte, *v.*, satisfy

săt′ĕl-līte, *n.*, small body revolving around larger one   [tion

sā′tĭ-āte, *v.*, satisfy fully;

săt′ĭn, *n.*, smooth shiny fabric; **-y** *a.*

săt′īre, *n.*, literary ridicule; **rist; rize; tirical; tiri-cally**

săt′ĭs-fȳ, *v.*, fulfill needs, please; **fier; faction; factory**

săt′ū-rāte, *v.*, soak thoroughly; **tor; tion**

săuce, *n.*, liquid served with food

său′cȳ, *a.*, rude, impudent; **cily; ciness**   [heat

său′nà, *n.*, bath of hot, dry

săun′têr, *v.*, walk idly

său′sàge, *n.*, chopped, spicy meat in casing

său-te′ (tā), *v.*, fry quickly

săv′àge, *a.*, primitive, wild; crude; **-ry; -ly; -ness**

sāve, *v.*, keep safe, rescue, preserve for future, avoid waste; **-r; -able**

săv′ĭng, *n.*, reduction, (pl.) money saved   [saves

sāv′ior (yŏr), *n.*, one who

sā′vŏr, *n.*, special quality of taste or smell; **-less; -ous; -y** *a.;* **-ily; -iness**

săv′vȳ, *n.*, shrewdness; *v.*, understand; *a.*, shrewd

săw, *n.*, cutting tool with series of sharp teeth

săx′ȯ-phōne, *n.*, woodwind instrument; **phonist; phonic**

săy, *n.*, chance to speak, power; *v.*, express in words, state; **-er**

săy′ĭng, *n.*, expression of

wisdom   [sore; **-by** *a.*

scăb, *n.*, crust formed over

scăb′bård, *n.*, sword holder   [**-ness**

scăb′roŭs, *a.*, rough; **-ly;**

scăf′fŏld, *n.*, temporary framework for workers

scăld, *v.*, burn with hot liquid or steam

scāle, *n.*, weighing instrument, ratio of size, graduated series; fish's hard covering; *v.*, go up, weigh, remove scales

scăl′lĭŏn, *n.*, onion

scăl′lŏp, *n.*, shellfish, curved fancy edge

scăl′pĕl, *n.*, surgical knife

scămp, *n.*, rascal; **-ish**

scăm′pêr, *v.*, run hurriedly

scăn, *v.*, glance at quickly, examine; **-ner**

scăn′dàl, *n.*, disgrace, slanderous talk; **-ize; -izer; -ization; -ous; -ously; -ousness**

scănt, *a.*, meager, not enough; **-y** *a.;* **-ily; -iness**

scāpe′gōat, *n.*, one blamed for others' mistakes

scăr′àb, *n.*, beetle, its image cut on stone

scārce, *a.*, rare; **city; -ly; -ness**   [**scary** *a.*

scāre, *n.*, fear; *v.*, frighten;

scârf, *n.*, cloth worn about neck, head or shoulders

scâr′lĕt, *n.*, *a.*, bright red

scăth′ĭng, *a.*, harsh; **-ly**

scăt′têr, *v.*, throw about loosely

scăv′ĕng-êr, *n.*, collector of disgarded things

scė-nār′ĭ-ō, *n.*, outline of play, script of movie

scēne, *n.*, place setting, view, part of play, emotional display; **scenic**

scē′nêr-ȳ, *n.*, painted surroundings for play, view outdoors

scĕnt, *n.*, *v.*, smell

scĕp′têr, *n.*, ruler's rod of authority

schĕd′ūle (skĕd), *n.*, list,

scheme 146 **scurrilous**

timed plan; v., place in schedule, plan

schēme (skēm), n., plan, secret project; v., plot; **matize; matic; matically**

schĭsm (skĭsm), n., split; **matic; matical; matically**

schĭz-ȯ-phrē'nĭ-à (skĭz), n., mental disorder; **ic** n., a.

schŏl'ȧr (skŏl), n., learned person, pupil; **-ship; -ly** a.

schȯ-lăs'tĭc (skȯ), a., of school, academic; **-ally**

school (skul), n., place for learning, group, group of fish; v., instruct

scī'ĕnce, n., systematized knowledge, group of facts; **entist; entific; entifically**

scĭn'tĭl-lāte, v., sparkle, be clever; **tor; tion**

scī'ȯn, n., bud, offspring

scĭs'sȯrs, n., cutting tool with opposing blades

scŏff, n., v., jeer, ridicule; **-er; -ingly** [**-er**

scōld, v., find fault angrily;

scō-lĭ-ō'sĭs, n., curvature of spine; **otic**

scŏnce, n., candleholder on wall

scōne, n., tea cake

scōop, n., small shovel; v., take up and carry, dig; **-er**

scōot'êr, n., child's two-wheeled vehicle, small motorcycle

scōpe, n., extent, range of understanding

scôrch, v., burn lightly

scōre, n., mark, notch, debt, points made in game, rating, twenty; v., mark, tally, make point(s); **-r**

scôrn, n., contempt; v., reject; **-er; -ful; -fully; -fulness** [bing; **-er**

scour, v., clean by rub-

scoûrge, n., whip, punishment [spy, search

scout, n., v., (one sent to)

scrăg'glȳ, a., ragged; **gliness**

scrăm, v., get out

scrăm'ble, v., climb hurriedly, struggle, mix; **-r**

scrăp, n., bit, discarded piece, fight; v., junk

scrătch, n., skin wound; v., cut surface, rub, write hurriedly; **-er; -y** a.; **-ily; -iness**

scrāwl, v., write carelessly; **-er; -y** a.

scrāw'nȳ, a., skinny; **niness**

scrēam, n., loud, high piercing sound; **-er**

scrēen, n., partition, coarse mesh of wire, surface to show movies on; v., separate, protect, sift; **-er; -able; -less**

scrēw, n., grooved naillike fastener; v., twist, fasten

scrībe, n., writer

scrĭm'måge, n., confused struggle

scrĭmp, v., be frugal; **-er; -y** a.; **-ily; -iness**

scrĭpt, n., handwriting, copy of play

scrĭp'tûre, n., Bible

scrōll, n., roll of paper with writing

scrō'tŭm, n., testicles' pouch; **tal** [pilfer; **-r**

scrouͤnge, v., (coll.) beg,

scrŭb, n., stunted tree; a., undersized; **-by** a.; **-bily; -biness** [clean; **-ber**

scrŭb, v., rub hard to

scrŭff, n., nape of neck

scrŭmp'tiouͤs, a. (coll.) delicious; **-ly; -ness**

scrū'tĭ-nȳ, n., close examination; **nize; nizer**

scū'bȧ, n., underwater breathing apparatus

scŭd, v., move swiftly

scŭf'fle, n., v., fight

scŭlp'tûre, n., art of carving, modeling and welding; **tor; tural; turally**

scŭm, n., filth, impurities; **-my** a. [**-ness**

scûr'rĭl-ouͤs, a., vulgar; **-ly;**

scûr'rÿ, v., run hastily

scûr'vÿ, n., disease; a., vile; **vily; viness**

scüt'tle, v., move quickly

scÿthe, n., tool with long blade for cutting

sēa, n., body of salt water

sēa'fār-êr, n., sailor

sēal, n., sea mammal with flippers, official mark; v., close securely, certify

sēam, n., line made by joining two pieces; v., join

sēam'strėss, n., woman who sews for money

se'ånce (sā), n., meeting of spiritualists

sēar, v., burn the surface

sêarch, n., inquiry; v., ex- amine; **-er; -able; -ing; -ingly**

sēa'sïck, a., of nausea from travelling on sea; **-ness**

sēa'sòn, n., time of year, spring, summer, autumn or winter; v., add spices, herbs to food, mature; **-er** [for food

sēa'sòn-ïng, n., flavoring

sēat, n., place to sit, part one sits on; v., put on seat; **-ing** n.

sēa'wŏr-thÿ,a., fit to travel on sea

sė-cēde', v., withdraw from; **-r; cession; ces- sional**

sė-clūde', v., isolate; **clu- sion; clusive; clu- sively; clusiness**

sėc'ònd-hånd', a., used previously

sėc'rėt,n., a., (something) hidden from others, mys- terious: **recy; -ive; -ively; -iveness; -ly**

sėc'rė-tār-ÿ, n., corre- sponding or recording officer, cabinet minister; **tariat** n.

sė-crēte', v., hide, dis- charge body substance; **tion; tory**

sėct, n., group with same beliefs; **-arian** a.

sėc'tion, n., part; v., cut into divisions; **-al**

sė-cūre', v., protect, make firm, get; a., safe, stable; **-r; rity; curance; cura- ble; -ness; -ly**

sė-dăn', n., enclosed au- tomobile

sė-dāte', v., reduce ex- citement; a., serious, calm; **tion**

sĕd'ėn-tār-ÿ, a., sitting

sĕd'ï-mėnt, n., matter set- tling to bottom of liquid; **-ation; -al; -ary**

sė-dūce', v., lead astray; **-r; duction; -ment; duc- tive; ductively; duc- tiveness; ducible**

sĕd'ū-loŭs, a., working hard; **lity; -ly; -ness**

sēe, n., bishop's official seat; v., look at, under- stand, make sure, meet

sēed, n., plant part from which new one grows, source; v., plant or re- move seeds; **-er; -less**

sēed'ÿ, a., shabby; **seed- ily; seediness**

sēem'lÿ, a., handsome; **liness** [**-age; -y** a.

sēep, v., leak out, ooze;

sēer'sŭck-êr,n., light fab- ric

sēe'säw, n., plank for rid- ing up and down

sēethe, v., boil, be very angry

sĕg'mėnt, n., part, divi- sion; **-ation; -ary; -al; -ally**

sĕg'rė-gāte, v., set apart from group; **tion; tionist; tive** [ing net

seine (sān), n., large fish-

seïs'mïc, a., of earth- quake; **-ity; mism, mol- ogy; mologist; -ally**

sēize, v., take forcibly; **-r; seizable**

sĕl'dòm, adv., rarely; **-ness**

sė-lĕct', v., choose; a., chosen; **-or; -ion; -ness; -ive; -ivity; -ively; -ive- ness**

sĕlf, *n.*, one's own person

sĕlf´ĭsh, *a.*, too interested in oneself; **-ly; -ness**

sĕlf´lĕss, *a.*, interested in others; **-ly; -ness**

sĕlf-rīght´eoŭs, *a.*, feeling morally superior; **-ly; -ness**   [**-ness**

sĕlf´sāme, *a.*, identical;

sĕlf-wĭll´, *n.*, stubbornness

sĕll, *v.*, trade for money, deal in, betray; **-er**

sė-măn´tĭcs, *n.*, study of words and meanings; **ti-cist; tic**   [ance

sĕm´blȧnce, *n.*, appear-

sē´mĕn, *n.*, male reproductive fluid

sė-mĕs´têr, *n.*, half year, college term

sĕm´ĭ-nâr, *n.*, course for research or advanced study

sĕm´ĭ-năr-ў, *n.*, school for clergymen; **narian** *n.*

sĕn´ȧte, *n.*, lawmaking assembly; **tor; torial**

sĕnd, *v.*, cause to go or be carried; **-er**

sē´nīle, *a.*, of old age, mentally feeble; **nility; -ly**   [rank; **-ity**

sēn´iŏr, *a.*, older, of higher

sĕnse, *n.*, ability to feel, hear, see, smell and taste, feeling, sound judgment, meaning; *v.*, perceive, understand; **sory** *a.*

sĕnse´lĕss, *a.*, foolish, meaningless; **-ly; -ness**

sĕn´sĭ-ble, *a.*, wise, aware; **bility; bly**

sĕn´sŭ-ȧl, *a.*, of bodily pleasure; **-ism; -ist; -ity; -ize; -istic; -ly**

sĕn´tĕnce, *n.*, group of words stating a thought, judge's decision

sĕn´tĭ-mĕnt, *n.*, feeling opinion

sĕn-tĭ-mĕn´tȧl, *a.*, emotionally nostalgic; **-ity; -ism; -ist; -ize; -ization; -ly**

sĕn´tĭ-nĕl, *n., v.*, guard

sĕn´trў, *n.*, guard

sĕp´ȧ-rāte, *v.*, divide, keep apart; *a.*, **(rȧte)** distinct; **tor; tion; tive; -ly; -ness**

sĕp´ŭl-chêr, *n.*, tomb; **chral**

sē´quĕl, *n.*, result

sē´quĕnce, *n.*, succession, order, series; **quent; quential; quentially**   [seize

sė-quĕs´têr, *v.*, seclude,

sē´quĭn, *n.*, small shiny ornament

sĕr-ė-nāde´, *n.*, outdoor lover's music; **-r**

sĕr-ėn-dĭp´ĭ-tў, *n.*, good luck

sė-rēne´, *a.*, calm; **renity; -ly; -ness**

sêrf, *n.*, person bound to master's land; **-dom**

sêrge, *n.*, twilled fabric

sē´rĭ-ȧl, *n.*, separately published episodes

sē´rĭēs, *n., pl.*, number of related things coming in order; **riate; ration; rial; rially**

serĭ-grăph, *n.*, original print by silkscreen

sē´rĭ-oŭs, *a.*, thinking deeply, important, dangerous; **-ly; -ness**

sêr´mon, *n.*, serious speech, religious lecture; **-ize; -ic**

sêr´rȧte, *v.*, make toothlike notches on edge; **tion**

sē´rŭm, *n.*, watery animal fluid, liquid antitoxin; **rous; rology; rologist**

sêr´vȧnt, *n.*, one hired to perform services for another; **-less**

sêrve, *v.*, assist, spend time, supply, offer food; **-r**

sêr´vĭce, *n.*, job, ceremony, assistance; *v.*, repair, supply; **-able; -ability; -ableness; -ably**

sêr´vĭ-tūde, *n.*, slavery

sĕs´ȧ-mē, *n.*, edible seed

sĕs´sion, *n.*, meeting of a group, period of time

sĕt, *n.,* stage scenery, group of like things or people, firmness; *v.,* put, arrange, become hard or firm, establish start; *a.,* established, rigid, ready

sē'tà, *n.,* bristle

sĕt-tēe', *n.,* sofa

sĕt'tle, *v.,* arrange, go to live, calm, sink, decide, pay; **-r; -ment**

sĕv'êr, *v.,* cut, separate; **-ance; -able; -ability**

sē-vēre', *a.,* harsh, strict, serious; **verity- -ly; -ness**

sew (sō), *v.,* fasten with needle and thread; **-er**

sēw'êr, *n.,* underground pipes to carry water and waste; **sewage**

sex, *n.,* one of two divisions of living things: male or female, living reproduction; **-ual; -uality; -less; -lessly; -lessness; -ly**

sĕx'tón, *n.,* church official

sĕx'ÿ, *a.,* sexually exciting; **sexily; sexiness**

shăb'bÿ, *a.,* worn out, disgraceful; **bily; biness**

shăck, *n.,* small crude cabin

shăck'le, *n.,* wrist or ankle restraint, fastener; *v.,* hamper

shāde, *n.,* part darkness caused by blocking light, color gradation, small degree; *v.,* screen from light; **-r; -less; shady** *a.;* **shadily; shadiness**

shăd'ōw, *n.,* dark image cast by body in light, small amount; *v.,* follow; **-er; -less; -y** *a.*

shăft, *n.,* long, slender part, arrow, vertical tunnel

shăg, *n.,* long, rough nap, disorderly mass; **-gy** *a.;* **-gily; -giness**

shāke, *n.,* tremor; *v.,* move with abrupt, brisk motions, tremble, upset; **-r;**

-able; shaky *a.*

shāle, *n.,* rock of clay

shăl-lŏt', *n.,* small onion

shăl'lōw, *a.,* not deep; **-ly; -ness**

shăm, *v.,* pretend; *a.,* false

shăm'bles, *n., pl.,* disorderly scene

shāme, *n.,* feeling of having lost respect, dishonor; *v.,* disgrace; **-ful; -fully; -fulness; -less; -lessly; -lessness**

shăm-pōo', *n., v.,* (soap to) wash hair

shăn'tÿ, *n.,* small, run-down dwelling

shāpe, *n.,* physical form, *v.,* form, mold; **-less; -lessly; -lessness; -ly; -liness**

shāre, *n.,* one's portion; *v.,* divide, participate in together

shârk, *n.,* large fish

shāve, *v.,* cut off, scrape into thin slices, graze; **-r; -n** *a.*

shāwl, *n.,* large cloth worn on head and shoulders

shēaf, *n.,* bundle

shēath, *n.,* close fitting case

shĕd, *n.,* small building; *v.,* flow, radiate, lose

shēen, *n.,* brightness

shēep'ĩsh, *a.,* shy; **-ly; -ness**

shēer, *n., v.,* swerve; *a.,* transparent, pure; **-ly; -ness**

shēet, *n.,* large thin piece of cloth, paper, etc.

shĕll, *n.,* hard outer covering, framework; *v.,* remove shell

shĕl-lăc', *n., v.,* varnish

shĕl'têr, *n.,* covered protection; *v.,* protect; **-er; -less**

shĕlve, *v.,* put on shelf

shĕp'hêrd, *n.,* one who tends sheep

shêr'bét, *n.,* frozen dessert

shêr'rÿ, *n.,* wine

shiēld, *n.,* thing that protects, protective armor;

v., defend, screen; **-er**

shift, *n.*, change, work period; *v.*, move from one to another; **-er; -able**

shift′less, *a.*, lazy; **-ly; -ness**

shim′mer, *v.*, shine; *a.*, wavering light

shine, *n.*, brightness, polish; *v.*, emit light, glow; **-r; shiny** *a.*

shin′gle, *n.*, thin piece of wood to cover roof, woman's short haircut

ship, *n.*, large water vessel; *v.*, transport; **-per; -ment; -ping** *n.;* **-pable**

ship′wright, *n.*, one who makes and repairs ships

shirk, *v.*, neglect work; **-er**

shiv′er, *n.*, splinter; *v.*, shake, shatter; **-y** *a.*

shoal, *n.*, school of fish, shallow place in water; **-y** *a.*

shoat, *n.*, young hog

shock, *n.*, sudden impact, great surprise, extreme nerve stimulation; *v.*, startle; **-er**

shod′dy, *a.*, cheap, inferior; **dily; diness**

shoot, *n.*, new growth; *v.*, move quickly, send forth, discharge a gun, photograph; **-er**

shop, *n.*, place to sell goods or do work; *v.*, buy; **-per** [store; **-er**

shop′lift, *v.*, steal from

shore, *n.*, edge of land bordering water; *v.*, prop, make stable

short, *a.*, low in height, brief, lacking; *adv.*, abruptly; **-en; -ly**

short-change′, *v.*, cheat by not returning change due; **-r**

short′com-ing, *n.*, defect

short′en-ing, *n.*, making short, edible fat for cooking [ing

short′hand, *n.*, speed writing

short′wave′, *n.*, radio band for broadcasting

shoul′der, *n.*, joint connecting arm to body; *v.*, push or hold with shoulder [-er

shout, *n.*, loud call or cry;

shove, *n.*, *v.*, push; **-r**

show, *n.*, display, trace, pretense entertainment; *v.*, bring into view, complete exhibit, point out; **-er**

show′er, *n.*, rain, party for an occasion, bath with spraying of water; *v.*, pour forth

shred, *n.*, torn strip, fragment; *v.*, tear

shrew, *n.*, nagging woman; **-ish; -ishly; -ishness**

shrewd, *a.*, clever, astute; **-ly; -ness**

shrill, *a.*, piercing in tone; **-y** *adv.;* **-ness**

shrimp, *n.*, small edible shellfish

shrine, *n.*, sacred place

shrink, *v.*, become smaller, contract, avoid; **-age; -able**

shriv′el, *v.*, shrink and become wrinkled

shroud, *n.*, burial cloth

shrub, *n.*, bush; **-bery; -by** *a.;* **-biness**

shuck, *v.*, remove pod, husk or shell [ror

shud′der, *v.*, shake in hor-

shuf′fle, *v.*, drag feet as walking, mix; **-r**

shun, *v.*, keep away from

shush, *int.*, be quiet

shut, *v.*, close, lock up, stop [opening

shut′ter, *n.*, cover for an

shut′tle, *n.*, *v.*, (thing on which to) go back and forth

shy, *a.*, shrinking from notice, bashful; **-ly; -ness**

sib′ling, *n.*, child born of same parents as another child

sick, *a.*, in bad health, disgusted, upset; **-ness; -en; -ening; -ish; -ly; -liness** [tool

sick′le, *n.*, curved cutting

side, *n.,* right or left half, bounding line, position, surface; *a.,* of side, secondary

side′bûrns, *n.,* hair growing in front of ears

side′lŏng, *a.,* sloping, indirect; *adv.,* on side

sī-dê′rē-ál, *a.,* of stars; **-ly**

side′splĭt-tĭng, *a.,* causing laughter

sĭd′ĭng, *n.,* covering for outside wall

sī′dle, *v.,* move sideways

siêge, *n.,* persistent attack, blockade [range

sī-ĕr′rȧ, *n.,* mountain

sī-ĕs′tȧ, *n.,* afternoon nap

sĭft, *v.,* pass through a sieve, distinguish; **-er**

sīght, *n.,* seeing, view, aiming device; *v.,* see

sīght′lĕss, *a.,* blind; **-ly; -ness**

sign, *n.,* something to convey meaning, symbol, display board; *v.,* write one's name, signal

sĭg′nȧl, *n.,* notice to impel action; *v.,* communicate; **-er; -ize; -ly**

sĭg′nȧ-tûre, *n.,* one's name written by oneself; **tory** *a.*

sĭg′nĕt, *n.,* official seal

sī′lĕnt, *a.,* not speaking, quiet; **lence; lencer; -ly**

sĭl-hŏu-ĕtte′, *n.,* black outline of thing

sĭl′ĭ-cón, *n.,* nonmetallic chemical element

sĭlk, *n.,* fine soft fiber from silkworm; **-en; -y** *a.*

sĭll, *n.,* bottom of door or window frame

sĭl′lỹ, *a.,* ridiculous, of little sense, foolish; **lily; liness** [fodder

sī′lō, *n.,* tower for storing

sĭlt, *n.,* fine-grained sediment

šĭl′vêr-wāre, *n.,* household articles made of silver

sĭm′ĭ-lȧr, *a.,* nearly the same; **-ity; -ly**

sĭm′mêr, *v.,* boil gently

sĭm′ple, *a.,* easy, not complex, plain, natural, common; **plicity; plify; plifier; plification; -ness**

sĭm′ū-lāte, *v.,* pretend; **tor; tion; tive**

sī-mŭl-tā′nē-oŭs, *a.,* done at same time; **neity; -ly; -ness**

sĭn, *n.,* breaking moral law; *v.,* do wrong; **-ful; -fully; -fulness**

sĭn-cēre′, *a.,* truthful, honest, genuine; **cerity; -ly; -ness**

sĭn′eẁ, *n.,* tendon; **-y** *a.*

sĭng, *v.,* produce music with voice; **-er; -able**

sĭnge, *v.,* burn slightly

sĭn′gle, *a.,* one only, alone, unmarried; **gly**

sĭng′sŏng, *n.,* monotonous rhythm [ous

sĭn′ĭs-têr, *a.,* evil, dangerous

sĭnk, *v.,* go under water, descend, lower; **-er; -age; -able**

sĭn′ū-oŭs, *a.,* crooked; **-ly**

sī′nŭs, *n.,* air cavity in skull

sī′phȯn, *n., v.,* (tube to) drain liquid from one container to another

sī′rėn, *n.,* warning signal with wailing sound

site, *n.,* piece of land, location

sĭt-ū-ā′tion, *n.,* position, state; **-al; -ally**

sĭz′ȧ-ble, *a.,* quite large; **bly; -ness**

size, *n.,* amount of space occupied, graded measures

sĭz′zle, *v.,* hiss when hot

skĕl′ė-tȯn, *n.,* animal's bony framework, outline; **tal** [-ally

skĕp′tĭc, *n.,* doubter; **-al; -ally**

skĕtch, *n.,* rough drawing, outline; **-er; -y** *a.*

skī, *n.,* shoe runner for gliding on snow or water; **-er**

skĭll, *n.,* expertness, art, craft; **-ful; -fully; -fulness**

skĭl′lėt, *n.,* frying pan

skĭm, v., remove floating matter from liquid, glance over; **-mer**

skĭmp, v., be stingy; **-y** a., **-ily; -iness**

skĭn, n., outer covering; v., remove skin from; **-less**

skĭp, v., jump from leg to leg, omit

skĭr'mĭsh, n., brief fight

skĭrt, n., woman's garment from waist down; v., go along edge

skĭt, n., short play

skĭt'tĭsh, a., lively, nervous; **-ness; -ly**

skŭlk, v., lurk stealthily

skŭnk, n., mammal emitting foul odor, (coll.) offensive person

skȳ, n., air above, heavens

skȳ'lĭght, n., window in ceiling

slăb, n., flat, broad piece

slăck, a., loose, slow, lax; **-er; -ness; -en; -ly**

slăm, n., noisy impact; v., shut, throw or hit forcibly

slăn'dêr, n., false statement said about another; **-er; -ous** [guage

slăng, n., informal lan-

slănt, n., slope, attitude, bias; v., incline, distort

slăp, n., v., hit with palm of hand; adv., straight; **-per** [rough play

slăp'stĭck, n., comedy with

slăsh, v., cut or whip viciously, reduce; **-er**

slăt, n., thin strip

slăugh'têr, n., brutal killing; **-ous; -ously**

slāve, n., person totally owned by another; **-ry**

slāy, v., kill; **-er**

slēa'zȳ, a., flimsy; **ziness; zily**

slĕdge'hăm-mêr, n., long, heavy hammer

slēek, a., glossy, stylish; **-ness; -en; -ly**

slēet, n., partially frozen rain

slĕn'dêr, a., small in width, thin; **-ness; -ize; -ly**

sleuth, n., detective

slīce, n., thin, cut piece, part; v., cut into slices; **-r**

slĭck, n., oily film on water; v., a., (make) glossy; a., clever; **-ness; -ly**

slīde, n., sliding, surface on which to slide, photographic transparency; v., move smoothy on surface, slip; **-r**

slīght, v., neglect; a., thin; **-ness; -ly**

slīme, n., wet slippery matter; **slimy**

slĭng, n., v., (looped or hanging band used to) support, carry, throw

slĭnk, v., sneak, lurk; **-y** a.; **-ingly**

slĭp, n., woman's undergarment, error, small piece of paper; v., go quietly or quickly, slide accidently, err

slĭt, n., narrow opening; v., cut open; **-ter** [a.

slĭth'êr, v., slide, glide; **-y**

slĭv'êr, n., splinter

slŏb'bêr, v., drip saliva from mouth, drool; **-er; -y** a. [phrase

slō'găn, n., motto, catch

slōop, n., sailing vessel

slŏp, n., unappetizing food mixture; v., splash; **-py; -piness; -pily**

slōpe, n., raising or falling plane; v., go up or down at an angle

slŏt, n., narrow opening, position

slŏth, n., tree-dwelling mammal, laziness; **-ful; -fulness; -fully**

slōugh, n., swamp

slough (slŭf), v., shed, discard

slŏv'ên-lȳ, a., careless in appearance; **liness**

slōw, a., taking a long time, dull; v., make slow; **-ness; -ly**

slŭg, n., small land mollusk, false coin; v., hit hard

slŭm, n., poor, over-

crowded neighborhood
slŭm'bêr, n., v., sleep; **-er; -ous**

slŭmp, n.,v., fall, decline

slŭr, n., insult; v., say indistinctly, slander

slûrp, v., drink or eat noisily   [snow

slŭsh, n., partly melted

slŭt, n., slovenly woman

slŷ, a., skillful at deceit; **-ness; -ly**

smăck, n., sharp noise, loud kiss, slap, trace; v., make a smack; **-er**

smăll, a., little, limited in size, trivial; **-ness; -ish**

smăll'pŏx, n., contagious disease

smârt, v., cause pain; a., sharp, intelligent, stylish; **-ness; -en; -ly**

smăsh, v., break violently, hit; **-er**   [amount

smăt'têr-ĭng, n., small

smēar, n., smudge mark; v., rub, spread dirt, slander; **-y** a.

smĕll, n., quality perceived through nose, odor; v., detect a smell, sniff; **-er**

smĕlt, n., small silvery fish; v., melt ore or metal; **-er**

smile, n., grin; v., curve mouth upward to show pleasure; **-r; smilingly**

smīte, v., strike, distress; **-r**

smĭth, n., one who makes or repairs metal things

smŏck, n., protective outer garment

smŏg, n., fog and smoke

smōke, n., vapor arising from fire; v., give off smoke, use cigarettes, etc.; **-r; -able; -less; smoky** a.

smōl'dêr, v., burn without flame, be supressed

smôr'gàs-bôrd, n., many foods served buffet style

smŏth'êr, v., keep from getting air, suffocate, stifle; **-er; -y** a.

smŭdge, n., dirty spot; v., soil; **smudgy**

smŭg, a., annoyingly self-satisfied; **-ness; -ly**

smŭg'gle, v., import or export illegally; **-r**

smŭt, n., dirty matter, pornography; **-ty** a.

snăg, n., rough, sharp part, hidden difficulty; v., tear on snag; **-gy** a.

snāil, n., mollusk with spiral shell   [reptile

snāke, n., long limbless

snăp'shŏt, n., photograph

snâre, n., trap

snârl, n., v., growl, tangle; **-y** a.

snătch, n., v., grab; n., brief period, bit; **-er**

snēak, v., move or act underhandedly; **-y** a., **-iness; -ily**

snēer, v., smile scornfully; **-er; -ingly**

snēeze, v., exhale breath from mouth and nose in explosive action; **-r**

snĭck'êr, v., laugh slyly; **-ingly**   [**-ness; -ly**

snīde, a., malicious;

snĭff, v., breathe in through nose forcibly; **-er**

snĭp, v., cut quickly with scissors; **-per**

snipe, v., shoot from a hidden place; **-r**

snŏb, n., one who acts superior; **-bery; -bish; -bishness; -bishly**

snōoze, n., v., (coll.) nap; **-r**   [while asleep; **-r**

snôre, v., breathe loudly

snôrt, v., breath making harsh sound; **-er; -ingly**

snōw, n., flakes of frozen water vapor from sky; **-y** a.   [**-ber; -by** a.

snŭb, v., show contempt;

snŭff, n., smokeless tobacco; v., inhale through nose, put out candle

snŭg, a., warm and cozy, tight in fit; **-gery; -ness; -ly**

sōak, v., make very wet, take in; **-age**

S T

sōap, *n.,* washing substance; **-y** *a.;* **-iness; -ily**

sōap'bŏx, *n.,* improvised platform

sôar, *v.,* fly high in air; **-er**

sŏb, *v.,* cry aloud; **-ingly**

sŏc'cêr, *n.,* team ball game

sō'ciál, *a.,* of people, of society; **-ity; -ize; -izer; -ization; -ly**

sō'ciál-ĭsm, *n.,* public ownership of industry; **ist; istic; istically**

sŏ-ci'é-tȳ, *n.,* community of people, all people, wealthy class; **tal**

sō-cĭ-ŏl'ŏ-gȳ, *n.,* study of society and human relations; **gist; logical**

sŏck, *n.,* short stocking; *v.,* hit hard

sŏck'ĕt, *n.,* hollow part into which a thing fits

sŏd'dĕn, *a.,* soaked, soggy; **-ness; -ly**

sō'di-ŭm, *n.,* soft metallic element

sŏd'ŏm-ȳ, *n.,* abnormal sexual behavior

sôft, *a.,* pleasing to senses, yielding easily to touch, smooth, mild, easy; **-ness; -en; -ener; -ly**   [ball

sôft'băll, *n.,* kind of base-

sôft'ȳ, *n.,* sentimental person   [**giness; gily**

sŏg'gȳ, *a.,* wet and heavy;

sŏil, *n.,* top layer of earth, ground, stain; *v.,* make dirty

sō'joûrn, *n., v.,* visit; **-er**

sŏl'áce, *n., v.,* comfort; **-r**

sō-lăr'ĭ-ŭm, *n.,* glassed-in room exposed to sun

sŏl'dier (jêr) *n.,* member of army; **-y; -ly** *a.;* **-liness**

sōle, *n.,* bottom of foot; fish

sōle, *a.,* single, alone; **-ly**

sŏl'ĕmn, *a.,* sacred, formal, serious, awesome; **-ity; -ify; -ize; -ness; -ly**

sŏ-lĭc'ĭt, *v.,* seek, ask for **-ation; -ant** *n., a.*

sŏ-lĭc'ĭ-tŏr, *n.,* lawyer

sŏl-ĭ-dăr'ĭ-tȳ, *n.,* complete unity

sŏ-lĭl'ŏ-quȳ, *n.,* talking aloud to oneself; **quize**

sŏl'ĭ-tār-ȳ, *a.,* alone, single; **tariness; tarily**

sŏ-lū'tion, *n.,* answer, being dissolved

sŏl'vĕnt, *n.,* solution; *a.,* able to pay debts, dissolving; **vency**

sō-măt'ĭc, *a.,* of the body; **-ally**   [**-ness; -ly**

sŏm'bêr, *a.,* gloomy, sad;

sŏme'bŏd-ȳ, *pro.,* a person   [time

sŏme'dāy, *adv.,* at a future

sŏme'how, *adv.,* in an unknown way   [body

sŏme'óne, *pro.,* some-

sŏm'êr-săult, *n.,* turning the body head over heels

sŏme'tĭmes, *adv.,* occasionally

sŏme'whĕre, *adv.,* at an unknown place

sō'nánt, *a.,* of sound; **nance**

sŏ-nā'tá, *n.,* musical piece

sŏng, *n.,* music to be sung; **-ster**

sŏn'ĭc, *a.,* of sound

sŏn'nĕt, *n.,* poem with fourteen lines

sŏ-nô'roŭs, *a.,* rich in sound; **nority; -ness; -ly**

sŏŏt, *n.,* black particles of smoke; **-y** *a.*

sŏŏthe, *v.,* calm, pacify; **-r; soothingly**

sŏŏth'sāy, *v.,* predict; **-er**

sŏph'ĭsm, *n.,* false reasoning

sŏ-phĭs'tĭ-cāt-ĕd, *a.,* knowledgeable, complex; **tion**

sŏ-prä'nō, *n.,* highest singing voice

sôr'cêr-ȳ, *n.,* witchcraft; **cerer; cerous; cerously**

sôr'dĭd, *a.,* dirty, mean; **-ness; -ly**

sôre, *n.,* infected spot on body; *a.,* painful, distressing; **-ness; -ly**

sŏ-rôr'ĭ-tȳ, *n.,* woman's club

sŏr′rĕl, *n.*, *a.*, (horse of) reddish-brown

sŏr′rŏw, *n.*, mental pain, sadness, distress; *v.*, grieve; **-er**; **-ful**; **-fulness**; **-fully**

sor′rў (sâr), *a.*, feeling regret, grieved, poor; **riness**; **rily**

sôrt, *n.*, type; *v.*, arrange, classify; **-er**; **-able**

soûf-fle′ (flā), *n.*, light, puffy baked dish

sōul, *n.*, spiritual part of person, vital part; **-ful**; **-fulness**; **-fully**; **-less**

sŏūnd, *n.*, inlet of sea

sōūnd, *a.*, in good condition, valid, deep; **-ness**; **-ly**

soūr, *a.*, tasting unplesant and sharp, fermented; **-ness**; **-ly**

sôurce, *n.*, starting point

sŏūth, *n.*, direction to left when facing sunset; *a.*, *adv.*, in or of south; **-erly** *a.*, *adv.*; **-ern** *a.*; **-ward**, **-wardly** *a.*, *adv.*

soū-vĕ-nǐr′, *n.*, thing kept as a reminder

sŏv′er-eǐgn, *n.*, *a.*, (person) supreme in power; **-ty**

sŏw, *n.*, adult female pig

sōw, *v.*, plant seed, scatter; **-er**

soy′bēan (sōǐ), *n.*, plant of legume family, seed

spå, *n.*, mineral spring, health resort

spāce, *n.*, unlimited expanse, area, room; **-less**

spā′cioŭs, *a.*, vast, large; **-ness**; **-ly**

spāde, *n.*, digging tool, black card suit

spå-ghĕt′tĭ, *n.*, long thin noodles

spăn, *n.*, measurement, extent, period of time; *v.*, reach across; **-ner**

spăn′gle, *n.*, small decorative metal piece; **gly** *a.*

spănk, *v.*, hit on buttocks as punishment; **-ing** *n.*

spâr, *n.*, long thick pole; *v.*, box with fists, dispute

spāre, *n.*, extra part; *v.*, save, give up; *a.*, extra; **-r**; **-ness**; **-ly**

spârk, *n.*, particle of fire or electricity, trace; *v.*, stir up; **-er**

spâr′kle, *n.*, *v.*, glitter

spârse, *a.*, meager; **-ness**; **-ly**

spăsm, *n.*, sudden muscle contraction; **-odic**; **-odical**; **-odically**

spăt, *n.*, *v.*, quarrel

spā′tiàl, *a.*, of space; **-ity**; **-ly** [drops

spăt′têr, *v.*, splash in

spăt′ū-là, *n.*, utensil with flexible blade

spăwn, *n.*, mass of eggs, or young; *v.*, produce young

spēar, *n.*, long pointed weapon

spēar′mǐnt, *n.*, fragrant plant for flavoring

spě′ciàl, *a.*, distinctive, extraordinary; **-ty**; **-ize**; **-ization**; **-ly**

spē′cǐēs, *n.*, *pl.*, distinct kind, biological classification

spĕ-cǐf′ǐc, *a.*, definite, explicit; **-ity**; **-ally**

spĕc′ǐ-mĕn, *n.*, sample

spĕck, *n.*, particle

spĕc′tå-cle, *n.*, unusual display, (pl.) pair of eyeglasses; **cular** *a.*; **cularly**

spĕc′tå-tŏr, *n.*, onlooker

spĕc′têr, *n.*, ghost; **tral** *a.*; **trality**; **tralness**; **trally**

spĕc′trŭm, *n.*, band of colors formed by diffusing light

spĕc′ū-lāte, *v.*, ponder, take business risk; **tor**; **tion**; **tive**; **tively**

spēech, *n.*, talk, address given to audience; **-less**; **-lessness**; **-lessly**

spēed, *n.*, quick motion; *v.*, move rapidly, aid; **-er**; **-y** *a.*

S
T

spéed-ŏm'é-têr, *n.,* device showing rate of speed

spĕll, *n.,* charm, period of time

spĕll, *v.,* give letters in word in order, signify; **-er; -ing** *n.*

spĕnd, *v.,* use up, pay out money; **-er** [derer

spĕnd'thrĭft, *n.,* squan-

spêr-măt-ò-zō'ŏn, *n.,* male reproductive cell; **zoal; zoan** *a.;* **zoic**

spĕw, *v.,* vomit, gush forth; **-er**

sphēre, *n.,* round body, ball; **spheric; spherical; spherically**

sphĭnx, *n.,* statue with human head and lion's body

spī'dêr, *n.,* eight-legged animal that spins web; **-y** *a.*

spīke, *n.,* large nail, sharp-pointed projection; *v.,* fasten [**-age**

spĭll, *v.,* drop, overflow;

spĭn, *n.,* ride; *v.,* twist fibers into thread, make a web, rotate; **-ner; -ning** *n.* [vegetable

spĭn'ăch, *n.,* green leafy

spĭn'dle, *n.,* rod used in spinning thread

spine, *n.,* backbone, quill, thorn; **nal; nous; spiny** *a.* [**-ness; -ly**

spine'lĕss, *a.,* cowardly;

spĭn'ĕt, *n.,* upright piano

spĭn'stêr, *n.,* older unmarried woman

spī'răl, *n.,* coil, helix; *a.,* circling around a center; **-ly** [a point

spire, *n.,* thing tapering to

spīr'ĭt, *n.,* soul, ghost, courage, meaning, (pl.) frame of mind; **-less; -lessness; -lessly**

spīr'ĭt-ū-ăl, *n.,* Negro folk song; *a.,* of spirit, religious; **-ity; -ize; -ization**

spĭt, *n.,* rod to roast meat over fire, saliva; *v.,* eject from mouth; **-ter**

spite, *n.,* malice; *v.,* hurt; **-ful; -fulness; -fully**

splăsh, *v.,* scatter liquid; **-er; -y** *a.*

splēen, *n.,* abdominal organ

splĕn'dĭd, *a.,* brilliant, grand, glorious; **dor** *n.;* **dorous; drous; -ness; -ly**

splīce, *v.,* join together; **-r**

splĭnt, *n.,* device to hold broken bone together

splĭn'têr, *n.,* sliver; *v.,* break into small parts; **-y** *a.*

splĭt, *n.,* break; *v.,* separate, break, divide; **-ter**

splûrge, *n.,* (coll.) showy display; *v.,* be extravagant; **-r**

spŏil, *n.,* conquered property; *v.,* damage, ruin, overindulge; **-er; -age**

spōke, *n.,* wheel brace, ladder rung

spōkes'măn, *n.,* one who speaks for another

spònge, *n.,* porous plant-like animal of sea, absorbent material; *v.,* absorb, wipe clean; **-r; gy** *a.;* **giness**

spŏn-tā'nē-oŭs, *a.,* occurring naturally; **neity; -ness; -ly**

spōōk, *n.,* ghost; *v.,* haunt, frighten; **-y** *a.*

spōōl, *n.,* cylinder for thread, wire, etc.

spô-răd'ĭc, *a.,* happening from time to time; **-ally**

spôre, *n.,* reproductive cell

spôrt, *n.,* athletic game, fun; *v.,* play; *a.,* informal; **-er; -ive; -iveness; -ively; -ful; -fully; -y** *a.;* **-ness; -ily**

spŏt, *n.,* small area different from the rest, *v.,* stain, locate; **-ter; -less; -lessness; -lessly; -ty** *a.;* **-tiness; -tily**

spŏūse, *n.,* partner in marriage; **spousal**

spoŭt, *n.,* lip or tube for

pouring liquid; *v.*, shoot out; **-er; -less**

sprāin, *v.*, twist a muscle

sprāwl, *v.*, spread limbs to relax; **-er; -y** *a.*

sprāy, *n.*, mist of fine liquid drops; *v.*, apply a spray; **-er**

sprĕad, *n.*, extent, cover; *v.*, stretch out, scatter, cover; **-er**

sprēe, *n.*, lively time

sprĭng, *n.*, leap, resilient coil, source of water, season for beginning plant growth; *v.*, bounce, rise, come from

sprĭn'kle, *v.*, scatter in drops or particles

sprĭnt, *n., v.*, race fast

sprŏut, *n.*, new growth; *v.*, begin growing

sprȳ, *a.*, active, agile; **-ness; -ly**

spŭnk, *n.*, (coll.) courage; **-y** *a.;* **-ness; -ily**

spŭr, *n., v.*, (pointed attachment to horseman's heel to) urge to action

spū'rĭ-oŭs, *a.*, artificial; **-ness; -ly**   [-er

spŭrn, *v.*, reject scornfully;

spŭrt, *n.*, sudden burst of energy; *v.*, gush

spŭt'nĭk, *n.*, manmade satellite

spȳ, *n.*, one who spies; *v.*, watch closely and secretly

squăb, *n.*, young pigeon

squăb'ble, *n., v.*, quarrel

squăd, *n.*, small group

squăll, *n.*, violent storm; shrill cry; *v.*, scream harshly   [fully

squăn'dêr, *v.*, use waste-

squăre, *n.*, figure with four equal sides, city block; *v.*, adjust; multiply by itself; *a.*, squarelike, straight, even, fair; **-ness; -ly**

squăsh, *n.*, fleshy vegetable, tennislike game; *v.*, crush, suppress; **-y** *a.*

squăt, *v.*, crouch, settle public land; *a.*, short and

thick; **-ter; -ty** *a.*

squăw, *n.*, Indian woman

squēal, *n.*, shrill cry or sound; *v.*, (coll.) informer; **-er**

squēam'ĭsh, *a.*, easily nauseated or shocked; **-ness; -ly**   [hug

squēeze, *v.*, press closely,

squĕlch, *v.*, suppress

squĭd, *n.*, ten-armed sea mollusk

squĭg'gle, *n.*, short curved line; **gly** *a.*

squīre, *n.*, country gentleman [body; **-y** *a.*

squîrm, *v.*, twist and turn

squîr'rĕl, *n.*, tree-dwelling rodent   [jet; **-er**

squîrt, *v.*, shoot liquid in

stăb, *n.*, wound; *v.*, pierce with something sharp; **-ber**

stā'ble, *n.*, building for horses and cattle

stā'ble, *a.*, firm, enduring; **bility; bilize; bilizer; bilization; bly**

stăff, *n.*, rod or stick, group of workers

stăg, *n.*, male deer, party for only men

stāge, *n.*, platform, theater, growth period; *v.*, present

stăg'gêr, *v.*, move unsteadily; **-er**   [ing; **-ly**

stăg'gêr-ĭng, *a.*, astonish-

stăg'nănt, *a.*, not moving, foul; **nancy; nate; nation; -ly**

stāid, *a.*, settled, steady; **-ness; -ly**

stāin, *n., v.*, spot, dishonor, color; **-er; -able; -less; -lessly**

stāke, *n.*, pointed stick, wager, prize; *v.*, mark off, hitch

stă-lăc'tīte, *n.*, lime deposit hanging from cave; **titic**

stă-lăg'mīte, *n.*, lime deposit sticking up from cave floor; **mitic**

stāle'māte, *n.*, deadlock

stălk, *n.*, plant stem; *v.*,

S
T

walk or spread grimly;
-er

stall, *n.,* animal compartment in stable, booth; *v.,* delay

stăl′liŏn, *n.,* male horse

stăl′wȧrt, *a.,* strong, sturdy; **-ness; -ly**

stăm′ĭ-nȧ, *n.,* endurance

stăm′mêr, *v.,* talk with involuntary pauses, stutter; **-er; -ingly**

stămp, *n.,* gummed paper for postage, mark from die, sign; *v.,* put foot down forcibly, imprint mark; **-er** [rush

stăm-pēde′, *n.,* headlong

stănce, *n.,* standing posture [support beam

stăn′chiŏn, *n.,* upright

stănd, *n.,* position, halt, platform, booth; *v.,* be or set upright, tolerate, remain, rank; **-er**

stănd′ȧrd, *n.,* established rule or model, basis of measurement; *a.,* typical; **-ize; -izer; -ization**

stănd′ĭn, *n.,* substitute

stănd′pŏint, *n.,* point of view

stănd′stĭll, *n.,* halt

stăn′zȧ, *n.,* division of poem; **-ic**

stā′ple, *n.,* main commodity; *a.,* principal

stā′ple, *n.,* U-shaped wire fastener; *v.,* fasten with staple; **-r**

stâr, *n.,* heavenly body, flat figure with five or six points, celebrated person; *a.,* outstanding

stâr′board, *n.,* ship's right side when facing bow

stârch, *n.,* carbohydrate food substance, clothes stiffener; **-y** *a.;* **-iness; -ily**

stāre, *v.,* look intently; **-r**

stârk, *a.,* prominent, bare, rigid, utter; **-ness; -ly**

stârt, *n.,* beginning, shock; *v.,* set into motion, move suddenly; **-er**

stârve, *v.,* suffer from hunger; **vation**

stāte, *n.,* condition, political unit; *v.,* declare; *a.,* formal

stāte′mėnt, *n.,* declaration, financial account, bill

stăt′ĭc, *n.,* electrical interference; *a.,* motionless; **-ally**

stā′tion, *n.,* assigned place, stopping place, position

stā′tion-âr-ȳ, *a.,* fixed, unchanging

stā′tion-ĕr-ȳ, *n.,* writing supplies

stȧ-tĭs′tĭcs, *n.,* science of numerical data; **cian** *n.;* **cal; cally**

stăt′ūe, *n.,* carved or modeled figure; **uary**

stăt′ûre, *n.,* height, level of attainment

stăt′ŭs, *n.,* position

stăt′ūte, *n.,* law; **tory** *a.*

stäunch, *v.,* stop flow; *a.,* firm, loyal; **-ness; -ly**

stāve, *n.,* barrel slat

stāy, *n., v.,* support, stop, delay, continuing; *v.,* remain

stĕad, *n.,* position for a replacement

stĕad′ȳ, *a.,* fixed, regular; **steadiness; steadily**

stĕal, *v.,* take without permission; **-er**

stĕalth, *n.,* secret behavior; **-y** *a.;* **-iness; -ily**

stēam, *n.,* water vapor; **-y** *a.;* **-iness; -ily**

stēel, *n.,* tough metal of iron and carbon; **-y** *a.;* **-iness**

stēep, *v.,* soak in liquid

stēep, *a.,* having sharp slope, extreme; **-ness; -en; -ly**

stēe′ple, *n.,* high tower on building [**-able**

stēer, *v.,* guide, direct; **-er**

stēer′ȧge, *n.,* poorest accommodations aboard ship

stein, *n.,* beer mug

stĕl′lȧr, *a.,* of star, important

stĕm, n., main upward axis of plant, stemlike thing; v., derive, stop; **-less**

stĕnch, n., offensive odor

stĕn'cĭl, n., cut-out pattern; v., make or mark with stencil; **-er**

stē-nŏg'rȧ-phў, n., shorthand writing; **pher; graphic; graphical; graphically**

stĕp'lăd-dêr, n., ladder with flat rungs and wide base

stĕr-ē-ȯ-phŏn'ĭc, a., of sounds from two or more directions; **ny; -ally**

stĕr'ē-ȯ-tȳpe, n., fixed pattern

stĕr'īle, a., unable to reproduce, not stimulating, free of germs; **rility; lize; lizer; lization**

stĕr'lĭng, n., real silver; a., excellent

stĕr'nŭm, n., breastbone

stĕth'ȯ-scōpe, n., device to hear chest sounds; **py; scopic; scopical; scopically**

stē'vė-dȯre, n., one who loads and unloads ships

stew, n., mixture of meat and vegetables; v., boil slowly

stew'ȧrd, n., one in charge; **-ess** n.; **-ship**

stĭck'lêr, n., uncompromising person

stĭck'ў, a., adhesive, humid; **stickiness; stickily**

stĭff, a., hard to bend, firm, rigid; **-ness; -en; -ish; -ly**

stĭ'fle, v., smother, suppress; **-r; fling; flingly**

stĭg'mȧ, n., mark of disgrace, plant part; **-tize; -tization; -tic; -tical; -tically**

stĭll, n., device for distilling liquids

stĭll, a., quiet, inactive; adv., continuously, yet; **-ness; -y** a., adv.

stĭll'bôrn, n., dead at birth

stĭlt, n., supporting pole

stĭlt'ėd, a., raised, pompous; **-ness; -ly**

stĭm'ū-lāte, v., excite; **-r; tor; lant,** n., a.; **lus** n.; tion; tive

stĭn'gў, a., miserly; **giness; gily**

stĭnt, n., limit, task; v., restrict; **-er**

stĭ'pĕnd, n., fixed payment; **-iary** a.

stĭp'ple, v., mark with dots

stĭp'ū-lāte, v., specify, require; **tor; tion; tory**

stĭr'rŭp, n., footrest on saddle

stĭtch, n., single loop in sewing; v., sew; **-er; -ery**

stŏck, n., lineage, supporting part, livestock, goods in store, share in a business; v., supply; a., common

stŏck-āde', n., enclosure, jail

stŏck'brō-kêr, n., agent for stocks and bonds; **-age**

stŏck'ĭng, n., closefitting cover for leg and foot

stŏck'pīle, n., supply in reserve; **-r**

stŏck'ў, a., short and heavy; **stockiness**

stō'ĭc, n., a. (one who is) indifferent; **-al; -ally**

stōke, v., feed full, fill; **-r**

stōle, n., large shoulder scarf [**-ness; -ly**

stŏl'ĭd, a., unexcitable;

stōne, n., hard nonmetallic mineral matter, rock

stōol, n., backless seat, feces

stōop, n., small porch; v., bend body forward, lower oneself

stŏp'găp, n., temporary substitute

stôr'ȧge, n., place for keeping goods

stôre, n., supply, place to sell goods; v., put aside for future

stôrk, n., large wading bird

stôrm, n., atmospheric disturbance wind, rain,

S T

snow, etc.; v., attack; **-y** a.

stô′rȳ, n., series of connected events, tale, one level of building

stŏŭt, a., fat, brave; **-ness; -ish; -ly**

stŏve, n., device for heating or cooking

stŏw, v., pack away; **-age**

străd′dle, v., put leg on either side; **-r**

strāfe, v., attack with gunfire; **-r**

straight (strāt), a., not crooked, even, sincere; v., directly; **-en**

straight-fôr′ward (strāt), a., direct, honest; **-ness; -ly**

strāin, n., effort, breed; v., stretch or exert to utmost, filter, strive hard; **-er**

strāit, n., narrow waterway, emergency

strănd, n., shore, thread; v., be helpless; **-er**

strănge, a. unfamiliar, foreign. odd; **-r; -ness; -ly**

străn′gle, v., choke;ʼ**-r**

străp, n., leather strip; **-less**

străt′à-gĕm, n., trick

străt′ė-gȳ, n., plan, maneuver; **gist; gic; gical; gically**

străt′ô-sphēre, n., upper atmosphere

strā′tŭm, a., layer

străw, n., hollow grain stalk, tube used for sucking; **-y** a. [fruit

străw′bĕr-rȳ, n., small red

strāy, v., roam; a., lost, incidental; **-er**

strēam, n., small river; n., v., flow [banner

strēam′ĕr, n., ribbonlike

strēam′līne, v., design for efficiency; **-d**

strēet′câr, n., passenger car on rails

strĕngth, n., strong quality, durability, force; **-en; -ener**

strĕn′ū-oŭs, a., showing great effort; **-ness; -ly**

strĕss, n., strain, emphasis, tension; **-ful; -fully**

strĕtch, v., reach out, extend; **-ability; -able; -y** a.

strī′āte, v., make with lines; **tion**

strĭck′ĕn, a., afflicted

strĭct, a., exact, closely enforced; **-ness; -ly**

strĭc′tûre, n., sharp criticism

strīde, n., long step

strī′dĕnt, a., shrill; **dence; dency; -ly**

strīfe, n., struggle, discord

strīke, v., hit, sound by hitting, ignite, find, stop work for new demands; **-r** [**-ly**

strīk′ĭng, a., outstanding;

strĭn′gĕnt, a., strict; **gency; -ness; -ly**

strĭp, n., narrow piece, runway; v., remove covering, deprive

strīpe, n., long narrow mark

strĭp′lĭng, n., grown boy

strīve, v., try hard, fight; **-r**

strŏke, n., sudden action, single effort, sound from striking; v., caress

strŏll, v., walk leisurely; **-er**

strông′-ârm, a., physical force [place

strông′hōld, n., fortified

strŏn′tĭ-ŭm, n., chemical element

strŭc′tûre, n., building, organization; v., organize; **tural; turally**

strŭg′gle, n., great effort; n., v., conflict; **-r**

strŭm, v., stroke strings of instrument

strŭt, v., walk arrogantly

strȳch′nīne, n., poisonous substance

stŭb, n., short remaining piece; v., hit against

stŭb′bôrn, n., unyielding, resistant; **-ness; -ly**

stŭc′cō, n., coarse plaster

stŭd, n., ornamental nailhead, wall support, male breeder   [room

stŭ'dĭ-ō, *n.*, artist's work-

stŭd'ў, *n.*, *v.*, act to acquire knowledge, examine carefully; *n.*, place to study; **dious; diousness; diously**

stŭff, *n.*, substance, objects; *v.*, fill, pack; **-er**

stŭl'tĭfў, *v.*, make absurd; **fier; fication**

stŭm'ble, *n.*, error; *v.*, miss one's step, happen; **-r; blingly**

stŭmp, *n.*, remaining part; *v.*, speak on tour; **-y** *a.*

stŭn, *v.*, shock, make unconscious; **-ner**

stŭnt, *n.*, daring trick; *v.*, hinder growth

stŭ'pė-fў, *v.*, shock, amaze; **fier; faction; facient**

stŭ-pĕn'doŭs, *a.*, astonishing; **-ly**

stŭ'pŏr, *n.*, loss of senses, lethargy; **-ous**

stŭr'dў, *a.*, physically strong, firm; **diness; dily**

stŭr'geŏn, *n.*, large fish

stŭt'tėr, *v.*, talk with involuntary repeat of sounds; **-er**   [eyelid

stў, *n.*, pigpen, swelling of

stўle, *n.*, manner, artistic expression, fashion; **stylist; stylize**

stў'lŭs, *n.*, marking tool

stў'miė, *v.*, obstruct

suàve, *a.*, smoothly gracious; **suavily; -ness; -ly**   [rank

sŭb-ăl'tėrn, *a.*, of lower

sŭb-cŏn'scioŭs, *a.*, happening without awareness; **-ness; -ly**

sŭb'cŭl-tùre, *n.*, culture within larger society; **tural**

sŭb-dĭ-vīde', *v.*, divide land into smaller areas

sŭb-dūe', *v.*, conquer, lessen; **duct; dual; duable**

sŭb'jĕct, *n.*, one controlled, theme, course of

study, word discussed

sŭb-jĕct', *v.*, control, undergo; **-ion**

sŭb-jĕc'tĭve, *a.*, of one's own feelings; **tivity; -ness; -ly**

sŭb'jŭ-gāte, *v.*, control, conquer; **tor; tion**

sŭb'lĭ-māte, *v.*, express impulses in acceptable forms; **tion**

sŭb-līme', *a.*, exalted, splendid; **limity**

sŭb-mêrge', *v.*, put under water; **gence; gible**

sŭb-mĭt', *v.*, yield, surrender; **-ter; mission; missive; missiveness; missively; -table**

sŭb-poē'nà, *n.*, written order to appear in court

sŭb-scrībe', *v.*, agree to pay, support; **-r; scription**

sŭb-sīde', *v.*, sink lower, abate; **-nce**   [illiary

sŭb-sĭd'ĭ-ār-ў, *n.*, *a.*, aux-

sŭb'sĭ-dў, *n.*, grant of money; **dize; dizer; dization**

sŭb-sĭst', *v.*, exist, remain alive; **-ence; -ent**

sŭb'stànce, *n.*, essence, matter, character

sŭb-stăn'tĭ-āte, *v.*, prove; **tor; tion; tive**

sŭb'stĭ-tūte, *n.*, one in place for another; *v.*, replace; **tion; tive; tional; tionally; tionary; tutable**   [action

sŭb'têr-fūge, *n.*, evasive

sub-tle (sŭt'l), *a.*, delicate, clever, keen; **-ty; -ness; -ly**

sŭb-trăct', *v.*, take away from; **-er; -ion; -ive**

sŭb'ûrb, *n.*, residential district near city; **-anize; -anization; -an** *a.*

sŭb-vêrt', *v.*, destroy, undermine; **-er; version; versive; versiveness; versively**

sŭc-cēed', *v.*, follow, achieve goal; **-er**

sŭc-cĕss, *n.*, favorable re-

S
T

sult, gaining wealth; **-ful; -fulness; -fully**

sŭc-cĕs'siŏn, *n.,* following in order, series; **sor; sive; siveness; sively; -al; -ally**

sŭc-cĭnct', *a.,* briefly and clearly stated; **-ness; -ly**

sŭc'cŏr, *n., v.,* help

sŭc'cū-lĕnt, *a.,* juicy; **lence; lency; -ly**

sŭc-cŭmb', *v.,* yield, die

sŭck, *v.,* draw into or up, dissolve in mouth; **-er**

sŭck'le, *v.,* suck at breast; **-r**

sū'crōse, *n.,* pure sugar

sŭd'dĕn, *a.,* unexpected, abrupt; **-ness; -ly**

sŭds, *n., pl.,* foam of soapy water; **-y** *a.*

sūe, *v.,* take legal action against, plead; **-r**

sū'ĕt, *n.,* hard animal fat

sŭf'fĕr, *v.,* experience pain or grief, endure; **-er; -ance; -ing** *n.;* **-able**

sŭf-fī'ciĕnt, *a.,* as much as is needed; **ciency; -ly**

sŭf'fŏ-cāte, *v.,* deprive of air; **tion; tive; catingly**

sŭf'frăge, *n.,* right to vote

sŭf-fūse', *v.,* overspread; **sion; sive**

sŭg'ăr, *n.,* sweet crystalline carbohydrate; **-like; -less; -y** *a.*

sŭg-gĕst', *v.,* bring to mind, propose; **-er; -ion; -ive; -iveness; -ively; -ibility; -ible**

sū'ĭ-cide, *n.,* killing oneself; **dal; dally**

sŭit, *n.,* set of clothes or playing cards, legal action; *v.,* be right for, please; **-ability; -able; -ableness; -ably**

suite (swēt) *n.,* set of rooms of furniture

sūit'ŏr, *n.,* man wooing woman

sŭl'fûr, *n.,* chemical element; **-ic; -ous**

sŭlk, *v.,* be aloof and ill-humored; **-y** *a.;* **-iness; -ily**

sŭl'lĕn, *a.,* silently resentful; **-ness; -ly**

sŭl'ly, *v.,* soil, stain

sŭl'trў, *a.,* hot and humid; **triness; trily**

sŭm, *n.,* whole amount, amount of money; *v.,* total; **-mation; -mational**

sŭm'mĭt, *n.,* highest point

sŭm'mŏn, *v.,* order to come; **-er**

sŭmp'tū-oŭs, *a.,* costly, lavish; **-ness; -ly**

sŭn'bûrn, *n.,* skin inflammation for exposure to sun

sŭn'daē, *n.,* ice cream topped with syrup

sŭn'dêr, *v.,* break apart; **-ance; -able**

sŭn'drў, *a.,* various

sŭn'glăss-ĕs, *n., pl.,* tinted eyeglasses for protection from sun

sŭnk'ĕn, *a.,* submerged, depressed

sŭn'nў, *a.,* bright like sunshine; **niness; nily**

sŭn'tăn, *n.,* skin's darkened condition from exposure to sun

sū'pêr, *a.,* outstanding, large

sū-pĕrb', *a.,* splendid; **-ness; -ly**

sū'pêr-chărge, *v.,* increase power; **-r**

sū-pêr-fĭ'ciăl, *a.,* on the surface, obvious; **-ity; -ness; -ly**

sū-pêr'flū-oŭs, *a.,* excessive; **-ness; -ly**

sū-pêr-ĭm-pōse', *v.,* put on top of; **position**

sū-pêr-ĭn-tĕnd'ĕnt, *n.,* one in charge

sū-pē'rĭ-ŏr, *a.,* higher, better, greater; **-ity; -ly**

sū-pêr'lă-tĭve, *n.,* highest degree; *a.,* exceeding all; **-ness; -ly**

sū-pêr-sēde', *v.,* replace; **-r; dure; -nce**

sū-pêr-sŏn'ĭc, *a.,* faster than speed of sound, beyond human hearing; **-s**

sū-pêr-stĭ'tion, *n.,* belief

in magic or charm; **tious; tiousness; tiously**

sü′pêr-vīse, v., oversee, direct; **sor; sion; sory**

sŭp′pêr, n., evening meal

sŭp-plănt′, v., replace; **-er; -ation**

sŭp′ple, a., flexible; **-ness; -ly**

sŭp′plė-mėnt, n., added part; **-ation; -al, -ary**

sŭp′plĭ-cāte, v., ask humbly; **tion; pliance; pliant** n., a.; **tory**

sŭp′plÿ, n., available amount; v., meet needs of, furnish; **plier**

sŭp-pôrt′, n., aid; n., v. (that which can) hold up, help, be in favor of, maintain; **-er; -ive; -able; -ably**

sŭp-pŏs′ĭ-tô-rÿ, n., medicine put into a body passage

sŭp-prĕss′, v., put down by force, stop; **-or; -ion; -ive; -ively; -ible**

sü-prĕme′, a., highest, utmost; **premacy; -ness; -ly** [charge, overload

sûr′chârge, n., v., oversure (**sôr**), a., without doubt, certain; **-ty; -ly**

sûrf, n., sea waves at shore

sûr′fāce, n., exterior; v., rise to top; a., superficial

sûr′feït, n., excess

sûrge, n., sudden rush, wave; v., increase suddenly

sûr′gêr-ÿ, n., medical treatment by operations; **geon** n.; **gical; gically**

sûr′lÿ, a., bad-tempered; **liness**

sûr-mīse′, n., v., guess

sûr-mŏunt′, v., overcome, rise above; **-able**

sûr′nāme, n., family name

sûr-prīse′, n., unexpected event; v., come upon unexpectedly; **prising; prisingly**

sûr-rė′àl-ĭsm, n., modern art movement; **ist; istic; istically**

sûr-rĕn′dêr, n., yielding; v., give up

sûr-rĕp-tĭ′tioŭs, a., secret; **-ness; -ly**

sûr′rėy, n., horse-drawn carriage with top

sûr′rȯ-gāte, n., v., substitute

sûr-rŏund′, v., enclose

sûr-vey′ (vā), n., detailed inspection, view; v., examine, determine land boundaries; **-or; -ing** n.

sûr-vīve′, v., continue to live; **vor; vorship; vival; vivability; vivable**

sŭs-cĕp′tĭ-ble, a., easily affected; **bility; -ness; bly** [mise

sŭs-pĕct′, v., distrust, sur-

sŭs-pĕnd′, v., stop temporarily, exclude, hang; **pension; pensive**

sŭs-pĕnd′êrs, n., shoulder straps to hold up pants

sŭs-pĕnse′, n., anxious uncertainty; **-ful**

sŭs-pĭ′ción, n., suspecting, trace; **cious; ciousness; ciously**

sŭs-tāin′, v., support, endure; **-er; -ment; -able**

sŭs′tė-nȧnce, n., nourishment

sü′tûre, n., join by sewing

swăb, n., (thing used to) clean or medicate

swăd′dle, v., bind in cloth

swăg′gêr, n., v., strut

swämp, n., wet, spongy land; v., flood, overwhelm; **-ish; -y** a.; **-iness**

swănk, a., ostentatiously stylish; **-y** a.; **-iness; -ily**

swarm (swôrm), n., v., (colony of bees that) fly together

swarth′ÿ (swôrth), a., darkish; **swarthiness; swarthily**

swăsh′bŭck-lêr, n., swaggering fighting man; **ling** n. [-ter

swăt, n., quick sharp hit;

swătch, n., sample of cloth

swăthe, v., wrap a band-

S
T

age around; **-r**

swāy, *n.,* power; *v.,* move back and forth, lean, influence; **-er**

sweār, *v.,* vow, curse; **-er**

swĕat, *n.,* salty liquid given off from skin; *v.,* give forth sweat; **-y** *a.;* **-iness; -ily**

sweep, *n.,* flowing movement, extent; *v.,* clean with broom, win; **-er**

sweep'stākes, *n.,* lottery

sweet, *n.,* candy; *a.,* tasting like sugar, pleasant; **-en; -ener; -ening** *n.*

sweet'heârt, *n.,* lover

swĕll, *n.,* bulge, increase; *v.,* become larger, expand; **-ing** *n.*

swĕl'têr, *v.,* feel intense heat

swĕrve, *v.,* turn aside; **-r**

swĭll, *n.,* garbage; *v.,* drink greedily

swĭm, *v.,* move through water, be dizzy; **-mer; -ming** *n.*

swĭn'dle, *n., v.,* cheat, fraud; **-r**

swine, *n.,* pig

swĭng, *n.,* swinging motion; *v.,* sway when hanging; **-er**

swĭrl, *v.,* twist; **-y** *a.*

swĭsh, *n.,* sharp, hissing sound; **-y** *a.*

swĭtch, *n.,* stick for whipping, control device; *n., v.,* lash, shift, change

swĭtch'bôard, *n.,* control panel for electrical circuits

swĭv'ĕl, *v.,* rotate

swŏl'lĕn, *a.,* swelling

swŏon, *n., v.,* faint; **-er**

sword (sôrd), *n.,* weapon with sharp blade

sўc'ȯ-phȧnt, *n.,* one seeking favors by flattery; **phancy; -ish; -ishly; -ic; -ically**

sўl'lȧ-bŭs, *n.,* summary of course of study

sўl'lȯ-gĭsm, *n.,* form of reasoning; **gize; gistic; gistical; gistically**

sўlph, *n.,* thin graceful woman   [est

sўl'vȧn, *a.,* wooded, of for-

symbol, *n.,* representation, sign; **-ize; -izer; -ization; -ism; -ist; -istic; -istically; -ic; -ical; -ically**

sўm'mĕ-trў, *n.,* balance of opposite parts; **trize; trization; trical; trically**

sўm'pȧ-thў, *n.,* sharing another's feeling, agreement; **thize; thizer; thizingly; thetic; thetically**

sўm'phȯ-nў, *n.,* harmony, musical composition for orchestra; **phonic; phonically**

sўm-pō'sĭ-ŭm, *n.,* meeting with intellectual discussion

sўmp'tȯm, *n.,* outward sign, indication; **-atic; -atically**

sўn'ȧ-gŏgue, *n.,* Jewish place of worship

sўn'chrȯ-nīze, *v.,* regulate together; **-r; zation; nous; nousness; nously**

sўn'drōme, *n.,* set of symptoms in a disease; **dromic**

sўn'ȯd, *n.,* council of churches; **-al; -ical; -ically**

sўn'ȯ-nўm, *n.,* word with same meaning as another; **-ic; -ical; -ous; -ously**

sўn-ŏp'sĭs, *n.,* summary; size; **optic; optical; optically**

sўn'tăx, *n.,* word arrangement in sentence; **tactic; tactical; tactically**

sўn'thĕ-sĭs, *n.,* uniting parts into whole; **size; sizer**

sў-rĭnge', *n.,* ball with tube for drawing in or ejecting liquid   [uid; **-y** *a.*

sўr'ŭp, *n.,* sweet thick liq-

sўs'tĕm, *n.,* plan, method, orderly arrangement; **-atize; -atizer; -atiza-**

tab 165 **tarnish**

tion; -atic; -atical; -ati-
cally

T

tăb, *n.,* small flat, (coll.)
bill for expenses

tăb'êr-năc-le, *n.,* place of
worship; **nacular**

tā'ble, *n.,* furniture of flat
surface and legs, sys-
tematic list; *v.,* postpone

tăb'lĕt, *n.,* flat inscribed
stone slab, writing pad,
compressed piece of
medicine

tă-boo', *n.,* sacred or social prohibition; *a.,* for-
bidden

tăc'ĭt, *a.,* silent, implied;
-ness; -ly

tăck, *n.,* short nail, course
of action, ship's course;
v., fasten with tack,
change course

tăck'le, *n.,* equipment; *v.,*
undertake, bring down
football carrier

tăct, *n.,* diplomatic skill;
-ful; -fulness; -fully;
-less;   -lessness;
-lessly

tăc'tĭcs, *n., pl.,* skillful
method; **tic; tical; tically**

tăc'tĭle, *a.,* of touch; **tility**

tăf'fў, *n.,* chewy candy

tăg, *n.,* label, chase game;
v., fasten tag, touch; -ger

tāil, *n.,* rear part, appen-
dage to body's hind part;
v., (coll.) follow; -less

tāint, *v.,* spoil; -less

tāke, *n.,* amount taken; *v.,*
get hold of, seize, obtain,
use, receive, lead, carry;
-r; -able

tāke'ôff, *n.,* leaving the
ground   [control

tāke'ō-vêr, *n.,* assuming

tăl'cŭm, *n.,* body powder

tāle, *n.,* story, be

tăl'ĕnt, *n.,* natural ability;
-ed   [-ical

tăl'ĭs-măn, *n.,* charm; -ic;

tălk, *n.,* speech, discussion, rumor; *v.,* say
words, gossip; -er;

-ative

tăll, *a.,* high; -ness

tăl'lōw, *n.,* animal fat; -y *a.*

tăl'lў, *n., v.,* record, score;
v., agree

tăl'ŏn, *n.,* claw

tăm, *n.,* flat, round cap

tăm-bóu-rine', *n.,* hand
drum with jingling metal
discs

tāme, *v., a.,* (make) domestic, gentle, obedi-
ent; -r; -ness; -less;
-able; -ly

tămp, *v.,* pack down; -er

tăm'pêr, *v.,* interfere; -er

tăn, *n., a.,* yellowish
brown; *v.,* make hide into
leather, become sun-
burned, heat

tăn'á-gêr, *n.,* songbird

tăn'dĕm, *n.,* horse team,
bicycle for two; *adv.,* one
behind another

tăng, *n.,* strong taste or
odor; -y *a.*; -iness

tăn'gĕnt, *a.,* touching at a
point; **gency; -ial**

tăn'gĭ-ble, *a.,* real; **bility;**
-ness; bly

tăn'gō, *n.,* dance

tănk, *n.,* large container,
large armored vehicle

tănk'êr, *n.,* vehicle carrying liquids

tăn'tá-līze, *v.,* tease; -r;
zation; lizingly

tăn'tá-moŭnt, *a.,* equal

tăn'trŭm, *n.,* fit of temper

tāpe, *n.,* strong narrow
strip   [*v.,* lessen

tā'pêr, *n.,* slender candle;

tăp'ĕs-trў, *n.,* cloth with
woven designs

tāpe'wŏrm, *n.,* worm living
in intestines

tăp-ĭ-ō'cá, *n.,* starchy food

tā'pîr, *n.,* hoglike mammal

tăp'rŏot, *n.,* main root

târ, *n.,* thick dark liquid
made from coal

târ'dў, *a.,* late, slow; **tar-
diness; tardily**

târ'gĕt, *n.,* thing aimed at

tăr'ĭff, *n.,* tax

târ'nĭsh, *n.,* dullness,
stain; *v.,* discolor; -able

târ-päu'lĭn, *n.,* water-proofed canvas

tăr'rÿ, *v.,* linger, stay

tårt, *n.,* pastry

tårt, *a.,* sour; **-ness; -ly**

târ'tår, *n.,* deposit on teeth

tăsk, *n.,* assigned work; *v.,* labor

tăs'sĕl, *n.,* ornamental tuft of threads

tāste, *n.,* sense, flavor, sample, liking; *v.,* detect flavor in mouth, experi-·ence; **-r; -less; -less-ness; -lessly**

tăt'têr, *n.,* rag, shred

tăt'tle, *v.,* tell tales; **-r**

tăt-tōō', *v.,* mark skin with permanent design

täunt, *n.,* scornful remark; *v.,* ridicule; **-er; -ingly**

taupe (tōp), *n., a.,* brown-ish gray   [**-ly**

täut, *a.,* tight, tense; **-ness;**

tăv'êrn, *n.,* place for sell-ing liquor   [yellow

täw'nÿ, *n., a.,* brownish

tăx, *n.,* payment required by government, burden; *v.,* levy, strain; **-er; -ation; -ability; -able**

tăx'ĭ-căb, *n.,* automobile for hire

tēa, *n.,* beverage made from leaves, afternoon meal

tēach, *v.,* impart knowl-edge, instruct; **-er; -ing** *n.;* **-ability; -able; -able-ness**

tēak, *n.,* yellowish brown wood   [grayish blue

tēal, *n.,* wild duck, dark

tēam, *n.,* group working together

tēam'stêr, *n.,* truck driver

tēar, *n.,* liquid drop from eye; **-y** *a.;* **-iness; -ily; -ful; -fulness; -fully; -less;   -lessness; -lessly**   [dash; **-er**

teăr, *v.,* force apart, rip,

tēase, *v.,* comb out, annoy, poke fun; **-r; teasingly**

tēat, *n.,* nipple

tĕch'nĭ-căl, *a.,* of mechan-ical arts, skilled; **-ly**

tĕch-nĭ-căl'ĭ-tÿ, *n.,* detail

tĕch-nïque', *n.,* method

tē'dĭ-oŭs, *a.,* boring, tire-some; **dium** *n.;* **-ness; -ly**   [or football

tēe, *n.,* holder for golf ball

tēem, *v.,* pour, swarm

tēens, *n., pl.,* years from thirteen through nine-teen

tēethe, *v.,* grow teeth

tĕl'ė-căst, *n., v.,* broadcast of television; **-er**

tĕl'ė-grăph, *n., v.,* (device to) send message elec-trically by wire; **-er; -y; -ic; -ically**

tė-lĕp'å-thÿ, *n.,* thought transference;   **thist; pathic; pathically**

tĕl'ė-phōne, *n.,* electrical device to convey speech; **-r; phonic; phonically**

tĕl'ė-scōpe, *n.,* instrument that makes objects seem nearer; **scopic; scopi-cally**

tĕl'ė-vĭ-sion, *n.,* transmis-sion of scenes by radio waves; **vise; -al; -ally**

tĕl'ĕx, *n.,* teletypewriter with a dial

tĕll, *v.,* say, relate, recog-nize, order; **-er; -able**

tĕll'êr, *n.,* counter, bank cashier

tĕll'tāle, *a.,* revealing

tĕl-lū'rĭ-ŭm, *n.,* chemical element

tė-mĕr'ĭ-tÿ, *n.,* rash bold-ness; **erarious**

tĕm'pêr, *n.,* state of mind, mood, rage; *v.,* reduce intensity; **-er; -ability; -able**   [paint

tĕm'pêr-å, *n.,* water-base

tĕm'pêr-a-mėnt, *n.,* frame of mind

tĕm'pêr-åtₑ, *a.,* moderate; **ance; -ness; -ly**

tĕm'pêr-a-tùre, *n.,* degree of hot and cold, fever

tĕm'pėst, *n.,* violent storm; **-uous;   -uousness; -uously**

tĕm'ple, *n.,* place for worship, area on head between eye and ear

tĕm'pō, *n.,* rate of speed

tĕm'pȯ-rār-ȳ, *a.,* of limited time; **rariness; rarily**

tĕm'pȯ-rīze, *v.,* delay, evade; **-r; zation**

tĕmpt, *v.,* lure, attract; **-er; -ation; -ing; -able**

tė-nā'ciŏŭs, *a.,* holding fast, retentive; **nacity; -ness; -ly**

tĕn'ȧnt, *n.,* one renting living space; **ency; -able; -less** [inclined

tĕnd, *v.,* take care of, be

tĕn'dêr, *n., v.,* offer; **-er**

tĕn'dêr, *a.,* delicate, soft, gentle; **-ness; -ly**

tĕn'dêr-fŏŏt, *n.,* beginner

tĕn'dêr-lŏĭn, *n.,* choice cut of meat

tĕn'dȯn, *n.,* fibrous cord connecting muscle to bone; **dinous**

tĕn'ė-mėnt, *n.,* slum apartment house

tĕn'nĭs, *n.,* sport played with racket and ball

tĕn'ȯr, *n.,* high male voice, general meaning

tĕnse, *n.,* verb form of time

tĕnse, *a.,* showing strain, anxious; **sion; sity; sive; sile** *a.*

tĕn'tȧ-cle, *n.,* long flexible growth on head; **tacular**

tĕn'tȧ-tĭve, *a.,* temporary; **-ness; -ly**

tĕn'ū-oŭs, *a.,* thin, flimsy; **nuity; -ness; -ly**

tĕn'ûre, *n.,* right or time holding a position

tĕp'ĭd, *a.,* lukewarm; **-ity; tepefy; -ness; -ly**

têr'bĭ-ŭm, *n.,* metallic element

têrm, *n.,* set period of time, contractual condition, word

têr'mĭ-nāte, *v.,* end; **tor; tion; tive**

têr-mĭ-nŏl'ȯ-gȳ, *n.,* system of terms; **gist; logical; logically**

têr'mite, *n.,* insect of colony eating wood

têrn, *n.,* sea bird

tĕr'rȧce, *n.,* reused flat land, paved garden area

tĕrrȧ-cŏt'tȧ, *n.,* unglazed earthenware

têr'rāin, *n.,* land features

tĕr-rār'ĭ-ŭm, *n.,* container for small garden [**-ly**

tĕr-rĕs'trĭ-ȧl, *a.,* earthly;

tĕr'rĭ-ble, *a.,* frightful, extreme, very bad; **bly**

tĕr-rĭf'ĭc, *a.,* dreadful, (coll.) great; **-ally**

tĕr'rĭ-fȳ, *v.,* frighten; **-ingly**

tĕr'rĭ-tȯ-rȳ, *n.,* land region, area as part of country; **rial; riality; rialism; rialize; rialization; rially**

tĕr'rȯr, *n.,* intense fear

tĕr'rȯr-ĭsm, *n.,* intimidation by force and threats; **ist; ize; ization** [**-ly**

têrse, *a.,* concise; **-ness;**

tĕst, *n.,* examination, trial; *v.,* try, take test; **-er; -able**

tĕs'tȧ-mėnt, *n.,* Bible part, legal will; **-al**

tĕs'tĭ-cle, *n.,* male sex gland; **ticular**

tĕs'tĭ-fȳ, *v.,* give evidence; **fier; fication**

tĕs'tĭ-mō-nȳ, *n.,* proof

tĕs'tȳ, *a.,* irritable; **tiness; tily** [disease

tĕt'a-nŭs, *n.,* infectious

tĕth'êr, *n., v.,* rope to confine animal

tĕxt, *n.,* wording, main part of book, subject; **-ual**

tĕx'tĭle, *n., a.,* (fabric) that has been woven

tĕx'tûre, *n.,* appearance or feel of surface; **tural; turally**

thănk, *v.,* express gratitude; **-ful; -fulness; -fully; -less; -lessness; -lessly**

thătch, *n.,* roof of straw, etc.

thāw, *v.,* melt

thē'ȧ-têr, *n.,* place for viewing plays, etc., drama; **atrics; atrical; atric; atrically**

thĕft, *n.,* stealing

thē'ĭsm, *n.*, belief in God; **ist; istic; istically**

thēme, *n.*, topic, short essay, main tune; **matic**

thĕn, *adv.*, at that time, next, therefore, besides

thē-ŏl'ô-gÿ, *n.*, study of God and religions; **gist; logical; logically**

thē'ô-rĕm, *n.*, statement that can be proved; **-atic**

thē'ô-rÿ, *n.*, unproven idea, guess; **rize; rizer; rization; retical; retically**

thĕr-à-peū'tĭc, *a.*, serving to cure; **-s; -al; -ally**

thĕr'à-pÿ, *n.*, treatment of disease; **pist**

thĕre'à-bouts, *adv.*, near that place   [that

thĕre-ăf'têr, *adv.*, after

thĕre'fôre, *adv., conj.*, as a result of this

thĕre-tô-fôre', *adv.*, up to then

thĕre-ŭp-ŏn', *adv.*, at once

thêr'mal, *a.*, of heat; **-ly**

thêr-mô-dÿ-năm'ĭcs, *n.*, relationship of heat and mechanical power; **ic**

thêr-mŏm'ê-têr, *n.*, device to measure temperature; **try; metric; metrically**

thêr'mô-stăt, *n.*, device to regulate temperature

thê-sau'rŭs (sô), *n.*, book of words

thē'sĭs, *n.*, unproved premise, lengthy research paper

thī'à-mīne, *n.*, vitamin B₁

thĭck, *a.*, of great depth, not thin, dense; **-ness; -en; -ener; -ening** *n.*; **-ish; -ly**   [of plants

thĭck'ĕt, *n.*, dense growth

thĭef, *n.*, one who steals

thĭeve, *v.*, steal; **-ry; thievish**

thĭm'ble, *n.*, protective cap for finger when sewing

thĭn, *a.*, of little depth, slender, sparce, sheer; **-ness; -ly**

thĭnk, *v.*, use mind, consider, reason, recall; **-er;**

-ing *n., a.;* **-able**

thĭrst, *n.*, need for water; **-y** *a.;* **-iness; -ily**

thĭs'tle, *n.*, prickly plant

thông, *n.*, leather strap

thô'răx, *n.*, body between neck and abdomen

thô'rĭ-ŭm, *n.*, chemical element

thŏrn, *n.*, sharp point on plant; **-y** *a.;* **-iness**

thŏr'ôugh, *a.*, complete, very exact; **-ness; -ly**

thŏr'ôugh-brĕd, *n., a.*, (animal) of pure breed

thou, *pro.*, you

thôugh, *adv., conj.*, nevertheless

thôught, *n.*, act or result of thinking, idea; consideration; **-ful; -fulness; -fully; -less; -lessness; -lessly**

thrăsh'êr, *n.*, songbird

thrĕad, *n.*, fine, spun cord, groove on screw; **-er; -like** *a.*   [shabby

thrĕad'bāre, *a.*, worn,

thrĕat, *n.*, sign of danger, intention to hurt; **-en; -ener; -eningly**

thrĕsh, *v.*, beat grain out of husk; **-er**

thrĕsh'ōld, *n.*, doorway, entrance

thrĭft, *n.*, careful money management; **-y** *a.;* **-iness; -ily; -less; -lessness; -lessly**

thrĭll, *n.*, excitement; *v.*, excite; shiver; **-er**

thrive, *v.*, prosper, succeed

thrŏb, *v.*, vibrate strongly; **-ber; -bingly**

thrŏe, *n.*, struggle

thrŏm-bō'sĭs, *n.*, blood clot; **botic**   [chair

thrône, *n.*, king's official

thrông, *n., v.*, crowd

thrŏt'tle, *n.*, valve controlling power flow

thrôugh, *a.*, open, finished; *adv.*, in and out, to the end; *prep.* from end to end, by way of

thrōw, *v.*, send through air

from hand, hurl, direct;
-er

thrŭsh, *n.*, songbird, infant disease in mouth

thrŭst, *n.*, shove, sudden attack; *v.*, push with force

thŭg, *n.*, hoodlum; **-gery; -gish**   [nearest wrist

thŭmb, *n.*, thick finger

thŭmp, *n.*, heavy blow, its sound; **-er**

thŭn′dêr, *n.*, loud sound after lightning; **-ous; -ously**

thwart (thwôrt), *v.*, frustrate, hinder; **-er**

thȳme, *n.*, herb

thȳ′rŏid, *n.*, gland in neck that regulates growth

tī-ār′á, *n.*, woman's crownlike headdress

tĭck, *n.*, light tapping sound, insect, mattress covering

tĭck′ĕt, *n.*, paper giving one a right, label, list of candidates

tide, *n.*, regular rise and fall of ocean

tī′dȳ, *a.*, neat, orderly; **diness; dily**

tie, *n.*, neckwear, link railroad beam; *v.*, connect as with string, etc., make knot, equal a score

tiĕr, *n.*, row of seats

tĭff, *n.*, argument

tĭght, *a.*, close fitting, compact, taut, constricting; **-ness; -en; -ly**

tile, *n.*, piece of glazed clay for covering floor or roof

tĭll, *n.*, cash drawer; *prep; conj.*, until   [**-age**

tĭll, *v.*, cultivate land; **-er;**

tĭlt, *n., v.*, slope, slant

tĭm′bêr, *n.*, wood for building, trees

time, *n.*, duration, period, measured interval, tempo, occasion

time′lĕss, *a.*, eternal; **-ness; -ly**

time′lȳ, *a.*, done at suitable time; **liness**

tĭm′ĭd, *a.*, shy, afraid; **-ity; -ness; -ly**

tĭm′pá-nĭ, *n.*, set of kettle drums

tĭn, *n.*, soft metallic element; **-ny; -niness; -nily**

tĭn′dêr, *n.*, dry easily flammable material

tine, *n.*, prong

tĭnge, *n.*, tint, slight trace; *v.*, color, give a trace

tĭn′gle, *n., v.*, sting, prickle; **-r; gly** *a.*; **glingly**

tĭn′kêr, *v.*, mend, fuss aimlessly; **-er**

tĭn′sĕl, *n.*, decorative stripes of foil; *a.*, gaudy; **-ly** *a.*

tĭnt, *n.*, shading of color; **-er**

tĭp, *n.*, pointed end, light blow, warning, secret information; *v.*, give money for service, tilt, overturn

tĭp′sȳ, *a.*, shaky, somewhat drunk; **siness; sily**

tī′rāde, *n.*, long, angry speech

tire, *n.*, rubber wheel for vehicle; *v.*, become weary, lose strength

tĭred, *a.*, fatigued, stale; **-ness; -ly**

tĭs′sŭe, *n.*, body substance, thin paper or cloth

tithe, *n.*, tenth part of income paid to church; **-r; tithable**

tĭt′ĭl-lāte, *v.*, excite; **-r; tion; tive**

tī′tle, *n.*, name, word showing rank, legal right; **titular** *a.*; **titularly**

tĭt′mouse, *n.*, small bird

tĭz′zȳ, *n.*, state of excitement

to (tōō), *adv.*, forward; *prep.*, toward, as far as, on, until, for, as compared with   [imal

tōad, *n.*, froglike land an-

tōad′stōol, *n.*, poisonous mushroom

tōad′ȳ, *n.*, sycophant; *v.*, flatter; **-ism**

to-băc'cō, *n.,* plant, its leaves used to smoke

to-bŏg'gàn, *n.,* flat sled without runners

to-gĕth'êr, *adv.,* in one group, at same time, in agreement

tŏil, *n.,* hard work; *v.,* labor; **-er; -ful; -some** *a.;* **-someness; -somely**

tŏi'lĕt, *n.,* fixture receiving body waste, grooming; **-ry**

tō'kĕn, *n.,* sign, keepsake, metal piece for fare

tŏl'êr-ànce, *n.,* enduring another's way; **ant; antly**

tōll, *n.,* tax, charge, number lost; *v.,* ring bell; **-er**

tŏm, *n.,* male of some animals

tŏm'à-hăwk, *n.,* light ax

to-mā'tō, *n.,* red fruit, eaten as vegetable

tomb (tōomb), *n.,* chamber for dead; **-like**

tōme, *n.,* large scholarly book [drum

tŏm'-tŏm, *n.,* primitive

tŏn, *n.,* two thousand pounds; **-nage**

tōne, *n.,* musical sound, attitude, style, shade; **tonal; tonality; tonally**

tŏngs, *n., pl.,* hinged device for seizing and lifting

tòngue, *n.,* movable structure in mouth; **-less**

tŏn'ĭc, *n.,* substance that invigorates; **-ally**

tŏn'sĭl, *n.,* tissue at back of mouth; **-lar**

tōo, *adv.,* in addition, very

tōol, *n.,* work instrument

tōoth, *n.,* bony structure set in jaw, toothlike part; **-like** [**-ness; -ly**

tōoth'sòme, *a.,* tasty;

tŏp, *n.,* highest part or rank, spinning toy; *v.,* be better

tō'păz, *n.,* gem

tŏp'ĭc, *n.,* subject for discussing or writing; **-al; -ality; -ly**

tŏp-nŏtch', *a.,* first-rate

to-pŏg'rà-phў, *n.,* science of geographic features and maps; **pher; graphic; graphical; graphically**

tŏp'ple, *v.,* fall over

tŏp'sў-tûr'vў, *a., adv.,* upside down, in disorder; **viness; vily**

tôr'mĕnt, *n.,* suffering; *v.,* **(tôr-mĕnt')** cause agony; **-or; -ingly**

tôr-nā'dō, *n.,* violently whirling funnellike cloud

tôr-pē'dō, *n.,* explosive missile or its case

tôr'rĕnt, *n.,* violent flow; **-ial; -ially**

tôr'rĭd, *a.,* very hot; **-ity; -ness; -ly** [**-ally**

tôr'sion, *n.,* twisting; **-al;**

tôr'sō, *n.,* trunk of body

tôrte, *n.,* rich cake

tôr'toïse, *n.,* land turtle

tôr'tûre, *n.,* inflicting great pain, agony; *v.,* torment; **-r; turous; turously**

tŏss, *n.,* pitch; *v.,* throw about, fling; **-er**

tō'tàl, *n.,* whole amount; *v.,* add; *a.,* complete; **-ity; -ize; -izer; -ly**

tō-tăl-ĭ-tār'ĭ-àn, *a.,* of dictatorship; **-ism**

tōte, *v.,* carry

tŏt'têr, *v.,* be unsteady; **-y** *a.;* **-ing; -ingly**

tŏu'căn, *n.,* tropical bird

tŏuch, *n.,* tap, sense of feeling, small amount, contact; *v.,* feel; come into contact with, mention; **-er; -able; -ability**

tŏu-che' (shā), *int.* expression to acknowledge a point

tough (tŭf), *a.,* hard to chew, cut, break, etc., strong, difficult; **-ness; -en; -ly** [wig

tŏu-pee' (pā), *n.,* man's

tŏur, *n.,* trip, circuit; **-ist**

tŏur'nà-mĕnt, *n.,* contest

tŏur'nĭ-quĕt, *n.,* device to stop bleeding

tŏu'sle, *v.,* dishevel

tōw, *v.,* pull, drag; **-er;**

-age

tŏw'ĕl, *n.,* cloth or paper for drying

tŏw'êr, *n.,* high narrow structure; *v.,* rise high; **-ing**

tŏwn, *n.,* small city, business district

tŏx'ĭn, *n.,* poison; **ic; icant** *a.*

trāce, *n.,* sign, small amount; *v.,* follow the trail, copy; **-r; -able; -ability; -ableness; -ably**

trā'chē-à, *n.,* windpipe; **-l**

trà-chō'mà, *n.,* eye infection; **-tous**

trăck, *n.,* mark left as evidence, path, parallel rails for train, running sports; *v.,* follow the track, leave footprints; **-less**

trăct, *n.,* area, booklet

trăc'tà-ble, *a.,* manageable; **bility; -ness; bly**

trăc'tion, *n.,* pulling, adhesive friction

trāde, *n.,* skilled work, buying and selling; *v.,* swap, buy and sell; **-r**

trāde'mârk, *n.,* manufacturer's distinguishing mark

trà-dūce', *v.,* slander, betray; **-r; -ment**

trăf'fĭc, *n.,* business, vehicles or people on street; *v.,* trade; **-ker**

trăg'ė-dў, *n.,* serious drama ending unhappily

trāil, *n.,* path; *v.,* track, follow behind

trāin, *n.,* thing that drags, procession, series, connected railroad cars; *v.,* guide, instruct; **-er; -ee; -ing** *n.*

trāit, *n.,* characteristic

trāi'tŏr, *n.,* unfaithful person; **-ous; -ousness; -ously**

trămp, *n.,* vagrant; *v.,* walk heavily, hike; **-er**

trăm'ple, *v.,* step on, crush; **-r**

trănce, *n.,* altered consciousness, daze

trăn'quĭl, *a.,* calm; **-ity; -ize; -izer; -ization; -ness; -ly**

trăns-ăct', *v.,* do, complete; **-or; -ion; -ional**

trăn-scĕnd', *v.,* excel; **-ent; -ence; -ency; -ently**

trăn-scrībe', *v.,* write out; **-r; script; scription; scriptional**

trăns'fêr, *n., v.,* move or change to another; **-rer; -ence; -al** *n.;* **-ential; -able**

trăns-fôrm'êr, *n.,* device that changes voltage

trăns-fū'sion, *n.,* transfer of blood to another

trăns-grĕss', *v.,* sin, break law; **-or; -ion; -ive**

trăn'siėnt, *a.,* temporary; **science; sciency; -ly**

trăn-sĭs'tŏr, *n.,* small electronic device; **-ize**

trăn-sĭ'tion, *n.,* change, passing stage; **-ary; -al; -ally**

trăns-lāte', *v.,* put into different language; **tor; tion; tional; latable**

trăns-lĭt'êr-āte, *v.,* express in alphabet of another language; **tion**

trăns-mĭs'sion, *n.,* transmitting, auto part sending power to wheels; **-al**

trăns-mūte', *v.,* transform; **tation; tational; tative; mutable; mutably**

trăn'sŏm, *n.,* small window over doorway

trăns-pār'ėnt, *a.,* easily seen through, clear; **ency; -ness; -ly**

trăn-spīre', *v.,* happen

trăns-plănt', *v.,* move from one to another; **-er; -ation; -able**

trăns-pōse', *v.,* interchange; **-r; sition; posable**

trăns-vêrse', *a.,* across, crosswise; **sal** *n.;* **-ly**

trăns-vĕs'tĭte, *n.,* one

S
T

dressing in clothes of opposite sex

trăp, *n.*, device for catching animals; *v.*, catch; **-per**

tră-pēze', *n.*, high swing

trăp'pĭngs, *n.*, adornments

trȧu'mȧ, *n.*, shock; **-tize; -tic; -tically**

trăv'ãil, *n.*, hard work, agony; *v.*, work

trăv'ĕl, *n.*, trip; *v.*, go from place to place; **-er; -ler**

trȧ-vêrse', *v.*, move across

trăv'ĕs-tȳ, *n.*, farcical imitation

trăwl, *n.*, fishing net

trāy, *n.*, flat carrying board

trēach'ĕr-oŭs, *a.*, disloyal, unsafe; **ery; -ness; -ly**

trĕad, *v.*, walk, trample

trĕad'mĭll, *n.*, monotonous routine

trēa'sŏn, *n.*, betrayal of one's country; **-ous; -able; -ably**

trĕas'ûre, *n.*, stored wealth; *v.*, value greatly

trēat, *n.*, delight, something paid by another; *v.*, deal with, pay another's expense, give medical care; **-ment**

trēa'tĭse, *n.*, formal composition

trēa'tȳ, *n.*, agreement between nations

trĕ'ble, *n.*, highest musical part, *v.*, *a.*, triple

trēe, *n.*, large woody plant

trĕk, *n.*, slow journey; *v.*, travel slowly; **-ker**

trĕl'lĭs, *n.*, lattice for plants

trĕm'ble, *v.*, shake, quiver; **-r; bly** *a.*; **blingly**

trĕ-mĕn'doŭs, *a.*, great; **-ness; -ly**

trĕnch, *n.*, long ditch

trĕnd, *n.*, general direction, current style

trĕp-ĭ-dā'tion, *n.*, fear

trĕs'pȧss, *v.*, sin, intrude another's land or privileges; **-er**

trĕss, *n.*, lock of hair

trĕs'tle, *n.*, framework for

support [**-ic**

trī'ăd, *n.*, group of three;

trī'ȧl, *n.*, test, formal court hearing, effort

trībe, *n.*, primitive communal group; **tribal; tribally**

trĭb-ū-lā'tion, *n.*, affliction

trī-bū'nȧl, *n.*, court of law

trĭb'ū-tār-ȳ, *n.*, river flowing into larger one

trĭb'ute, *n.*, forced payment, praise

trĭck, *n.*, clever act; *n.*, *v.*, (thing done to) deceive or outwit; **-er; -ery; -ish; -ishness; -y** *a.*; **-iness; -ily**

trīed, *a.*, proven

trī'fle, *n.*, thing of little value, dessert; *v.*, deal lightly; **-r**

trĭg'gêr, *n.*, gun lever

trĭg-ȯ-nŏm'ė-trȳ, *n.*, mathematics of angles and lines; **ric; rical; rically**

trĭll, *n.*, vibrating sound

trĭl'liȯn, *n.*, number followed by twelve zeros; **-th** *a.*

trĭl'ō-gȳ, *n.*, set of three plays or books

trĭm, *n.*, good condition, decoration; *v.*, make neat, clip, decorate; *a.*, neat; **-mer; -ness; -ly**

trĭn'kĕt, *n.*, trifle, small ornament

trĭp, *n.*, short course of travel; *v.*, stumble, skip, err

trī'plĕt, *n.*, group of three, three of same birth

trī'pŏd, *n.*, three-legged stand, stool, etc.

trīte, *a.*, worn-out, stale; **-ness; -ly**

trī'ümph, *n.*, victory, success; **-al; -ant** *a.*; **-antly**

trĭv'ĕt, *n.*, small stand for hot dishes [**matters**

trĭv'ĭ-ȧ, *n.*, *pl.*, unimportant

trōll, *v.*, fish with moving line; **-er** [**car**

trŏl'lēy, *n.*, electric street-

trŏl'lŏp, *n.*, prostitute

trŏm-bōne', *n.*, brass horn

with sliding tube; **bonist**

tro͞op, *n.*, military unit, group of people; *v.*, go in group

trō'phȳ, *n.*, prize or memento for victory

trŏp'ĭc, *n.*, one of two latitudes on either side of equator; (pl.) hot region between these latitudes; **-al; -ally**

trou'ble, *n.*, distress, difficulty, bother; *v.*, disturb; **-r; -some** *a.;* **-someness; -somely**

trough (trôf), *n.*, long, narrow container for animal's food and water

tro͞upe, *n.*, company of actors; **-r**

trous'seau (sō), *n.*, bride's clothing, linens, etc.

trōw'el, *n.*, hand tool for smoothing, scooping, etc.

tru'ant, *n.*, *a.*, (one) absent without permission; **ancy**

truce, *n.*, halt in fighting

truc'u-lent, *a.*, fierce, harsh; **lency; lently**

true, *a.*, loyal, factual, real; **-ness; truly**

truf'fle, *n.*, edible fungus

tru'ĭsm, *n.*, statement of truth; **istic**

trump, *n.*, playing card of highest suit

trum'pet, *n.*, brass horn; **-er** [**tion**

trun'cāte, *v.*, cut off a part;

trun'cheon, *n.*, club, authority [*v.*, roll; **-r**

trun'dle, *n.*, small wheel;

truss, *n.*, framework for support, bundle; *v.*, fasten; **-er; -ing** *n.*

trust, *n.*, faith, custody, business monopoly, care of another's property; *v.*, believe in, rely on; **-er; -ee; -eeship; -ful; -fulness; -fully; -less**

truth, *n.*, being true, real fact; **-ful; -fulness; -fully**

trȳ, *n.*, *v.*, attempt; *v.*, test, determine judicially

trȳst, *n.*, appointment to meet

tŭb, *n.*, large open container, especially for washing

tu'bà, *n.*, large brass horn

tu'bêr, *n.*, fleshy part of underground stem

tū-bêr-cū-lō'sĭs, *n.*, infectious disease of lungs; **lar; lous**

tŭck, *n.*, sewed fold; *v.*, gather into folds, wrap snuggly, cram; **-er**

tŭf'fét, *n.*, low stool

tŭft, *n.*, cluster of hairs or feathers; **-er; -y** *a.*

tŭg'bòat, *n.*, small boats for pulling ships

tŭ-ĭ'tion, *n.*, charge for instruction; **-al**

tŭm'ble, *n.*, fall, confusion; *v.*, do acrobatics, fall suddenly [**glass**

tŭm'blêr, *n.*, acrobat,

tū'mĭd, *a.*, swollen; **-ity; -ness; -ly**

tū'mör, *n.*, abnormal body growth or swelling; **-ous**

tū'mŭlt, *n.*, uproar, confusion; **-uous; -uousness; -uously**

tŭn'drà, *n.*, nearly treeless plains of arctic area

tūne, *n.*, musical pitch, melody, agreement; *v.*, put in tune; **-r; -ful; -fulness; -less; -lessness; -lessly**

tŭng'stèn, *n.*, heavy metallic element

tū'nĭc, *n.*, loose, belted garment

tûr'bàn, *n.*, cloth wrapped around head

tûr'bĭd, *a.*, muddy, not clear; **-ity; -ness; -ly**

tûr'bĭne, *n.*, engine powered by air, steam or water

tûr'bòt, *n.*, edible fish

tŭ-rēen', *n.*, large deep dish with lid

tûrf, *n.*, grass-covered layer of earth

tûr'gĭd, *a.*, swollen, pomp-

S
T

ous; **-ity; -ness; -ly**

tûr'mŏil, *n.,* confusion, uproar

tûrn'cōat, *n.,* traitor

tûr'nĭp, *n.,* plant with edible leaves and root

tûrn'pīke, *n.,* highway with toll [platform

tûrn'tā-ble, *n.,* rotating

tûr'pĭ-tūde, *n.,* vileness

tûr'quōise, *n., a.,* (gem of) greenish-blue

tûr'rĕt, *n.,* small tower on building [in shell

tûr'tle, *n.,* reptile encased

tŭsk, *n.,* long projecting animal tooth

tŭs'sle, *n., v.,* struggle

tū'tŏr, *n.,* private teacher, guardian; *v.,* teach; **-age; -ship; telage; -ial**

tŭx-ē'dō, *n.,* man's semiformal jacket

twēak, *n.,* twisting pinch

twēed, *n.,* rough wool fabric; **-y** *a.;* **-iness**

twēez'êrs, *n., pl.,* small pincers

twĭd'dle, *v.,* toy with, twirl; **-r; dly** *a.*

twĭg, *n.,* small tree branch

twī'līght, *n.,* subdued light after sunset

twĭll, *n.,* rubbed cloth

twĭn, *n.,* one of a pair that are alike; *a.,* paired

twīne, *n.,* strong cord

twĭnge, *n.,* sudden pain

twĭn'kle, *n., v.,* sparkle; **-r; kling** *n.*

twĭst, *n.,* thing twisted; *v.,* wind together, put out of shape, turn; **-er**

twĭtch, *n.,* quick slight jerk

twĭt'ter, *v.,* chirp, chatter, flutter; **-er; -y** *a.*

two'fold (tōo), *a.,* double; *adv.,* twice

tȳ-cōon', *n.,* industrialist

tȳpe, *n.,* group having common characteristics, metal pieces for printing; *v.,* classify, use typewriter; **-able**

tȳ'phoid, *n.,* infectious disease; **-al** [phonic

tȳ-phōon', *n.,* hurricane;

tȳ'phŭs, *n.,* infectious disease; **phous**

tȳ'rȧnt, *n.,* cruel, absolute ruler; **anny; annize; annizer; rannical; rannically; annous; annously**

tȳ'rō, *n.,* beginner

tzâr, *n.,* czar

U

ū-bĭq'uĭ-toŭs, *a.,* being everywhere; **uity; -ness; -ly** [gland

ŭd'dêr, *n.,* mammary

ŭg'lȳ, *a.,* unpleasant to see, bad; **liness; lify; lily**

ū'kāse, *n.,* official order

ū-kŭ-le'lē (lā), *n.,* small guitarlike instrument

ŭl'cêr, *n.,* open sore; **-ous; -ously**

ŭl-tē'rĭ-ŏr, *a.,* beyond what is said; **-ly**

ŭl'tĭ-mȧte, *a.,* farthest, final, utmost; **macy; -ness; -ly** [mand

ŭl-tĭ-mā'tŭm, *n.,* final de-

ŭl'trȧ, *a.,* extreme

ŭl-trȧ-sŏn'ĭc, *a.,* beyond human hearing; **-s; -ally**

ŭl'ū-lāte, *v.,* wail; **tion; lant**

ŭm-bĭl'ĭ-cŭs, *n.,* navel; **cal**

ŭm-brĕl'lȧ, *n.,* cloth covered frame as rain protector [judge

ŭm'pīre, *n.,* game or sports

ū-nȧn'ĭ-moŭs, *a.,* agreeing completely; **nimity; -ly**

ŭn-, *prefix* not, reverse of,

ŭn-ȧp-prōach'ȧ-ble, *a.,* aloof, unmatched; **bility; -ness; bly**

ŭn-ȧp-prō'prĭ-āt-ĕd, *a.,* not granted for use

ŭn-ârmed', *a.,* defenseless

ŭn-ȧsked', *a.,* not invited

ŭn-ȧs-sŭm'ĭng, *a.,* modest

ŭn-ȧt-tăched', *a.,* not connected, unmarried

ŭn-ȧt-tĕnd'ĕd, *a.,* neglected

ŭn-băl′ănced, *a.,* not equal, mentally ill

ŭn-beăr′à-ble, *a.,* not tolerated; **-ness; bly**

ŭn-bė-cŏm′ĭng, *a.,* unattractive; **-ness; -ly**

ŭn-bė-liĕv′à-ble, *a.,* incredible; **bly**

ŭn-bĕnd′, *v.,* relax, straighten

ŭn-bŏs′ŏm, *v.,* reveal

ŭn-bûr′dėn, *v.,* reveal, disclose

ŭn-căn′nў, *a.,* eerie; **ni-ness; nily**

ŭn-cĕr-ė-mō′nĭ-oŭs, *a.,* informal; **-ness; -ly**

ŭn-cŏn-cêrn′, *n.,* apathy; **-ed; -edness; -edly**

ŭn-cŏn-dĭ′tion-ál, *a.,* absolute, **-ly**

ŭn-cŏn′scion-à-ble, *a.,* unreasonable; **bly**

ŭn-coŭ′ple, *v.,* unfasten

ŭn-coûth′, *a.,* crude; **-ness; -ly**

ŭnc′tion, *n.,* annointment with oil; **tuous; tuous-ness; tuously**

ŭn′dėr-, *prefix,* beneath, below normal, too little

ŭn′dėr, *a.,* lower; *adv.,* beneath; *prep.,* lower than, covered, controlled by

ŭn′dėr-brŭsh, *n.,* shrubs below large trees

ŭn-dėr-clăss′màn, *n.,* student below senior

ŭn-dėr-cŏv′êr, *a.,* secret

ŭn′dėr-dŏg, *n.,* one expected to lose

ŭn-dėr-gō′, *v.,* experience

ŭn-dėr-grăd′ū-àte, *n.,* college student not ready to receive degree

ŭn′dėr-ground′, *a., adv.,* below ground, secret

ŭn-dėr-hănd′ėd, *a.,* secret, sly; **-ness; -ly**

ŭn′dėr-lĭng, *n.,* subordinate

ŭn-dėr-mīne′, *v.,* dig beneath, weaken

ŭn-dėr-nēath′, *a.,* lower; *adv., prep.,* below

ŭn-dėr-pĭn, *n.,* support from below; **-ning** *n.*

ŭn-dėr-prĭv′ĭ-lėged, *a.,* poor

ŭn-dėr-sīgn′, *v.,* sign name at end

ŭn-dėr-stănd′, *v.,* know meaning of, infer, take as fact, learn

ŭn-dėr-stănd′ĭng, *n.,* knowledge, intelligence, agreement

ŭn-dėr-stāte′, *v.,* say too weakly   [tute actor

ŭn′dėr-stŭd-ў, *n.,* substi-

ŭn-dėr-tāke′, *v.,* agree to do, promise; **taking** *n.*

ŭn-dėr-tāk′êr, *n.,* funeral director

ŭn′dėr-weâr, *n.,* clothes worn under outer clothes

ŭn′dėr-wŏrld, *n.,* hell, organized crime

ŭn′dėr-wrīte′, *v.,* agree to buy or pay

ŭn-do′(dōō), *v.,* open, destroy; **-ing** *n.*

ŭn-drĕss′, *v.,* remove clothing

ŭn-dūe′, *a.,* excessive, improper; **duly**

ŭn′dū-lāte, *v.,* move in waves; **tion; tory; lant**

ŭn-êarth′, *v.,* dip up, learn

ŭn-êarth′lў, *adv.,* weird

ŭn-ēas′ў, *a.,* uncomfortable, perturbed; **easi-ness; easily**

ŭn-ė-quĭv′ŏ-cál, *a.,* clear; **-ly**   [tant; **-ly**

ŭn-ė-vĕnt′fŭl, *a.,* unimpor-

ŭn-fāil′ĭng, *a.,* certain; **-ly**

ŭn-fōld′, *v.,* open, reveal

ŭn-fôr-gĕt′à-ble, *a.,* never to be forgotten; **bly**

ŭn-fôrmed′, *a.,* shapeless

ŭn-fôr′tu-nàte (chu), *a.,* unlucky; **-ly**

ŭn-foŭnd′ėd, *a.,* not based on truth

ŭn-fûrl′, *v.,* unfold

ŭn-gāin′lў, *a.,* clumsy; **li-ness**   [**ness**

ŭn-gŏd′lў, *a.,* wicked; **li-**

ŭn′guênt, *n.,* ointment

ŭn-hăp′pў, *a.,* unlucky, sad; **piness; pily**

ŭn-hĕalth′ў, *a.,* sickly, harmful; **healthiness**

ū-nĭ-căm'êr-ål, *a.*, of single legislature

ū'nĭ-côrn, *n.*, mythical one-horned horse

ū'nĭ-fôrm, *n.*, official clothes of group; *a.*, all alike, unchanging; **-ity; -ly**

ū'nĭ-fȳ, *v.*, combine into one; **fier; fication; fiable**

ū-nĭ-lăt'êr-ål, *a.*, of one side; **-ism; -ly**

ūn'ĭón, *n.*, joining, united group; **-ize**

ū-nīque', *a.*, one and only, unusual; **-ness; -ly**

ū'nĭ-sòn, *n.*, harmony, agreement

ū'nĭt, *n.*, one, single part, fixed amount; **-ary**

ū-nīte', *v.*, join into whole

ū'nĭ-tȳ, *n.*, oneness, agreement

ū-nĭ-vêr'sål, *a.*, of all, present everywhere; **-ity; -ize; -ly**

ū'nĭ-vêrse, *n.*, world

ū-nĭ-vêr'sĭ-tȳ, *n.*, school of higher learning

ūn-kĕmpt', *a.*, not neat; **-ness** [**-ness; -ly**

ūn-lăw'fŭl, *a.*, illegal;

ūn-lĕad'ĕd, *a.*, not containing lead

ūn-lêarn', *v.*, forget

ūn-lĕss', *conj.*, *prep.*, except [not like

ūn-līke', *a.*, not alike; *prep.*

ūn-māke', *v.*, revert to original, ruin

ūn-măn'nêr-lȳ, *a.*, rude; **liness**

ūn-mêr'cĭ-fŭl, *a.*, cruel; **-ly**

ūn-nêrve', *v.*, upset

ūn-ŏc'cū-pīed, *a.*, empty, idle [qualed

ūn-păr'ål-lĕled, *a.*, une-

ūn-prĕc'ĕ-dĕnt-ĕd, *a.*, unique

ūn-quĕs'tion-à-ble, *a.*, certain; **bly**

ūn-răv'ĕl, *v.*, undo threads, make clear; **-ment** [ble

ūn-rĕ-lĕnt'ĭng, *a.*, inflexi-

ūn-rĕst', *n.*, angry discon-

tent

ūn-rūl'ȳ, *a.*, hard to restrain; disorderly; **ruliness**

ūn-sā'vŏr-ȳ, *a.*, disgusting; **voriness; vorily**

ūn-scāthed', *a.*, unharmed

ūn-sĕt'tle, *v.*, disturb; **-d**

ūn-sīght'lȳ, *a.*, ugly; **liness**

ūn-sōŭnd', *a.*, defective, not safe; **-ness; -ly**

ūn-spēak'å-ble, *a.*, wicked; **bly**

ūn-strŭc'tûred, *a.*, loose

ūn-sŭng', *a.*, not honored

ūn-tĕn'å-ble, *a.*, not defensible; **bility**

ūn-tĭl', *prep.*, up to the time of, before; *conj.*, to the point, before

ūn-toŭch'å-ble, *n.*, *a.*, (one that) should not be touched; **bility**

ūn-trŭth'fŭl, *a.*, dishonest; **-ness; -ly**

ūn-veil' (vāl), *v.*, reveal; **-ing** *n.*

ūn-wŏnt'ĕd, *a.*, rare

ŭp, *a.*, *adv.*, *prep.*, to a higher place or condition

ŭp-brāid', *v.*, scold

ŭp'brĭng-ĭng, *n.*, child's training

ŭp'grāde, *n.*, upward slope; *v.*, raise upward

ŭp-hēav'ål, *n.*, violent change

ŭp-hōld', *v.*, support; **-er**

ŭp'kēep, *n.*, maintenance

ŭp-ŏn', *adv.*, *prep.*, on

ŭp'pêr, *a.*, higher than

ŭp-pêr-clăss'màn, *n.*, junior or senior student

ŭp'pêr-mōst, *a.*, highest

ŭp'rīght, *a.*, straight up, honest, just; **-ness; -ly**

ŭp'rīs-ĭng, *n.*, revolt

ŭp'rôar, *n.*, loud commotion; **-ious; -iousness; -iously**

ŭp-rōot', *v.*, pull up by roots, remove

ŭp'sĕt, *n.*, disorder, unexpected defeat; *v.*, (ŭp-sĕt) overturn, defeat, disturb; **-ter**

ŭp′shŏt, *n.,* outcome

ŭp′stāirs′, *a., adv.,* on upper level

ŭp-stănd′ĭng, *a.,* erect, honorable

ŭp′stårt, *n., a.,* (one) newly rich or powerful

ŭp′tĭght′, *a.,* very tense

ŭp′-tô-dāte′, *a.,* most recent

ŭp′wård, *a., adv.,* toward higher place

ū-rā′nĭ-ŭm, *n.,* radioactive metallic element

ûr′bán, *a.,* of city; **-ism; -ize; -ization**

ûr-bāne′, *a.,* refined, suave; **banity**

ûr′chĭn, *n.,* mischievous child

ûrge, *n.,* impulse; *v.,* persuade, provoke; **-r**

ûr′gĕnt, *a.,* needing immediate action; **gency; -ly**

u′rĭne, *n.,* liquid body waste; **nate; nation; nary**

ûrn, *n.,* footed vase

ū-rŏl′ô-gȳ, *n.,* medicine of urinary system; **gist; logic; logical; logically**

ŭs, *pro.,* objective case of **we**

ŭs′å-ble, *a.,* fit for use; **bility; -ness; bly**

ŭs′åge, *n.,* treatment, habit

ūse, *n.,* (ūs) worth, function; *v.,* (ūz) put into action, treat, consume; **-er; -less; -lessness; -lessly** [**-ly**

ūse′fŭl, *a.,* helpful; **-ness;**

ŭsh′êr, *n., v.,* (one who can) show the way

u′sū-ål, *a.,* common, expected; **-ness; -ly**

u′sū-rȳ, *n.,* lending money at high interest rate; **rer; rious; riousness; riously**

ū-sûrp′, *v.,* take without right; **-er; -ation; -ingly**

ū-tĕn′sĭl, *n.,* tool, implement [*a.*

u′têr-ŭs, *n.,* womb; **terine**

ū-tĭl′ĭ-tȳ, *n.,* usefulness, public service giving power; **lize; lizer; lization; tarian**

ŭt′mōst, *n., a.,* greatest, farthest

ū-tō′pĭ-à, *n.,* ideal society of perfection; **-n** *a.*

ŭt′têr, *v.,* express with voice; **-er; -ance; -able**

ŭt′têr, *a.,* complete; **-ness; -ly**

ŭx-ô′rĭ-oŭs, *a.,* submissive to one's wife; **-ly**

V

vā′cånt, *a.,* empty; **cancy; -ness; cate; -ly**

văc-cīne′, *n.,* preparation to cause immunity to a disease

văc′ĭl-lāte, *v.,* waver, show indecision; **tor; tion; tory; lant; lating; latingly**

văc′ū-ŭm, *n.,* completely empty space

vå-gār′ȳ, *n.,* odd action or idea; **garious**

vā′grånt, *n.,* idle wanderer; **grancy; -ly**

vāgue, *a.,* not clear, undefinite; **-ness; -ly**

văl-ė-dĭc′tô-rȳ, *n.,* school farewell speech; **rian** *n.*

văl′iånt, *n.,* brave; **iance; iancy; -ly**

văl′ĭd, *a.,* being legal, sound; **-ity; -ness; -ate; -ly**

văl′lēy, *n.,* area between hills

văl′ūe, *n.,* worth in money, importance; *v.,* place value on, regard highly; **-r; uation; uate; uator**

vălve, *n.,* device that controls flow of liquid; **vular**

văn′dål, *n.,* one who purposely destroys property; **-ism; -ize**

vāne, *n.,* swinging device that shows wind direction [front

văn′guård, *n.,* group in

U Z

văn'ĭ-tў, *n.*, false pride

văn'quĭsh, *v.*, conquer, defeat; **-er**

vā'pör, *n.*, mist, gas; **-ize; -izer; -like; -ish; -ous**

văr'ĭ-cōse, *a.*, swollen; **cosity**

vâr'nĭsh, *n.*, liquid to make surface glassy; **-er**

vār'ў, *v.*, change, differ

văs'cū-lȧr, *a.*, of body or plant vessels; **-ity**

văs-ĕc'tȯ-mў, *n.*, male operation for sterility

văs'sȧl, *n.*, feudal tenant, underling; **-age** [**-ly**

văst, *a.*, very great; **-ness;**

vȧude'vĭlle, *n.*, stage show of many acts

väunt, *n.*, *v.*, boast; **-er; -ed; -y** *a.*

vēer, *v.*, deviate, shift; **-ingly**

vĕg-ė-tār'ĭȧn, *n.*, one eating no meat; **-ism**

vē'hė-mėnt, *a.*, showing strong feeling; **mence; mency; -ly**

vein (văn), *n.*, blood vessel to heart, mineral deposit, leaf tube, quality; **-y** *a.*

vė-lŏc'ĭ-tў, *n.*, speed

vĕnd, *v.*, sell; **-or; -ee; -ition; -ible**

vĕn'ȇr-āte, *v.*, respect deeply; **tor; tion; able; ability; ableness; ably**

vė-nė're-ȧl, *a.*, of sexual intercourse

vē'nĭ-ȧl, *a.*, pardonable; **-ity; -ly**

vĕn'ȯm, *n.*, animal poison; **-ous; -ousness; -ously**

vĕnt, *n.*, outlet, escape; *v.*, let out, relieve feelings

vĕn'trĭ-cle, *n.*, *a.*, lower chamber of heart

vĕn'ūe, *n.*, locality of trial

vė-răn'dȧ, *n.*, porch

vėr-bā'tĭm, *n.*, word for word

vėr'dĭct, *n.*, legal decision

vėr'ĭ-fў, *v.*, prove to be true; confirm; **fier; fication; fiable**

vėr'mĭn, *n.*, troublesome

animal or insect; **-ous**

vêr-năc'ū-lȧr, *a.*, of commonly spoken language; **-ly**

vêr'sȧ-tĭle, *a.*, skilled in many areas; **tility; -ly**

vêr'sion, *n.*, translation, report; **-al**

vêr'tė-brȧte, *n.*, animal with segmented spine

vêr'tĕx, *n.*, top, corner point

vêr'tĭ-gō, *n.*, dizziness

vĕs'tĭge, *n.*, trace; **tigial; tigially**

vĕt-ėr-ĭ-năr'ў, *n.*, medicine of animals; **narian**

vētō, *n.*, power to reject; *v.*, prevent from becoming law; **-er**

vi'ȧ-ble, *a.*, workable; **bility; bly**

vi'brȧte, *v.*, quiver, swing; **tor; tion; tory**

vi-cār'ĭoŭs, *a.*, experienced by imaginary participation; **-ness; -ly**

vĭ-cĭn'ĭ-tў, *n.*, nearness, neighborhood; **nal**

vĭ-cĭs'sĭ-tūde, *n.*, constant change, shifting circumstances; **dinary; dinous**

vĭc'tȯ-rў, *n.*, winning, success; **tor; rious; riously**

vie, *v.*, compete; **-r**

view, *n.*, seeing, sight, scene, opinion; *v.*, look at, consider; **-er; -less; -lessly**

vĭg'ĭl, *n.*, night watch

vĭg'ör, *n.*, strength, energy; **-ous; -ousness; -ously**

vīle, *a.*, disgusting, very bad; **-ness; -ly**

vĭm, *n.*, energy

vĭn'dĭ-cāte, *v.*, clear name, absolve; **tor; tion; tive; tory**

vĭn'ė-gȧr, *n.*, sour liquid from fermenting liquor; **-y** *a.*

vi'ȯ-lāte, *v.*, break law, desecrate, rape; **tor; tion; tive**

vi'pêr, *n.*, venomous snake, spiteful one; **-ous; -ously**

vĭr'ĭle, a., manly; **rility**

vĭr'tūe, n., moral good-
ness, value; **tuous;
tuousness; tuously**

vī'rŭs, n., microscopic
agent causing disease

vī'sion, n., seeing, mental
image, foresight; **-al**

vĭs'ĭt, v., go or come to
see, stay as a guest; **-or;
-ation; -ational; -able**

vī'tȧ-mĭn, n., organic food
substance for good
health; **-ic**

vī'tĭ-āte, v., spoil; **tor; tion;
able**

vĭv'ĭd, a., lively, bright, active; **ify; ifier; ification;
-ness; -ly**

vō-cā'tion, n., career,
trade; **-al**

vōĭce, n., sound made by
mouth, opinion; v., utter;
**-less; -lessness;
-lessly**

vŏl'ȧ-tĭle, a., changeable,
explosive; **tility; -ness**

vŏl'lĕy, n., discharge of
firearms, burst of words;
-er

vŏl'ume (yŭm), n., book,
space occupied, bulk;
**minous; minosity; min-
ousity**

vȯ-lŭp'tū-oŭs, a., sensual;
-ness; -ly

vȯ-rā'cioŭs, a., greedy,
hungry; **racity; -ness;
-ly**

vōte, n., formal choice, decision reached; v., cast
a vote; **-r** [antee

voŭch, v., uphold, guar-

vōw, n., holy or solemn
pledge; v., promise; **-er**

vŭl'cān-ize, v., treat crude
rubber; **zation**

vŭl'nêr-ȧ-ble, a., easily
hurt; **bility; bly**

W

wȧd, n., small soft mass;
v., crumple, roll up; **-der**

wāde, v., walk in shallow
substance, do with ef-
fort; **-r**

wā'fêr, n., thin flat cracker

wȧf'fle, n., batter cake with
gridlike surface

wȧft, v., float; **-er**

wȧg, v., move back and
forth; **-ger**   [gage in

wāge, n., salary; v., en-

wā'gêr, n., v., bet; **-er**

wāif, n., homeless person

wāil, n., pitiful cry; v., cry
with grief; **-er; -ful; -fully**

wāin'scȯt, n., paneling on
lower part of wall

wāist, n., body between
ribs and hips

wāit, v., remain in readiness, serve food; **-er;
-ress**   [-r

wāive, v., give up rights;

wāke, v., come out of
sleep, become alert; **-n;
-ner; -ful; -fulness;
-fully**

wāke, n., track gone before

wȧlk, n., walking, path; v.,
go along on foot; **-er**

wȧll, n., upright structure,
building side

wȧl'lȧ-bȳ, n., small kan-
garoolike animal

wȧl'lĕt, n., pocket case for
money

wȧl'lȯp, n., hardblow; v.,
strike; **-er**

wȧl'lōw, v., roll in mud,
indulge oneself; **-er**

wȧl'nŭt, n., tree, nut, wood

wȧl'rŭs, n., large sea
mammal

wȧltz, n., ballroom dance
with three-fourth time;
-er   [-ness; -ly

wȧn, a., pale, sickly;

wȧnd, n., thin rod

wȧn'der, v., go aimlessly,
stray; **-er**

wāne, v., fade, decline; **-y**
a.   [need

wȧnt, n., v., lack, desire,

wȧn'tȯn, a., immoral,
senseless; **-ness; -ly**

wȧp'ī-tĭ, n., large deer

war (wôr), n., armed con-
flict, hostility; v., fight;
-like   [bird; **-r**

war'ble (wôr), v., sing like

ward (wôrd), n., one under

guardian's care, division
of hospital, jail or city;
v., turn aside

war'dén (wôr), n., head of
prison

ward'rōbe (wôrd), n.,
movable closet, clothes
supply   [pottery

wāre, n., kind of goods,

wāre'hoŭse, n., storage
building   [conflict

war'fāre (wôr), n., armed

warm (wôrm), v., a., (make
or be) of moderate heat,
friendly, lively, angry; **-th**
n.; **-ness; -ly**

warn (wôrn), v., tell of danger, inform; **-ing** n.

warp (wôrp), n., distortion,
lengthwise thread; v.,
distort, pervert; **-er**

war'rȧnt (wôr), n., legal
sanction, n., v., guaran-
tee; **-or; -ee**

war'rȧn-tȳ (wôr), n., guar-
antee

wart (wôrt), n., small tu-
morous growth on skin

wāsh, n., clothes to be
washed; v., clean with
water, purity; **-er; -ing** n.;
-able   [sect

wȧsp, n., large stinging in-

wāste, n., empty land refuse, neglect, excre-
ment; v., use up, make
weak, consume; **-r; -ful;
-fulness; -fully**

wȧtch, n., guarding, small
timepiece; v., guard, be
alert, observe; **-er; -ful;
-fulness; -fully**

wä'têr, n., colorless liquid
of rivers, etc., rain, body
fluid; v., supply water,
-y a.; **-iness; -less;
-lessness**

wä'têr-crĕss, n., plant, its
leaves used in salad

wä'têr-frȯnt, n., land at
edge of river, etc.

wä'têr-līl-ȳ, n., aquatic
flowering plant

wä'têr-lŏgged, a., soaked

wä'têr-mĕl-ȯn, n., large
melon with juicy red pulp

wä'têr-shĕd, n., area

drained by river

wä'têr-wȯrks, n., system
of public water supply

wätt, n., unit of electrical
power; **-age**

wāve, n., curving swell in
water, curls, hand signal
rise; v., move to and fro;
wavy a.; **-less; -like**

wăx, n., plastic substance
made by bees, similar
substance; v., polish,
with wax, become
larger; **-en** a.

wāy, n., route, course,
method, manner, wish

wāy'fār-êr, n., traveler

wāy-lāy', v., ambush; **-er**

wāy'wȧrd, a., disobedient,
erratic; **-ness; -ly**

wĕak, a., lacking strength,
or power, deficient; **-en;
-ener**

wĕak'nĕss, n., fault, fondness

wĕalth, n., riches, large
amount; **-y** a., **-iness;
-ily**

wĕan, v., stop suckling,
withdraw in degrees
from habit

wĕap'ȯn, n., device used
for fighting; **-ry**

wear, n., fashion, damage;
v., have on body, impair
by use, tire, last; **-able;
-ability**

wēa'rȳ, a., tired; **riness;
risome** a.,; **riless; rily**

wēas'ĕl, n., small slender
mammal

wĕath'êr, n., condition of
atmosphere; v., survive

wĕave, v., interlace
threads to make fabric;
-r

wĕb, n., woven network
animal membrane con-
necting digits

wĕd'dĭng, n., marriage
ceremony

wĕdge, n., wood or metal
piece tapered to point;
v., jam in

wēe, a., very small

wĕed, n., undesired plant;
v., remove; **-er; -less;**

-y *a.*

weep, *v.,* shed tears, mourn; **-er; -y** *a.*

wee'vil, *n.,* beetle

weight (wāt), *n.,* heaviness, importance; **-less; -lessness; -y** *a.;* **-iness**

weird, *a.,* very strange, mysterious; **-ness; -ly**

weld, *v.,* unite by fusing; **-er; -ability; -able**

wel'fāre, *n.,* prosperity, public agencies giving aid to needy

well, *n.,* shaft to tap underground water, source; *v.,* pour forth; *a.,* in good health; *adv.,* satisfactorily, prosperously

well-brĕd', *a.,* courteous

well-măn'nêred, *a.,* courteous [intentions

well-mēan'ĭng, *a.,* of good

well-ôff', *a.,* prosperous

welt, *n.,* raised ridge on skin, shoe leather piece

welt'êr, *n.,* confusion; *v.,* wallow

wench, *n.,* young woman

wend, *v.,* go on

west, *n.,* direction left of one facing north; *a., adv.,* in, of or to west; **-ern** *a.;* **-erly; -ward** *a., adv.,* **-wardly**

wet, *v., a.,* (become) soaked with liquid, rainy; **-ter; -ness; -tability; -table; -tish**

whāle, *n.,* large fishlike mammal

wharf (wôrf), *n.,* platform to dock ships

whåt, *pro.,* which thing, event, etc.?, that which; *a.,* which kind of, as much as; *adv.,* how, in part; *int.,* exclamation of surprize

whåt'nŏt, *n.,* nondescript thing or person

wheat, *n.,* cereal grass, its grain; **-en** *a.*

whee'dle, *v.,* coax

wheel, *n.,* disk turning on axis; *v.,* roll, turn; **-er**

wheel'chāir, *n.,* mobile chair for one unable to walk

wheeze, *v.,* breathe with difficulty; **-r; wheezy** *a.;* **wheezingly**

whelp, *n.,* puppy

when, *adv.,* at what time or point?; *conj.,* if, at that time

where, *adv.,* in or at what place?; *conj.,* at that place

where'with-āl, *n.,* necessary means, ex. money

whet, *v.,* sharpen, stimulate; **-ter**

wheth'êr, *conj.,* in either case that

whet'stōne, *n.,* abrasive stone for sharpening tools

which, *a., pro.,* what one or ones, that

whiff, *n.,* light puff or smell

while, *n.,* time period; *v.,* spend time; *conj.,* during the time that

whim, *n.,* passing notion; **-sical; -sicality; -sically**

whim'pêr, *n., v.,* cry in broken sounds; **-ingly**

whip, *n.,* rod with strap; *v.,* beat, move suddenly; **-per; -ping**

whip'lăsh, *n.,* sudden jolt of neck

whip'pĕt, *n.,* small greyhoundlike dog

whir, *v.,* move with buzzing sound

whirl'pōol, *n.,* water in whirling motion

whisk, *n., v.,* (utensil or small broom to) brush quickly

whisk'êrs, *n., pl.,* hair growing on face

whis'tle, *n.,* clear, shrill sound; *n., v.,* (device to) make whistling sound; **-r; ling** *n.*

whit, *n.,* least bit

white, *n.,* color of white; *a.,* of color of snow, pale, pure, of light skin; **-n; -ner; -ness; -ly**

white-cŏl'lår, *a.,* of cleri-

U
Z

cal and professional workers

whĭth'êr, *a.,* where

whĭt'tle, *v.,* cut wood shavings, reduce gradually; **-r**

who (hū), *pro.,* what or which person, that

whôle (hōl), *a.,* entire, unity; **-ness**

whole'sāle (hōl), *n.,* selling large amounts to retailer; *a.,* extensive; **-r**

whole'sŏme (hōl), *a.,* healthy, morally good; **-ness; -ly**

whoop (hūp), *n.,* loud shrill shout

whŏp'pêr, *n.,* something very large, lie

whore (hŏr), *n.,* prostitute

whose (hūz), *pro.,* of who or which

whȳ, *adv.,* for what reason?; *conj.,* because of which

wĭck, *n.,* cord in candle

wĭck'ĕd, *a.,* morally bad; **-ness; -ly** [twig

wĭck'ĕr, *n.,* thin flexible

wĭde, *a.,* of great extent, ample; *adv.,* to full extent; **-ness; -n; -ner; -ly**

wĭeld, *v.,* handle with skill, use; **-er; -y** *a.*

wĭe'nêr, *n.,* smoked sausage

wĭg, *n.,* false covering of hair [gler; gly *a.*

wĭg'gle, *v.,* twist and turn;

wĭg'wăm, *n.,* Indian tent

wĭld, *a.,* in its natural state, uncivilized, unruly, imprudent; **-ness; -ly**

~~wĭl'dêr-nĕss, *n.,* uninha~~bited, wild area

wile, *n.,* sly trick

wĭll, *n.,* choice, determination, wish, legal paper disposing of property after death; *v.,* choice, bequeath

wĭll'ĭng, *a.,* consenting, done readily; **-ness; -ly**

wĭl'lōw, *n.,* tree

wĭlt, *v.,* become limp, droop

wī'lȳ, *a.,* sly

wĭn, *v.,* gain victory, achieve, get; **-ner**

wĭnce, *v.,* draw back; **-r**

wĭnd, *n.,* moving air; **-less; -lessness; -lessly; -y** *a.;* **-iness; -ily**

wĭnd, *v.,* twist around, tighten spring, ex. clock; **-er; -ing** *n.*

wĭnd'băg, *n.,* great talker who says little

wĭnd'fäll, *n.,* stroke of luck

wĭn'dŏw, *n.,* glass opening in building; **-less**

wĭnd'pĭpe, *n.,* trachea

wĭnd'shĭeld, *n.,* glass screen in car's front

wĭne, *n.,* liquor fermented from grapes; **-ry**

wĭng, *n.,* feathered limb of bird, winglike part; **-less**

wĭnk, *n.,* instant; *v.,* close and open eyelid quickly; **-er** [**-ness; -ly**

wĭn'sŏme, *a.,* charming;

wĭn'têr, *n.,* coldest season of year; **try** *a.;* **triness; trily** [**-r**

wĭpe, *v.,* rub clean or dry;

wĭre'tăp, *n., v.,* (device to) secretly intercept information; **-per**

wĭse, *a.,* having good judgment, learned; **-ly**

wĭse'crăck, *n.,* flippant remark

wĭsh, *n., v.,* want, desire, request; **-er; -ful; -fulness; -fully**

wĭst'fŭl, *a.,* yearning; **-ness; -ly**

wĭt, *n.,* good sense, cleverness; **-less; -lessness; -lessly**

wĭtch, *n.,* woman supposedly having magical power

wĭth, *prep.,* in company of, concerning, of same opinion as, because of, using

wĭth-dräw', *v.,* remove from, go away; **-er; -al** *n.*

wĭth'êr, *v.,* dry up, wilt

wĭth-hōld', *v.,* keep back,

refuse; **-er**

wĭth-stănd', v., endure

wĭt'nĕss, n., testimony, firsthand observer of occurrence; v., testify

wĭt'tÿ, a., cleveriy amusing; **tiness; tily**

wĭz'ărd, n., magician; **-ry**

wĭz'ĕned, a., withered

wōe, n., sorrow, trouble; **-ful; -fulness; -fully**

wŏk, n., metal cooking pan

wŏlf, n., flesh-eating doglike mammal; **-ish**

wŏl-vêr-īne', n., large weasellike animal

wŏm'ăn, n., adult female; **-hood; -ish; -ishness; -ishly; -ly**

womb (wūmb), n., uterus

wŏm'băt, n., burrowing marsupial

wŏn'dêr, n., astonishment, miracle; v., marvel, be curious; **-ment**

wŏnt, n., habit; a., accustomed; **-ed; -edness**

wōo, v., court, coax

wŏod, n., hard material under tree's bark, lumber; **-en; -enness; -y** a.; **-iness**

wŏod'cŏck, n., game bird

wŏod'pĕck-êr, n., bird that pecks holes in wood

wŏod'wŏrk, n., wooden doors, frames, etc.

wŏol, n., hair of sheep, yarn or cloth from wool; **-en** a.; **-ly** a.; **-liness**

wŏrd, n., unit of language, sound or sounds having meaning, promise; v., phrase; **-age; -less**

wŏrk, n., effort put forth, result, job; v., exert oneself, operate; **-er; -able; -ability; -ableness**

wŏrk'măn-shĭp, n., skill of workman [ercise

wŏrk'ŏut, n., strenuous ex-

wŏrld, n., plant earth, universe, sphere

wŏrm, n., long slender creeping animal; **-like; -y** a.; **-iness**

wŏr'rÿ, n., troubled state;

v., feel uneasy; **rier; riment; risome**

wŏrse, a., less good, more ill; **-n**

wŏr'shĭp, n., religious service, extreme devotion; v., pray, adore; **-er**

wŏrst, a., least good, lowest

wor'stĕd (wŏos), n., smooth wool fabric

wŏrth, n., material value, importance; a., deserving equal in value; **-y** a.; **-iness; -ily; -less; -lessness; -lessly**

woŭnd, n., injury; v., hurt

wrăn'gle, n., v., quarrel; **-r**

wrăp, n., outer covering; v., enclose in covering, envelop

wrăth, n., anger; **-ful; -fulness; -fully; -y** a.

wrēak, v., inflict, give vent to; **-er**

wrēath, n., ring of leaves

wrēathe, v., make wreath, encircle

wrĕck, n., destruction, ill person; v., damage, ruin; **-er; -age**

wrĕn, n., songbird

wrĕnch, n., v., twist; n., tool to turn nuts

wrĕst, v., take by force; **-er**

wrĕs'tle, v., struggle, force opponent to ground; **-r; tling** n. [son

wrĕtch, n., miserable per-

wrĕtch'ĕd, a., miserable, poor; **-ness; -ly**

wrĭg'gle, v., twist and turn; **-r; gly**

wrĭn'kle, n., tiny ridge; v., crease; **kly**

wrĭst, n., joint between hand and forearm

wrĭt, n., formal legal order

write, v., form visible letters or words, be author of; **-r; writing** n. [-r

wrīthe, v., squirm in pain;

wrŏng, n., violation; v., treat badly; a., unlawful, improper, false; adv., incorrectly; **-er; -ness; -ful; -fulness; -fully; -ly**

wrôught, a., formed, shaped by hammering

wrȳ, v., twist; a., distorted; **-ness; -ly**

X

xē'bĕc (zē), n., small ship

xē'nŏn (zē), n., colorless gaseous chemical element

xĕn-ȯ-phō'bĭ-ȧ (zĕn), n., fear of strangers; **phobe** n.; **bic**

xė-rŏg'rȧ-phȳ (zė), n., process of copying written material; **phic**

X-rāy, n., v., (radiation used to) photograph or treat body tissues

xȳ'lȯ-phōne (zī), n., musical percussion instrument

Y

yăcht, n., small pleasure ship; **-sman** n.; **-ing** n.

yăk, n., large ox

yăm, n., edible root

yănk, n., v., pull, jerk

yȧrd, n., length measure of three feet, land around building; **-age**

yȧrn, n., spun strand of fiber, (coll.) tale

yāwl, n., small sailboat

yāwn, v., open mouth wide when sleepy or bored; **-er**

yēar, n., period of 365 days; **-ly** a., adv.

yēar'lĭng, n., one year old animal [n.

yêarn, v., desire; **-er; -ing**

yēast, n., frothy substance used as fermenting or leavening agent; **-y** a.

yĕll, n., v., shout, scream; **-er**

yĕl'lōw, n., color; a., of ripe lemon color; **-ness**

yĕn, n., strong desire

yeō'mȧn, n., naval clerk

yĕs, n., affirmative reply; adv., it is so

yĕt, adv., now, still; conj., however

yiēld, n., product; v., produce, surrender, grant; **-er**

yō'dėl, v., sing with abrupt alternating sounds; **-er**

yō'gȧ, n., body exercising system

yōke, n., wooden neck harness for oxen, slavery, thing that binds, garment pair at shoulders; v., harness, join together

yōlk, n., yellow of egg

yŏn'dêr, a., adv., farther

yôre, n., adv., (time) long ago

yŏung, a., being in early period of life, fresh; **-ster; -ling** n.; **-ish**

yôur-sĕlf', pro., reflexive or intensive form of you

yŏuth, n., state of being young, young people; **-ful; -fulness; -fully**

yŭc'cȧ, n., shrub

yūle, n., Christmas

yŭm'mȳ, a., (coll.) delicious

Z

za'ny, n., clown; comical foolish; **niness; nily**

zarf, n., an ornamental holder for a hot coffee cup, used in the Levant

zax, n., a tool for trimming slates

zeal, n., enthusiasm, passion; **-ous; -ousness; -ously**

zeal-ous, adj., eager in the pursuit of an object, enthusiastic

ze'bra, n., striped horse like mammal

ze-bec, n., a small three-masted ship, sometimes seen in the Mediterranean

ze'-bu, n., the Indian ox or cow, with long ears and a large hump on the shoulders

Zech-a-ri-ah, *n.*, a book of the Old Testament containing the message of the Hebrew prophet Zechariah

zed, *n.*, the English name for the last letter of the alphabet

ze'nith, *n.*, highest point; **-al**

zeph'yr, *n.*, soft gentle breeze

ze-ta, *n.*, in the Greek alphabet, the sixth letter

Zep'-pe-lin, *n.*, a cigar-shaped dirigible balloon, named after its inventor, Count von Zeppelin of Germany , and able to fly long distances and to carry a large weight: used by Germany in bombing raids over England and France during the World War

ze-ro, *n.*, a cipher, nothing; neutral point (°) on a scale, of temperature, etc., from which reckoning begins: zero hour, the hour fixed for beginning a military engagement, as an advance or attack

zest, *n.*, flavor, enthusiasm; **-ful; -fullness; -fully; -y** *a.*

zig-zag, *n.*, a course or line the direction of which changes in sharp turns or angles alternately to left and right

zilch, *n.*, nothing

zinc, *n.*, bluish-white metallic element

zip, *n.*, energy; *v.*, fasten zipper; **-py** *a.*

zir'con, *n.*, mineral

zith'er, *n.*, stringed instrument

zo'-di-ac, *n.*, imaginary belt near sun's path divided into twelve signs; **-al**

zo-ic, *adj.*, pertaining to, or connected with, animal life; containing fossils or preserved animals or plants: said of rocks

zone, *n.*, distinct area; *v.*, divide into districts; **zonal**

zoo, *n.*, a park or other large enclosure in which live animals are kept for public exhibition; a zoological garden

zo'-ol'o-gy(zu), *n.*, science of animals and animal life; gist; logical; logically

zoom, *v.*, make a loud buzzing sound, rise rapidly

zo-ot-o-my, *n.*, the dissection of animals, especially of animals other than man

zounds, *interj.*, an exclamation expressing anger or wonder;

Zu-lu, *n.*, one of a warlike native tribe of Natal, South Africa

zwie-back, *n.*, a kind of biscuit or roll first baked in a loaf and then cut and toasted

zy'gote, *n.*, fertilized egg

zy-mol-o-gy, *n.*, the science or study of the principles of fermentation.

U
Z

Directory of Computer Terms and Meanings

The computer has become commonplace in most homes and businesses. The following section of computer terms will help in your understanding of this important area of interest.

Adapter: A circuit as an interface board that serves between the system unit, typically a motherboard and the devices that attach to it.

Address: A location where a piece of information is stored within the computer.

Alphanumeric: An association of characters whose group is comprised of both Alphabetic (A-Z) and Numeric (0-9) symbols.

ANSI: American National Standards Institute. An organization that develops standards and guidelines for both the computer and electronics industries.

ASCII: American Standard Code for Information Interchange. A code used by computers to represent characters such as letters, numbers punctuation marks and other symbols.

Asynchronous: A term used typically to describe a method of data transfer. The timing of which is not directly tied to an external clock. but instead dictated by either of the computers involved in the communication.

Backup: A process of copying data from one type of media to another, for the purpose of preventing data loss in the event the original may become unusable.

Baud: A term used to describe the rate at which data is transferred between two computers. As originally used it was equivalent to the number of bits transmitted per second.

Binary: The Base 2 numbering system used by computers comprised of 1's and 0's.

BIOS: Basic Input/Output System. The part of a computer operating system that is responsible for communications with the machines peripheral components such as the monitor, printer, and keyboard.

Bit: The smallest unit of measure used by computers. The electronic equivalent to a switch which can be either on; high or 1 or off; low or 0. Eight associated bits comprise one byte.

Boot: A term to turning on of a computer and the subsequent describe the loading of its operating system.

Buffer: A section allocated to of memory temporarily store data during transfer.

Bug: A glitch or error in the expected operation of a program.

Byte: The equivalent of one character, typically eight bits.

Clock: A time regulated electronic signal used by the computer to coordinate its operation.

Cluster: The allocation for disk files. Clusters are smallest unit of comprised of one or more sectors.

CPU: Central Processing Unit. The main computer chip used within a computer where the bulk of the processing of data is done. Can also refer to the chassis or box in which this chip is located.

Cursor: The small flashing mark usually a line or box that appears on your computer screen signifying the location of where typed key will be located.

Directory: A location on a disk where the names, locations and other information related to files located on that disk are kept.

DMA: Direct Memory Access. An electronic path within a computer for high-speed data transfer. The computers CPU is not utilized in this operation that neither the transfer or system is impacted.

Disk: A magnetic storage device used to store computer information.

Encryption: A method of securing data by changing the codes to unrelated characters which can later be deciphered by use of a key, usually algorithm.

File: A collection of related information or instructions that is usually stored on a disk.

Fixed Disk: A non removable magnetic storage device which retains its memory after power to the computer is turned off. Also referred to as a hard disk.

Format: Preparing a magnetic disk or tape so that data may be stored. This process typically deletes any prior information stored while also checking for any defects or flaws in the surface being prepared.

Gigabyte: A quantity of storage approximately equivalent to one billion bytes. Exactly 1,073,741,824 bytes.

Head: The electromagnetic component responsible for reading and writing information on magnetic media.

I/O: Input/Output. A term used to relate to the flow of information to or from a source.

Interface: To attach through a common point of access two disparate systems.

Interrupt: Abbr. IRQ. An electrical signal with a computer used to temporarily suspend a task in process so that another task may be performed.

Kilobyte: Abbr. Kbyte. or KB. A quantity of storage approximately equivalent to one thousand bytes. Exactly 1024 bytes.

Logical Drive: A function of creating through the operating system the appearance of a specific physical device, but instead may represent another disk drive or directory.

Megabyte: Abbr. Mbyte. or MB. A quantity of storage approximately equivalent to one million bytes. Exactly 1,048, 576 bytes.

Memory: The electronic components within a computer used to temporarily hold information as its being processed. Also referred to as RAM.

Modem: Modulator/Demodulator. A device used to interface computers to telephone lines to link them together. A modem must be in use at each computer to translate the digital signals to its telephone line in compatible analog form.

Network: The linking of several computers together so that physical and data resources may be shared.

Output: Data that is sent to a device such as a monitor, printer, speaker or another physical device.

Parallel: The process of transferring data where the electrical signals are sent over multiple wires simultaneously.

Parity: A method of

insuring data integrity by adding an extra bit to each byte in a process similar to check summing.

Partition: A section of a hard disk that has been set aside for use by an operating system.

Peripheral: A piece of equipment connected to the computer. Some typical examples are modems, monitors, printers and disk drives.

Port: The connector that allows for the attaching of external peripherals.

Program: A series of instructions which allow a computer to perform a specific task.

Random-Access Memory: Abbr. RAM. The memory accessed by the computer to run a program or temporarily store data. This memory is cleared and the data lost when the computer is turned off.

Read-Only Memory: Abbr. ROM. This type of memory has the information permanently placed into it which cannot be altered. The information contained in ROM is not lost when power is turned off.

Sector: A sub section of a track of a disk. The size of a sector may vary depending on the drive and operating system in use.

Serial: The process of transferring data or executing tasks one after the other in succession.

Terminal: A separate piece of equipment that is used to input and process information to prepare it for its end use. A complete computer processing station.

Terminate and Stay Resident: Abbr. TSR. A program that remains in memory after it has been loaded and exited.

Track: On a disk it represents one of the concentric circles in which data stored. On a tape the concept is similar but data is stored in parallel lines extending the entire tape length.

Virus: A program designed to attach itself to other programs for the purpose of being unknowingly propagated from computer to computer. The affects of a virus may range from a simple annoyance to the loss of data.

METRIC CONVERSION CHART
APPROXIMATIONS

When You Know	Multiply by	To Find
Length		
millimeters	0.04	inches
centimeters	0.04	inches
meters	3.3	feet
meters	1.1	yards
kilometers	0.6	miles
Area		
square centimeters	0.16	square inches
square meters	1.2	square yards
square kilometers	0.4	square miles
hectares 10,000m^2	2..5	acres
Mass and Weight		
grams	0.035	ounce
kilograms	2.2	pounds
tons (l000kg)	1.1	short tons
Volume		
millimeters	0.03	fluid ounces
liters	2.1	pints
liters	1.06	quarts
liters	0.26	gallons
cubic meters	35	cubic feet
cubic meters	1.3	cubic yards
Temperature (exact)		
Celsius temperature	9/5, + 32	Fahrenheit temp.
Fahrenheit temperature	-32, 5/9 x remainder	Celsius temp.
Length		
inches	2.5	centimeters
feet	30	centimeters
yards	0.9	meters
miles	1.6	kilometers
Area		
square inches	6.5	square centimeters
square feet	0.09	square meters
square yards	0.8	square meters
square miles	2.6	square kilometers
acres	0.4	hectares
Mass and Weight		
ounces	28	grams
pounds	0.45	kilograms
short tons (2000 lb)	0.9	tons
Volume		
fluid ounces	30	milliliters
pints	0.47	liters
quarts	0.95	liters

WEIGHTS AND MEASURES

U.S. Customary Unit	U.S. Equivalents	Metric Equivalents

Length

inch	0.083 foot	2.54 centimeters
foot	1/3 yard. 12 inches	0.3048 meter
yard	3 feet. 36 inches	0.9144 meter
rod	51/2 yards. 161/2 feet	5.0292 meters
mile (statute, land)	1,760 yards. 5,280 feet	1.609 Kilometers
mile (nautical international)	1.151 statute miles	1.852 kilometers

Area

square inch	0.007 square foot	6.4516 square centimeters
square foot	144 Square inches	929.030 square centimeters
square yard	1,296 square inches. 9 square feet	0.836 square meter
acre	43,560 square feet. 4,840 square yards	4,047 square meters
square mile	640 acres	2,590 square kilometers

Volume or Capacity

cubic inch	0.00058 cubic foot	16,387 cubic centimeters
cubic foot	1,728 cubic inches	0.028 cubic meter
cubic yard	27 cubic feet	0.765 cubic meter

U.S. Customary Liquid Measure	U.S. Equivalents	Metric Equivalents
fluid ounce	8 fluid drams 1.804 cubic inches	29,573 milititers
pint	16 fluid ounces 28,875 cubic inches	0.473 liter
quart	2 pints. 57.75 cubic inches	0.946 liter
gallon	4 quarts. 231 cubic inches	3l.785 liters
barrel	varies from 31 to 42 gallons, established by law or usage	

U.S. Customary Dry Measure	U.S. Equivalents	Metric Equivalents
pint	1/2 quart. 33.6 cubic inches	0.551 liter
quart	2 pints. 67.2 cubic inches	1.101 liters
peck	8 quarts. 537.605 cubic inches	8.810 liters
bushel	4 pecks. 2,150.42 cubic inces	35.238 liters

SPECIAL OFFER
REFERENCE LIBRARY

THE WEBSTER'S FRENCH-ENGLISH ENGLISH-FRENCH DICTIONARY **$5.95**

THE WEBSTER'S HOME MEDICAL DICTIONARY **$5.95**

THE WEBSTER'S SPANISH-ENGLISH ENGLISH-SPANISH DICTIONARY **$5.95**

THE WEBSTER'S CONCISE DICTIONARY **$7.95**

ROGET'S THESAURUS **$5.95**

THE WEBSTER'S CROSSWORD PUZZLE DICTIONARY **$5.95**